Directory of
VOLUNTEERING
& EMPLOYMENT
OPPORTUNITIES

By Jan Brownfoot and Frances Wilks

A Directory of Social Change Publication

Directory of Volunteering & Employment Opportunities
with charities and voluntary organisations

Edited by Jan Brownfoot and Frances Wilks

First published in 1993
Second edition 1995

Copyright © 1995, Directory of Social Change,
24 Stephenson Way, London NW1 2DP
The Directory of Social Change is a registered
educational charity, Charity No. 800517

Printed and bound in Britain by Page Bros., Norwich
Cover design by Kate Bass
Designed and typeset by Linda Parker

ISBN 1-873860-71-4

Acknowledgements

The Directory of Volunteering and Employment
Opportunities was first produced for Charityfair 93,
the national charity exhibition held annually at the
Business Design Centre. The second, enlarged and
revised edition has been produced for Charityfair 95.
The publication of this book was made possible
through the generous support of Whitbread PLC.
The publishers are grateful for this support for the
encouragement of volunteering and for providing
better information on employment opportunities
in the charity sector.

The *Directory of Volunteering and Employment
Opportunities* is accompanied by a practical guide
*How to Work for a Charity on a Paid or Voluntary
Basis (by Jan Brownfoot and Frances Wilks).*

Many people assisted in the preparation of this
volume. We would particularly like to acknowledge
and thank all the people from every type of charity
and voluntary organisation who provided the
information from which this Directory has been
compiled.

Lastly, our thanks to all the organisations that agreed
to our use of their logos on the cover of this book. We
regret that we could not use more of them.

Contents

Directory of Organisations

Introduction

We are pleased to present a second, enlarged and revised edition of the *Directory of Volunteering and Employment Opportunities* - DOVEO for short. When the Directory was first produced in 1993 it was the first publication of its kind specifically about people and job opportunities in the voluntary sector. Since then it has been a source of reference for all sorts of people seeking all sorts of opportunities in the sector. These range from caring work with disabled people to using professional skills as a trustee of a campaigning organisation, from finding out about environmental volunteering to looking for a paid job. Everyone - whether a housewife or a company director, whether at school or retired - can do something to contribute. It has also been a source of information for people wanting to find out about the many services that the voluntary sector offers from self-help groups to specialist legal advice centres, from respite care to dramatic or musical entertainments for residential homes and hospices.

More than 23 million people volunteer in the United Kingdom each year and the possibilities are endless. This book lists only some of them, but also provides pointers and suggestions for finding out about many, many more. As the voluntary sector grows in importance and size, so too do the jobs within it. Indeed, the range now rivals that in the commercial sphere. As this book was revised, it was very noticeable that many organisations were reporting a substantial increase in the numbers of their paid staff during the last two years. This can only be good news for those looking for work in the voluntary field. At the same time it is strikingly clear that increasingly the route into many charities is via volunteering.

In this second edition we have included more regional organisations as well as a European perspective. With changing economic and political dynamics, we feel this is important. We have also added sections on the psychology of volunteering whether for fun or for a career change, and on how volunteering can contribute to getting a paid job. And, if you are already employed, there is information on volunteering as an employee.

We hope you will enjoy this second edition and find it useful.

Jan Brownfoot and Frances Wilks

The Voluntary Sector for Beginners

by Michael Norton

What is the voluntary sector?

Activity in our society is divided into three sectors:

- The Commercial Sector or Private Sector which operates for profit in manufacturing or selling goods or in the provision of services. Of course, not all businesses actually make a profit.
- The Statutory Sector which consists of government bodies, local councils, health authorities and other official agencies and other government bodies providing services directly or indirectly. Many services are provided in this way, including health services, education, social services and other services of community benefit. There is often some legal (or statutory) requirement for the service to be provided, although sometimes the services are provided at the discretion of the public body as being in the public interest.
- The Voluntary Sector which consists of a whole range of independent organisations which operate on a not-for-profit basis. These may provide services for public benefit or to meet the needs of particular groups of people. Many of the organisations which comprise the voluntary sector are charities.

At one time it was quite simple to define which sector was responsible for doing what. Business made and sold things. Government provided basic services to people who need them. The voluntary sector met needs that nobody else was responsible for or was doing anything about. Today it is not so simple.

Many basic services are now provided by the voluntary sector. Housing Associations are responsible for building and managing a large part of the nation's public housing programme. They are charities, but they carry out this work with large amounts of government support. The move to community care and the development of purchaser-provider systems in the health service will result in many more voluntary sector organisations being involved in delivering basic services.

Many statutory services are being reconstituted as voluntary bodies. For example, schools are being encouraged to opt out of local authority control and become charities. Some local arts centres and museums, once owned and run by the local authority, are being established as independent organisations having to seek at least some of their funding from new sources.

Income generation is a phenomenon which is being adopted in both the statutory sector and the voluntary sector, and is forcing a much more business-like approach. The private sector itself is becoming increasingly interested in tendering for and running social and welfare services on behalf of government – 1992 saw the opening of the first privately-run prison.

Now there is a great deal of overlap between the three sectors, and there are also cases of partnerships being formed by business, government and independent agencies to work together to solve problems or provide services.

What is a voluntary organisation?

Voluntary organisations are quite different from businesses or statutory organisations. The main points that characterise a voluntary organisation are:

- They are cause-led. They are established to do something specific, rather than make a profit or because there is some legal or community responsibility to see that something is done.
- They are set up by concerned individuals. It is a fundamental right in Britain for people to associate and set up organisations on matters of concern to them, provided that such organisations are not against the public interest (such things as promoting racial hatred or encouraging terrorism would be banned). Even the National Trust was set up in this way by a group of people concerned about the disappearance of Britain's countryside and Scope (formerly the Spastics Society) by a group of parents with children with cerebral palsy. If there is a cause that concerns you, you are free to set up a voluntary organisation to do something about it.
- They are established not-for-profit. This means that any money they have must be spent for the purposes of the organisation. They are often subsidised through fundraising or getting grants, or through the contribution of volunteers.
- They are controlled by a committee of volunteers, who receive no payment for this work (although they may have expenses reimbursed).
- The purposes of the organisation, the area in which it can operate, and the rules and regulations for operating the organisation are set out in its constitution.

These then are the main common features shared by voluntary organisations. There are also many differences:

- Size and scale of operation: The voluntary sector includes large national organisations such as the Royal National Lifeboats Institution and Oxfam both of which are widely known but also the committee that runs the Village Hall or the Canal Preservation Society and other areas of very local or specialist interest.
- Staffing and funding: The sector ranges from organisations run entirely by volunteers to those which employ professional staff to do the administration or carry out the charity's work. It includes endowed organisations that have an investment income to spend; but it also includes organisations which have to raise money in order to be able to carry out their work, and organisations that get by without needing money at all.
- Nature of activity: The sector covers almost every conceivable type of interest and activity. Some are national, some regional, some local; some have networks of local branches or affiliates; some are international, with overseas branches or activities. Some are set up for mutual aid or self-help by a group of people with a direct interest or concern with the problem that they are motivated to do something about it. Some are set up to deliver services, anything from meals-on-wheels to drugs counselling. Some are involved in advocacy, advising people and helping them obtain what is due to them in welfare benefits, for example. Some are primarily campaigning organisations, set up to seek some change in the law or in public opinion. Some are set up to protect or promote the interests of their members, for example professional bodies.

What is a charity?

Not all voluntary organisations are charities. But all charities are voluntary organisations. Examples of voluntary organisations that are not charities include campaigning organisations (such as Amnesty International and the Campaign for Real Ale), professional interest groups (such as trade unions), self-help groups (such as the tenants association for a block of flats) which do not benefit a wide enough section of the public to qualify as a charity, co-operatives and friendly societies, or organisations operating in fields which are not deemed to be charitable (such as sports clubs). Then there are those organisations whose work is charitable, but which choose not to register or which have not got round to registering as a charity.

A charity has a specific legal definition. It is a body set up for public benefit with purposes that the law has decided are charitable. The law stems from an Act of Parliament in 1601 known as the Statute of Elizabeth. This set out a whole range of purposes which were deemed to be charitable at the time. Over the years, from time to time the Courts have had to decide whether a particular activity is charitable, and in doing this have extended or clarified the definition of what is charitable.

In the late 19th Century, Lord Macnaghten, a prominent judge, categorised four types or 'heads' of charity: trusts for the relief of poverty and distress; trusts for the advancement of education for public benefit; trusts for the advancement of religion for public benefit; and trusts for other purposes beneficial to the community.

Note that there has to be public benefit. Organisations set up for private benefit cannot be charities. In a court case an enclosed order of nuns tried to argue that they should be given charitable status, but the court held that there was no public benefit – the prayers offered by the nuns on behalf of the outside world could not be shown to be beneficial!

The fourth category is a catch-all category which enables new purposes to be given charitable status when a new need emerges. In recent years the promotion of racial equality, the provision of services to gay and lesbian people and organisations set up to help those who have Aids or who are HIV-positive have all been awarded charitable status.

Once a charity is set up, its objects or purposes are set out in its constitution, as is the beneficial area where it is allowed to provide benefit. Some charities have wide purposes – some are even permitted to do anything that is deemed to be charitable. Others have narrowly defined purposes – for example, the Winston Churchill Memorial Trust has been established to promote non-academic education. The trustees or managing committee of the charity, who are responsible for running the organisation, may have to decide a strategy, a policy and priorities for its work. These must always be within the charity's permitted objects. If they are outside, the trustees will be acting improperly and be in breach of trust. The policy of the Winston Churchill Memorial Trust is to provide bursaries for people to study their trade, profession or hobby by visits to locations overseas.

Similarly, the trustees must operate within the beneficial area defined in the constitution. Again, this can be quite widely drawn or very narrowly described. There are local charities, whose activity is restricted to a particular district, parish, town or region; there are national charities able to operate anywhere in Britain; there are international charities with a global remit; there are as yet no charities established with an extra-terrestrial beneficial area (for example to relieve distressed astronauts)! Sometimes it is quite difficult to determine where exactly the beneficial area is, as boundaries change – the County of Rutland, the ancient parish of St James within may no longer be on the map.

Most charities are constituted so that the objects of the charity cannot be changed.

The trustees must work within the constitution, and they can only meet needs that they are permitted to. They should try to interpret the charity's objects, which may have been determined many centuries ago, in the light of present conditions. For example, in Victorian times, there were many charities set up to relieve girls in moral danger, as a result of sexual harassment of servant girls. Today such a charity might be concerned with Rape Crisis counselling or running a Women's Refuge, which it could do quite properly within its objects.

Charities exist in perpetuity – or rather, for so long as they continue to have resources. Where a charity can no longer fulfil its original purposes, then it can apply to the Court (in England and Wales to the Charity Commission) for the purposes to be changed. This is done through a process called 'cy pres' which allows the charity to change its objects to something near to the original purposes or intentions.

A charity is normally not allowed to pay its trustees (members of its governing body) any remuneration for work undertaken in respect of their trusteeship, and this is almost always prohibited in the constitution of the charity. It must also operate for charitable purposes only – which means that it is unable to undertake any but incidental trading activities, except where these directly fulfil the objects of the charity – this includes charging for charitable services (such as a fee for an educational course, a charge for publications or the provision of training). Selling products made by beneficiaries or donated items of clothing and bric-a-brac is also permitted. Where the charity wishes to undertake commercial trading, such as the operation of a gift shop at a tourist site, then this will normally be done through a separate trading company that the charity will set up specially for the purpose.

Charities are not allowed to engage in political activity, except where this is of a non-party political nature and where it is an ancillary (not a main) activity which is undertaken to further the charity's objects.

In England and Wales, most charities have to register with the Charity Commission, which supervises their activity and maintains records which are open to public scrutiny. In Scotland and in Northern Ireland, no registration procedure currently exists, and application for charitable status is usually made to the Inland Revenue, which is responsible for granting tax relief to charities.

The benefits of being a charity include:

- Being able to say that you are a charity. This can be extremely useful when fundraising or applying for a grant. However, simply being a charity does not mean that you are a well-run or even a good organisation. There are effective and efficient charities, and there are ineffectual charities and even charities expressly set up to dodge tax. There is currently a proposal around to create a Charity Standards Council to accredit charities which meet certain operational criteria.
- Tax benefits and rate reliefs. A wide range of tax and rate relief is available to charities. These include tax relief on large donations (Gift Aid), on Deed of Covenant donations, on donations made regularly by deduction of sums from your pay by your employer to be given to charities of your choice and on legacies; rate relief on premises occupied by the charity; and certain VAT reliefs; these reliefs are worth many hundreds of millions of pounds each year.

Many voluntary organisations are charities – there are some 170,000 bodies registered with the Charity Commission and it is estimated that there are more than 250,000 active charities in the UK today, with over 4,000 new charities being registered every year. There are many more voluntary organisations that are not charities. These do not enjoy the tax reliefs and other benefits available to charities.

Legal status and liabilities

Besides its charitable status (which it may or may not have), the organisation also has a legal status. There are two main types of legal status that voluntary organisations have:

- Unincorporated status. This includes trusts, associations and societies. With unincorporated status, the organisation does not have any legal personality, which means that it is the trustees or managing committee who enter into agreements or contracts (such as funding agreements, contracts of employment, leases or other contracts) rather than the organisation itself.
- Incorporated status. This includes organisations established as companies limited by guarantee or as industrial and provident societies. Here the organisation does have its own legal personality.

The liabilities of the trustees or managing committee members depends on the legal status of the organisation. With an unincorporated body, members of the committee are all personally liable for any debts or claims on the organisation. With incorporated bodies, this liability is limited to a nominal sum, usually £1. All committee members are personally responsible, whatever the status of the organisation, if they act outside their powers or are otherwise in 'breach of trust'. This degree of personal liability can cause problems, although it is now possible for trustees and committee members to insure themselves against any personal liability.

Organisational structure

All voluntary organisations have a top Board which is responsible for controlling the affairs of the organisation. This Board is usually known as the Trustees or the Managing Committee. The function of this group of people is to oversee the work of the organisation, to invest its assets and manage its property properly, to see that it is operating constitutionally, to decide priorities and to see that the organisation has sufficient resources available for it to be able to carry out its work. In doing this work, the Committee can decide to do everything itself. It can decide to use volunteers to help out. It can decide to appoint and pay people to do the work, appointing staff on a full-time or a part-time basis, or employing a consultant on a retainer. Or a mixture of any or all of these.

Where the work is delegated to staff or volunteers, the committee still retains responsibility for the proper functioning of the organisation. Certain members of the Committee have special positions and functions: the Chair or Chairperson, who is the figure head of the organisation, and who is also responsible for seeing the proper functioning of the committee; the Hon. Secretary, for seeing that all legal duties of the organisation are properly undertaken; and the Hon. Treasurer, for seeing that the finances are in order and proper accounts are prepared and examined as required by the constitution and the Charities Act.

The rules as to who can become a member of the committee are almost always set out in the constitution. Often the committee itself is responsible for finding and appointing new members. Some have a process of election or appointment of representatives from other bodies. Most, especially smaller and local charities, would be interested in hearing from someone who would like to serve as Committee Member or Trustee, especially where that person has relevant skills, experience or enthusiasm and the time to make an effective contribution. The charity cannot offer any form of payment or honorarium in return, but can reimburse out-of-pocket expenses.

The Managing Committee may also establish sub-committees with a delegated responsibility to oversee particular functions, such as long-range strategy and development, undertaking a capital appeal, communications, specialist matters of concern to the charity, etc. These committees will seek to appoint appropriate people to serve as members, which may also include Managing Committee members or members of staff alongside those specially appointed for their particular skills and experience.

There may also be people who serve in an honorary capacity, such as a President, or Vice-Presidents, or Patrons. These people do not have legal duties, and are in effect simply lending their name (and prestige) to the organisation. They may also help out in a voluntary capacity.

Many charities use volunteers to help out in the work. Sometimes these volunteers fulfil an administrative function, staffing the office, answering the phone, doing the book-keeping, administering Deeds of Covenant, etc. Sometimes they help out in the actual work of the charity, for example working on a helpline, doing practical conservation work, or organising a soup run for the homeless. Most volunteers receive no payment for their work, although there is nothing (apart from benefit rules for those in receipt of welfare benefits) to prevent them from doing so. Some receive some form of honorarium as recognition for their work, some get any expenses reimbursed, such as travel to the office or a lunch allowance. Some charities take on volunteers on an ad hoc basis. Some actively recruit and have a formal selection and induction process.

Where does the money come from?

There are five main sources of income for charities:

- Investment income. Many charities have some form of endowment, which can include property and investments. For example, Eton College owns a slice of Swiss Cottage in North West London, and the Wellcome Trust owns a very substantial slice of the pharmaceutical firm that shares its name. Even quite small charities may have some assets, even a temporary cash surplus, which can be invested to generate an income.
- Earnings. A major source of income is derived from the sale of services. Some charities, such as Barnardos, run residential facilities where charges are made either to local authorities or to the residents. Some make charges to clients for services. Some sell expertise through consultancy and training. Some engage in commercial trading activity, such as through the sale of Christmas cards and promotional items, which they will usually do through a separate trading company.
- Donations from members and supporters. This includes everything from membership subscriptions and Deeds of Covenant to occasional donations, big gifts and a legacy made through a Will.
- Grants from public sources such as the local authority, a central government department, a TEC (training and enterprise council), or a body such as the Arts Council or the Housing Corporation. And grants from private bodies such as a grant-making trust or foundation or support in some form from a company.
- Fundraising activities. Anything from a gala premiere of the latest blockbuster film to a coffee morning or a sponsored slim or swim, from a public collection in the street to the sale of raffle tickets.

....

II Although as a Justice of the Peace (JP) you have to give 26 days of voluntary work a year, 2 days a month minimum – which is a fairly hefty commitment – I decided to apply to volunteer as a JP for several reasons. Although I enjoy my freelance work in training very much, part of me was unfulfilled. I often feel quite isolated from some of the difficulties and problems that people living around me face. I live in a mixed community in London and I wanted to be part of bringing justice to it. And I love the intellectual challenge of being a JP Also there's a part of me that likes the theatricality of law courts... Secretly I always wanted to be a barrister, so this fulfils that part of me, too. I'm afraid I do my voluntary work as a JP for some purely selfish, personal reasons but I hope that I also give something back to others at the same time. *II*
A-M G, professional trainer and volunteer JP, London

....

Fundraising is now an extremely important part of many organisations' activity. They need to get the money before they can do the work. They have to bring considerable ingenuity to bear on this aspect of their work, as very many organisations are seeking support from sources which seem to have less and less money available to give. Some of this fundraising is extremely public through Telethons such as Comic Relief and Children in Need, through press advertising, or through appeal letters sent out in their millions by direct mail. Some is very private, involving people asking the very rich discreetly but persuasively.

Many organisations now have specialist fundraisers to do this work, and there is even an Institute of Charity Fundraising Managers to set standards. Some organisations use volunteers to help raise money, and in a recent survey of volunteering over 60 % of all volunteers undertook fundraising work.

Where do you fit in, and how to find out more?

You can fit in anywhere. You can ask to become a volunteer. You can seek employment by responding to a job opportunity. You can even ask to become a Trustee or Committee Member. If you are famous enough, you could even ask to become a patron! And you can set up a charity or voluntary organisation yourself to tackle a problem or issue that you are particularly interested in or concerned with.

To begin finding out what is available you could contact a number of information providing services. These include Councils of Voluntary Service: most local areas have a body which is responsible for co-ordinating voluntary activity and supporting voluntary organisations in their area. The address can be obtained from your local Reference Library. Some Councils of Voluntary Service operate or liaise closely with a Volunteer Bureau, which promotes volunteering and volunteer opportunities in the area.

You may want to find out more about an existing organisation. The first step is to ask to see a copy of their Annual Report. Most organisations would be happy to let you have a copy. If they are a charity, they are obliged to send a copy to the Charity Commission for the public record. You might even drop by to see their staff, their premises or their work.

There are a number of directories and publications which could be of interest. Here are a few:

Charities and voluntary organisations

Charity Trends: an annual review of the income and trends in the voluntary sector (published by Charities Aid Foundation (CAF))

Voluntary Agencies Directory: a guide to over 2,000 national voluntary organisations and what they do (published by National Council for Voluntary Organisations (NCVO))

How to Work for a Charity on Paid or Voluntary Basis (published by the Directory of Social Change (DSC))

Charity law and structure

Charitable Status: a practical handbook, An introductory guide to setting up a charity, (published by the Directory of Social Change)

Charity Commission leaflets – The Commission publishes a wide range of free leaflets. **Voluntary but Not Amateur** and **Just About Managing** – two simple to understand books on setting up and running a charity (London Voluntary Service Council – available from DSC)

Accounting and Financial Management for Charities – a basic guide to charity accounts and how to understand them (published by Directory of Social Change)

The Effective Trustee – a guide in three parts for intending and serving trustees. Volume One covers roles and responsibilities (published by the Directory of Social Change)

Fundraising
All published by the Directory of Social Change

Raising Money from Trusts, a basic guide for intending applicants

Raising Money from Industry, a basic guide for intending applicants

The Central Government Grants Guide: a guide to how central government makes grants available

The Complete Fundraising Handbook

Writing Better Applications

Tax Effective Giving

Useful addresses:
The Charity Commission,
St Alban's House, 57-60 Haymarket, London SW1Y 4QX

The Charities Aid Foundation,
48 Pembury Road, Tonbridge, Kent TN9 2JD

The National Council for Voluntary Organisations,
Regent's Wharf, 8 All Saints Street, London N1 9RL

The Directory of Social Change,
24 Stephenson Way, London NW1 2DP

Volunteering and Employment Opportunities – An Overview

by Jan Brownfoot and Frances Wilks

The Relationship between Paid and Voluntary Work in the Voluntary Sector

Many people who now have paid jobs in a voluntary organisation started their career in the voluntary sector as volunteers. Similarly, some people who may have had paid work in a voluntary organisation, and are now retired, still work there – but as volunteers. Increasingly the route into many charities is as a volunteer.

An interesting psychological relationship exists between working for money and working for free in the voluntary sector. In almost no other job sector do people offer their time and skills freely. This is, arguably, what makes the voluntary sector a vibrant and interesting place to be, but it can also lead to a variety of tensions and problems.

These may take the form of a lack of communication, unclear boundaries about work responsibilities between paid workers and volunteers, difficult or stressful working relationships, an 'unpleasant' atmosphere and competitiveness. Some of these can be the result of unsatisfactory management. From the volunteer's perspective the keys to overcoming these are to be very clear about **why** you're volunteering and to have an understanding of **what** your presence may mean to the organisation and its staff.

Why Volunteer?

In choosing a charity to volunteer with the one essential criterion is that you are in sympathy with and share the organisation's ideals and objectives. Beyond that, each person's reasons for volunteering are different. It helps to be aware of yours as they are the key to a successful volunteering experience.

You may want to volunteer for personal or career reasons or a mixture of both. Personal reasons may include that you:

- feel strongly about a charity's cause and want to help
- have a year off to fill before going to college or starting a training course
- have a friend, who is a volunteer, who is asking you to help
- have time available on a regular basis and want to do something useful
- want to meet new friends.

If you are thinking more about developing your career, ask yourself whether you:

- want to learn a new skill?
- are trying to improve your employment prospects and add to your CV (Curriculum Vitae)?
- need specific practical experience before applying for a training course?
- think you might like to work in the voluntary sector but want to check it out first?

Whatever your reason(s) for volunteering, it is essential that your voluntary work meets your needs. Although you are not getting paid, it must bring you certain rewards and help you achieve your aims. For example, if you want to meet new people there is no point in volunteering in a situation where you are expected to work alone. Similarly, if you want to acquire new skills, your volunteer job needs to include some training or new experience.

The Psychology of Working in a Voluntary Organisation

Once you have identified your motivations (and they may be more complex than those outlined above), you need to research the right organisation for you and negotiate the right job for yourself (See next chapter Seeking Employment and Volunteer Opportunities). Once inside the voluntary organisation, you need to understand how the other staff may regard you.

Many voluntary organisations, especially the smaller organisations (but some of the larger ones too) work on extremely tight budgets in terms of money, time, resources and staff. The stress level among workers can be high. Sometimes staff may resent volunteers because they are taking up valuable resources in terms of training and management without any immediate return being obvious.

Also, staff can find volunteers threatening. This may be for all sorts of reasons including the fact that volunteers can be genuinely looking for work. Sometimes paid staff fear that their own jobs are at risk from a volunteer who is 'too successful'. It is up to those in management positions within the organisation to set the tone and establish clear guidelines for involving volunteers. Good communication with paid staff, setting agreed boundaries and careful induction are essential. If, as a volunteer, you find you are being treated in a way that is inappropriate and unacceptable, you should have no hesitation about approaching management or senior personnel within the organisation and discussing your views with them.

Many organisations have limited office space. It may not be possible to give a volunteer his or her own working area: you will have to be flexible about this. The most important thing is to be very clear about the task you have to do and to carry it out as efficiently and reliably as you can. Remember that many voluntary organisations are dependent on their volunteers to get the work done. But be very clear also about the boundaries of your own work, what it does and does not include, and where your responsibility begins and ends.

Although you may need to be aware of the above, people typically have enjoyable and rewarding volunteering experiences. Many volunteers stay with an organisation to which they feel committed for years. Conversely many voluntary organisations endorse just how important, if not vital, their volunteers are and retain them for years. If appropriate, they may offer them a paid job. The fruit of the collaborative partnership between employee and volunteer is evident in the long term success of a charity.

The Government's Make a Difference Initiative

The value of volunteers and the huge contribution they make to communities and life in the UK has now been formally recognised by the British Government.

In March 1994 the Government launched its 'Make a Difference' Volunteering Initiative, which reflects a desire to see an increase in the already high levels of volunteering. It wants to involve people who are not yet active volunteers and is determined to expand people's knowledge of volunteering opportunities so they are able to get involved. By setting up a team to focus on volunteering, the Initiative aims to encourage an integrated approach to developing effective local voluntary action through linking together those in the business, voluntary and public sectors.

Employers, voluntary organisations and public service providers will all be encouraged to promote and diversify volunteering by building partnerships, endorsing and publicising the value and importance of volunteers, and identifying unmet needs.

Accordingly, the Initiative is founded on the belief that overcoming obstacles to volunteering involves three positive steps:

1. raising awareness
2. making it easier for people to get and stay involved
3. developing a wider range of appropriate opportunities.

Developed through emerging local 'Make a Difference' partnerships, the Initiative will be underlain and supported by

- the UK Make a Difference Team – which will develop a UK volunteering strategy
- the Make a Difference Development Programme of grants to projects that fulfil the above three steps
- Make a Difference Action Plans to get government departments and agencies to 'think volunteering'.

The strategy will provide those involved in volunteering with a framework to ensure that the benefits of volunteer participation are spread throughout the UK. Businesses are especially encouraged to get their staff to volunteer to expand the idea of employee volunteering. But the aim is also to get those already involved as volunteers to promote the message that volunteering is fun.

Progress with the Initiative

As of October 1994, 27 winning groups with innovative schemes to encourage more people to take part in volunteering had been selected from more than 250 entries for the Development Programme grants. The winning groups, 17 from various parts of England, four from Scotland and three each from Wales and Northern Ireland, are all formed of partnerships between the private, voluntary and/or public sectors. They range from Councils for Voluntary Service (CVSs) and Volunteer Bureaux to Rural Community Councils and Employee Volunteering groups, with an equally wide range of projects targeting new volunteers in such categories as young, elderly, disabled or unemployed people, ethnic minority groups, and/or employee volunteers. Nearly £500,000 has been allocated among the 27 groups to support their exciting approaches to finding new ways of raising people's awareness of what voluntary action can achieve, and promoting the use and effectiveness of volunteers.

To find out more about the projects and the Initiative in each part of the UK you could contact the Home Office (0171-273 4600), the Scottish Office (0131-244 4951), the Welsh Office (01222-825645) or the Northern Ireland Office (01232-520700). From 1 March 1995 you can also try phoning the newly launched national telephone helpline which aims to put people in touch with local volunteering agencies. The idea is that anyone, any where in the UK, will be able to pick up a telephone and dial a single national phone number to find out where they can go to get more information on local volunteer opportunities. One call will be able to advise you about how to get involved in volunteering initiatives in your own area. The phone line is an information, not a placement, service, and should prove to be a useful new resource. The telephone number is 0345-221133.

Getting Paid Work

Range and Scope

The voluntary sector is diverse and wide-ranging. This is reflected in the types of employment opportunities in voluntary organisations. The larger charities, which generally have more jobs available, recruit staff regularly for full-time posts offering a range of opportunities. Some also offer seasonal work opportunities. Smaller charities have far fewer paid staff and correspondingly far fewer recruitment opportunities. Some may employ a new staff member only once in five or more years. However, if the work they do interests you, it is worthwhile contacting them. They may have a need for volunteers, if not for paid staff, or they may be able to put you in touch with other agencies working in the same field.

Finding out about opportunities

Most voluntary organisations use press advertising in one form or another to recruit staff. The Guardian on Mondays and Wednesdays is the most commonly used national paper for advertising job vacancies. The Independent's charity section on Thursdays is growing in importance. The Times is used by some. More specialist papers such as The Voice, the Pink Paper, the Asian Times and the Caribbean Times regularly carry advertisements for positions.

Where jobs are advertised depends largely on the status of the post. Professional, executive and more specialised posts tend to appear in national newspapers, but specialist journals and magazines are also used. These can include Community Care, the British Medical Journal (BMJ), Disability News or ecology and environmental publications. Local papers are frequently used to advertise clerical and more general administrative jobs, and some higher paid posts too. Branches of national voluntary organisations which recruit and manage their own staff, are also likely to use local and/or regional papers more. The publications that each organisation typically uses to advertise vacancies are generally listed in its entry in this Directory.

Few agencies appearing in the Directory use recruitment consultants. If and when they do, such consultants are approached to hire senior level executive and professional staff. Consultants include Charity Appointments, Charity Recruitment and Charity People. More generally, and for less senior posts, staff recruitment agencies, perhaps local to the organisation, are used. These can include agencies such as Reed and Graduate Careers. Job centres are popular for finding staff for certain administrative and secretarial positions. A few organisations rely on more informal methods, such as word of mouth, often through their members.

Voluntary organisations are becoming increasingly professional in their recruitment procedures. Many have already, or are implementing, written policy methods for employing staff. Many are already equal opportunities employers and most of the rest have some commitment towards developing equal opportunities policies. Many also follow formal procedures for recruiting staff. These include the use of printed application forms which need to be accompanied by succinct, well presented curriculum vitaes (CVs), followed by formal interviews.

Types of Employment Opportunities

As voluntary organisations adapt to changing economic and social conditions, so the range of employment opportunities in them continues to expand.

The variety of job opportunities in many voluntary sector bodies is now as wide as that in the commercial sector. Voluntary organisations need directors and chief executives, public relations (PR) and publicity managers, accountants and treasurers, heads of research and information, marketing and merchandising organisers, administrators and assistants of all kinds. Apart from these positions, an organisation may require specialist trained and qualified staff to achieve its aims. These might include people with medical, educational, social work or scientific backgrounds. In organisations using significant numbers of volunteers, volunteer co-ordinators may be employed. If the organisation is structured regionally, it may require regional co-ordinators or development officers, who might also be responsible for setting up more local branches.

All voluntary organisations need administrative and secretarial skills. Jobs can vary from director of administration to a part-time clerical assistant. In local branches of a national society or association, a single administrator or branch coordinator may be responsible for the day to day running of the branch. In these situations, support staff may work only a couple of days a week, doing the accounts or organising fund raising.

A number of voluntary organisations also offer seasonal employment. Charity Christmas card shops are well-known. Other opportunities include running holiday schemes for disabled children, such as the National Federation of Gateway Clubs – Gateway – organises for those with learning difficulties, or being leaders of volunteers who sign up for holiday conservation projects, as happens with Cathedral Camps. Similarly, Contact a Family runs summer and Christmas play schemes which require short-term employees.

Job opportunities are not always immediate. For example the Tracheotomy Patients' Aid Fund lets people start as volunteers by setting up self-help groups. In the next twelve months some of these volunteers will then be appointed as paid regional co-ordinators as funding becomes available. Indeed, volunteering for an organisation may be one way into paid employment (see section on volunteering below).

Other employment possibilities exist that are concerned with the voluntary sector, but are in commercial rather than voluntary organisations. Some of these are concerned with fundraising from the private and statutory sectors. Charity in Commerce for example, a small commercial promotions company set up in High Wycombe in 1993 (01494-712623), aims to promote and achieve donating through payroll giving, 'Workaid' and 'Give as You Earn' schemes for charities from employees. Keen to develop a network of national outlets, during 1995 the company was seeking to expand in various parts of England and in Wales. Particularly interested in recruiting returners and those who have been made redundant in middle age, it offers many opportunities and full training is given.

Applying for a Job

Voluntary organisations are keen to recruit people who share their aims and ideals, and who already have knowledge and experience of how the voluntary sector works. So experience of working with a voluntary organisation, whether in a paid or a voluntary capacity, is always beneficial.

As a general rule voluntary organisations do not welcome 'cold' applications for jobs. It is usually better to apply for a post you see advertised, rather than to 'spray and pray' the organisations of your choice with speculative letters and CVs. But you may find it useful to contact the personnel department/representative in those in which you would really like to work. You may get to meet them and be able to discuss possible opportunities and find out when vacancies are likely to occur. You might even find yourself being recruited as a volunteer.

Getting Voluntary Work

The many different types of voluntary organisations – social welfare, educational, developing countries, environmental to name a few – have many different aims and objectives. Some offer practical assistance, some raise funds for others to carry out major projects, yet others exist to change opinions and legislation through advocacy and lobbying. Most use volunteers in some way.

Apart from the agencies that make up the voluntary sector itself, statutory organisations are now offering and developing volunteer opportunities. In the health sector the Royal Borough of Kensington and Chelsea advertised in early 1995 for volunteers to be trained to work with young people in a health setting and support the Health Information Projects' afternoon 'drop in' session. In Berkshire, the local authority's Cultural Services runs an innovative scheme for delivering library books to house-bound people using volunteers. A wide range of possibilities exists in the field of education too. One recent initiative is 'The Place to Be' or P2B which is a network of over 100 volunteer therapists of different kinds who work in schools in London with primary school children who have a variety of problems, ranging from attempted suicide to shyness. Even if you are unemployed it is still possible to volunteer. Many organisations use unemployed volunteers and put them on Employment Training schemes, devised by the Employment Service for people on benefit.

Opportunities for volunteering in the voluntary sector are numerous. They can include stuffing envelopes, running a fundraising campaign or counselling on a telephone helpline. You could be a trustee or a stamp licker. You might be able to use your work experience or professional skills, or do something using totally different skills just for a change. The range of opportunities in any given organisation depends on its size, the nature of its work and its attitudes to, and dependence, on volunteers. Another factor is the availability of funding to employ paid staff. Most volunteers are used in administration and fundraising. However, there are also some very imaginative uses of volunteers. Pets as Therapy uses canine volunteers together with their owners. House of Light Trust is keen to recruit volunteer carers who see this work as a first step to entering one of the caring professions.

How many volunteers an organisation requires depends on its approach and on its size. Some organisations use only one or two; others, like the National Trust, involve thousands. Some depend on volunteers to do virtually all their work.

An estimated 23 million people volunteer in the UK every year. Among just the

....

*"*I am a volunteer advocate for an autistic man who lives alone and needs assistance with getting and maintaining a service to help him cope. You don't need any qualifications , but you do need a lot of confidence and some assertiveness in dealing with the professionals. I got involved partly through professional interest and partly because I thought I could help him and his parents have a better quality of life. I feel what I do is very powerful because no one can put me in a professional box. So I find it very rewarding because I have a sense of making a difference, of making people live up to what they say they will do, making the system work, and fighting hypocrisy. *"* Bill Goodyear, Volunteer Advocate

....

organisations appearing in this Directory which have indicated approximately how many volunteers they involve, the numbers amount to over 5 million. People often volunteer for more than one organisation, perhaps a sports club or the local school, as well as for a charity which interests them. Many organisations are actively seeking more volunteers to help with a wide variety of kinds of work.

Types of Volunteer Opportunities
Below are listed some examples of volunteer opportunities, illustrating also the kinds of skills involved, which we have found are needed. You may wish to use this as a tick list to identify the sorts of work you would like to do as a volunteer.

☐ Administrative work	☐ Holiday hosting
☐ Advice giving	☐ Information giving
☐ Advocacy	☐ Library/resource centre management
☐ Assessing grant applications	☐ Lobbying/campaigning
☐ Auditing	☐ Management committee membership
☐ Aviculture	☐ Play schemes
☐ Befriending	☐ Praying
☐ Bird wardens	☐ Press and PR
☐ Book-keeping	☐ Public speaking
☐ Cafe/restaurant management	☐ Railway 'navvying'
☐ Computer inputting	☐ Reading
☐ Cooking	☐ Reception work
☐ Counselling	☐ Research
☐ Database development/management	☐ Riding
☐ Driving	☐ Running self-help groups
☐ Escorting disabled people etc	☐ Sailing
☐ Exercising animals	☐ Shopping
☐ Fundraising	☐ Swimming
☐ Gardening	☐ Trustees
☐ Helping at festivals	☐ Youth work

Having identified some of your skills, how would you go about discovering where to go next for information? Although it may not be immediately apparent where to look in this directory for such opportunities, some of the examples given are actually quite easy to take forward. For example, almost all voluntary organisations need administrative assistance and fundraising; most require people to serve in management committees. So, if you have such skill(s) you should have a fairly wide choice of agencies: decide on the type of charity you'd like to work with and contact them.

If your ability and interests are more specialist, you may have to do some lateral thinking and some research. One clue is to think what sort of voluntary organisation might need your interest or skill. Suppose, for example, you are interested in railway 'navvying'? This will probably be required by an organisation that runs and/or restores railway lines. This is a form of recreation, as well as of conservation. So start by delving in this directory under 'Recreation and Leisure' and 'Environment and Conservation'. There is only one entry concerned with railways: the Association of Railway Preservation Societies which, from the information given, obviously has links with a wide range of organisations concerned with railways. You could then try phoning the

Association and explaining your interest and the information you want to someone like the Information Officer.

If, however, you wanted to set up a self help group, the place to start would be in 'Counselling and Self Help'. You might also look in 'Family and Community Matters' too. But supposing you wanted to volunteer for holiday hosting or teaching swimming to disabled people? The most effective starting places then will be in the list of 'Organisations at a glance' under their subject headings, such as 'Recreation' and 'Sports', and also in the alphabetical index, picking out any with appropriate names. You could also consult some of the books in the 'Useful Publications' list, most of which should either be in your public library or be available on inter-library loan.

Employee Volunteering/Employees in the Community
Volunteering as an employee is another way of getting involved as a volunteer. If you are in paid employment your company may already have an employee volunteering scheme. If not, then why not help get one started? The Government's Make a Difference Initiative is keen to expand and develop employee volunteering. From just one or two schemes a few years ago like that of Whitbread's, the idea is now catching on all over the UK. Such schemes benefit communities and community projects by providing a range of skills and resources that otherwise may not be available or affordable to the groups involved. The schemes also benefit the company and the employers, especially in contributing to positive public relations, as well as by enabling employees to develop new skills, and assisting management/staff communications. The kinds of work done are very wide ranging – any thing from fundraising to organising events for sick or disabled children, from visiting elderly people to working on projects with young offenders.

Any employee volunteering scheme needs enthusiasm and energy from the volunteers and the positive support of management. You need to want to volunteer and to be committed to whatever scheme you get involved in. If you want to help start a scheme you will need to work with other interested colleagues to research the possibilities locally and get suggestions. To help decide which local organisations you want to work with, you could draw up a short list and invite them to make a presentation. You might also get in touch with agencies that can give advice such as your local volunteer bureau (which might become a partner with you), the Volunteer Centre UK, and Action: Employees in the Community, tel: 0171-629 2209. Setting up an employee volunteering scheme needs genuine and sustained commitment, but the rewards are considerable, and should be fun too. There are also various events and awards available that reward both employees and companies for their initiatives and involvement.

Becoming a charity trustee
Another form of volunteering is to serve as a member of the managing committee or as a trustee. The titles used vary. The trustees are the group of people who ultimately control the organisation, even though they may employ staff or use volunteers to carry out the actual work done. They are almost always unpaid, and if the organisation is a charity, then they cannot be paid for the work they put in as a trustee – although they may have their out-of-pocket expenses reimbursed.

If you do want to serve as a trustee, you should first understand the legal responsibilities of the role and the amount of time and commitment that it will involve.

And if you still feel that this is the right step, then approach the organisation you would like to work with direct and ask. Being a trustee is a rewarding role in itself – as you are with your co-trustees at the helm of the organisation and are in a position actually to do something about a problem or need you feel strongly about. But it can also be a help if you are looking for employment in the voluntary sector, as it can only add to your experience and demonstrate your commitment.

Opportunities for volunteering in Europe, and in other areas overseas

Many of the organisations listed in this directory have links with similar organisations overseas. The development of these international connections is partly due to a growing awareness that voluntary organisations in different countries can learn from each other's research and expertise. But it is also due to a realisation that they share many issues and experiences in common, despite considerable differences in culture, language and environment. Thus some of the links are with English-speaking countries, notably Australia, New Zealand and the USA. Others are with countries throughout the developing world. Increasingly they are with European organisations, both in those countries that belong to the European Union (EU), and those that do not.

As relations with Europe via the EU have increased, and as recent developments in Eastern Europe have led to changes in political philosophies and governments, so the opportunities for volunteering throughout Europe have begun, and continue, to expand. Although European countries generally lack the size and diversity of the Voluntary Sector in the UK, nevertheless some have a significant, and growing, number of established voluntary organisations, while in others these are rapidly being set up and/or expanded eg in Poland, Roumania and Russia. Through these links and through developing intra-European organisations, many volunteering opportunities are already available in a diversity of voluntary agencies, from children to environment, from disability to education.

Whether within Europe or over a wider area of the world, some of the connections are formal; others are informal. Sometimes groups of charities in various countries join together to form a consortium or umbrella organisation serving a common interest. Thus DEBRA (Dystrophic Epidermolysis Bullosa Research Association) co-ordinates the European Network of EB Support Groups, while the Association of Railway Preservation Societies in the UK has set up Federail, representing railway preservation societies throughout Europe. L'Arche Worldwide has over 100 centres; while Cheshire Homes Far Eastern Region, part of the world-wide Cheshire homes network, has 40 autonomous Cheshire homes throughout the Asia/Pacific area, with more planned.

A wide variety of organisations has connections of various kinds with overseas counterparts. Community Service Volunteers (CSV) has links with Volonteurop for Europe and with Energise Inc. for the USA. The UK Sports Association has links with most EU member states, plus Romania, Poland and Estonia. Catholic Aids Link (CAL) has contacts with similar organisations world-wide, and with EUROCASO – church-based, grass-roots HIV organisations. Some British organisations have very specific or close contacts with a limited range of agencies overseas. Green Light Trust in Suffolk for example has developed links with the East Sepik Council of women (ESCOW) among only a few others. Every year young British people interested in conservation go to work on projects organised by the Australian Trust for Conservation Volunteers (ATCV) through its links with the British Trust for Conservation Volunteers (BTCV). Similarly, the RSPCA has set up training schemes in India and Eastern Europe, as well

....

II Established in 1988, Green Light Trust (GLT) gained charitable status in 1990. We set it up in response to the destruction we saw when we travelled to the East Sepik region in Papua New Guinea (PNG). Now we have a programme of education through action incorporating creative workshops, environmental theatre productions and grassroots projects, including planting community woodland in Suffolk. We work to unite environmental and cultural understanding and reawaken people's connection with nature, especially children's. Being responsible for the environmental side is challenging, exciting and very rewarding. We hope that through GLT we can demonstrate that even with a very small administrative base and no bureaucracy, we can have a wide influence by inspiring and motivating other people to take action. *II*
Richard Edmunds, Environmental Director, Green Light Trust

....

as linking up with animal welfare schemes world-wide.

Some organisations affiliate themselves to others for mutual benefit. Hearing Dogs UK for example is affiliated to Fedics in Italy and Hearing Dogs in France. Some agencies form associations of individual national organisations. Thus Young Enterprise Europe has members groups from across the continent united by the common purpose of enabling young people to learn about the world of work 'by doing', in an international perspective supported by business sector volunteers. Programmes of European events are organised annually, Young Enterprise companies meet at a specially initiated European Trade Fair and informal exchanges take place. Apart from exhibitions and trade fairs, sometimes international conferences are arranged to share and develop knowledge and experience across frontiers. In 1994 the British Association of Counselling together with the European Association for Counselling and other counselling organisations and individuals throughout Europe set up and ran a major international conference on aspects of cross-border counselling and psychotherapy in Europe.

As international involvement and relationships grow some organisations find that their original base is no longer the most appropriate one. Mobility International for example, formerly a UK-based organisation, has moved its headquarters location from London to Brussels. Others may have a base, but much of the actual work takes place in seminars, workshops and projects in widely disparate parts of the world, as happens with Working Partners and WOMANKIND Worldwide. Working Partners, which began in 1989 as 'Spouses for Development' and changed its name in 1992, is an affiliate of the United Nations Association of the UK, which in turn is affiliated to the World Federation of United Nations Associations (WFUNA) with member associations in 80 countries world-wide. Thus Working Partners, headquartered in London but acting globally, is the only international, non-governmental organisation (NGO) specifically

....

II I decided to volunteer for Working Partners because I support the objectives of helping the spouse/partner to use their skills in an effective manner when people are posted overseas. This gives them a sense of self esteem and benefits the developing country. Also, because Working Partners needs to be more widely known, as a journalist I can help publicise the cause, and contribute to changing government policies on the international movement of labour. It enables me to meet people from many different cultures and backgrounds too, and to extend my own network of contacts world-wide. *II* *Matt George, journalist and volunteer with Working Partners*

....

representing the interests of partners (including men) from diplomatic, military and commercial companies who want to develop their skills and careers in the host country, and contribute to international development, while accompanying their employed partner on an overseas posting. By late 1994 volunteer co-ordinators had already been appointed in 16 countries.

The variety and possibilities are considerable. If you are interested in volunteering/ working overseas, whether close to home in Europe or further afield, why not pick the type of organisation and the area in which you are interested and then simply see what is available.

Further information

The agencies below can provide advice and further information about various aspects of the voluntary sector.

Action: Employees in the Community, 8 Stratton Street, London W1X 5FD

The Charity Commission
St Alban's House, 57-60 Haymarket, London SW1 4QX
This is the regulatory body for charities in England and Wales. It publishes a range of literature about charities and the roles and responsibilities of trustees.

National Council for Voluntary Organisations
8 Regent's Wharf, All Saints Street London N1 9RL
NCVO is the national agency promoting voluntary action. It has a special unit dealing with trusteeship issues.

The Trustee Register.
c/o Reed Charity Fund 114 Peascod Street Windsor SL4 1DN
People wishing to service as charity trustees can put their name on the Trustee Register.

The Volunteer Centre UK, Carriage Row, 183 Eversholt Street, London NW1 1BU

Seeking Volunteering & Employment Opportunities

How to set about seeking opportunities

To join a voluntary agency, whether in a paid or voluntary capacity, you need to decide first what kind of work you want to do in what type of organisation. What appeals most? What do you feel you can best do? How can you make an effective contribution? Would you prefer administrative work in a charity dealing with children, or being a driver for an organisation helping sick, elderly, or disabled people, or buddying work with those suffering from Aids/HIV?

Once you have decided, the best next step is to contact an appropriate organisation in your local area. If you can't find one, then intermediary bodies which act as national federations or associations for (smaller) local groups, should be able to help you with suggestions and contacts. This Directory primarily covers national agencies, although a selection of smaller regional and/or local ones has also been included.

These intermediary organisations represent their affiliated member groups across the country. The members, however, are independent and autonomous at local level. They may be guided by a national constitution, but they decide locally, usually through a management committee, how best to put the constitution into practice, and what aspects of the aims and objectives to concentrate on.

There is a wide range of intermediary and national organisations with affiliated local branches. Many of these organisations appear in the Directory and are a good starting point for making contact with their local branches. A few examples, with their areas of interest, include:

ACRE – Action with Communities in Rural England – which supports the development of rural community projects

Age Concern – providing services for elderly people

Alzheimer's Disease Society – for people with dementia and their carers

Association of Community Health Councils – for local health bodies

British Association of Friends of Museums – for museums around the country

Business in the Community – for employee volunteering

Civic Trust – for local amenity groups

Hospices Information Service – for hospices country-wide

Mencap – for people with learning difficulties and their carers

National Association of Volunteer Bureaux – for local volunteer bureaux

Youth Clubs UK – for local youth clubs

and many, many more.

There are also national and intermediary organisations, themselves registered charities, which fulfil an umbrella role and provide services for their members who are also voluntary organisations. Some examples of these include the National Council for Voluntary Child Care Organisations, the British Refugee Council and the Federation of Independent Advice Centres (FIAC). If you are interested in the area covered by such agencies, each has lists of its member organisations, usually in the Annual Report, which will provide you with a good cross-section of the charities and other organisations working in the field.

Apart from getting in touch with umbrella or national organisations, there are also regional sources of information. If you live in Scotland, Wales, or Northern Ireland you can contact local agencies which have been set up to promote and support volunteering within their own region. They are:

Volunteer Development Scotland, 80 Murray Place, Stirling FK8 2BX, tel: 01786-479593; fax: 01786-447148

Volunteer Development Scotland promotes volunteering and makes connections between volunteering and voluntary bodies, central and local government, the private sector (commerce, industry, etc), and political, social and legal institutions throughout Scotland. As well as working on various programmes, including 'Make A Difference' and the Scottish Employee Volunteering Initiative, the agency also runs an information service. The requests it receives include those for information about volunteering, legal aspects, training, and screening of volunteers, among others. The agency also maintains a list of Scottish Volunteer Bureaux.

Wales Council for Voluntary Action, Cyngor Gweithredu Gwirfoddol Cymru, Llys Ifor, Crescent Road, Caerffili, Mid Glamorgan CF8 1XL, tel: 01222-869224; fax: 01222-860627.

The Council promotes volunteering throughout Wales, has offices in both north and south Wales, and produces a directory of Welsh voluntary organisations, many of whom involve volunteers.

Northern Ireland Volunteer Development Agency, Annsgate House, 70-74 Ann Street, Belfast BT1 4EH, tel: 01232-236100; fax: 01232-237570

The Agency promotes volunteering in Northern Ireland and supports volunteer-involving organisations through the provision of a Volunteer Development Forum and a Volunteering Development Training Group. A wide range of publications is produced including *Residential Volunteer Opportunities in Northern Ireland*.

Some of the entries in the directory are themselves specific to a particular regional or local area, although the 'market' or audience they serve may come from further afield. Examples include the Wales Youth Agency, the Warwickshire Association for the Blind, and Gainsborough's House Society in Sudbury, Suffolk.

Becoming a Volunteer (or an Employee)

It is worth bearing in mind how important volunteers are to voluntary sector organisations. In time, commitment, resources and other ways, it is said that volunteers bring into charities as much as fund raisers do in financial terms. Remember also that volunteering can often be a way of eventually getting into paid employment. Or you can volunteer simply because you want to. Before you contact a voluntary organisation, it is best to ask yourself some preliminary questions and to develop some awareness about the voluntary sector and how it works.

Ask yourself first what are your aims and objectives in seeking paid or voluntary work? Voluntary sector work can be very rewarding, and offers satisfaction, personal fulfilment and useful experience, even if you don't receive any pay. Whether doing voluntary or paid work, you will be an ambassador for the organisation, so to be effective you need to understand – and share – its aims and its 'mission statement'.

You will need to make some initial decisions
● what type of organisation do you want to be involved in?
● will your involvement be voluntary or paid (if possible) or even a mixture of both?
● what would you like to do? – work similar to the usual work you do or have done, or something completely different?
● do you want to undertake a specific task, such as fundraising?
● do you want to gain some administrative experience perhaps, or are you hoping to prepare for vocational training?
● do you want to use your existing skills or develop new ones?
What time will you have available
● daily/weekly, seasonal, regular/irregular?
Do you want
● to be involved intensively for a short period of time, e.g. two weeks each summer, or three months abroad?
● to have a regular commitment for a few hours a week or a month?
● to travel overseas or work just round the corner?

If you are volunteering it is important to clarify how much time you can realistically give. It is often better for a voluntary organisation to have someone for a couple of hours regularly than for a whole day intermittently.

Voluntary organisations need and value reliability from their volunteers. They also ask for commitment, enthusiasm, patience and flexibility. Some ask for interest in the subject of their work, which may mean being good with particular types of people, such as children or the elderly. Others require personal experience of the organisation's work – for example to have had a urostomy or a child with a stoma, or to be physically disabled or a carer for someone who is.

Volunteering is for everyone. It transcends race, age and gender. There are possibilities for people who are disabled too. Traditionally volunteers have come from the leisured middle classes. Nowadays people from a wide range of backgrounds are volunteering in their own communities. Everyone has something to offer. Certain agencies have been set up to promote opportunities: for instance, the 'Resource Unit for Black Volunteering' promotes the involvement of black people as volunteers. There is also widespread interest in promoting volunteering among the long-term unemployed. Employees, too, are

....

❝ I worked for fourteen years as a wig maker. The money was good but the work was very repetitive. I wanted a new experience, so when I was offered redundancy, I took it and decided to retrain for another career. I took an Employment Training course and then went on a work placement for a small charity. Well, the amazing thing was that when I was due to finish my placement a big cheque came in which has enabled the charity to take me on full-time at a proper wage. I really feel volunteering is a wonderful way to prove yourself as capable of a job – especially if you're a bit older. It really shows you have commitment and gives you a reference and enormously valuable experience. If you go on placement as a volunteer, and they can see that you're willing, they'll probably give you a chance. ❞ *Denise, PA to the Director of a small charity*

....

increasingly volunteering in the community. 'Business in the Community' helps companies establish or extend employee volunteering programmes.

You will need to assess what skills you particularly can offer. Voluntary organisations need many different types of skills, perhaps those which you have taken for granted. Do a skills audit on yourself. List everything you can do, whether or not the skills are 'professional' or not. Being a 'good listener', for example, is considered a social skill. It could be the first step to becoming a counsellor, after training. Everyday abilities, such as driving and reading, are valued too. Secretarial skills, such as word processing, telephone answering or filing, are always needed.

Once you have listed your various skills, decide which ones you most want to offer. Is your professional ability in accountancy or word-processing? Or would you prefer to develop completely new skills, perhaps learn how to fundraise or to care for an elderly person as a visiting care attendant?

Strategic Volunteering

You may have decided that you would like to pursue a career for which you have not yet got the right experience or skills. This might be as an administrator, a bookkeeper, or an advisor, or perhaps the necessity of training for one of the counselling/caring professions. Alternatively, you may want to develop your committee skills by serving as a trustee or extend your media contacts with a stint as a volunteer PR assistant in a charity. The possibilities are limitless. But to get the most out of your volunteering you will need to develop a strategy based on the following:

- assessment of your current skills and attributes
- research into the skills and attributes you will need
- search for the organisation in which you can acquire the skills and attributes you need
- effective presentation of your new skills on your CV and at interviews.

Many people possess skills and attributes which they don't recognise as important or useful. Carrying out your own Skills and Attributes Audit, perhaps with a friend, is a good way of discovering hidden or unsuspected abilities. This process will help you prepare your CV more effectively. As a general rule, a skill is something you can **do** eg teaching, counselling, word processing, and an attribute is something you **are** eg a good listener, a left hander.

Begin by asking yourself – and your friend if you are working together – what you have already done. For example you may have

- worked in bank for 30 years and been made redundant. Your abilities might include: financial skills, money management, managing staff, dealing with customer complaints, coping with new technology, negotiating with many different types of people
- managed a household. This has required: an ability to juggle three or more things at once, controlling a household budget, organisational and inter-personal skills, as well as being able to plan menus, cook, sew and clean
- just left school. Perhaps you: edited the school magazine, helped to run a club or society, argued for a cause you really believe in at a school debate.

As important as skills and attributes is the confidence that comes from the subtle amalgam of both of them. Confidence is based on knowing you have usable, valuable abilities, and having had a positive experience of using them. The word 'confidence' comes from the Latin word meaning 'faith', and means that you believe you have the

II My two main interests are art and psychology. I'm doing an NVQ Level 3 in Business Administration following a BA in Fine Art which I completed last summer. Part of the business course means doing a volunteer placement for one day a week which I am doing at ACT (Arts Counselling Trust). I was immediately drawn to it as it offers creative arts therapies – painting, clay, music, movement and drama – to people in prison and on probation. I do every kind of work here: cash, newsletters, phone calls, typing, making orders, telephone work. It's wonderful experience learning how a small charity runs and also finding out how art therapy has to be supported by an good firm structure. It's not like a mere job – it's a real introduction to a world I want to be in. It's made everything make sense. *II*   *Mary, volunteer placement with ACT (Arts Counselling Trust)*

ability to do something. Volunteering is an excellent way to develop confidence.

Once you have established what skills and attributes you already possess, you will then have to decide what else you must acquire as part of your strategic plan. Working with a friend or buddy is a good way to do this as you can take it in turns to interview each other and tease out what it is that you each really need in terms of training and experience.

Once you have compiled a list of your needs – and each person's will, of course, be unique – you can then set about finding the right charity in which to volunteer. Under the **Opportunities for Volunteers** section in each organisation's entry in this directory, you will find details of any training that is offered. Examples of training include in data base/word processor, telephone answering, retailing, basic first aid, listening and counselling skills.

However, useful experience doesn't just come in the form of training. Many of the volunteer opportunities listed here are in the areas of fundraising and administration. Fundraising encompasses all sorts of skills including financial management, creative thinking, planning an event, presenting an argument for an important cause, and perhaps contributing something which is saleable, such as clothes or home-made marmalade. Many of these skills are very useful in the job marketplace, as are administrative skills. Recruiting volunteers to set up support or local groups is another common need of many charities, and offers invaluable experience in organisational and inter-personal skills, such as persuading other people to join in and help, setting aims and objectives, chairing meetings, and planning agendas.

Once you have chosen the organisation you most want to volunteer with, made contact, and been accepted, you will need to negotiate with them a contract that allows you to follow your strategic course, while also fulfilling their requirements. Be careful not to allow yourself to get side-tracked into an area that takes you away from your own goals. Since it is likely that at some time in the future you will want to ask the organisation for a reference, remember as a volunteer to treat your volunteering with the same seriousness you would a paid job. The key points are: professionalism and reliability. Be professional in your attitude, your behaviour and your work, and be absolutely reliable. Asking for regular assessments if possible will help you monitor your progress.

Finally, remember to write up your new found skills and attributes on your CV (Curriculum Vitae). Illustrate them with examples of work, whether voluntary or paid. For further help with your CV, see Appendix 2 'How to Write a Successful CV' in *How to Work for a Charity – on a Paid or Voluntary Basis* by Jan Brownfoot and Frances Wilks.

Joining a Voluntary Organisation

Once you have answered the questions above and decided what agencies or area of voluntary work you would like to be involved with, you will need to get in contact and offer your skills. It is probably best to try in your local area first. Various organisations can put you in touch (see below). There are several ways of volunteering locally:

1. Use this Directory to target local groups or ask charities that you are interested in for a list of local groups. Check if there is a local branch of the charity of your choice in your area. If not, you might consider starting one up.
2. Contact the Volunteer Centre UK in London for suggested organisations. The Centre has established a national database called Signposts.
3. Contact your local Volunteer Bureau. Bureaux have information on a wide range of local organisations and groups which need volunteers.
4. Phone the national Volunteer phone line.
5. Make direct contact with a particular organisation which you would like to work for. Look in the telephone directory, Thompson's Directory or Yellow Pages for their number.
6. Look out for advertisements or articles in your local paper about local voluntary organisations and campaigns. If none of these can give you any specific names, ask in your local library.

Contacting a voluntary organisation

You can make a direct approach. A preliminary phone call can identify who you should contact. If in doubt about who to ask for, talk to the Personnel Department or, in smaller agencies, the Director. Some agencies, such as Christian Aid, Help the Aged, the National Trust, and Barnardos, employ volunteer co-ordinators. Others are best contacted through project managers who manage local projects for national organisations like the National Association for the Care and Resettlement of Offenders NACRO. In the entries in this Directory the name of a person, a job title and/or a department is/are given as the relevant contact.

Make an appointment to see the appropriate person if possible. Otherwise write to them indicating your interest and what you can offer. Ask for some information, such as the Annual Report or an explanatory leaflet on the organisation. Suggest an informal meeting.

You may then have to fill in an application form and attend a formal interview. Some agencies ask for references, too. In addition those organisations working with vulnerable people and children are usually required to seek police screening for both paid and voluntary helpers.

Once you have been accepted in the organisation you will need to agree your involvement. This can include

- getting a clear job description
- establishing the place and space where you will be working
- identifying whether you will need any training
- agreeing the days and hours of work
- ascertaining who you will be supervised by
- clarifying what expenses, if any, will be paid.

In the Directory, the minimum commitment requested by each organisation is indicated where relevant. Some agencies are more flexible than others on this matter. Most voluntary organisations now offer some expenses, typically for travel, and often for lunch too. Other expenses can often be negotiated. A few agencies pay volunteer allowances, especially those who need volunteers on an extended basis, such as VSO (Voluntary Service Overseas) or those using holiday camp leaders.

Networking
Finally some comments about the importance of networking when volunteering/ working in the voluntary sector may be useful. There are several sorts of networking:
- informal networking within an organisation
- group networking – where individuals meet to discuss issues and share information
- professional networking – a way of increasing your professional contacts.

Informal Networking
Many people find out about opportunities within an organisation by practising a form of networking. This involves making contacts with people you meet and talking to them. It's an effective way of finding out what's going on internally, and what the needs and opportunities are. You can then see whether you, or someone you know, could be of benefit to the situation. This may be by providing specialist information, sharing contacts perhaps with the press, or identifying someone you know as suitable for a job vacancy.

Informal networking can be especially useful if you are a volunteer as you may hear of a job going in another department which would be worth while applying for. Even if the organisation has an equal opportunities programme, you, or the person you suggest, will be no worse off than any outside candidates and the 'inside knowledge' may prove beneficial.

The best way of networking from within is to develop working relationships which are relaxed and friendly. Always be professional, but be on the lookout for any suggestions that you can make that would be of benefit to the organisation. The key to successful networking is not to look for opportunities that might benefit you, but to build a reputation for being a person who is genuinely friendly, helpful, knowledgeable, and wants to contribute positively.

Group Networking
This is where a group of friends get together regularly to share information. The group may meet in someone's house, a local centre or a Jobclub. The benefits are that you can give each other support and encouragement, and that you can pool ideas, knowledge and resources. Sometimes, a person in such a network will hear of a job that is not suitable for them, but which they can suggest to others in the group.

Courses such as those run by Working for a Charity, encourage participants to keep in touch with each other afterwards. The Charity Forum, a national membership organisation for people working in fundraising and marketing in the voluntary sector, arranges lunchtime talks once a month in London which provide opportunities to meet other people working in the sector.

Professional Networking
This is the process by which you use personal contacts to assist you in your job search. A fuller account of how to do this is given in *How To Work for a Charity – on a Paid or Voluntary Basis*. Basically, networking in this way involves talking to people you know

or are put in contact with and finding out information from them. Doing this may lead to a job – but information, not employment, is the primary aim.

Make a list of all the people you know in the area of the voluntary sector that you want to work in. For example a good friend of your uncle might be the Honorary President or on the Management Committee of a small charity. He/she will not be in a position to offer you a job but will be able to give you two vital pieces of information:
● a insider's view of what a charity is like and how it functions
● suggestions as to named contacts you might approach.
Follow this up by approaching the contacts and asking for an interview or a meeting, not a job. For people you don't know it's probably a good idea to write a letter explaining why you want to see them and saying that you will phone them in a few days. Gaining knowledge by talking to people active in the type of organisation you want to join will not only give you invaluable information, but also a confidence which will be noticeable when you eventually go for an interview.

Often when people say they were in the right place at the right time, it means they have been networking at some level. One woman who was keen to get a job in a voluntary organisation wrote around 100 letters and followed these up with almost the same number of interviews. Some months later, she was offered the perfect job.

And Finally...

Not all the information you may need can be given in the space of one book. At the end of this Directory we have included a selected list of publications and some useful addresses in case you want to find out more. Apart from these, one of the most important sources of information in the voluntary sector is people. In the course of your own work - whether as a volunteer or an employee - you will meet a rich variety of people who will be able to tell you their own stories. How they found the right organisation, how they got the job they wanted, or perhaps how they started a charity themselves! Reflecting the diversity of the voluntary sector, each one will be unique.

The people we have met ourselves while researching for this Directory and for *How to Work for a Charity* have frequently been inspirational. So it is appropriate these introductory chapters should end with the words of one such volunteer of long standing.

....

When my sight got much worse through a condition I've had since birth, I rather despaired of ever finding anything worthwhile to do. I volunteered for a charity, not because I wanted to but because someone asked me and I went along not really expecting very much. Since then I've volunteered in many different ways, and they've often led to paid work. I've also learnt one important lesson: You only get out of life what you put in. I now put a lot into it and get so much out of it. At the moment as a volunteer I'm doing a report for the Victoria and Albert Museum on access for disabled people. Fingers crossed, it may lead to a job. My disability is still there but it's a far less significant part of my life. I've discovered there's so much more to life - of real worth, ideas to be enjoyed, people to be encountered, needs to be fulfilled.
Humphrey Selfe, broadcaster and volunteer at the Victoria and Albert Museum, London

....

How to Use This Directory

The starting point for the second edition of this Directory was its predecessor, the first edition, which in turn developed out of the Directory of Social Change's database and various published guides, including The Voluntary Agencies Directory published by the Bedford Square Press of the National Council for Voluntary Organisations (NCVO). We are also grateful to the people who wrote to us with suggestions for improving the second edition – we have tried to include as many of them as possible. Among other sources of information and assistance are the regional agencies for volunteer promotion in Scotland, Wales and Northern Ireland, staff of the Make a Difference Initiative at the Voluntary Service Unit of the Home Office, and a wide variety of publications.

The changes in this second edition include an increase in the number of entries from 500 to over 650. Not only are there more overall, but there is a wider range of organisations. We have listed some which are very local, others which only operate in a particular region or county. We have also updated and amended as far as possible the existing entries from DOVEO 1, eliminating any which have shut down or are no longer relevant. We have also increased and refined the number of subject categories into which the entries are grouped.

The Directory is now divided into 32 subject categories. Organisations are then listed alphabetically within each category. In determining an entry's alphabetical listing, words such as 'The' are omitted. It is the next main word eg National or Society, that applies. Look under the category which interests you and then look alphabetically for the organisation's name. Some organisations could logically have a listing in more than one category. Where this is the case, they are cross-referenced to their most important category, which is where their entry appears.

Each entry is laid out in exactly the same way beginning with the organisation's name, address and phone number. The information included on each is relatively brief. The contact given might be a named individual, or a person's position, or a department within the organisation which can help with details about volunteering or employment opportunities. You may be able to phone a particular individual or you may have to ask for the specific department and explain why you are contacting them.

The section on **Main Activities** covers the organisation's aims and objectives, as well as what it does in practice. The **Opportunities for Volunteers** indicates whether the organisation uses volunteers and, if so, in what ways. Some organisations prefer people to contact them direct for any detailed information, so the details under their entry may be very brief.

The **Opportunities for Employment** section gives you, as far as possible, an indication of the size of an organisation's staff, how often it recruits and where posts are advertised. Because of the competition for paid posts, it is best not to simply send off your CV to an organisation you may be interested in working for. Find out first whether there are any possible vacancies, and look out for advertisements and any other evidence that the organisation is interested in recruiting staff eg ask at your local job centre.

Further Information outlines what else is available and also any other relevant addresses. The great majority of organisations publish annual reports. Many have other publications such as leaflets and posters. As these can cost a considerable amount to produce, a factor of particular importance to the very small organisations, and as large numbers of copies may not be readily available, it is preferable to write for copies, asking also whether any charges are made. Stamped addressed envelopes (SAEs) are appreciated.

A very few of the agencies in the Directory do not have either volunteering or employment opportunities currently. Where there is no information available it means the organisation is not looking for volunteers and/or for paid employees at the moment. However, such organisations may seek people in the future. Alternatively, they may be able to put you in touch with other organisations active in the same area of work which may require volunteer help or could need to recruit paid employees. They have been included in the Directory for information purposes because in some instances they are the only voluntary agency working in their particular field of interest.

This Directory and the Future

This is the second time this Directory has been published. We realise that, despite considerable research effort, there are organisations involving volunteers which are not included here. If your organisation would like an entry in a subsequent edition of this Directory, please write to the following address: Directory of Volunteering and Employment Opportunities, Directory of Social Change, 24 Stephenson Way, London NW1 2DP – and we will ensure you are sent a questionnaire to fill in.

We are also very interested in getting feedback from people who use this Directory. We would particularly appreciate hearing from volunteers about their experiences of volunteering, including those who have found that volunteering acted as a bridge to paid employment. Do write to us at the Directory of Social Change at the above address.

Organisations at a Glance

Advice
Lambeth Social Services, Voluntary Sector Unit
London Advice Services Alliance (LASA)
National Association of Citizens Advice Bureaux (NACAB)

Aids/HIV
AIDS Care Education & Training (ACET)
Aids Helpline (NI)
Body Positive
Catholic Aids Link (CAL)
Crusaid
Crusaid Scotland
IMMUNITY Legal Centre
London Lighthouse
National Aids Trust (NAT)
Positively Women

Animals
The Blue Cross Animal Welfare Society
British Union for the Abolition of Vivisection (BUAV)
Humane Research Trust
National Canine Defence League (NCDL)
People's Dispensary for Sick Animals
Pets As Therapy (PAT)
PRO Dogs National Charity (PRO Dogs)
Royal Society for the Prevention of Cruelty to Animals (RSPCA)
Southern Marine Life Rescue (SMLR)
Wood Green Animal Shelters (WGAS)
World Society for the Protection of Animals (WSPA)

Bereavement
The Compassionate Friends (TCF)
CRUSE Bereavement Care
Jewish Bereavement Counselling Service
London Association of Bereavement Services (LABS)
National Association of Bereavement Services (NABS)
Wandsworth Bereavement Service

Broadcasting
Broadcasting Support Services (BSS)
Campaign for Press and Broadcasting Freedom (CPBF)
Deaf Broadcasting Council (DBC)
Voice of the Listener and Viewer (VLV)

Caring

The Befriending Network
Break
Cancer Care Society (CARE)
Cancer Relief Macmillan Fund
CARE for People with a Mental Handicap (CARE)
Christian Concern for the Mentally Handicapped (A Cause for Concern)
Crossroads (Association of Crossroads Care Attendant Schemes Ltd)
Guideposts Trust Ltd
Jewish Care
Medical Foundation for the Victims of Torture
National Autistic Society
National Society for Epilepsy
The Stroke Association
Tactent, Cancer Support – Scotland
Tracheotomy Patients Aid Fund (TPAF)
Turning Point

Charity Support

Charities Advisory Trust
Charities Aid Foundation (CAF)
Charity Christmas Card Council (4C)
Charity Projects Comic Relief
REACH
Swanley District Volunteer Bureau

Children

Action for Sick Children
Aid for Children with Tracheostomies (ACT)
Barnardos London Division
The Boys' Brigade
The British Institute for Brain Injured Children (BIBIC)
Cancer and Leukaemia in Childhood Trust (CLIC UK)
Child Growth Foundation (CGF)
Child Poverty Action Group (CPAG)
ChildLine
The Childlink Adoption Society
Children in Wales /Plant yng Nghymru
Children's Country Holidays Fund (CCHF)
The Children's Society
The Children's Trust
Fair Play for Children
Foundation for the Study of Infant Deaths (FSID)
HAPA (formerly Handicapped Adventure Playground Association)
Hyperactive Children's Support Group (HACSG)

Multiple Births Foundation
NASPCS, the Charity for Incontinent and Stoma Children
National Association for Gifted Children (NAGC)
National Association of Toy and Leisure Libraries/Play Matters
National Childminding Association (NCMA)
National Children's Home (NCH)
National Deaf Children's Society (NDCS)
National Foster Care Association (NFCA)
National Playbus Association (NPA)
National Society for the Prevention of Cruelty to Children (NSPCC)
Pestalozzi Children's Village Trust
Pre-school Playgroups Association (PPA)
RESPITE
Save the Children Fund (SCF)
St Piers Lingfield
Thomas Coram Foundation for Children

Counselling & Self Help

Abuse in Therapy Support Network
ACCEPT
Acceptance (Helpline and Support Group for Parents of Lesbians and Gay Men)
Action on Phobias Associations Scotland (AOPAS)
Al-Anon Family Groups UK and Eire (AFG)
Alcohol Concern
Alcohol Counselling and Prevention Services (ACAPS)
Alcoholics Anonymous (AA)
Anorexia and Bulimia Nervosa Association (ABNA)
Arthritis Care (Wales)
The Arts Counselling Trust (ACT)
APA (Association for the Prevention of Addiction)
Association for Stammerers (AFS)
BACUP (British Association of Cancer United Patients)
Behçet's Syndrome Society
British Association for Counselling (BAC)
CALL (Cancer Aid and Listening Line)
Cancer Link
Catholic Marriage Advisory Council (CMAC)
Child Abuse Survivor Network
City and Hackney Alcohol Counselling Service (City and Hackney ACS)
Contact a Family
Counsel and Care
Drug and Alcohol Women's Network (DAWN)
Drugline

Fellowship of Depressives Anonymous (FDA)
Gender Dysphoria Trust International (GDTI)
Guillain-Barré Syndrome Support Group
 (GBS Support Group)
The Haemophilia Society
Herpes Association
Ileostomy and Internal Pouch Support Group
 (IA)
Let's Face It – Support Network for Facially
 Disfigured
Life for the World Trust
London Lesbian and Gay Switchboard
Lowe Syndrome Association (LSA)
Lupus UK
Mind over Matter (MOM)
Myalgic Encephalomyelitis Association (ME
 Association)
National Agoraphobic Society
National Marriage Guidance Council (Relate)
National Rett Syndrome Association (NRSA)
National Society for Epilepsy (NSE)
The Neurofibromatosis Association
New Approaches to Cancer
Psoriasis Association
QUIT – Helping Smokers to Quit
Release
The Samaritans
The Society for Mucopolysaccharide Diseases
 (The MPS Society)
St Marylebone Healing & Counselling Centre
STEPS (National Association for Children
 with Lower Limb Abnormalities)
Victim Support

Disability

Access Committee for England
Action for Blind People
Action for Dysphasic Adults
Afterwards
The Arthrogryposis Group (TAG)
Arts Disability Wales (ADW)
ASPIRE (Association for Spinal Injury
 Research, Rehabilitation & Reintegration)
Association for Spina Bifida &
 Hydrocephalus
British Deaf Association (BDA)
British Retinitis Pigmentosa Society
Brittle Bone Society
Camphill Village Trust (CVT)
Camping for the Disabled
Citizen Advocacy Alliance (CAA)
Citizen Advocacy Information and Training
 (CAIT)
CMT International UK
The Commonwealth Society for the Deaf

Crypt Foundation
DIAL UK (Disablement Information &
 Advice Lines)
Disability Law Service (Network for the
 Handicapped Ltd)
Disability Scotland
Disabled Housing Trust (DHT)
Disabled Living (DL)
Disabled Living Foundation (DLF)
Disabled Motorists' Federation (DMF)
The Disablement Income Group (DIG)
Elfrida Rathbone
Friends of the Young Deaf (FYD)
Gift of Thomas Pocklington
Graeae Theatre Company
Greater London Association of Disabled
 People (GLAD)
The Guide Dogs for the Blind Association
 (GDBA)
Hearing Dogs for the Deaf
Holiday Care Service
House of Light Trust
I CAN (Invalid Children's Aid Nationwide)
In Touch Trust
The International Autistic Research
 Organisation/ Autism Research Ltd
International Disability Education and
 Awareness (IDEA)
L'Arche
The Leonard Cheshire Foundation
MENCAP, Royal Society for Mentally
 Handicapped Children and Adults
Mobility Information Service
Mobility International
Mobility Trust
Music for the Disabled
Myotonic Dystrophy Support Group
National Association of Deafened People
 (NADP)
National Deaf-Blind League
National Disability Arts Forum
National Federation of Gateway Clubs
 (Gateway)
Nystagmus Action Group (NAG)
One-To-One
Outset
Paddington Integration Project (PIP)
Paradise Community
Phab, Physically Disabled and Able Bodied
Prader-Willi Syndrome Association (UK)
Ravenswood Foundation
Riding for the Disabled Association (RDA)
Royal National Institute for Deaf People
Royal National Institute for the Blind (RNIB)

SOS Stars Organisation Supporting Action
    for People with Cerebral Palsy
Spinal Injuries Association (SIA)
Sue Ryder Foundation
Treloar Trust
United Response
Urostomy Association
Warwickshire Association for the Blind
    (WAB)
Winged Fellowship Trust (WFT)

Education

ADFAM National
ADiTi - The National Organisation of South
    Asian Dance
African Caribbean Library Association
Anthrosophical Society in Great Britain
British Association for Early Childhood
    Education
British Association for the Advancement of
    Science
British Dyslexia Association (BDA)
Business In The Community (BITC)
Campaign for State Education (CASE)
Community Transport Association Ltd
The Dyslexia Institute
Endeavour Training
Family Education Trust (FET)
ICOM (Industrial Common Ownership
    Movement)
Inter-Action
The Marine Society
Mary Ward Centre
Midwives Information and Resource Service
    (MIDIRS)
The National Association for Special
    Education Needs (NASEN)
National Confederation of Parent Teacher
    Associations (NCPTA)
The National Star Centre, College of Further
    Education
Network 81
Notting Dale Urban Studies Centre
Parent Partnership Project
Sing for Pleasure
United Kingdom Council for Overseas
    Student Affairs (UKCOSA)
Volunteer Reading Help
Workers' Educational Association (WEA)
Worldaware
Worldwide Education Service (WES)

Elderly People

The Abbeyfield Society
Age Concern England

Age Concern, Kensington and Chelsea
Age Exchange/Age Exchange Theatre Trust
Anchor Housing
Centre for Policy on Ageing (CPA)
Contact the Elderly
Daybreak (Wales) Ltd
Friends of the Elderly (FOTE)
Help the Aged
Methodist Homes for the Aged / Methodist
    Homes Housing Association Limited
National Benevolent Fund for the Aged
    (NBFA)
The Royal Agricultural Benevolent
    Institution
The Royal Surgical Aid Society (RSAS)
Semi Care Trust (Support the Elderly
    Mentally Infirm)
The Sons of Divine Providence

Environment & Conservation

Action with Communities in Rural England
    (ACRE)
British Trust for Conservation Volunteers
    (BTCV)
British Trust for Ornithology (BTO)
Campaign for Nuclear Disarmament (CND)
Capital Transport Campaign
Cathedral Camps
Centre for Alternative Technology (C.A.T.)
Chelsea Physic Garden
Civic Trust (Community Action)
Council for the Protection of Rural England
    (CPRE)
Earthwatch Europe
Free Form Arts Trust Limited
Friends of the Earth (FoE)
The Georgian Group
Green Light Trust
Greenpeace
Groundwork
Inland Waterways Association (IWA)
Kent Trust for Nature Conservation
Land Use Volunteers (LUV)
London Wildlife Trust (LWT)
The Nansen Society
National Federation of City Farms (NFCF)
The National Trust for Places of Historic
    Interest
National Trust for Scotland
Neighbourhood Energy Action (NEA)
Open Spaces Society (OSS) (formally the
    Commons, Open Spaces and Footpaths
    Preservation Society)
Peace People Farm Project
Pedestrians Association

Royal Society for the Protection of Birds
(RSPB)
Scottish Conservation Projects Trust (SCP)
Tidy Britain Group
Tim Lilley Fundraising Consultancy
Transport 2000
Trust for Urban Ecology (TRUE)
Wildfowl and Wetlands Trust (WWT)
The Wildlife Trusts (formerly the Royal
Society for Nature Conservation, RSNC)
The Woodland Trust

Ethnic Minorities
Confederation of Indian Organisations (CIO)
Migrant Resource Centre
West Glamorgan Race Equality Council

Family & Community Matters
Brent Family Service Unit (FSU)
Community Matters
CRY-SIS Support Group
Divorce Conciliation & Advisory Service
(DCAS)
Exploring Parenthood Trust
Families Need Fathers
Family Mediation Scotland (FMS)
Family Service Units (FSU)
Family Welfare Association (FWA)
HALOW (Help and Advice Line for
Offenders, Wives and Families)
Home-Start Consultancy
Independent Adoption Service
Kith and Kids
National Council for One Parent Families
(NCOPF)
National Council for the Divorced and
Separated (NCDS)
National Family Mediation Service (NFM)
PARENTLINE
Parent Network
Parent to Parent Information on Adoption
Services
Parents Against Injustice (PAIN)
Parents Aid
Parents Anonymous London (PAL)
Prisoners Families and Friends Service
Prisoners Wives and Families Society (PWFS)
Stepfamily (National Stepfamily Association)
Working for Childcare

Health & Medicine
Action for Victims of Medical Accidents
Alzheimer's Disease Society (ADS)
The Amarant Trust
Aperts Syndrome Support Group

Arthritis & Rheumatism Council for Research
(ARC)
ASH (Action on Smoking and Health)
Association for Glycogen Storage Disease
(UK) (AGSD (UK))
Association for Improvements in the
Maternity Services (AIMS)
Association of Community Health Councils
for England and Wales (ACHCEW)
Baby Life Support Systems, BLISS
British Colostomy Association
British Council for Prevention of Blindness
(BCPB)
British Diabetic Association (BDA)
British Heart Foundation (BHF)
The British Kidney Patient Association
(BKPA)
British Liver Trust
British Lung Foundation
British Migraine Association
British Organ Donor Society (BODY)
British Polio Fellowship
Brook Advisory Centres
Cancer Research Campaign
Casualties Union
Child
Child Accident Prevention Trust (CAPT)
Cleft Lip And Palate Association (CLAPA)
DEBRA (Dystrophic Epidermolysis Bullosa
Research Association)
Down's Syndrome Association (DSA)
The Dystonia Society
Elimination of Leukaemia Fund (ELF)
Family Planning Association (FPA)
Fight for Sight
Health Rights Ltd
Help to Hand
Huntington's Disease Association
Imperial Cancer Research Fund
Institute for Complementary Medicine
Institute of Cancer Research ICR
International Centre for Active Birth
Iris Fund for Prevention of Blindness
ISD (Institute for the Study of Drug
Dependence)
LEPRA (The British Leprosy Relief
Association)
Leukaemia Research Fund
Medical Aid for Palestinians (MAP)
Medical Aid for Poland Fund (MAP)
Motor Neurone Disease Association (MNDA)
Muscular Dystrophy Group of Great Britain
and Northern Ireland
Myasthenia Gravis Association

National Ankylosing Spondylitis Society
(NASS)
National Association for Colitis and Crohns
Disease (NACC)
National Association for the Relief of Paget's
Disease (NARPD)
National Asthma Campaign
National Eczema Society (NES)
National Federation of Kidney Patients
Associations
National Meningitis Trust
National Reye's Syndrome Foundation of the
UK (Reye's Syndrome Foundation)
Neuroblastoma Society
Noonan Syndrome Society (NSS)
Parkinson's Disease Society of the UK
The Raynaud's & Scleroderma Association
Re-Solv
Research into Ageing
Research Trust for Metabolic Diseases in
Children
St Andrews Ambulance Association
St John Ambulance (part of the Order of St
John)
Sickle Cell Society
TOFS Tracheo-Oesophagal Fistula Support
UK Band of Hope
UK Thalassaemia Society
UKAN Narcolepsy Association (UK)
Vitiligo Society

Hospitals & Hospices
Help the Hospices
Hospice Information Service
National Association of Hospice Volunteer
Co-ordinators
National Association of Hospital
Broadcasting Organisations
National Association of Leagues of Hospital
Friends
National Association of Voluntary Help
Organisations
St Christopher's Hospice
Trinity Hospice

Housing & Homelessness
The Almshouse Association (The National
Association of Almshouses)
Carr-Gomm Society
The Central and Cecil Housing Trust
(formerly Cecil Houses)
Centre for Accessible Environments
Centrepoint
CHAR, Housing Campaign for Single People
CRISIS

The Depaul Trust
English Churches Housing Group (ECHG)
Homes for Homeless People Project
Housing Associations Charitable Trust
(HACT)
Keychange (formerly Christian Alliance)
Leaving Home Project (LHP)
Manna Drop-In Centre
National Association for Voluntary Hostels
(NAVH)
SHAC, the London Housing Aids Council
The Simon Community
Stonham Housing Association
Vision Homes Association

Human Rights & Civil Liberties
Amnesty International, British Section (AIBS)
Anti-Slavery International (ASI)
INTERIGHTS – The International Centre for
the Legal Protection of Human Rights
Liberty (National Council for Civil Liberties)
Survival International

Law & Justice
Children's Legal Centre
Community of the Peace People
The Corrymeela Community
The Howard League for Penal Reform
International Voluntary Service (IVS)
Latin American Women's Rights Service
(LAWRS)
Law Centres Federation (LCF)

Lobbying & Campaigning
Carers National Association
English Collective of Prostitutes
The Jubilee Centre
National Federation of Consumer Groups
(NFCG)
National Peace Council (NPC)
Peace Pledge Union (PPU)
Society for the Protection of Unborn Children
(SPUC)
Stonewall Lobby Group

Mental Health
African-Caribbean Mental Health
Association (ACMA)
Ex-Services Mental Welfare Society
First Steps to Freedom (FSTF)
Hamlet Trust
Lothlorien (Rokpa Trust)
Manic Depression Fellowship (MDF)
Mental After Care Association (MACA)

The Mental Health Foundation
Mental Health Matters
MIND (National Association for Mental
Health)
National Schizophrenia Fellowship (NSF)
Northern Ireland Association for Mental
Health
Portia Trust
The Richmond Fellowship
The Richmond Fellowship International
Schizophrenia Association of Great Britain

Museums, the Arts & Festivals

Academy of Indian Dance
ArtLink Live
Artsline
Berwick Studios, Printmaking Museum and
Workshop
British Association of Friends of Museums
(BAFM)
Drama Association of Wales
Gainsborough's House Society
Godalming Museum
Ironbridge Gorge Museum Trust
John King Workshop Museum
Museum of Women's Art (MWA)
Museums Association
Quay Theatre
Quicksilver Theatre for Young Children
Riverside Studios
Tate Gallery
The Upper Wharfdale Museum Society
Victoria & Albert Museum
The Victorian Society
Yorkshire Sculpture Park

Overseas & the Developing World

ActionAid
Action Health 2000
African Medical & Research Foundation
(AMREF)
Appropriate Health Resources and
Technologies Action Group (AHRTAG)
Book Aid International
British Executive Service Overseas (BESO)
Catholic Fund for Overseas Development
(CAFOD)
Catholic Institute for International Relations,
CIIR
Christian Aid
The Christian Children's Fund of Great
Britain
Christians Abroad
East European Partnership
GAP Activity Projects (GAP) Ltd

The Great Britain-China Centre
Health Unlimited
Indian Volunteers for Community Service
(IVCS)
International Cooperation for Development
International Health Exchange (IHE)
The Karuna Trust
Médecins Sans Frontières (MSF) (UK)
OWA – One World Action
Oxfam
The Project Trust
Raleigh International
Skillshare Africa
SOS – Children's Villages UK
Tear Fund
Third World First (3W1)
Tools for Self Reliance
UNICEF – The United Nations Children's
Fund
Voluntary Service Overseas (VSO)
Volunteer Missionary Movement (VMM)
War on Want
WaterAid
World Vision (UK)
WWF-UK (World Wide Fund for Nature)
WWOOF (Working for Organic Growers)

Recreation & Leisure

Association of Railway Preservation Societies
Countrywide Holidays
Duke of Edinburgh's Award/Gwobr Dug
Caeredin
English National Association of Visually
Handicapped Bowlers (ENAVHB)
Festival Welfare Services (FWS)
Ffestiniog Railway
Jubilee Sailing Trust
National Association of Round Tables of
Great Britain and Ireland (RTBI)
National Federation of Eighteen Plus Groups
(18 Plus)
National Playing Fields Association
(Scotland), NPFA (Scotland)
Railworld
Share Holiday Village
SPLASH (Single Parent Links and Special
Holidays)
Wandsworth Blind Bowling Club and
London Blind Rambling Club
Yoga for Health Organisation
Youth Hostels Association (YHA)

Religious Affairs

Africa Inland Mission (AIM)
Baptist Missionary Society

Christian Action
Church Army
Church Lads and Church Girls Brigade
CONCERN Worldwide
Crosslinks
The Mothers' Union (MU)
Pax Christi
Scripture Union
SGM International
TF8
TOC H
Torch Trust for the Blind
Union of Muslim Organisations of UK and Eire

Social Welfare

Association of Jewish Refugees (AJR)
Bangladesh Association
The Bourne Trust
British Association of Settlements and Social Action Centres (BASSAC)
British Limbless Ex-Servicemen's Association (BLESMA)
British Red Cross
Camphill – Rudolf Steiner – Schools
Centre for Armenian Information and Advice (CAIA)
The Clubhouse
Community Development Foundation (CDF)
Daycare Trust/National Childcare Campaign
Ethiopian Community in Britain (ECB)
Family Holiday Association (FHA)
Fire Services National Benevolent Fund
The Forces Help Society and Lord Roberts Workshops
Gingerbread
Headway, National Head Injuries Association Limited
Institute for Social Inventions
Jesuit Volunteer Community in Britain (JVC)
League of Jewish Women
Leukaemia Care Society
The Malcolm Sargent Cancer Fund for Children
Missions to Seamen (Flying Angel)
Multiple Sclerosis Society of Great Britain and Northern Ireland
National Association for the Care and Resettlement of Offenders (NACRO)
National Association of Laryngectomee Clubs (NALC)
National Council on Gambling (NCG)
The National Society for Mentally Handicapped People in Residential Care (RESCARE)

The Natural Death Centre
The Network
Norwood Child Care
Parents at Work (formerly the Working Mothers Association)
PSS
Royal British Legion
Royal British Legion Women's Section
Royal National Lifeboat Institution (RNLI)
Royal National Mission to Deep Sea Fishermen
The Royal Society for the Prevention of Accidents (ROSPA)
Salvation Army
Shaftesbury Society
Sheffield Community Transport (SCT)
Sick Children's Trust
Society of Voluntary Associates (SOVA)
Soldiers', Sailors', and Airmen's Families Association (SSAFA/FHS)
Women's Royal Voluntary Service (WRVS)

Sports

British Blind Sport (BBS)
The British Disabled Water Ski Association
The British Ski Club for the Disabled (BSCD)
British Sports Association for the Disabled (BSAD)
Calvert Trust
Great Britain Wheelchair Basketball Association (GBWBA)
Greater London Sports Association (GLSA)
National Association of Swimming Clubs for the Handicapped (NASCH)
The Pony Club
UK Sports Association for People with Learning Disability

Support for Volunteering

Community Service Volunteers (CSV)
Federation of Independent Advice Centres (FIAC)
National Association of Councils for Voluntary Service (NACVS)
National Association of Volunteer Bureaux (NAVB)
National Council for Voluntary Youth Services
Returned Volunteer Action
The Volunteer Centre UK

Women

Asian Women's Resource Centre (AWRC)
The Feminist Library

GFS Platform for Young Women
Junior League of London (JLL)
La Leche League (Great Britain), (LLL(GB))
London Lesbian Line – also known as
   Women's Referral and Information
   Services (WRIS)
London Rape Crisis Centre
Maternity and Health Links
Meet-a-Mum Association (MAMA)
National Alliance of Women's Organisations
   (NAWO)
National Association of Ladies Circles of
   Great Britain and Ireland (NALC)
National Association of Widows (NAW)
National Association of Women's Clubs
   (NAWC)
National Childbirth Trust (NCT)
The National Council of Women of Great
   Britain (NCW)
National Federation of Women's Institutes
   (NFWI)
National Free Church Women's Council
   (NFCWC)
National Women's Register (NWR)
The Pankhurst Trust
Townswomen's Guilds (TG)
WOMANKIND Worldwide
Women's Design Service (WDS)
Women's Health
Women's Nationwide Cancer Control
   Campaign (WNCCC)
Women's Voice
Young Women's Christian Association of
   Great Britain (YWCA of GB)

Youth

Association for Jewish Youth (AJY)
Baptist Youth Ministry
British Youth Council
Catholic Youth Services (CYS)
Council for Wales of Voluntary Youth
   Services, CWVYS
Crusaders
The Duke of Edinburgh's Award
FAIRBRIDGE
The Guide Association
Jewish Lads and Girls Brigade (JLGB)
London Union of Youth Clubs
Methodists Association of Youth Clubs
   (MAYC)
NABC Clubs for Young People (NABC-CYP)
National Federation of Young Farmers Clubs
   (NFYFC)
National Youth Agency (NYA)

Northern Ireland Children's Holiday Scheme
   (NICHS)
The Prince's Trust and the Royal Jubilee
   Trusts
QISP – Quaker International Social Projects
Sail Training Association
The Scout Association
Sea Ranger Association (SRA)
Student Community Action Development
   Unit (SCADU)
The Trident Trust
Turkish Youth Association
Wales Youth Agency (WYA)
The Woodcraft Folk
Young Men's Christian Association (YMCA)
Youth Access
Youth Clubs UK

Advice

Many problems in life can be solved by the right piece of advice at the right time. This is the role of advice giving organisations who generally focus on finding a solution to a problem. The network of Citizens Advice Bureaux (CABx) offers a nationwide advice service.

Many other voluntary organisations offer specific advice in various forms. Other sections which may be of interest include: Aids/HIV, Counselling and Self-Help, Health and Medicine, Social Welfare.

ADiTi - The National Organisation of South Asian Dance, *see Education*

Afterwards, *see Disability*

Alcohol Counselling and Prevention Services (ACAPS), *see Counselling and Self-Help*

The Asian Women's Resource Centre, *see Women*

Baptist Youth Ministry, *see Youth*

The Bourne Trust, *see Social Welfare*

The British Ski Club for the Disabled, *see Sport*

Business in the Community (BITC), *see Education*

Centre for Armenian Information and Advice (CAIA), *see Social Welfare*

Community Development Foundation (CDF), *see Social Welfare*

Council for Wales of Voluntary Youth Services (CWVYS), *see Youth*

Families Need Fathers, *see Family & Community Matters*

Family Service Units (FSU), *see Family & Community Matters*

Fire Services National Benevolent Fund, *see Social Welfare*

First Steps to Freedom, *see Mental Health*

Lambeth Social Services, Voluntary Sector Unit

91 Clapham High Street
Clapham, London SW4 7TF
Tel: 0171-926 4809
Fax: 0171-926 5140

Contact
Mrs Verna Lindsay, Development Officer

Main Activities
The Unit, as part of the Lambeth Social Services Department, provides a central focus for voluntary work in the borough. It promotes volunteering in Lambeth, brings together potential volunteers and those needing them, and helps create volunteering opportunities of various kinds. Volunteers are supported by the Development Officer through the Volunteer's Forum, which gives volunteers the opportunity to meet, socialise, and raise issues and needs. Apart from serving and working with local voluntary groups and statutory organisations, and with

individuals interested in volunteering, the Unit also has responsibility for grants funding and training for the voluntary sector.

Opportunities for Volunteers
The Unit itself does not use volunteers, but actively recruits and places them in the voluntary sector. Potential volunteers phone or write in, and informal interviews are then held during office hours. Two character references are taken; those wishing to work with children must also be police checked. Volunteers are then placed according to wishes, skills and ability. Lambeth welcomes volunteers from all sections of the community regardless of background, gender, race, age or disability. An Introduction to Volunteering and other training is available, together with the Volunteer's Forum Support Group.

Opportunities for Employment
Apart from the Voluntary Services Development Officer there are some paid seasonal opportunities available, including odd jobs/gardening and working with voluntary groups in the local area. Any positions are advertised throughout the Borough. A formal equal opportunities policy is in operation.

Further Information
A leaflet 'Become a Volunteer' describing the Unit's work is available.

London Advice Services Alliance (LASA)

Universal House
88-94 Wentworth Street
London E1 7SA
Tel: 0171-377 2748
Fax: 0171-247 4725

Contact
Appeals Team for volunteering; Marion Fitzpatrick, Director re employment opportunities

Main Activities

LASA is a second tier organisation providing support services to a range of advice agencies and law centres. Services include training in welfare benefits, representation at tribunals for clients referred by agencies, computer development and support, information, research and policy work in the advice sector. LASA works with advice networks to encourage co-operation between them, as well as providing direct advice, information and consultancy services to agencies.

Opportunities for Volunteers

LASA bases its work around paid staff but there are some opportunities eg appeals team (volunteers need experience in social security law and tribunal representation), computer development, and administrative support. Volunteers are always needed for appeals representation and should already be trained in this. Commitment is a minimum seven hours weekly. Travel and lunch expenses are paid.

Opportunities for Employment

LASA has fifteen full- and two part-time staff, of which three are in the Appeals Team. Vacancies may sometimes occur.

Further Information

Annual report available.

Maternity and Health Links, *see Women*

National Alliance of Women's Organisations (NOWA), *see Women*

National Association of Citizens Advice Bureaux (NACAB)

Myddleton House
115-123 Pentonville Road
London N1 9LZ
Tel: 0171-833 2181
Fax: 0171-833 4371

Contact

Local Citizens Advice Bureaux for volunteering; Director of Personnel for employment opportunities

Main Activities

Provision of free, impartial and confidential advice to the public, on a wide range of subjects, through 750 CABx (Citizens Advice Bureaux) throughout England and Wales. NACAB provides consultancy and guidance to the Bureaux which are members. There are also 18 area offices. NACAB's budget is nearly £13.5 million annually, plus £31.2 million CAB core funding.

Opportunities for Volunteers

Volunteers are essential to NACAB - 12,000 volunteers work in Citizens Advice Bureaux and a further 10,000 serve on management committees. Volunteers are generally needed in most CABx and all receive extensive training. Recruitment is by application to the bureau manager or through a volunteer bureau. Six hours commitment a week over a year is requested. Local CABx have application forms (addresses etc in phone directories).

Opportunities for Employment

NACAB employs 380 full-time and 30 part-time staff. It recruits nearly 100 people a year, in various work areas, depending on turn-over. Posts are advertised in the national media, especially The Guardian.

Further Information

Annual report and various publications are available. Sister organisations are:

Citizens Advice Scotland, 26 George Street, Edinburgh EH8 9LD

Northern Ireland Citizens Advice Bureaux, 11 Upper Crescent, Belfast BT7 1NT

Parent Partnership Project, *see Education*

Parents at Work, *see Social Welfare*

Phab, Physically Disabled and Able Bodied, *see Disability*

Trinity Hospice, *see Hospitals & Hospices*

Wales Youth Agency (WYA), *see Youth*

Women's Design Service, *see Women*

Aids/HIV

T he last few years have seen a huge increase in voluntary organisations that care for and advise people who are affected by Aids/HIV. Services include day and residential care, counselling, alternative therapies, befriending, support, education, and self-help groups.

AIDS Care Education & Training (ACET)

PO Box 3693
London SW15 2BQ
Tel: 0181-780 0400 (General Enquiries)
Tel: 0181-780 0455 (London Homecare)
Fax: 0181-780 0450

Contact
Sheila Murphy, Volunteer Trainer Co-ordinator

Main Activities
ACET is a national Christian charity with two main objectives:

1) to provide practical home care for those ill with HIV/Aids irrespective of background, sexuality, ethnic origin or lifestyle. Services include full nursing assessment, liaison with doctors, specialists and other services and practical care, housework, transport to clinics, shopping, nightsitting.

2) to reduce the number of new infections through a schools education programme, professional training and education awareness initiatives.

ACET has inter-denominational links with many UK churches, plus eight regional offices, and three overseas offices in Uganda, Romania and Thailand.

Opportunities for Volunteers
Volunteers are central to ACET's work providing practical home care for those with HIV/Aids, including housework and driving. ACET would like to use more. Recruitment is by application and

applicants must have good support from within a church. Commitment is flexible, but volunteers are needed especially in the day time, and in London. A full training programme is given. Travel expenses are offered.

Opportunities for Employment
ACET recruits five or six staff a year. All staff should have the support of a church. Posts are advertised in The Guardian, based on an equal opportunities policy. ACET employs 43 full-time and 4/5 part-time staff.

Further Information
Annual Report, newsletters and fact sheets, including a school pack, are available.

Aids Helpline (NI)

24 Mount Charles
Belfast BT7 1NZ
Tel: 01232-249268
Fax: 01232-329845

Contact
The Director

Main Activities
Aids Helpline (NI) has the joint aims of providing support to people with HIV and carrying out HIV prevention work. The work involves counselling, training, as well as operating telephone helpline service and an information centre.

Opportunities for Volunteers
Volunteers are central to service provision and take part in all areas of work including working on the telephone helpline, training and home support. Volunteers also help to fundraise. Minimum commitment is ten hours a month.

Opportunities for Employment
There are six full-time members of staff. There is an formal equal opportunities policy and posts are advertised in the Belfast Telegraph.

Further Information
The Annual Report, membership application forms, a list of local groups and Helpline services leaflets are available on request. Information Manual is also available at a cost of £10.

Body Positive

51B Philbeach Gardens
London SW5 9EB
Tel: 0171-835 1045

Contact
Mike Campling

Main Activities
A self-help organisation for people affected by HIV/Aids. Provides a telephone support line, hospital visiting, counselling, and helps run a range of support groups, including those for women and young people. Has a national network of 30 local groups.

Opportunities for Volunteers
Volunteers help in the office, the drop-in centre and with running the local groups. Work includes administration, fundraising, counselling on the telephone helpline, and support visits/writing to those with HIV/Aids in hospitals and prisons. More volunteers are welcome. Apply to above office. Training is given as necessary. Travel and lunch expenses are offered.

Opportunities for Employment
Body Positive employs sixteen full-time staff. No other details on employment are available.

Further Information
The Annual Report, regular newsletter and information sheets on HIV and on Body Positive are available.

Catholic Aids Link (CAL)

PO Box 646
London E9 6QP
Tel: 0171-485 7298

Contact
Martin Pendergast, Convenor

Main Activities
Offers non-judgmental spiritual, emotional, practical and financial help to those affected by HIV/Aids. Organises training, support groups and conferences. National organisation with local contacts.

Opportunities for Volunteers
Volunteers are essential and are needed to fundraise and give administrative support. An understanding of HIV/Aids and a knowledge of and a sensitivity to Catholic issues useful. Travel expenses are offered.

Opportunities for Employment
There are no paid staff.

Further Information
Annual Report and newsletter/leaflets available.

Crusaid

1 Walcott Street
London SW1P 2NG
Tel: 0171-976 8100
Fax: 0171-976 8200

Contact
Chris Markham, Volunteer Co-ordinator

Main Activities
Raises funds for care and relief for those affected by Aids in Britain. Annual budget £1 million.

Opportunities for Volunteers
Volunteers are needed for fundraising and administrative work. Write or telephone for an application form.

Opportunities for Employment
There are four staff.

Further Information

Annual Report available. For Scotland, contact: Crusaid Scotland, see entry below.

Crusaid Scotland

8 Frederick Street
Edinburgh EH2 2HB
Tel: 0131-225 8910

Contact

David McNally

Main Activities

Crusaid Scotland raises funds for projects involved in education, prevention and care in the field of HIV infection and Aids. It is a national organisation with local groups. It was set up in 1988 and the annual budget is £200,000.

Opportunities for Volunteers

About 30 volunteers carry out a variety of tasks including: administrative support, fundraising, organising local groups, public relations, and management/ trusteeship. Travel and out-of-pocket expenses are offered.

Opportunities for Employment

There is one full-time and one part-time member of staff.

Further Information

Annual Report, list of local groups, Friends leaflet, newsletter and introduction sheet are available on request.

IMMUNITY Legal Centre

1st Floor, 32-38 Osnaburgh Street
London NW1 3ND
Tel: 0171-388 6776

Contact

Ceri Hutton, Director

Main Activities

IMMUNITY Legal Centre promotes the legal rights of people with HIV/Aids by providing a free legal service and by undertaking social policy work. Annual budget is £250,000.

Opportunities for Volunteers

A volunteer programme is currently being developed. The Centre is particularly interested to hear from people who have admin., fundraising, legal, research or writing skills.

Opportunities for Employment

There are six staff. There is an equal opportunities policy and posts are advertised in The Guardian and The Voice.

Further Information

Annual Report, leaflet and business plan are available on request.

London Lighthouse

111-117 Lancaster Road
London W11 1QT
Tel: 0171-792 1200
Fax: 0171-229 1258

Contact

Volunteer Co-ordinator; Personnel Department re employment

Main Activities

A residential and support centre for people affected by HIV/Aids. Offers a range of services, including counselling, complementary therapies, home support, drop-in, residential and day care, and education and training. Serves people primarily in the Thames/Greater London area. Annual budget £4.35 million (1992/93).

Opportunities for Volunteers

About 140 volunteers work in the main Lighthouse building providing administrative support, help with fundraising, and information giving, and working in the cafe, in day care, the residential unit, reception and as drivers. Another 200 or so volunteers help in the community (ie home support). Lighthouse particularly welcomes more volunteers as day-time drivers with their own vehicle, and those from the black and ethnic communities. Commitment is negotiable, but usually over six months. Travel and lunch expenses are paid. Full training is given. Recruitment is by application, and through various in-house methods. Because Lighthouse is lucky to have the support of many would-be volunteers, so recruitment is sometimes closed. It is then worthwhile contacting other Aids organisations.

Opportunities for Employment
Lighthouse employs about 160, including full-time, part-time, and sessional staff. Recruitment occurs occasionally. Training and qualifications are needed for nursing and counselling positions; community services staff often have a public sector background. Vacancies are advertised in The Guardian, the Evening Standard, The Voice and the gay press. Lighthouse is an equal opportunities employer.

Further Information
Lighthouse publishes an annual report, various pamphlets on its services, a support group booklet and Lighthouse News.

National Aids Trust (NAT)

14th Floor, Euston Tower
286 Euston Road
London NW1 3DN
Tel: 0171-383 4246
Fax: 0171-972 2885

Contact
Dr Les Rudd, Director

Main Activities
NAT is a grant-making trust and development agency which promotes voluntary sector responses to Aids/HIV throughout the UK. It is not a direct service agency but brokers for other organisations.

Opportunities for Volunteers
Volunteers give administrative support and help with various projects. Travel and lunch expenses are offered.

Opportunities for Employment
There is one member of staff. Jobs are advertised in The Guardian.

Further Information
Annual Report is available on request.

Positively Women

5 Sebastian Street
London EC1V 0HE
Tel: 0171-490 5515

Contact
Maggie Stewart

Main Activities
Positively Women offers peer support by and to women with HIV/Aids. The organisation offers telephone and one-to-one counselling and there are support groups as well as hospital and home visits.

Opportunities for Volunteers
There are eleven volunteers who offer a very valuable service in specific therapies eg shiatsu, massage, acupuncture, healing.

Opportunities for Employment
There are twelve full-time and two part-time members of staff.

Further Information
A wide range of leaflets on various aspects of HIV/Aids and women is available on request.

Animals

The Blue Cross Animal Welfare Society

Home Close Farm
Shilton Road, Burford
Oxon OX18 4PF
Tel: 01993-822651
Fax: 01993-823083

Contact
Andrea Frazer, Information Officer

Main Activities
Blue Cross is an animal welfare society that treats the animals of people unable to afford a private vet. Also offers a home-finding service for cats, dogs and other pets. A national organisation, it has three hospitals, one clinic and eleven re-homing centres. Head Office is in Burford, Oxfordshire.

Opportunities for Volunteers
Volunteers are needed at all locations for reception duties, kennel cleaning and exercising animals. A caring attitude towards people and animals is essential. Regular weekend work is involved and training is provided where appropriate. No remuneration is offered. Contact as above, or through Yellow Pages directories.

Opportunities for Employment
Blue Cross has a total of 250 full-time staff. It recruits specialist veterinary surgeons and nurses each year. Posts are usually advertised in the Veterinary Record.

Further Information
Annual Report, and leaflets on the organisation and animal care, are available.

British Union for the Abolition of Vivisection (BUAV)

16A Crane Grove
London N7 8LB
Tel: 0171-700 4888
Fax: 0171-700 0252

Contact
Bob Garner, Director

Main Activities
Campaigns for the total abolition of vivisection. Lobbies Parliament and provides information to the press and public. National, with one office only. Annual expenditure £1.6 million in 1992/93.

Opportunities for Volunteers
Up to ten volunteers are used in the office for administration and fundraising work. BUAV would welcome more, all year round, especially for administrative support. Recruitment is by application in writing, and through in-house drives. There is no minimum commitment. Basic induction is given. Travel and lunch expenses are offered.

Opportunities for Employment
BUAV recruits a varying number of people each year. Posts are advertised internally first, and then in appropriate media. There are 32 full-time staff and BUAV has an equal opportunities policy.

Further Information
Annual Report and various publications on BUAV's work are available.

Hearing Dogs for the Deaf, see *Disability*

Humane Research Trust

Brook House
29 Bramhall Lane South
Bramhall, Cheshire SK7 2DN
Tel: 0161-439 8041
Fax: 0161-439 3713

Contact
Mrs M Pritchard, or headquarters

Main Activities
The Humane Research Trust raises money through voluntary fundraising efforts to finance medical research projects to both advance research and replace live animals in laboratory experiments. Works as a responsible partner with researchers and is non-confrontational. Has a number of local support groups.

Opportunities for Volunteers
Volunteers are extremely important and undertake administrative and fundraising work in both head office and the local groups. More are needed, especially to provide support for quarterly mailings (8,000 a time) and to compile fundraising packs. Contact head office for details.

Opportunities for Employment
There are very few employment opportunities.

Further Information
An Annual Report, leaflets, quarterly newsletters and merchandise lists are available.

National Canine Defence League (NCDL)

17-26 Wakely Street
London EC1V 7LT
Tel: 0171-837 0006

Contact
Head Office

Main Activities
Promotes the welfare of dogs. Undertakes rescue, rehabilitation and re-homing of

dogs through a network of fifteen rescue centres which provide for lost and unwanted dogs throughout the UK. NCDL's policy is that no healthy dog in its care is ever destroyed. Campaigns locally and nationally, and offers dog owners advice and assistance. Membership is available. Relies entirely on donations and contributions. National with 23 local support groups.

Opportunities for Volunteers
Volunteers are used year round in administrative and fundraising work, and for general help at rescue centres/kennels. NCDL is keen to enlist more volunteer help. Recruitment is ad hoc by application to head office. Prospective volunteers need a love of dogs and a general concern for animal welfare. Training is given. Minimum commitment is 30 minutes a week, any day between 9 am and 5 pm. No remuneration is offered.

Opportunities for Employment
Staff are recruited as required in both the rescue centres and at head office. Posts are advertised in appropriate papers and through recruitment agencies. NCDL employs 80 full-time staff.

Further Information
Many leaflets on dog ownership, a list of local groups and the Annual Report are available.

People's Dispensary for Sick Animals (PDSA)

Whitechapel Way
Priorslee, Telford
Shropshire TF2 9PQ
Tel: 01952-290999
Fax: 01952-291035

Contact
Local appeals managers and shops - list available from head office

Main Activities
Provides free veterinary treatment for sick and injured animals whose owners cannot afford private fees. There are 72 local offices and 74 shops.

Opportunities for Volunteers
Volunteers always needed for fundraising, clerical work and working in PDSA shops. Help particularly needed at holiday periods and for major campaigns. Induction and on-the-job training given.

Opportunities for Employment
There are 577 full-time and 185 part-time staff, with 100-150 recruited annually. Telephone canvassers for house-to-house campaigns needed. Jobs advertised in local and national media and in Job Centres.

Further Information
Annual Report, information leaflets and list of local contacts available from Head Office.

Pets As Therapy (PAT)

6 New Road
Ditton, Aylesford
Kent ME20 6AD
Tel: 01732-872222

Contact
Lesley Scott-Ordish

Main Activities
Provides community programme in which registered, friendly dogs regularly visit patients in hospitals, hospices and homes for elderly people. Makes provision for research into the social and health benefits from the companionship of dogs.

Opportunities for Volunteers
Suitable dogs accompanied by owners always required for visits to sick people. Volunteers are essential to the charity's work. Canine volunteers are required to have a temperament assessment to ensure friendly, well-balanced disposition. Free third party insurance for dogs available for owner members.

Opportunities for Employment
No information available.

Further Information
Full information pack available on request.

The Pony Club, *see Sports*

PRO Dogs National Charity (PRO Dogs)

Rocky Bank
4 New Road, Ditton
Aylesford, Kent ME20 6AD
Tel: 01732-848499

Contact
Lesley Scott-Ordish

Main Activities
Promotes higher standards of dog ownership and a better understanding of the value of dogs to society. Undertakes educational programmes and provides information on related subjects.

Opportunities for Volunteers
Volunteers needed for educational work in schools, running annual Walkover Britain event, and media promotion. Volunteers are especially needed for fundraising and to serve on a panel of expert volunteers who specialise in a particular subject about dogs.

Opportunities for Employment
No information available.

Further Information
Information sheets available on request.

Royal Society for the Prevention of Cruelty to Animals (RSPCA)

Causeway, Horsham
West Sussex RH12 1HG
Tel: 01403-264181
Fax: 01403-241048

Contact
Branches Department

Main Activities
RSPCA promotes kindness and prevention of cruelty to animals. National organisation with 200 local branches and 135 affiliated organisations.

Opportunities for Volunteers
Volunteers are vital to the RSPCA which is undertaking a recruitment drive throughout 1995. They are needed to campaign, fundraise and give administrative support at branch level. Other tasks include education, public speaking and helping with the re-housing of unwanted animals. Minimum commitment varies. Training is available. There are currently about 5,000 active volunteers.

Opportunities for Employment
There are 1,050 staff. About 100 are recruited each year. Potential Inspectors are welcome to apply for training intake 1995. Jobs are advertised in The Guardian, The Telegraph and the Sussex press. There is a formal equal opportunities policy.

Further Information
Annual Report and various pamphlets on animal welfare available. For Scotland, contact: Scottish Society for Prevention of Cruelty to Animals, 19 Melville Street, Edinburgh EH3 7PL, tel: 0131-225 6418. For Northern Ireland, contact: Ulster SPCA (inc), 11 Drumview Street, Lisburn, County Antrim BT27 6YF, Northern Ireland, tel: 018494-63993.

Southern Marine Life Rescue (SMLR)

60 Braishfield Road
West Leigh, Havant
Hampshire PO9 2HS
Tel: 01705-472151
Fax: 01705-552631

Contact
A D Williams, Chairman or C Morgan, Treasurer

Main Activities
SMLR is concerned with the rescue, rehabilitation and welfare of sick, stranded, injured or distressed marine mammals along the South Coast of Britain. Established in 1992, it has three regional groups under central control covering the South Coast of England, and sister groups in Wales. It also has links with similar groups overseas, including the European Cetacean Society, the Marine Mammal Rehabilitation Centre in The Netherlands, the Marine Mammal Stranding Centre in California, and the Project Jonah Rescue and Stranding Network in New Zealand. Annual budget is £3,000.

Opportunities for Volunteers
Volunteers entirely staff and run SMLR both administratively and in its rescue capability, with two in Head Office and 34 in the branches. They carry out the rescue function following training as first aiders for the animals. Their numbers are kept to a manageable level, and they also fundraise for the work, the only form of funding to date. More volunteers are needed continually, both as first aiders for the animals and administrators/fundraisers. First aid training, advice and information about marine animals are given, and support is on hand for all incidents. Enthusiasm is a pre-requisite and volunteers can be needed at very short notice when an incident occurs. Recruitment is ad hoc, on application and through in-house schemes. There is no minimum time commitment and no remuneration is offered.

Opportunities for Employment
There are no paid staff.

Further Information
The Annual Report is available for a fee of £1.50 to cover costs. After joining SMLR, a members information pack and newsletter are available. Currently membership is £15 per annum. A stamped, addressed A4 envelope is also requested. Other useful addresses: Dyfwr Cymru Marine Life Rescue (DCMLR), tel: 01545-580854 for North/mid Wales; and Severn Area Marine Life Rescue (SAMLR), c/o F.W.A.G., Elmbridge Court, Cheltenham Road, Gloucester for South Wales; British Divers Marine Life Rescue, tel: 01634-281680.

Wood Green Animal Shelters (WGAS)

Chishill Road
Heydon, Nr Royston
Herts SG8 8PN
Tel: 0763-838329

Contact
Michael Hawkins

Main Activities
Promotes all aspects of animal welfare and environmental issues through consultation, education and sheltering of animals. There are 35 local support groups. Annual budget is £3.5 million.

Opportunities for Volunteers
Volunteers are always needed to work on various projects, fundraise and give administrative support. Project work includes building shelters and animal care. Training is offered through WGAS's Education Centre. Particular need at weekends and Bank Holidays.

Opportunities for Employment

There are 150 full-time and 80 part-time staff. About 20 are recruited each year.

Further Information

Annual Report and newsletters available for supporters.

World Society for the Protection of Animals (WSPA)

2 Langley Lane
London SW8 1TJ
Tel: 0171-793 0540
Fax: 0171-793 0208

Contact

Jill Gray, Personnel Manager/Kay Cooper, Marketing Director

Main Activities

WSPA promotes animal protection internationally through campaigns. There are 300 affiliated organisations.

Opportunities for Volunteers

Volunteers are needed to give administrative support eg computer in-putting and sending out mailpacks. Basic computer training is provided and travel expenses are offered. Fundraising is also done by volunteers. There is also scope for volunteers to help with research and special projects.

Opportunities for Employment

There are 24 staff.

Further Information

Annual Report, general information, campaign leaflets and quarterly magazine available to supporters.

Bereavement

The Compassionate Friends (TCF)

53 North Street, Bristol BS3 1EN
Helpline: 0117-953 9639
Office: 0117-966 5202

Contact
John Gilbody

Main Activities
The Compassionate Friends is a nation-wide organisation of bereaved parents offering friendship and understanding to other bereaved parents. There are 210 local branches and the annual budget is £100,000.

Opportunities for Volunteers
There are approximately 400 volunteers, all of whom have been bereaved through the death of a son or daughter. In order to support other bereaved parents, potential volunteers must have been bereaved at least two years previously. Out-of-pocket expenses are offered.

Opportunities for Employment
There are no opportunities for employment.

Further Information
Annual Report and extensive publication list are available. Publications include: *No Death So Sad, Teenagers, Grieving Couples*, The Healing Process and a quarterly newsletter.

CRUSE
Bereavement Care

Cruse House, 126 Sheen Road
Richmond, Surrey TW9 1UR
Tel: 0181-940 4818
Cruse Bereavement Line: 0181-332 727
Fax: 0181-940 7638

Contact
Hilary Belton, Information Officer

Main Activities
Cruse offers help to all bereaved people, including children, by providing counselling for the individual and in groups. Advice and information on practical problems, and opportunities for social contact, are also available. A national organisation, Cruse has seven regional groups and 195 local branches, and offers membership.

Opportunities for Volunteers
Over 6,000 volunteers in the branches, and a few in head office, undertake administrative support, fundraising and counselling. Cruse is keen to enlist more in all these areas of work. Recruitment is through ad hoc applications, in-house schemes and advertising in local newspapers. Extensive training is given for counselling with on-going supervision. There is no specified time commitment for any type of volunteering. Travel expenses are offered.

Opportunities for Employment
Cruse employs twelve full-time and fourteen part-time staff. A number of people may be recruited each year. Any vacancies are advertised in appropriate local media, based on an equal opportunities policy.

Further Information
An Annual Report, a list of local groups, and a list for a wide range of publications, including for children, are available. Other contacts are:

Wales: Mrs Joan Morgan, Old Bedw Farmhouse, Nr Erwood, Bulith Wells, Powys LD2 3LQ. tel: 01982-560468

Scotland: Mrs Ruth Hampton, Cruse Bereavement Care, Scottish Headquarters, 18 South Trinity Road, Edinburgh EH5 3PN, tel: 0131-551 1511; fax: 0131-551 3058 (mark for the attention of Cruse)

Ireland: Mr Patrick Shannon, Cruse Bereavement Care, 50 University Street, Belfast BT7 1FY, tel: 01232-232695; fax and branch tel: 01232-232695

Northern: Ms Angela Cunningham, 1 Croftlands, Westbourne Road, Lancaster LA1 5DD, tel: 01524-842582

Central: Simon Godfrey, Suffolk House, 123 High Street, Cottenham, Cambs CB4 4SD. tel: 01954-250509.

Jewish Bereavement Counselling Service

Woburn House, Upper Woburn Place
London WC1H 0EZ
Tel: 0171-387 4300, extension 227
Fax: 0181-349 0839

Contact
Mrs J Epstein

Main Activities
Offers bereavement counselling and support on a one-to-one basis to members of the Jewish community. Organises a team of trained counsellors and provides information and speakers. The Service is London-based, but covers certain parts of London (NW, SW and Redbridge) only.

Opportunities for Volunteers
Counselling is on a voluntary basis and at present there are 40 volunteers working for the organisation. Recruitment is by application form with references to the office, followed by interview. On-going training and supervision are given. Minimum commitment is three hours a week over two years. Travel expenses are paid.

Opportunities for Employment
There is one part-time worker only and no other opportunities for employment.

Further Information
Leaflets are available.

London Association of Bereavement Services (LABS)

356 Holloway Road
London N7 6PN
Tel: 0171-700 8134

Contact
Maisie McKensie, Development Officer

Main Activities
LABS was set up in 1979 to offer advice, information and support to people who have been bereaved. There are 58 local branches in the London area and LABS is affiliated to the Association of Bereavement Services. Annual budget is £40,000.

Opportunities for Volunteers
Volunteers are involved with fundraising and in giving administrative support and are recruited via volunteer bureaux. Minimum time commitment is six months and travel expenses are offered.

Opportunities for Employment
There are two members of staff, one full-time and one part-time. An Equal Opportunities Policy is in place.

Further Information
The Annual Report is available.

National Association of Bereavement Services (NABS)

20 Norton Folgate
London E1 6DB
Tel: 0171-247 0617 (Admin)
Fax: 0171-247 0617

Contact
Carole Lambert

Main Activities
The National Association of Bereavement Services is a support organisation for bereavement services and acts as a referral agency by putting bereaved and

grieving people in touch with their most appropriate local service. It was founded in 1988 out of a concern to bring together individuals and groups who are actively involved in the care of the dying and the bereaved. NABS promotes networking, training and professional standards through its regional representatives, quarterly newsletter and annual training conference. The National Directory of Bereavement and Loss Services compiled by NABS is now available, as too are guidelines for setting up and running a bereavement counselling or support group.

Opportunities for Volunteers

Volunteers are involved in assisting the administrative and fundraising tasks at Head Office and at regional level. Volunteers are recruited locally to assist on committees and with member organisations. Knowledge of office systems or counselling useful. Training courses are offered for those wishing to become counsellors. Minimum commitment is four hours a week.

Opportunities for Employment

There are two staff.

Further Information

Leaflet, information pack and guidelines for setting up bereavement counselling or support group, available on request.

National Association of Widows (NAW), *see Women*

Trinity Hospice, *see Hospitals & Hospices*

Wandsworth Bereavement Service

66 Theatre Street
London SW15 5NF
Tel: 0171-223 3178

Contact

Alan Davidson, Co-ordinator

Main Activities

Wandsworth Bereavement Service offers one-to-one counselling and groupwork for those suffering from bereavement or loss in the London Borough of Wandsworth. It was set up in 1979 and the annual budget is £125, 000.

Opportunities for Volunteers

There are 80 volunteers who carry out crucial counselling and trusteeship roles. Training and travel expenses are offered. Time commitment is one hour per week for a minimum of eighteen months.

Opportunities for Employment

There are three full-time and two part-time staff. Recruits have a counselling/ therapy background and jobs are advertised in The Guardian, The Voice and the Pink Paper. A formal Equal Opportunities Policy is in operation.

Further Information

Leaflets on volunteer training, groupwork and the service generally are available. Other London Boroughs have similar Bereavement Services.

Broadcasting

Broadcasting Support Services (BSS)

252 Western Avenue
London W3 6XJ
Tel: 0181-992 5522

Contact

The office above

Main Activities

BSS provides various support services for television and radio broadcasts. These include helplines, other telephone services, publications, conferences, meetings and charitable appeals. It also runs the BBC Radio Helpline and national Aids helpline. It focuses on social action issues within broadcasting, covering many areas, ranging from elderly people to the environment. A national organisation, BSS has offices in Manchester, Glasgow and Cardiff, and many affiliated groups, including some in Europe with which it undertakes European initiatives.

Opportunities for Volunteers

BSS does not often use volunteers, except for donation-taking helplines for charitable appeals.

Opportunities for Employment

With around seventy full-time and fifty part-time staff, BSS recruits a number of people a year. Vacancies, with appropriate skill requirements, may occur in any of the departments. These include administration, accounting, languages and counselling. Posts are advertised in the national and specialist press, especially The Guardian, The Voice and the Pink Paper, and in the local press in each region. An equal opportunities policy operates. Any approaches for jobs should be via advertisements. BSS should not be contacted direct.

Further Information

The Annual Report is available on request, and an information pamphlet if a stamped addressed envelope is provided.

Campaign for Press and Broadcasting Freedom (CPBF)

8 Cynthia Street
London N1 9SF
Tel: 0171-278 4430
Fax: 0171-837 8868

Contact
Jo Treharne

Main Activities
CPBF campaigns for diverse, democratic and accountable media to challenge the monopoly ownership of the press and new broadcasting. It was set up in 1979. There are some specialist campaign groups within the organisation eg BBC, ownership and control. Annual budget is £35,000.

Opportunities for Volunteers
Volunteers are often asked to help on specific campaigns and are encouraged to take responsibility for that work. Volunteers are always needed for a variety of tasks and minimum training but maximum support is offered.

Opportunities for Employment
There are two part-time members of staff.

Further Information
Annual Report, bi-monthly journal 'Free Press' and codes of conduct on media sexism/racism/heterosexism available.

Deaf Broadcasting Council (DBC)

70 Blacketts Wood Drive
Chorleywood, Herts WD3 5QQ
Minicom only: 01923-283127
Typetalk: 0345-515152

Contact
Ruth Myers, Honorary Secretary

Main Activities
DBC works to ensure that broadcasters are aware of the needs of deaf, deafened and hard-of-hearing people, and aims to monitor services for quality and suitability. The consumer body for these viewers, the Council acts as a link between them and broadcasters. Covering England, Scotland and Wales, the DBC has a modest budget of £1,000 annually.

Opportunities for Volunteers
All committee members are volunteers. Volunteers also provide administrative support, help to organise the AGM, write the Annual Report and leaflets, and meet broadcasters. DBC is keen to attract more volunteers, especially those with knowledge of its area of work, to help check quality and programme accessibility. Recruitment is by application to DBC. There is no minimum commitment, but volunteers are particularly needed September to June. Travel expenses may be offered.

Opportunities for Employment
There are no paid staff because there are no funds.

Further Information
Annual Report and a leaflet are published, and Mailshot (a newsletter) is issued quarterly.

National Association of Hospital Broadcasting Organisations, *see Hospitals & Hospices*

Voice of the Listener and Viewer (VLV)

101 Kings Drive
Gravesend, Kent DA12 5BQ
Tel: 01474-352835

Contact
Jocelyn Hay, Chairman

Main Activities
VLV represents listeners and viewers on broadcasting issues. Has no religious,

political or commercial affiliations. Holds public meetings and lectures and produces regular newsletters/reports.

Opportunities for Volunteers

Volunteers are needed to fundraise and provide administrative support. Travel expenses are offered.

Opportunities for Employment

There are three part-time staff.

Further Information

Annual Report, membership leaflets and other information available.

Caring

There is a wide range of voluntary organisations which provide care. People may need care, support or befriending as a result of such experiences as: serious illness, bereavement, disability, homelessness, mental illness, or being a carer for a friend/family member with a disabling illness.

Various organisations exist to help people who cope with these situations, including: residential care eg community homes, centres and hostels, befriending schemes and self-help groups. A volunteer's role can be very varied. Some organisations require help with fundraising and administration, or with forming a local support group. Some require people to act as befrienders and carers, often in a one-to-one role.

As a befriender or carer, your role would be to give whatever practical and emotional support is needed. Examples of this include: help with the shopping, going to court with someone, cooking a meal, taking the person out for a meal/outing, sending a card/get well message, hospital visiting or just being there when someone wants to chat. All organisations who recruit volunteers as befrienders/carers should have a selection procedure, and offer training, on-going support and supervision.

Other sections to look in include: Aids/HIV, Bereavement, Counselling and Self-Help, Hospitals and Hospices -Volunteer Opportunities, Mental Health.

ADFAM National, see Education

Aid for Children with Tracheostomies (ACT), see Children

Alzheimer's Disease Society (ADS), see Health/Medicine

Aperts Syndrome Support Group, see Health & Medicine

Association for Glycogen Storage Disease (AGSD (UK)), see Health & Medicine

The Befriending Network

11 St Bernards Road
Oxford OX2 6EH
Tel: 01865-512405

Contact
Diana Senior

Main Activities
The Befriending Network aims to support people with a life threatening illness. It helps to provide trained volunteers who can visit regularly at home, to befriend a person who is ill, to help in whatever ways are appropriate and to give carers a break. The Network is working towards being nationwide; at present it has offices in Edinburgh, Oxford and London.

Opportunities for Volunteers
Volunteers are needed as befrienders. No particular skills are necessary. Minimum commitment is two or three hours a week. A training programme is offered.

Opportunities for Employment
There are no employment opportunities but transferable skills may be gained through the training and voluntary work.

Further Information
Information leaflets available and telephone enquiries are encouraged.

Break

27A Church Street, Sheringham
Norfolk NR26 8QR
Tel: 01263-822161
Fax: 01263-822181

Contact
Mr GM Davison, Chief Executive

Main Activities
Break provides holidays, respite care and day care for children and adults with learning disabilities. There are three local support groups. Main project locations are Hunstanton and Sheringham in Norfolk. Annual budget is £1.3 million.

Opportunities for Volunteers
Volunteers are needed to work as residential care assistants. Necessary personal qualities are patience and a caring nature. Minimum commitment is 40 hours a week for a period of between one and six months. Pocket money and UK travel expenses are offered.

Opportunities for Employment
There are 39 full-time and eleven part-time staff. Very low turnover of staff. Jobs are advertised in Eastern Daily Press and local job centres.

Further Information
Annual Report and information leaflet available.

British Colostomy
Association, see Health & Medicine

British Diabetic Association
(BDA), see Health & Medicine

British Retinitis Pigmentosa
Society, see Disability

Cancer Care Society (CARE)

21 Zetland Road, Redland
Bristol, Avon BS6 7AH
Tel: 0117-942 7419/923 2302

Contact
National Administrator

Main Activities
Provides emotional and practical support for anyone whose life has been affected by cancer. Services are free. National telephone helpline and a network of support groups. Two charity shops in Bristol. Subsidised holiday accommodation for members of the Society. Annual budget is £85,000.

Opportunities for Volunteers
Volunteers are needed to work in the CARE Charity shops in Bristol. Also needed are volunteers to help with fundraising.

Opportunities for Employment
There are six staff. Jobs are advertised in the Bristol Evening Post and journals relevant to post being advertised.

Further Information
Annual Report and information leaflets available.

Cancer Relief Macmillan Fund

15-19 Britten Street
London SW3 3TZ
Tel: 0171-351 7811

Contact
Personnel Manager

Main Activities
Supports and develops services to provide skilled care for people with cancer and their families, at every stage of the illness. Establishes Macmillan nurses, who are specialists in cancer care funds: in-patient and day care for cancer care;

gives financial help to people with cancer in financial need through patient grants. Macmillan also funds an education programme to improve doctors' and nurses' skills in cancer care, and finances four associated charities providing information for people with cancer.

Opportunities for Volunteers
Volunteers are used mainly to help with administrative and fundraising work. More are welcome. Opportunities vary according to local circumstances. Travel expenses may be offered. Approach head office for appropriate local contacts.

Opportunities for Employment
Macmillan has around 200 full-time staff. Vacancies are advertised in the local and national press as appropriate.

Further Information
Annual Report, information about the Fund, and a list of local groups, are available.

CARE for People with a Mental Handicap (CARE)

9 Weir Road, Kibworth
Leicester LE8 0LQ
Tel: 0116-279 3225

Contact
Mr G Slack

Main Activities
Provides residential and workshop facilities for adults with a learning disability. Emphasis is placed on providing satisfying and productive work activities. Main project locations are in Devon, Kent, Shropshire, Northumberland, Leicestershire, Lancashire, West Sussex and Wiltshire.

Opportunities for Volunteers
Volunteers are needed to support residents. Minimum commitment is 40 hours a week for six weeks. In-house training is provided. Volunteer allowance and board

and lodgings are offered.

Opportunities for Employment
There are 170 full-time and 47 part-time staff. Jobs are advertised locally and nationally where appropriate.

Further Information
Annual report and information sheet available.

Carers National Association,
see Lobbying & Campaigning

Christian Concern for the Mentally Handicapped (A Cause for Concern)

PO Box 351
Reading RG1 7AL
Tel: 01734-508781
Fax: 01734-391683

Contact
Personnel Officer

Main Activities
A charity concerned with the support and development of adults with learning disabilities (mental handicaps) through residential and day services and Causeway. There are 13 residential homes and two independent day services in England, Wales and Northern Ireland. Causeway raises awareness of the needs of people with learning disabilities and has a network of over 50 groups which offer people with learning disabilities spiritual ministry and practical help. Annual budget is £3 million.

Opportunities for Volunteers
A number of one-year full-time voluntary contracts are offered in 1995/6 (Sept-Aug). Applicants must be Christians. Board, lodging and pocket money are provided as well as valuable training and experience in the field of learning disability within a Christian context. Previous experience advantageous.

Unpaid voluntary helpers very welcome at all Services and Causeway groups.

Opportunities for Employment
Full-time and part-time opportunities occur mainly in residential or day services. Vacancies are usually advertised in local newspapers. All permanent staff are Christians and the Charity has 152 permanent staff.

Further Information
Annual Report, brochures on the work and a list of local groups available.

Crossroads (Association of Crossroads Care Attendant Schemes Ltd)

10 Regent Place, Rugby
Warwickshire CV21 2PN
Tel: 01788-573653
Fax: 01788-565498

Contact
Operations Director

Main Activities
Organises the development and support of local Crossroads schemes, which provide home care relief for carers looking after people with a wide range of disabilities and illnesses. Works to provide a high standard of care in association with statutory services. A national organisation covering all areas of the UK. Crossroads has 237 autonomous local branches. Annual budget is £850,000.

Opportunities for Volunteers
Over 2,000 volunteers support Crossroads work through fundraising and management committee membership. Volunteers are recruited mainly through local scheme supporters. No minimum commitment is required and no remuneration is offered.

Opportunities for Employment
Head Office employs 25 full-time and 25 part-time staff, while the branches employ varying numbers of co-ordinators and

care assistants to provide the local relief services. Various vacancies, with differing skill requirements, arise each year. Posts are advertised internally and in various newspapers, based on an evolving equal opportunities policy.

Further Information
Annual Report, a list of local groups and various pamphlets/leaflets and other publications (mostly for purchase) are available.

Disabled Living, see Disability

Families Need Fathers, see Family & Community Matters

Family Education Trust (FET), see Education

Family Service Units (FSU), see Family & Community Matters

Family Welfare Association (FWA), see Family & Community Matters

Guideposts Trust Ltd

Two Rivers, Station Lane
Witney, Oxon OX8 6BH
Tel: 01993-772886
Fax: 01993-778160

Contact
Clifford L Upex

Main Activities
Guideposts Trust helps people with mental illness, learning difficulties and the elderly mentally frail. Provides a Day Services Centre, residential and nursing homes and helps people to integrate into the local community. Main project locations are in Hertfordshire and

Oxfordshire at present. Annual budget is £450,000.

Opportunities for Volunteers
Volunteers are needed to do befriending, accountancy and fundraising. Befriending includes supporting people with mental health problems to integrate into the community. Good inter-personal skills and administrative skills are useful for the office-based jobs.

Opportunities for Employment
Recruits need to have experience in dealing with people with mental health problems. Jobs are advertised in professional magazines and local press.

Further Information
Annual Report available.

Huntington's Disease Association, see Health & Medicine

I CAN (Invalid Children's Aid Nationwide), see Disability

In Touch Trust, see Disability

Jewish Care

221 Golders Green Road
London NW11 9DQ
Tel: 0181-458 3282, extension 345
Fax: 0181-455 6214

Contact
Frances Harris or Carolyn Sumberg

Main Activities
Provides services for elderly, mentally ill, visually impaired and physically disabled people through a network of residential, day care and field services. Main areas are Greater London and South East England. Annual budget is £25 million.

Opportunities for Volunteers
Volunteers are vital. About 1,600

volunteers carry out a variety of tasks including managerial, fundraising and welfare work. Full training and travel expenses are offered.

Opportunities for Employment
There are 900 permanent staff. Approximately 200 are recruited each year. Professional skills associated with social work are useful. Jobs are advertised in Jewish Chronicle, Community Care, local newspapers and Job Centres.

Further Information
Annual Report and information leaflets and newsletter, *Volunteer News* available.

Leukaemia Care Society, see Social Welfare

London Lighthouse, see Aids/HIV

Medical Foundation for the Victims of Torture

96 Grafton Road
London NW5 3EJ
Tel: 0171-284 4321

Contact
The Administrator

Main Activities
The Medical Foundation for the Victims of Torture is a charity which provides care, support and rehabilitation for survivors of torture and their families. Treatment is through a combination of medicine, social work, psychotherapy, counselling and practical help. Established in 1986 and principally London based, with some work being carried out abroad eg training projects in certain countries.

Opportunities for Volunteers
There are currently 65 volunteers carrying out a variety of tasks including: administrative support, advice giving, counselling, fundraising, lobbying,

fundraising and research. Minimum commitment is a day per week. Travel and lunch expenses are provided.

Opportunities for Employment
There are eighteen full-time and fourteen part-time staff. Approximately two are recruited each year. Posts are advertised in The Voice and The Guardian. A formal Equal Opportunities Policy is in operation.

Further Information
The Annual Report and leaflets are available.

MENCAP (Royal Society for Mentally Handicapped Children and Adults), see Disability

Multiple Sclerosis Society, see Social Welfare

National Ankylosing Spondylitis Society (NASS), see Health & Medicine

National Association of Leagues of Hospital Friends, see Hospitals & Hospices

National Autistic Society

276 Willesden Lane
London NW2 5RB
Tel: 0181-451 1114
Fax: 0181-451 5865

Contact
Rachel Power, Personnel Training Officer

Main Activities
The Society offers families and carers information, advice and support. Aims to stimulate a greater understanding among professionals. Provides day and residential centres for children and adults with

autism. There are 90 local support groups.

Opportunities for Volunteers
Volunteers are increasingly important and are needed for a number of tasks eg classroom assistants, care staff. Relevant qualifications such as Teaching, Nursing, Occupational Therapy, Art and Craft etc. are very welcome. Personal qualities and ability to offer a regular commitment are important.

Opportunities for Employment
There are 660 staff. Jobs are advertised in local newspapers and professional journals such as Community Care and Social Work Today. Senior appointments are advertised in The Guardian.

Further Information
Annual Report, wide range of pamphlets and details of local groups available. For Scotland, contact: The Scottish Society for Autistic Children, 24d Barony Street, Edinburgh, Lothian EH3 6NY (Tel 0131-557 0474).

National Federation of Kidney Patients Associations, see Health & Medicine

National Society for Epilepsy

Chalfont St Peter
Gerrards Cross
Bucks SL9 0RJ
Tel: 01494-873991

Contact
Mr D Westcott, Fundraising Director

Main Activities
National Society for Epilepsy carries out research, rehabilitation and long term care of people with epilepsy. There are 40 local support groups. Annual budget is £5 million.

Opportunities for Volunteers
Volunteers are needed to staff a shop

and to fundraise. Ability to communicate with people is important. Minimum commitment is four hours a week. Lunch expenses are offered.

Opportunities for Employment
There are 240 full-time and 40 part-time staff. Approximately 75 people are recruited each year. An essential skill is some knowledge of caring in a residential setting. Jobs are advertised in The Guardian, Community Care, Nursing Times and local papers.

Further Information
Annual Report, information and videos available on request.

Norwood Child Care, *see Social Welfare*

PSS, *see Social Welfare*

St John Ambulance, *see Health & Medicine*

Sickle Cell Society, *see Health & Medicine*

The Stroke Association

CHSA House, Whitecross Street
London EC1Y 8JJ
Tel: 0171-490 7999
Fax: 0171-490 2680

Contact
Jenny Spreadborough, Director, Community Services

Main Activities
The Stroke Association is the only national organisation solely concerned with helping people who have suffered strokes and their families. Provides advice, welfare grants, local groups and Community services, family support and dysphasic support.

Opportunities for Volunteers
Volunteers are needed to help run stroke centres, to help stroke patients who have speech problems and to fundraise. Comprehensive initial and on-going training is offered as well as support from paid staff. A job description is available to potential volunteers who can then be put in touch with the centre closest to them. Minimum commitment is one hour a week. Travel expenses are offered if requested.

Opportunities for Employment
There are 54 full-time and 160 part-time staff. Vacancies are advertised in the local press.

Further Information
Annual report and publications list available.

Tactent, Cancer Support – Scotland

The Western Infirmary
Block C20, Western Place
100 University Avenue
Glasgow G12 6SQ
Tel: 0141-211 1930/31/32

Contact
David Brooks

Main Activities
Tak Tent provides information, support and training for cancer patients, friends and staff who care for them. Both practical and emotional support is provided through local groups and a newly established regional centre. There are twelve local support groups.

Opportunities for Volunteers
Volunteers are always needed to provide administrative support, fundraise and to organise local groups. Expenses are offered.

Opportunities for Employment
There are four staff.

Further Information
Annual Report, mission statement,

various leaflets and a list of local groups available.

Tracheotomy Patients Aid Fund (TPAF)

70 Medway
Crowborough TN6 2DW
Tel: 01892-652820

Contact
The Administrator

Main Activities
TPAF is the only UK charity concerned exclusively with the well-being of the respiratory disabled. It aims to make it possible for more of the respiratory disabled to leave hospital and receive care at home and thus acknowledges the need to give the afflicted and their carers vital support during the post-hospital adjustment period. The charity is currently planning to enlarge its local and regional representation.

Opportunities for Volunteers
TPAF is inviting applications from interested people who as national, regional, and local counsellors will give reassurance and comfort to the respiratory disabled. A medical background, although welcome, is not essential. Organisational ability and the quality of being a sympathetic listener is essential. It is envisaged that some of the volunteers will be eligible for remuneration within twelve months. The post of national or regional counsellor will probably best suit retired Army officers (of field rank) or hospital consultants. Other interested applicants may like to apply for the position of local co-ordinator. Write to the Administrator with a brief outline of present status.

Opportunities for Employment
There are none at present (see above).

Further Information
Annual Report and other information available on request.

Turning Point

New Loom House
101 Backchurch Lane
London E1 1LU
Tel: 0171-702 2300
Fax: 0171-702 1456

Contact
Louise Mussert, Fundraising Department

Main Activities
Turning Point helps people with drink, drug and mental health problems. Assists individuals to live independently in the community. Over 80 centres provide advice, information and confidential counselling. Annual budget is £14 million.

Opportunities for Volunteers
Volunteers are needed for fundraising, envelope stuffing, flag days and special events. Helplines in local centres are staffed by volunteers. Travel expenses are offered.

Opportunities for Employment
There are 348 full-time and 73 part-time staff. Six people job share. Project workers, nurses, managers and administrators are recruited from time to time.

Further Information
Annual Report, information leaflets and list of local groups available.

Warwickshire Association for the Blind (WAB), see Disability

Charity Shops

There are estimated to be over 6,000 charity shops in the UK selling mainly donated goods. They are an important feature of many high streets nowadays and are run by large, well-known voluntary organisations as well as by smaller, more local charities. They play an important fundraising role as well as acting as a public focus for the work of the charity. They also enhance the local community by selling (and re-cycling) one-off goods, often at very reasonable prices. Some shops are on a permanent basis – either owned or on long leases, and some are temporary – on a short-term, often rent-free basis. Additionally, some charities are diversifying their retail operation to include mail order.

Some shops are run totally by volunteers, others employ paid staff in a variety of jobs. Oxfam has the largest number of charity shops (over 850) which are run entirely by volunteers. It can take up to 50 or 60 volunteers to run an Oxfam shop. By contrast, the Notting Hill Housing Trust has over 30 permanent and temporary shops in the London area and only employs paid staff.

What Charity Shops sell

Charity shops sell a wide variety of goods, both second-hand and donated, as well as new. They include:

- donated clothes, including second-hand designer items
- second hand furniture, books and bric-à-brac
- items made by co-operative groups eg in a developing world project (Fair Trade and other projects) or a sheltered workshop
- items that have been specially produced to promote the charity eg National Trust shops selling their own branded goods

- new bought-in goods and special lines.

Additionally, there are three chains of temporary shops which sell charity Christmas cards in the run-up to Christmas each year (October-December): 1959 Group of Charities, Card Aid (Charities Advisory Trust), 4Cs (Charity Christmas Card Council)

Fair Trade and sustainable livelihoods

Some people also wish to support the developing world by buying products such as coffee and hand-made craft items which have been produced in small co-operatives. These co-operatives are usually too small to be able to market their goods commercially overseas. The charity sells the produce at cost price and the profit goes into providing the basic needs of life eg water and primary education. As a result, local communities are able to develop sustainable livelihoods.

What sort of people volunteer in a charity shop?

A very wide variety of people in terms of ages and skill background. Motivations vary greatly with different personal circumstances. They can include:

- wanting to gain an experience of retail work

- the need to keep skills fresh after a redundancy or during a time spent away from full-time employment looking after a family

- the opportunity for a retired or older person to apply their knowledge and pass on their experience

- the desire of a young person who has just left school or university to acquire skills and get valuable work experience

- the chance to make a contribution to something that is greater than self-interest.

What jobs do people do in a Charity shop?

This will vary with each charity. There is usually much work behind the scenes. Typically the jobs include:

- shop manager/shop leader - liaison between the organisation and the staff

- PR - outreach to local organisations asking for donated goods

- window decorating

- volunteer co-ordination

- sorting, pricing and perhaps ironing the donated goods

- decorating the shop

- serving the customers

- acting as treasurer.

How to volunteer

You may wish to volunteer in the most convenient charity shop to your home. In which case, drop in and ask about volunteering opportunities. Alternatively, you may wish to volunteer with a specific charity; in which case, contact the head office of the charity.

Paid Opportunities

The Notting Hill Housing Trust runs 23 charity shops throughout London. All their staff are paid. Card Aid (run by Charities Advisory Trust, see entry under Charity Support) runs Charity Christmas card shops each year and takes on staff between October and December.

Charity Support

Charities Advisory Trust

Radius Works
Back Lane
London NW3 1HL
Tel: 0171-794 9835
Fax: 0171-431 3739

Contact
Jacqui Caddick, Card Aid Shops co-ordinator

Main Activities
The Charities Advisory Trust advises charities on trading, supply and marketing of charity Christmas cards. Provides training and publications related to charity and museum trading. One national office and a network of retail sites. Annual budget is £500,000.

Opportunities for Volunteers
Volunteers are needed to work in charity Christmas card shops between October and December.

Opportunities for Employment
There are thirteen full-time and seven part-time staff. Approximately twenty new graduates are recruited for temporary jobs each year October–December. Jobs are advertised in national and local press.

Charities Aid Foundation (CAF)

48 Pembury Road
Tonbridge, Kent TN9 2JD
Tel: 01732-771333
Fax: 01732-773774

Contact
Linda Jordan, Personnel Manager

Main Activities
Provides financial and other services for charities and clients to ensure tax effective raising and distribution of funds. Includes donations, trusts, covenants, investments, pay roll giving, searches and

providing information. Based in Kent with two other branches.

Opportunities for Volunteers
CAF does not use volunteers, except for some short term work experience.

Opportunities for Employment
CAF employs 120 staff (full-time and part-time). It recruits between ten and fifteen people each year, especially for general and managerial posts, depending on business needs. Vacancies are advertised as relevant, including the national and local press. Various recruitment consultants are also used. CAF is developing an equal opportunities policy.

Further Information
Annual Report and other information available.

Charity Christmas
Card Council (4C)

49 Lambs Conduit Street
London WC1N 3NG
Tel: 0171-242 0546

Contact
Member charities for volunteering; Ian Black, Retail Manager, for employment opportunities

Main Activities
Retailing Christmas cards for 4C's 107 member charities. A national organisation, 4C operates in three regions Belfast, Leeds and Manchester, as well as London.

Opportunities for Volunteers
Volunteers are used for fundraising and to run retail outlets for Christmas cards from October to December. They are recruited through member charities and volunteer bureaux in the various regions. Training is given on site by shop managers. There is no minimum commitment. Travel and lunch expenses and a volunteer allowance are paid.

Opportunities for Employment
Between 35 and 60 staff are needed annually for the Christmas sales period. They must be enthusiastic, hard-working and able to deal with the public. Recruitment is through the member charities, using an equal opportunities policy.

Further Information
Annual report, list of member charities and mail order catalogue are available.

Charity Projects
Comic Relief

1st floor, 74 New Oxford Street
London WC1
Tel: 0171-436 1122
Fax: 0171-436 1541

Contact
Lorna MacKinnon

Main Activities
Creates new sources of money and distributes funds to specific projects run by charities in UK and Africa. Educates and informs public about the issues underlying their work.

Opportunities for Volunteers
Volunteers are needed to give administrative/clerical support throughout the organisation: fundraising, press, education, reception, grant-giving in UK and Africa. Volunteers need some Windows/Word Perfect and database experience necessary. Travel and lunch expenses are offered. Help is especially needed between January and March in the run-up to Comic Relief Week every two years.

Opportunities for Employment
There are 26 full-time staff. Extra staff are recruited to organise Comic Relief - for six months every two years. Jobs are advertised in The Guardian.

Further Information
Annual Report and educational materials available.

OWA – One World Action, *see*
Overseas & the Developing World

REACH

Bear Wharf, 27 Bankside
London SE1 9DP
Tel: 0171-928 0452
Fax: 0171-928 0798

Contact
Keith Galpin, Development Manager

Main Activities
REACH is a charity which finds part-time, expenses-only, voluntary jobs for retired or redundant business or professional men and women who want to use their skills to help charitable organisations. Usually has a large bank of extremely well-qualified people offering their services.

Opportunities for Volunteers
Approximately 700 volunteers each year are placed nationally according to their skills and experience. General management and financial skills are in particular demand. This job finding service is free.

Opportunities for Employment
There are three full-time staff, and two part-time supported by 22 volunteers.

Further Information
Annual Report, informational literature and a video available.

Swanley District Volunteer Bureau

Little Heath, St Mary's Road
Swanley, Kent BR8 8HA
Tel: 01322-669292

Contact
Pauline Long, Manager

Main Activities
Set up in 1977, the Bureau recruits, places and supports volunteers in Swanley and the northern parishes of Sevenoaks District Council. It is a local development agency for volunteering and for good practice in volunteering, and is a member of the Kent Association of Volunteer Bureaux. It also runs direct services including a befriending scheme and transport. The annual budget is £40,000.

Opportunities for Volunteers
Apart from placing hundreds of volunteers the Bureau itself involves 90 volunteers in head office and 25 at the new Ash Green sub-offices. The work they do includes administrative support, driving, befriending, and membership of the Management Committee. Volunteers are attracted through the local press, radio, displays, posters, talks and word of mouth, and are always needed across the whole area. The skills required vary greatly, there is no minimum commitment and travel expenses are paid.

Opportunities for Employment
The Bureau employs one full-time staff member and four part-time. Without further funding recruitment will only occur if a vacancy arises. An equal opportunities policy is in place.

Further Information
The Annual Report, newsletters, pamphlets and leaflets are available on request.

Children

Action for Sick Children

Argyle House
29-31 Euston Road
London NW1 2SD
Tel: 0171-833 2041
Fax: 0171-837 2110

Contact

For volunteering opportunities: for specific projects - Anne Fragniere, Director & Cheryl Hooper; for general/administrative - Anne Fragniere.

Main Activities

The main aims are to improve the quality of children's health services, to provide support for parents and carers, and to raise awareness of the needs of sick children. Set up in 1961, the organisation is national with 32 local branches, and sister agencies in Scotland and Wales. It is also involved with the European Association for Children in Hospital (EACH). The annual budget is £250,000.

Opportunities for Volunteers

Volunteers are extremely important. With insufficient staff at Head Office to deal with the workload, three volunteers help out. In the local branches volunteers act as ambassadors and do most of the work. This includes providing administrative support, giving advice and undertaking fundraising and research. Volunteers are used year-round and more are required, especially in Head Office. The skills needed include typing/word processor, administrative, organisational, telephone and/or research. On-going training and support are offered. Recruitment is generally ad hoc on application, but during 1994 a recruitment programme was initiated targeting specific groups (eg parents) using fliers, posters and local media. A regular commitment of time is asked for. Travel and out-of-pocket expenses are offered.

Opportunities for Employment

Eight full-time and one part-time staff members are employed. Funding prevents expansion, but should positions arise they are advertised in the national press or via recruitment consultants such as Charity People and Execucare. An equal opportunities policy is being implemented.

Further Information

The Annual Report, standard documents for health professionals, general and family information booklets, and parent advice leaflets are all available by writing in. Sister organisations are:

Action for Sick Children – Scotland
15 Smiths Place, Edinburgh
Tel: 0131-553 6553

Association for the Welfare of
Children in Hospital (Wales)
31 Penyrheol Drive, Sketty, Swansea

ActionAid, *see Overseas & the Developing World*

Association for Glycogen Storage Disease (AGSD (UK)),
see Health & Medicine

Aid for Children with Tracheostomies (ACT)

215A Perry Street
Billericay, Essex CM12 0NZ
Tel: 01277-654425
Fax: 01277-654425

Contact
Mrs J Simonds, Secretary

Main Activities

A national self-help group set up (in 1983) and run by parents of children with a tracheostomy. Provides practical advice and information on care and entitlements, organises study days for parents and professionals, and hires some medical equipment. Links together families and individual members (including health professionals) as requested. Also lobbies and promotes greater understanding of the condition.

Opportunities for Volunteers

Run by a volunteer committee of eight members, elected at the AGM, ACT could not exist without volunteers. The committee and others involved with ACT provide administrative support, fundraising and counselling, and undertake project work. Volunteers normally have to have experience of a tracheostomy. Certain out-of-pocket expenses are offered.

Opportunities for Employment
There are no paid staff.

Further Information
Annual Report, introductory factsheet and a handbook are published.

The Arthrogryposis Group (TAG), *see Disability*

Baptist Youth Ministry, *see Youth*

Barnardos London Division

Tanners Lane, Barkingside
Ilford, Essex IG6 1QG
Tel: 0181-551 0011

Contact
Ms A Matthews, Volunteer Co-ordinator

Main Activities

Involved in child care work, including 26 projects for children and young people from birth to sixteen years. Also runs day care and family centres, and helps young offenders, young people leaving care, and those with learning difficulties. Barnardos is a national organisation with seven regional divisions, including London.

Opportunities for Volunteers

Barnados uses volunteers for administrative, fundraising and project work. It welcomes more, especially during holiday periods. Recruitment is by application, via volunteer bureaux, and through in-house schemes. Prospective volunteers must provide personal details and referees, and attend an informal discussion. Minimum commitment is one hour a week over six months. Travel and lunch expenses are paid. Each regional division has its own contacts in both child care and appeals for initial inquiries about volunteering.

Opportunities for Employment
No details supplied - except that: posts are advertised internally, in local press and in The Guardian and The Voice, and there is an equal opportunities policy.

Further Information
Annual Report and list of local groups are available. In Scotland contact: Barnados Divisional Office, 235 Corstorphine Road, Edinburgh EH12 7AR, tel: 0131-334 9893. In Wales contact: Barnados Divisional Office, 11-15 Columbus Walk, Brigantine Place, Atlantic Wharf, Cardiff CF1 5BZ.

The Boys' Brigade

Felden Lodge, Felden
Hemel Hempstead
Hertfordshire HP3 0BL
Tel: 01442-231681
Fax: 01442-235391

Contact
Mr S Jones, Brigade Secretary

Main Activities
A national Christian uniformed youth organisation set up in 1883 and working for boys aged 6-18 years, in 2,500 companies, each attached to a church. Based on a membership of nearly 100,500 boys, the Brigade offers progressive programmes covering Christian leadership, community interests, physical activities and adventure. The Brigade has a national head quarters and thirteen regional offices. It is also active in Africa, Australia/New Zealand and the Far East, as well as having contacts with Christian youth organisations in Denmark, Sweden and Finland. Annual budget is around £2 million.

Opportunities for Volunteers
The officers leading the companies are all volunteers, and the Brigade is totally dependent on these voluntary leaders. Each company controls its own organisation and activities, and any volunteering opportunities are in these local branches. Volunteers need the ability to work with young people. Contact head quarters for further details and names of groups in specific areas.

Opportunities for Employment
The Brigade employs 26 full-time and sixteen part-time staff. Vacancies occasionally arise. Any posts are advertised in the religious press.

Further Information
The Annual Report, an information pack, the BB Gazette and various catalogues are available. Sister organisations are:

Boys' Brigade Scottish HQ, Carronvale House, Carronvale Road, Larbert, Stirlingshire FK5 3LH

Boys' Brigade Northern Ireland HQ, Rathmore House, 126 Glenarm Road, Larne, Co Antrim BT40 1DZ, N Ireland

Boys' Brigade Southern Ireland HQ, The Scots Centre, Lower Abbey Street, Dublin 1.

The British Institute for Brain Injured Children (BIBIC)

Knowle Hall, Knowle
Bridgwater, Somerset TA7 8PJ
Tel: 01278-684060
Fax: 01278-685573

Contact
Mrs E E Cozens, Regional Coordinator re volunteering; Mrs M Coulson, Administrative Director re employment

Main Activities
BIBIC teaches parents how to give their child appropriate stimulation to aid development and help overcome the problems created by the child's particular brain injury (eg learning difficulties, down's syndrome, cerebral palsy and spasticity). BIBIC has one national centre to which children go from all over the UK, and local affiliated societies/support groups dotted around the country for fundraising/ support. Annual budget of approximately £450,000.

Opportunities for Volunteers
Volunteers are involved in administrative support and fundraising. They are vital in raising both awareness nationwide and funds to enable BIBIC to continue helping more families. Over 50 work in head office and more than 150 in the local support groups. The families who bring children to BIBIC also volunteer. BIBIC is keen to involve more, all year round, especially for fundraising (eg street and supermarket foyer collections, manning stalls at fetes) and awareness raising. Volunteers with a knowledge of German, Polish and/or Dutch would also be helpful for translation purposes. BIBIC is aiming to establish a nationwide fundraising volunteer network. It seeks people with an ability to communicate well with the public and with their own transport (essential). Training is given as required. Recruitment is by application to BIBIC (phone or letter), in-house schemes, word-of-mouth, and through newspaper editorials. Expenses may be paid in certain circumstances.

Opportunities for Employment
BIBIC achieved its planned increases for 1992/93. It employs 31 full-time and five part-time staff. Any vacancies are advertised in local newspapers, specialist journals and The Times Educational Supplement. Clinical staff are recruited from those in an allied profession. An equal opportunities policy is in place.

Further Information
The Annual Report, a list of local groups, a brochure on BIBIC, various pamphlets, the Quarterly Newsletter and a 30-minute video 'Yesterday, Today, Tomorrow' are available.

Brent Family Service Unit, *see Family & Community Matters*

Cancer and Leukaemia in Childhood Trust (CLIC UK)

CLIC House
11/12 Fremantle Square
Cotham, Bristol BS6 5TL
Tel: 0117-9244333
Fax: 0117-9244409

Contact
Felicity Hanley, Executive Assistant or the Executive Director

Main Activities
Set up in 1976, CLIC is a rapidly-growing national children's charity. It provides care and support for children with cancer and leukaemia, and their families. The support is based on a unique model of care incorporating welfare, treatment and research. Regional programmes are provided in specific health authority areas. CLIC funds nurses, grants and home-from-

home facilities, as well as research at Bristol University. It offers information services country-wide. Based in Bristol, with an annual budget of approximately £2 million, CLIC has twenty six local branches.

Opportunities for Volunteers
CLIC uses some volunteers in head office and around 500 in the branches, mainly for administrative, fundraising and shop work. CLIC branches and its shops depend totally on volunteers. Volunteers are recruited via ad hoc approaches and applications to national office or individual branches. There is no set time commitment. Branches decide what expenses to allow for telephone and other costs.

Opportunities for Employment
Positions arise occasionally. All posts are advertised in the national and/or local press as appropriate. Contact the Executive Director for information.

Further Information
Various publications are available on request. These include the Annual Report, leaflets, the quarterly newspaper CLIC News and the appeals brochure. CLIC has also published 'The CLIC Story' and 'The CLIC Model of Care'. A more general 'Guide to UK Children's Cancer Charities' is available too.

Child Growth Foundation (CGF)

2 Mayfield Avenue
Chiswick, London W4 1PW
Tel: 0181-995 0257/0181-994 7625
Fax: 0181-995 9075

Contact
Mr T Fry, Honorary Chairman

Main Activities
The CGF is a small, self-help group which raises awareness of the importance of growth in a child as an indicator of a child's wellbeing. Set up in 1977, it provides support to parents of children with growth disorders, and educates the medical profession and the public on the importance of measuring the growth of children from birth. CGF also distributes money for research and organises conventions/meetings. A national (England-wide) organisation, CGF offers membership, and has five local support groups and eight affiliated organisations which fundraise.

Opportunities for Volunteers
Numerous volunteers are used in the branches to assist with fundraising, and at exhibitions and seminars. Recruitment is simply by people offering to help. There is no minimum time commitment. Travel expenses are offered.

Opportunities for Employment
With two full-time and four part-time staff, CGF has few employment opportunities and seldom recruits.

Further Information
Annual Report, a list of local groups, information on growth disorder and guides for parents are available.

Child Poverty Action Group (CPAG)

1-5 Bath Street
London EC1V 9DY
Tel: 0171-253 3406
Fax: 0171-490 0561

Contact
Debbie Haynes re volunteering; and Jean Ellis, Deputy Director re employment opportunities

Main Activities
A leading anti-poverty charity, CPAG was set up in 1965 and takes action for the relief of poverty among children and families with children. This includes publishing books and handbooks via its subsidiary CPAG Ltd, running training

courses, campaigning, educating the public and the media, and providing welfare benefit advice to welfare rights professionals. Based in London, CPAG has 40 local branches, and individual and organisational members. Its annual budget is £1 million.

Opportunities for Volunteers

CPAG uses volunteers mainly for book packing, particularly from September to February. As it cannot afford to employ any more staff, volunteers are very important to CPAG's work, especially in publications distribution. In future they may be needed to help with research and other activities too. Recruitment is via volunteer bureaux, from advertisements in shops and in Loot, Time Out and other magazines, and through application by letter. Prospective volunteers are interviewed. There is no minimum time commitment. Travel and lunch expenses are paid.

Opportunities for Employment

Between four and five staff might be recruited annually. Any vacancies are advertised in The Guardian, The Independent, The Voice and specialist magazines. CPAG has an equal opportunities policy. It employs nineteen full-time and four part-time staff.

Further Information

Annual Report and lists of books and guides are published.

ChildLine

Royal Mail Building
Studd Street, London N1 0QW
Tel: 0171-239 1000
Fax: 0171-239 1001

Contact

Sonia Tavares, Counselling Administration Officer or Annette Groark, Personnel Department (for administrative volunteering and employment)

Main Activities

Set up in 1986 ChildLine is a national telephone counselling service for children in trouble or danger. The service is confidential with a 24-hour, 365-days a year freephone number. A national organisation with head quarters in London and regional bases in Glasgow, Manchester, Nottingham, Swansea and Rhyl. Annual budget around £3 million.

Opportunities for Volunteers

Volunteers work as counsellors on the telephone lines as well as in fundraising and administration. There are around 300 active volunteer counsellors in the London base (24-hour service) and between 40 and 80 in the regional bases (services 6-9 hours daily). They are central to ChildLine's ability to respond to calls from young people. ChildLine is seeking more volunteers. Those wanting to volunteer as counsellors, if accepted, are given a twelve week counselling course plus on-going training. Volunteers in all other departments should preferably have some office experience. Recruitment is by application (phone or write to the above), in-house, through volunteer bureaux, and occasionally via publicity on television and in other media. Minimum commitment for counsellors is four hours a week over a year. For administration work it is flexible. Travel expenses are offered.

Opportunities for Employment

ChildLine employs 105 full-time and eighteen part-time staff. Recruitment depends on turnover and development strategy. In 1992 around fifteen people were taken on. Skills required depend on the job. Counselling supervisors, for example, preferably have a CQSW qualification or similar, and experience of supervising volunteers. Posts are advertised in national newspapers, especially The Guardian, and job centres. ChildLine is an equal opportunities employer.

Further Information

The Annual Report, information packs for both children and adults, and a list of regional offices are available on written request.

The Childlink Adoption Society

10 Lion Yard, Tremadoc Road
Clapham, London SW4 7NQ
Tel: 0171-498 1933
Fax: 0171-498 1791

Contact

Lisa Landells, Administrator

Main Activities

The Society places children for adoption, providing assessment, support and counselling for all the parties involved, together with post-adoption support. Set up in 1913 and London-based, the Society covers a 35 mile radius around London, and has an annual budget of £250,000.

Opportunities for Volunteers

There are no opportunities for volunteers.

Opportunities for Employment

The Society employs five full-time and five part-time staff. It might recruit one person a year with social work skills. Any posts are advertised in Community Care magazine, based on an equal opportunities policy.

Further Information

Annual Report and the Link Up fundraising brochure are available.

Children in Wales / Plant yng Nghymru

7 Cleeve House, Lambourne Crescent
Cardiff, South Glamorgan CF4 5GJ
Tel: 01222-761177

Contact

Eirwen Malin

Main Activities

Children in Wales promotes the interests of children, young people and their families. The organisation was set up in 1991, and covers all of Wales and has a strong bi-lingual policy. There are some local regional groups.

Opportunities for Volunteers

There are no opportunities at present but Children in Wales could refer potential volunteers on to an appropriate group working with children and young people.

Opportunities for Employment

There are three full-time and five part-time staff. Jobs are advertised in Western Mail and South Wales Echo. Competence in Welsh language helpful.

Further Information

Information leaflet, membership information, a list of local groups and a copy of the current newsletter are available on request.

Children's Country Holidays Fund (CCHF)

42/43 Lower Marsh
London SE1 7RG
Tel: 0171-928 6522
Fax: 0171-401 3961

Contact

Mark Godfrey, Recruitment Officer

Main Activities

CCHF provides summer holidays for socially disadvantaged London children aged 5-13. Set up in 1884, it is a national organisation, concentrating on the Greater

London area with 110 local affiliates. Annual budget is £400,000.

Opportunities for Volunteers

Volunteers are needed for a variety of jobs eg visiting London homes, camp supervising, hosting a child for ten days, escort duties. Over 2,500 are involved and are considered vital; CCHF could not operate without them. New graduates and returners are especially welcome, and it is an advantage to have experience of working with children. Training is provided. Volunteers are most needed in July and August.

Opportunities for Employment

There are eight full-time staff.

Further Information

Annual report, newsletters and information sheets on volunteer roles available.

Children's Legal Centre, *see* *Law & Justice*

The Children's Society

Edward Rudolf House
Margery Street
London WC1X 0JL
Tel: 0171-837 4299
Fax: 0171-837 0211

Contact

Personnel and Staff Development Department

Main Activities

Set up in 1881, the Society (one of the five major voluntary child care agencies) works with thousands of children, young people and their families in over 120 projects throughout England and Wales. The range of its work is enormous. For example, streetwork projects help young runaways at risk in cities. Family centres offer a safety valve to parents under pressure in areas of high unemployment. Children with learning difficulties or disabilities are given

respite care so their families can take a break. The Society is increasingly concerned to encourage everyone to listen more attentively to what children are telling us, and to address the social issues that concern them. It campaigns about a wide range of youth and family policy issues, from the rights of children with disabilities to decent accommodation for homeless families, and increased levels of welfare benefits for young people. Annual budget is approximately £23 million.

Opportunities for Volunteers

Volunteers play an important role in both the Society's fundraising and project activities throughout England and Wales. For example the shops, operation is run completely by volunteers, and the fundraising relies on them heavily. The skills needed vary with the project/activity. Anyone interested can obtain general information about opportunities from the Personnel and Staff Development Department at Head Office.

Opportunities for Employment

There are 1,300 staff employed on a full-time, part-time, temporary or sessional basis. About 240 people are recruited each year, including some for summer playschemes.

Further Information

Annual Report and publications available on request.

The Children's Trust

Tadworth Court
Tadworth, Surrey KT20 5RU
Tel: 01737-357171
Fax: 01737-373848

Contact

Rachel Turner, Voluntary Services Organiser

Main Activities

Formerly the Tadworth Court Trust and originally set up in 1927 as the country branch of Great Ormond Street Children's Hospital, the Children's Trust exists to offer appropriate care, treatment and education to children with exceptional needs and profound disabilities, and also to give support to their families. Its school and respite work is concentrated in southern England, while its rehabilitation unit operates UK-wide.

Opportunities for Volunteers
Volunteer helpers are needed to work directly with the children on a one-to-one basis. They are also required to help with fundraising, marketing, administrative support and general duties such as wheelchair maintenance and distributing post to the site. Volunteer helpers need to be friendly and understanding people who like children and have time to make a regular commitment. A police check is necessary.

Opportunities for Employment
There are 350 staff. There are seasonal recruitment opportunities for nursing and care staff between July and September.

Further Information
Annual Report and other information available.

Church Lads and Church Girls Brigade, *see Religious Affairs*

CRUSE – Bereavement Care, *see Bereavement*

Daycare Trust / National Childcare Campaign, *see Social Welfare*

Fair Play for Children

5 York Road
Bognor Regis PO21 1LW
Tel: 01243-869922 (day)
Tel: 01243-869022 (evening)

Contact
The Secretary

Main Activities
Set up in 1972, the organisation campaigns for the child's right to play (under the UN Convention), and provides information, advice, publications and guidelines for good practice. It is particularly interested in equal opportunities for children to access cultural and recreational resources, and in information and training concerning child protection in play work. A nationwide agency, it has around 450 member groups and networks amongst organisations directly involved in providing playwork facilities. It also has links with the European Playworkers Association, the International Association for the Child's Right to Play, and many smaller bodies. Annual budget is under £4,000.

Opportunities for Volunteers
Since there are no paid staff, volunteers are crucial. They are needed to act as regional co-ordinators and to provide help with training, publications and publicity. A wide range of skills is welcome. Opportunities are nationwide. Knowledge of children, playwork, youthwork, campaigning or training an advantage. Travel and lunch expenses are offered.

Opportunities for Employment
There are no paid staff.

Further Information
Annual Report and publications list available on request.

Families Need Fathers, *see Family & Community Matters*

Family Service Units (FSU), *see Family & Community Matters*

Foundation for the Study of Infant Deaths (FSID)

35 Belgrave Square
London SW1X 8QB
Tel: 0171-235 0965 (general enquiries)
Tel: 0171-235 1721 (Cot Death Helpline)
Fax: 0171-823 1986

Contact
Administration Officer or Appeals Manager

Main Activities
The Foundation has three main aims. It raises funds for research into the causes and prevention of cot death/sudden infant death syndrome. It supports and counsels bereaved families, and it also acts as a centre of information about cot death for health professionals and the public at large. Established in 1971 and a national organisation with head quarters in London, it is active in England, Wales and Northern Ireland. There are about 140 local FSID support groups across the country, and links with cot death organisations world-wide. Annual budget is around £1.5 million.

Opportunities for Volunteers
Head Office needs and uses volunteers to help mainly with clerical and administrative functions, including word processing, photocopying, envelope stuffing and use of the database. Appropriate skills are required. More volunteers are welcome, year round. Recruitment is ad hoc on application to the FSID, and through volunteer bureaux. There is no minimum commitment and no remuneration is offered. Local branches may also need volunteer help and can be contacted through head office.

Opportunities for Employment
Both full-time and part-time staff are employed. For details of any opportunities contact head office.

Further Information
The Annual Report and a wide range of information on cot death and the work of the Foundation are available. A list of the 140 local support groups is also available. For Scotland contact: The Scottish Cot Death Trust, Royal Hospital for Sick Children, Yorkhill, Glasgow G3 8SJ, tel: 0141-357 3946.

The Guide Association, *see Youth*

HAPA (formerly Handicapped Adventure Playground Association)

Fulham Palace, Bishop's Avenue
London SW6 6EA
Tel: 0171-736 4443
Fax: 0171-731 4426

Contact
Anne Melville, Administrative Assistant

Main Activities
HAPA, a registered charity set up in 1970, promotes good quality play provision for disabled children. It runs five fully-staffed adventure playgrounds for children with physical, mental and emotional disabilities in the London area, and also provides a national advice and information service on play and disability. Based in London, it has two local support groups. It is also a member of various national and international play organisations concerned with furthering the importance of play for children, especially those with special needs. Its annual budget is around £750,000.

Opportunities for Volunteers
Two volunteers work in head office on administrative support and fundraising, while approximately fifty work on the

playgrounds with the children. Volunteers also help by serving in the two associated shops, or supporting the play grounds through Friends groups. The voluntary management committee is interested in meeting possible new members. HAPA is seeking more volunteers, especially to work with children in the playgrounds during school holidays and half-terms. Experience of children and/or play, and/or disability are preferred, and arts/crafts skills/interest are useful. Support and training are available. More volunteers are also needed from time to time to work in the shops and to help with fundraising. HAPA recruits volunteers through volunteer bureaux, in-house contacts, play ground users and on application. There is a formal acceptance procedure. Minimum commitment is two hours a week. Reasonable travel and lunch expenses may be paid by arrangement.

Opportunities for Employment

Staff are recruited as vacancies occur through a formal procedure which follows the guidelines in HAPA's equal opportunities policy. Very limited opportunities for temporary paid employment also arise at short notice prior to holiday play schemes. Experience of working with disabled children and/or in play is required. Posts are advertised in the press, particularly The Guardian, The Voice and some local papers. HAPA employs 29 full-time and five part-time permanent staff.

Further Information

Annual Report, a list of local groups, information sheets (some free, some for sale), and a journal (£5 for three issues in 1994) are published. A video is available for sale or hire.

Green Light Trust, see
Environment & Conservation

Hyperactive Children's Support Group (HACSG)

71 Whyke Lane, Chichester
West Sussex PO19 2LD
Tel: 01903-725182, 10am to 3.30pm
Monday to Friday

Contact
Mrs Sally Bunday

Main Activities
HACSG, which was founded in 1977, offers support, counselling and practical support to families with a hyperactive child. It conducts research and promotes investigation into the incidence of hyperactivity in the UK, and its causes and treatments. It also disseminates findings. A national association, working throughout the UK and in Eire, HACSG has local groups and individual members. It also has links with related organisations concerned with allergies and family support in various parts of the world including Europe and Australasia.

Opportunities for Volunteers
Many of the volunteers are parents of hyperactive children as it is important to have some knowledge of the syndrome. However, volunteers who could help with committees, fundraising and administrative work would be very welcome. The Northern Group (Dewsbury) for example, needs help with fundays, meetings and generally extending the work. A Southern Regional Group to be started in 1995 will similarly need voluntary help. Volunteers are also needed to organise local groups and act as contacts for individual parents. Specific professional skills are useful eg teaching, nutrition, dietetics and physiotherapy.

Opportunities for Employment
There are three staff, together with one full-time volunteer at head office.

Further Information
The Annual Report, together with

introductory free literature for parents and low cost resource packs for professionals such as teachers, GPs and health visitors, are available.

International Centre for Active Birth, *see Health & Medicine*

In Touch Trust, *see Disability*

The Jewish Lads and Girls Brigade, *see Youth*

Multiple Births Foundation

Queen Charlotte's and Chelsea Hospital
Goldhawk Road, London W6 0XG
Tel: 0181-740 3519/20
Fax: 0181-748 4712

Contact
Ms Ruth Cockburn for volunteering; Mrs Faith Hallett, Administrative Director re employment

Main Activities
A professional organisation offering support and advice to parents of twins and triplets (and more). Also gives advice and training to professionals concerned with them. Runs clinics for multiple birth families in London, Birmingham and York, a media resource centre and study days. A national organisation with an annual budget of £200,000.

Opportunities for Volunteers
Volunteers help with administrative work and fundraising. They are also invaluable in offering practical support and advice to parents attending the twins clinics. Mothers of multiple birth children can become volunteers at the specialist clinics and at prenatal meetings. More such volunteer mothers with the ability to communicate, listen and support other

parents, are particularly needed. Training is available and volunteers are organised on a rota basis. Recruitment is in-house and through application by phone or in writing to the Foundation. Commitment is varied and flexible. Travel expenses are paid, plus telephone costs for volunteer co-ordinators.

Opportunities for Employment
The Foundation employs twelve staff, all part-time. Some positions may arise each year. There is a formal recruitment procedure and an equal opportunities policy. Skills needed can include medical, inter-personal and clerical. Recruitment is through the clinics, word of mouth, especially the fieldworkers, and the press.

Further Information
Annual Report and specialist leaflets are published.

NASPCS, the Charity for Incontinent and Stoma Children

National Advisory Service for Parents of Children with a Stoma
51 Anderson Drive
Valley View Park, Darvel
Ayrshire, Scotland KA17 0DE
Tel: 01560-322024

Contact
Mr J Malcolm, Chairman/National Organiser

Main Activities
A charity providing a contact and information service for parents on the practical, day-to-day management of aspects of coping with a child who has either a colostomy, ileostomy or urostomy. Also gives advice on incontinence encountered with bowel and bladder problems. A national organisation, with head quarters based in Scotland, NASPCS has one regional group and overseas members from nine other countries. It also has links

with the European Ostomy Association and the International Ostomy Association. The annual budget is £3,000.

Opportunities for Volunteers
Three volunteers run the service, under-taking all administrative, fundraising and counselling work. NASPCS is keen to recruit more from within the organisation. There is no formal time commitment required. Travel expenses are offered.

Opportunities for Employment
NASPCS has no paid staff and there are no employment opportunities.

Further Information
Contact head quarters.

National Association for Gifted Children (NAGC)

Park Campus
Boughton Green Road
Northampton NN2 7AL
Tel: 01604-792300

Contact
Peter Carey, Director

Main Activities
Set up in 1967, NAGC works for the welfare of gifted children, their parents and families. It also disseminates inform-ation concerning gifted children. Trained counsellors and advisers are available, while 35 local branches provide self-help and activities for parents and children. The annual budget is £100,000.

Opportunities for Volunteers
Volunteers are used primarily for admin-istrative support - photocopying, making up information packs and, if they have the necessary skills, for computer data filing and accountancy work. NAGC is keen to enlist more, particularly to help with its five or six mail shots each year. Recruitment is usually through volunteer bureaux. Minimum commitment is two hours a week, as available. Travel expenses are offered.

Opportunities for Employment
There are three full-time and one part-time staff members. Further general office assistance may be needed occasionally, although recruitment is rare. Posts may be available on a voluntary basis initially, advertised through volunteer bureaux, based on an informal equal opportunities policy. A volunteer may then be offered paid work later.

Further Information
Brochures, parents' and professionals' information packs and Annual Report are available. For Scotland contact NAGC Scotland (NAGCS):

Mrs S Divecha, 8 Castlehill Drive, Newton Mearns, Glasgow G77 5LB, tel: 0141-639 4797.

The National Association for Special Education Needs (NASEN), see Education

National Association of Toy and Leisure Libraries / Play Matters

68 Churchway
London NW1 1NT
Tel: 0171-387 9592
Fax: 0171-383 2714

Contact
Catherine Farrell

Main Activities
Toy libraries and leisure libraries loan care-fully chosen toys to families with young children, including those with special needs and learning difficulties. Set up in 1967 and UK-wide, the National Association also provides information and advice on the setting up of toy libraries. Annual budget (head quarters) is £320,000.

Opportunities for Volunteers
Administrative support and fundraising

help needed. Minimum commitment is seven hours per week.

Opportunities for Employment
There are four full-time and eight part-time staff. Jobs are advertised in the Hampstead and Highgate Journal.

Further Information
Annual Report and information available on request.

National Childminding Association (NCMA)

8 Masons Hill
Bromley,
Kent BR2 9EY
Tel: 0181-464 6164
Fax: 0181-290 6834

Contact
Marje Paling, Assistant Director Operations, re volunteering; Sarah Norrington re employment

Main Activities
NCMA promotes childminding as a quality childcare service for children under eight years for working parents, and works to improve its status and standards. Set up in 1977, it informs central and local government, parents, employers and childminders what constitutes best practice in childminding. It is also a membership organisation for childminders and others involved in early years childcare and education of young children. It covers twelve regions in England and Wales, has 1,200 local support groups, and over 50,000 members, including groups and individuals. Many of the groups, which the NCMA helps to support, are charities in their own right using a model constitution designed for local use. The NCMA also has links with the International Family Day Care Association.

Opportunities for Volunteers
Volunteers work in head office and the branches in administration, fundraising,

counselling and project work. They are vital in supporting staff in delivering training to members in the regional and county structures, and also as representatives from those structures on the NEC/Board of Trustees. Recruitment is mainly from among the membership. Minimum commitment varies from area to area. Travel and out-of-pocket expenses may be paid.

Opportunities for Employment
Occasional vacancies arise among the 23 full-time and seven part-time staff, including in fundraising. Any posts are advertised in the press, including The Guardian for specialised positions, and local papers for others. NCMA operates and is fully committed to a formal recruitment and an equal opportunities policy.

Further Information
Annual Report and publications list (send sae) are available. Sister organisations are:

Scottish Childminding Association, Room 15, Stirling Business Centre, Wellgreen, Stirling FK8 2DZ, tel: 01786-445377

Northern Ireland Childminding Association, 17A Court Street, Newtownards, Northern Ireland BT23 5NX, tel: 01247-811015.

National Children's Home (NCH)

85 Highbury Park
London N5 1UD
Tel: 0171-226 2033
Fax: 0171-226 1517

Contact
Regional staffing secretaries or Appeals offices re volunteering or employment; Personnel Department at Highbury office for administration posts

Main Activities
National Children's Home, set up over 125 years ago, is the UK's second largest

childcare charity, working with 16,000 children, young people and their families each year. Has around 200 projects throughout the UK including family centres, residential homes and schools, respite care facilities, sexual abuse treatment units and alternatives to custody schemes. NCH is regarded as a leader in social work development. It has nine Regional Social Work offices (eg Anglia, Woking, Warrington) and three Appeals offices, as well as its national office in North London. It also has projects in the Eastern Caribbean and Central America, and is a member of the International Forum for Child Welfare (IFCW) and its regional group the European Forum for Child Welfare.

Opportunities for Volunteers

Volunteers work in the projects and also in regional offices. Work includes administrative support, fundraising, and limited opportunities in counselling, caring and social welfare. Volunteers are essential to fundraising. A variety of skills are required ranging from driving and communication to social work. Recruitment is by application to the Regional or Appeals Offices which assess suitability and appropriate placements. There is no minimum commitment. Expenses may be paid.

Opportunities for Employment

NCH is a large employer with over 2,000 full-time and part-time staff. It recruits for social work, administrative, and appeals posts, requiring associated skills and qualifications. In some regions there are also seasonal play scheme jobs. Vacancies are advertised in the appropriate professional/ trade press (Community Care, Social Work Today), The Guardian and relevant local papers. NCH operates a formal recruitment policy with full job descriptions, and is an equal opportunities employer.

Further Information

The Annual Report, a list of local groups and a job opportunities leaflet are available.

National Deaf Children's Society (NDCS)

25 Wakefield Road
Rothwell, Haigh
Leeds LS26 0SF
Tel: 01532-823458

Contact
Julie Cook

Main Activities

NDCS enables deaf children to participate in society more fully and to achieve independence. Encourages them to maximise their skills. There are three centres with paid staff and 140 local groups of parents and professionals in the field.

Opportunities for Volunteers

Volunteers are needed locally to be part of registered associations, eg serving on management committees and parent support networks. Training is available.

Opportunities for Employment

There are 29 full-time staff. Skills needed are job specific but an awareness of deafness is always called for. Jobs are advertised in The Guardian, The Voice, Teletext and *No Need to Shout*.

Further Information

Annual Report and publications list available.

National Foster Care Association (NFCA)

Leonard House
5-7 Marshalsea Road
London SE1 1EP
Tel: 0171-828 6266

Contact
Ms S Tisdall, Administration Manager

Main Activities

A national charity set up in 1974 and working throughout the UK to promote and improve the quality of the foster care service. Provides advice, mediation and information, training, and membership services, and produces various publications. NFCA has offices in London and Glasgow, is membership based and also works with other organisations in Eastern Europe. Annual turnover is £1.4 million (1994).

Opportunities for Volunteers
The NFCA uses a small number of volunteers for administrative support. It is seeking more with appropriate skills for general accounts and occasional clerical help. Recruitment is by application to the central office. Commitment is flexible and travel expenses are paid.

Opportunities for Employment
There are 18 full-time and 14 part-time staff and one volunteer. Vacancies occasionally occur. Any recruitment is based on a written procedure in line with the equal opportunities policy. Posts are advertised in The Guardian, The Voice, the South London press and job centres.

Further Information
NFCA publishes a range of publications - leaflets, books, promotional literature and training manuals - and an annual report.

National Playbus Association (NPA)

AMF House
93 Whitby Road
Brislington, Bristol BS4 3QF
Tel: 0117-977 5375
Fax: 0117-972 1838

Contact
National Office for volunteering; Ms L Williams, General Manager (Administration) re employment

Main Activities
A national development agency working directly with all those interested in mobile community provision. Aims to benefit individuals and communities in areas of inadequate community provision, both urban and rural. Works mainly with children and young families, but also has projects with women, young people and health. Has a national office and eight regional groups, including Scotland, each with a committee structure. There are around 250 member projects sited in most major cities and in rural areas throughout the UK, with a few abroad (eg Germany). NPA's annual turnover is £289,000 (1993).

Opportunities for Volunteers
Volunteers work in national office (2) and in the projects (various) in administrative support and fundraising. More may be needed for individual projects, especially to work on play schemes and for bus cleaning and maintenance. Extra help is particularly needed with holiday play schemes at Christmas, Easter, half-terms and during the summer. Training can often be given on the job. Volunteers are frequently parents. But projects may also recruit through local advertisements, word of mouth and volunteer bureaux. Head Office has sometimes used REACH. Minimum commitment can be flexible, but on projects is often for the duration of the particular scheme. Travel expenses are usually paid and on some projects a small daily volunteer allowance also. Apply by letter or phone to national office.

Opportunities for Employment
Five full-time and six part-time staff are employed including those in the Scottish office. NPA has a small staff turn-over and recruits infrequently. Projects may have short-term sessional work available. Recruits need to understand the play world and play issues for under-eights and their families. Jobs are advertised among the membership, through the in-house magazine and mailings, in The Guardian, The Voice and the Caribbean Times, and in the local press. An equal opportunities policy is operational.

Further Information
The Annual Report, a publications list, pamphlets on technical services and information sheets, are available on request. Contacts for projects in local areas can also be supplied. In Scotland contact: the Mobile Projects Association Scotland (MPAS), 12 Picardy Place, Edinburgh EH1 3JT, tel: 0131-556 7580.

National Playing Fields Association (Scotland), see
Recreation & Leisure

National Society for the Prevention of Cruelty to Children (NSPCC)

67 Saffron Hill
London EC1N 8RS
Tel: 0171-242 1626

Contact
Ms Pam Medcalf, Personnel Manager

Main Activities
The NSPCC works to prevent children from suffering ill treatment, abuse and neglect. Set up in 1884, it assists and protects children at risk, and provides counselling and other help to abused children to help them overcome the effects of ill treatment. It has a country-wide network of 24-hour Child Protection Teams whose Child Protection Officers (CPOs) offer treatment, advice and consultation to families, professionals and other agencies. CPOs have statutory powers too. The NSPCC also runs various day care services (play groups, drop-in centres, etc). The Society is structured into eight regional groups and 76 local branches, including Northern Ireland, but does not operate in Scotland.

Opportunities for Volunteers
Volunteers work in head office and the branches primarily in administrative support and fundraising, although they are used throughout the organisation's activities. NSPCC is keen to enlist more volunteer help, and particularly needs people with office and typing skills. Volunteers are recruited by various methods, including ad hoc applications to head quarters and/or regional offices. No minimum commitment is required. Travel and lunch expenses are paid.

Opportunities for Employment
NSPCC recruits every year for both administrative and child protection team staff. Child Protection Officers (CPOs) require a CQSW qualification and two years experience. Posts are advertised in the national and local press. Recruitment of new graduates, returners and people with disabilities is particularly active. There are around 1,300 employees throughout the country.

Further Information
Annual Report, list of local groups and information leaflets are published.

Notting Dale Urban Studies Centre, see Education

Parent Network, see Family & Community Matters

Parent Partnership Project, see Education

Parents Against Injustice, see Family & Community Matters

Parents Aid, see Family & Community Matters

Pestalozzi Children's Village Trust

Sedlescombe, Battle
East Sussex, TN33 0RR
Tel: 01424-870444
Fax: 01424-870655

Contact
Nik Radcliffe, Director of Fundraising

Main Activities
Set up in 1958, the Trust educates poor children from rural areas in the developing world who would otherwise be unable to receive secondary education. Training is offered in management skills and modern technology. There are 50 local groups who support this work.

Opportunities for Volunteers
With a small staff volunteers are very important and are relied on for extra support. The skills required depend on whether the work is clerical, educational, fundraising/appeals, etc. Volunteers are used to organise an annual Open Day and to undertake farm and estate work. Many are gap-year students and the minimum commitment is 40 hours a week, usually over the spring and summer vacations. Applications should be made in writing to the Administrator.

Opportunities for Employment
There are 40 full-time, and ten part-time staff.

Further Information
Promotional literature is available.

The Pony Club, *see Sports*

Pre-school Playgroups Association (PPA)

61-63 Kings Cross Road
London WC1X 9LL.
Tel: 0171-833 0991
Fax: 0171-837 4942

Contact
John Randall

Main Activities
Set up in 1961 the PPA supports the work of nineteen thousand member playgroups throughout England who offer care and education to under-fives. There are 430 branches.

Opportunities for Volunteers
Volunteers work in both head office and the local branches. They fundraise and provide administrative support. PPA estimates that over 11,000 parents volunteer in the member groups and many others are on parent management committees. Travel and lunch expenses are offered.

Opportunities for Employment
There are 29 full-time staff. Three are recruited on average each year.

Further Information
Annual report and a list of groups available.

Quicksilver Theatre for Young Children, *see Museums, the Arts and Festivals*

Research Trust for Metabolic Diseases in Children (RTMDC), *see Health & Medicine*

RESPITE

13 Granville Road
Ilford, Essex IG1 4RU
Tel: 0181-518 4454
Fax: 0181-518 5829

Contact
Jenny Brock, Co-ordinator

Main Activities
Aims to provide respite to families with and carers of children with special needs by means of a domiciliary sitting service, and holiday play and activity schemes. Founded in 1988 Respite is a local voluntary organisation operating in the Redbridge area only.

Opportunities for Volunteers
Volunteers are essential for without voluntary input it would not be possible to provide the services Respite offers. Some volunteers carry out administrative tasks but most are needed as play and care workers for the holiday play and activity schemes and for the domiciliary sitting service. All these volunteers need to have experience of working with children with special needs, and more are required. Recruitment, which is ongoing, is by direct application or through the services of the Redbridge Volunteer Bureau. The time commitment required varies and can be at any time, including evenings and weekends, depending on the availability of the individual volunteer. Travel and out-of-pocket expenses are paid. Training includes initial induction and sessions on specific topics, and support is provided by experienced staff. Requests for an application pack can be made to the address above.

Opportunities for Employment
Staff consist of one full-time, two part-time and 12 temporary. The temporary staff are recruited each year for the holiday play and activity schemes. They are needed seasonally during Easter and summer, and must have experience of working with children with special needs. Positions are advertised through other agencies that work with children with special needs but general enquiries may be made directly to the Respite office. Respite is working towards an equal opportunities policy.

Further Information
An information leaflet is available through the Respite office.

Save the Children Fund (SCF)

17 Grove Lane
Camberwell,
London SE5 8RD
Tel: 0171-703 5400

Contact
Jennifer Sinclair

Main Activities
SCF works for the rights and welfare of children in the UK and in over 50 of the world's least developed countries. National organisation with 800 local branches and 150 shops. There are divisional offices in Wales, Scotland and Northern Ireland. Annual budget is £56 million.

Opportunities for Volunteers
Volunteers are always needed to help in shops and undertake fundraising activities eg coffee mornings, selling goods from the catalogue, concerts etc. Many are recruited through local branch networks and campaigns. Some volunteers become press secretaries, school speakers or trading secretaries. From time to time there is a need for volunteers to help with major campaigns or emergency disaster appeals at Head Office. Very occasionally volunteers work with children and their families.

Opportunities for Employment
There are approximately 700 full-time and 150 part-time staff. About 150 are

recruited each year. Jobs are advertised in local jobs centres, local and national newspapers as appropriate.

Further Information
Annual Report and information leaflets, including one on volunteering, are available from the Central Information Section.

The Scout Association, see Youth

Sea Ranger Association (SRA), see Youth

Sick Children's Trust, see Social Welfare

Stepfamily, see Family & Community Matters

SOS Stars Organisation Supporting Action for People with Cerebral Palsy, see Disability

St Piers Lingfield

St Piers Lane
Lingfield, Surrey RH7 6PW
Tel: 01342-832243
Fax: 01342-834639

Contact
Personnel Department

Main Activities
Set up in 1898, the organisation provides education, residential care and medical treatment for children aged 5–19 with epilepsy, learning difficulties and related neurological disorders. Annual budget is £6.5 million.

Opportunities for Volunteers
Volunteers are needed to assist with teaching, care and nursing throughout the school campus. They support the

professional staff in a lay capacity and are highly valued. All skills are welcomed and are used appropriately. Minimum commitment is five hours a week during term time. Travel and lunch expenses are offered. The Hospital is also hoping to create local fundraising groups.

Opportunities for Employment
There are 358 full-time and 116 part-time staff. About 30 people are recruited each year, often with skills such as educational, caring, medical, administrative. Jobs are advertised in local newspapers.

Further Information
Annual Report, general information and school brochures available.

The Thomas Coram Foundation for Children

40 Brunswick Square
London WC1N 1AZ
Tel: 0171-278 2424
Fax: 0171-837 8084

Contact
Richard Wyber

Main Activities
Primarily a child care charity providing services for children and young people. It also looks after the heritage/museum of the former Foundling Hospital.

Opportunities for Volunteers
Volunteers are welcomed to support the Foundation's work, especially in relation to the heritage activities.

Opportunities for Employment
There are no opportunities at present.

Further Information
Annual Review available.

TOFS Tracheo-Oesophagal Fistula Support, see Health & Medicine

Treloar Trust, *see Disability*

Volunteer Reading Help, *see Education*

Women's Royal Voluntary Service, *see Social Welfare*

The Woodcraft Folk, *see Youth*

Counselling & Self-Help

A great variety of organisations offer counselling and self-help. Some offer counselling in a face-to-face situation eg Relate, others on the telephone eg ChildLine, and others both eg the Samaritans. Others concentrate on setting up Self-Help Groups, which may be local or nationally organised.

Many people volunteer as counsellors as part of preparation for subsequent training as professional counsellors or psychotherapists. Counselling requires a level of self-knowledge and a willingness to explore issues which may feel uncomfortable or challenging. All voluntary organisations involving volunteer counsellors should offer training and on-going supervision and support.

Self-Help Groups offer many people an effective way of coping with a situation, illness or condition which would otherwise be very hard to bear. Some groups are set up by voluntary organisations, others by individuals who then create their own voluntary organisation or affiliate themselves with an existing one.

Other sections to look up include: Advice, Bereavement, Caring, Family and Community Matters, Mental Health.

Abuse in Therapy Support Network

c/o Women's Support Project
1700 London Road
Glasgow G32 8XD
Tel: 0141-554 5669

Contact
Co-ordinator

Main Activities
Abuse in Therapy Support Network offers confidential support and information for women who have been abused by someone in a position of trust eg therapist, counsellor, minister, priest.

Opportunities for Volunteers
Local groups and events are organised from time to time mainly by women who have had similar experiences themselves.

Opportunities for Employment
There are no opportunities for employment.

Further Information
Pamphlets, newsletters, recommended reading list available. Confidential Telephone Support Line: 013610-850227 (Tuesday, Thursday, Friday, Sunday 7-10 pm).

ACCEPT

724 Fulham Road
London SW6 5SE
Tel: 0171-371 7555

Contact
Anne Hunter, Director

Main Activities
ACCEPT provides a comprehensive range of non-residential services to individuals and their families who experience problems due to alcohol. There is a five week abstinence programme and evening groups.

Opportunities for Volunteers
Volunteers fundraise and provide administrative support. Travel and lunch expenses are offered. Minimum commitment is three hours a week.

Opportunities for Employment
There are six full-time staff and seven session workers. About two are recruited each year, often with counselling skills. Jobs are advertised in The Guardian, The Voice and in Job Centres.

Further Information
Annual Report and general information leaflet available on request.

Acceptance (Helpline and Support Group for Parents of Lesbians and Gay Men)

64 Holmside Avenue, Halfway Houses,
Sheerness
Kent ME12 3EY
Tel: 01795-661463

Contact
Jill and Gordon Green

Main Activities
Gives support by phone, literature and newsletters to the parents and families of homosexual people. Runs a national telephone helpline, organises meetings for parents to discuss their feelings, and disseminates information. Acceptance has a policy of strict confidentiality. It also lobbies, campaigns and seeks to educate the public and professionals. Based in Kent, Acceptance receives mail and calls nationwide. It relies entirely on donations to fund its work.

Opportunities for Volunteers
As a self-help and support group, Acceptance is a voluntary-run organisation. It would welcome help from suitable volunteers but, in dealing with such a sensitive issue, selection procedures are necessarily stringent. Contact the office for further details.

Opportunities for Employment
There are no paid staff and no employment opportunities.

Further Information
Annual Report, a list of local groups, booklets, posters and a newsletter (on annual subscription) are available.

Action on Phobias Associations Scotland (AOPAS)

6 Grange Street
Kilmarnock, Scotland
Tel: 01563-74144

Contact
Rosaline Rown, National Co-ordinator

Main Activities
AOPAS advises on help and self-help groups available to sufferers of panic attacks, anxiety, and all phobias. Information and videos are available. It is national organisation with self-help groups affiliated throughout Scotland.

Opportunities for Volunteers
Volunteers are very important to AOPAS. There are five in Head Office and a number running local branches. They fulfil various roles: counselling, setting up workshops, advice giving, administrative support. Travel and out-of-pocket expenses are offered.

Opportunities for Employment
There is one part-time worker at present.

Further Information
Annual Report, leaflets, cassettes and an information pack are available for a small charge to cover postage.

ADFAM National, see Education

Afterwards, see Disability

Association for Glycogen Storage Disease (AGSD (UK)), see Health & Medicine

Aid for Children with Tracheostomies (ACT), see Children

Al-Anon Family Groups UK and Eire (AFG)

61 Great Dover Street
London SE1 4YF
Tel: 0171-403 0888 (24-hour confidential service)

Contact
The Information Secretary

Main Activities
Offers help to families and friends of alcoholics and problem drinkers. Alateen, a part of Al-Anon, helps teenagers who are affected by another's drinking, usually a parent's. Organises group meetings and provides speakers. Runs a 24-hour confidential telephone service. An international organisation, the general office in London services nearly 2,000 local support groups in the UK, and has links with over 33,000 groups worldwide. AFG is funded entirely by voluntary contributions and the sale of literature.

Opportunities for Volunteers
Between twenty and 30 volunteers help in head office, but because of the confidential and specialist nature of the work, all are found from within the membership.

Opportunities for Employment
There are four full-time and six part-time staff. As with volunteers, all are recruited from within the membership.

Further Information
Leaflets and posters are available, with various publications for sale. Information about local group meetings can be obtained from the head office number (see above).

Alcohol Concern

Waterbridge House
32-36 Loman Street
London SE1 0EE
Tel: 0171-928 4644

Contact
Head Office; or local telephone directory for local organisations

Main Activities
Alcohol Concern aims to raise public awareness of the problems that alcohol can cause, improve services for those who drink too much and promote preventive action both locally and nationally. Alcohol Concern was set up in 1984 as an umbrella organisation representing the interests of all alcohol services, both statutory and voluntary.

Opportunities for Volunteers
Alcohol Concern does not involve volunteers itself but administers a national accreditation scheme for the training of volunteer counsellors by local agencies. Minimum commitment is four hours per month. Travel expenses and a 60 hour training course are offered. Qualities needed include empathy with others, and a non-judgmental attitude.

Opportunities for Employment
Local organisations recruit staff on an ad hoc basis. Jobs are generally advertised locally or in The Guardian.

Further Information
Annual report, leaflet about the Volunteer Alcohol Counsellors Training Scheme (available in 1995) and general information on Alcohol Concern available on request.

Alcohol Counselling and Prevention Services (ACAPS)

34 Electric Lane
Brixton, London SW9 8JT
Tel: 0171-737 3579
Fax: 0171-737 2719

Contact
Head Office as above

Main Activities
A local agency for the South East London boroughs of Lambeth, Lewisham and Southwark, ACAPS was set up in 1977. It offers alcohol education and prevention, group and individual counselling, and training in alcohol assessment and counselling. Annual budget is £250,000.

Opportunities for Volunteers
About 30 volunteers are involved in management/trusteeship, counselling and/or administrative support. More are needed and would be welcomed. Recruitment is via volunteer bureaux, in-house schemes and people simply applying since the agency is well known. Job descriptions and application forms are available. A minimum commitment of four hours a week is required and certain expenses are offered eg travel, sometimes lunch.

Opportunities for Employment
There are ten full-time paid staff. Up to two staff are recruited each year, the skills/experience required depending on the position. Jobs are advertised in the national, local and specialist ethnic press, and in mailings. An equal opportunities policy has been implemented.

Further Information
The Annual Report, and various leaflets about the agency, the service and drinking are available by written or verbal request.

Alcoholics Anonymous (AA)

General Service Office
PO Box 1, Stonebow House
Stonebow, York YO1 2NJ
Tel: 01904-644026 (admin)
Tel: 0171-352 3001 (helpline 10am-10pm)

Contact
Jim Keeney, General Secretary

Main Activities
A fellowship of men and women who share their experience, strength and hope with each other so that they may solve their common problem and help others to recover from alcoholism. A membership organisation, the main aim is to stay sober and help others achieve sobriety. AA is national, with around 3044 local support groups. Each group is autonomous and the aim is self-help not counselling.

Opportunities for Volunteers
Volunteers are found from among the membership only, and staff the telephone help lines 24 hours. Members are involved at local level and must have a desire to stop drinking. Anonymity and confidentiality form the foundation of the AA's traditions. Contact through local telephone directories or head office.

Opportunities for Employment
AA employs ten full-time staff. Opportunities for employment are very limited.

Further Information
The Annual Report, information sheets and a list of local groups are available.

Anorexia and Bulimia Nervosa Association (ABNA)

Tottenham Women & Health Centre
Tottenham Town Hall
London N15 4RB
Tel: 0181-885 3936

Contact
K Reeve

Main Activities
Anorexia and Bulimia Nervosa Association runs a helpline for parents, sufferers and friends. National organisation with office in London. Annual budget is £1,000.

Opportunities for Volunteers
Volunteers are needed to work on the helpline, fundraise and provide administrative support. Volunteers should preferably be ex-anorexics or ex-bulimics. General guidance and mutual support is offered.

Opportunities for Employment
There are no paid staff.

Further Information
General information leaflets are available (please enclose an SAE).

Aperts Syndrome Support Group, see Health & Medicine

Arthritis Care (Wales)

30 Brookfields
Crickhowell, Powys NP8 1DJ
Tel: 01873-811109

Contact
Senior regional Organiser

Main Activities
Arthritis Care aims to raise the quality of life for people with arthritis by offering information and support. There are 48 branches in Wales.

Opportunities for Volunteers
There are approximately three hundred volunteers in Wales who carry out a variety of tasks including: organising local groups, counselling, advice giving. Hospital information points are staffed by volunteers who supply information and support to people attending clinics. Arthritis Care visitors provide support for housebound and disabled people especially in rural areas. Minimum commitment is eight hours a week; travel expenses and out-of-pocket expenses are offered. There are induction and regular group meetings.

Opportunities for Employment
There are four members of staff.

Further Information
Annual Report and leaflets are available.

The Arts Counselling Trust (ACT)

PO Box 3875
London SW1V 9RZ
Tel: 0171-259 9104

Contact
Liza Davies, Director

Main Activities
The Arts Counselling Trust offers integrative creative therapy, counselling and pastoral care for offenders in prison and after release. ACT is planning to develop a residential centre.

Opportunities for Volunteers
Volunteers are required to provide services to families of offenders as well as pastoral care and social activity. Volunteers are needed also for administrative work, fundraising, research and to serve as trustees.

Opportunities for Employment
The organisation employs two full-time and four part-time staff. Creative therapists and trained counsellors are recruited from time to time.

Further Information
Annual Report, leaflets, and tri-annual newsletters are available on request. A contribution (£5 or £10 to cover costs) would be helpful.

APA (Association for the Prevention of Addiction)

27-39 Gt. Guildford Street
London SE1 0ES
Tel: 0171-620 0058

Contact
Victoria Parsons

Main Activities
APA provides care, support, information and advice for people experiencing drug and alcohol problems, their families and friends. Annual budget is £100,000.

Opportunities for Volunteers
APA is currently developing opportunities for volunteers. At present central office need volunteers to help with fundraising work. Computer skills are especially welcome. Managerial support is given.

Opportunities for Employment
There are forty staff. An equal opportunities policy is in place and jobs are advertised in The Guardian and other newspapers.

Further Information
Information leaflet on drugs, list of local groups and Annual Report are available on request.

Association for Stammerers (AFS)

15 Old Ford Road
London E2 9PL
Tel: 0181-983 1003 (admin)
Tel: 0181-981 8818 (Parents helpline)
Fax: 0181-983 3591

Contact
Peter Cartwright, Director

Main Activities
Helps stammerers with speech and related problems. Offers advice and information about speech therapy. Provides local self-help groups, open meetings and telephone links. Annual budget is £100,000.

Opportunities for Volunteers
Volunteers are needed to fundraise and give administrative support. There are also projects eg stammering pupils which needed help. Travel expenses are offered. AFS attempts to match the individual skills offered with the needs of the organisation.

Opportunities for Employment
There are three staff.

Further Information
Annual Report, further information and list of local self-help groups available.

BACUP (British Association of Cancer United Patients)

3 Bath Place, Rivington Street
London EC2 3JR
Tel: 0171-696 9003
Fax: 0171-696 9002

Contact
BACUP Cancer Counselling Service

Main Activities
Offers counselling, information and emotional support to cancer patients, families and friends. There is a national

telephone helpline and a London counselling service. Annual budget is £1.5 million.

Opportunities for Volunteers
Volunteers are needed to give counselling. Training and supervision are provided. Minimum commitment is four hours a week. Counselling skills and experience to Diploma level needed as well as commitment to personal therapy and supervision. Administrative assistance is sometimes required from time to time.

Opportunities for Employment
There are 40 full-time and six part-time staff. On average four or five are recruited each year. Jobs are advertised in The Guardian, Evening Standard, The Voice and the Pink Paper.

Further Information
Annual Report, pamphlets and BACUP news available on request.

Behçet's Syndrome Society

3 Church Close, Lambourn
Newbury, Berks RG16 7PU
Tel: 01388-71116

Contact
Honorary Secretary

Main Activities
The Society provides information, support and financial aid for sufferers of Behçet's Syndrome nationwide. Encourages networking amongst medical profession and research.

Opportunities for Volunteers
Volunteers are vital to the organisation and are needed to help with the production of the newsletter, publicity and marketing, driving and to act as advocates. An editorial, PR or journalistic background would be of use as would a knowledge of hospital structure and routines. Volunteers are also needed for street collections.

Opportunities for Employment
There are no paid staff.

Further Information
Annual Accounts and further information available on request.

Body Positive, see Aids/HIV

The Bourne Trust, see Social Welfare

Brent Family Service Unit, see Family & Community Matters

British Association for Counselling (BAC)

1 Regent Place
Rugby, Warwickshire CV21 2PJ
Tel: 01788-578328 (Information line)
Tel: 01788-550899 (Office)
Fax: 01788-562189

Contact
The main office

Main Activities
A membership organisation for counsellors and those using counselling skills, BAC is concerned with setting standards in practice and training, and with promoting awareness of counselling to the public. It organises conferences and provides informed comment on counselling issues. A national body, it is divided into specialist areas including medical, education and pastoral care, and has a number of affiliated local groups. It also has overseas members.

Opportunities for Volunteers
BAC uses volunteers from its membership only, for committee work (setting and operating policies, etc) and for producing its journal.

Opportunities for Employment
Nineteen full-time and three part-time

staff are employed, but few recruitment opportunities arise. Any vacancies are advertised in the in-house magazine, and require knowledge and expertise in counselling. BAC has an equal opportunities policy.

Further Information
An Annual Report, membership brochure and lists of local groups and of publications are available.

British Association of Settlements and Social Action Centres (BASSAC), *see Social Welfare*

British Colostomy Association, *see Health & Medicine*

British Diabetic Association (BDA), *see Health & Medicine*

British Polio Fellowship, *see Health & Medicine*

British Retinitis Pigmentosa Society, *see Disability*

CALL (Cancer Aid and Listening Line)

Swan Buildings, 20 Swan Street
Manchester M4 5JW
Tel: 0161-834 6551 (admin)
Tel: 0161-835 2586 Or 0161-434 8668
(Helpline)

Contact
Richard Lanyan, Co-ordinator

Main Activities
CALL provides emotional support and a 'listening ear' for cancer patients, their families and friends. There is a telephone helpline and a drop-in centre. Hospital visiting is arranged and there is a home visiting scheme. Operates in the Greater Manchester area and is the umbrella organisation for branches in Stockport, Wythenshawe and Trafford.

Opportunities for Volunteers
Volunteers are needed to fundraise and give administrative support. Helpline 'listening ears' are also needed, for which training is provided (course starts in January).

Opportunities for Employment
No information available.

Further Information
Annual Report and leaflet available on request.

Cancer Care Society (CARE), *see Caring*

Cancer Link

17 Britannia Street
London WC1X 9JN
Tel: 0171-833 2451

Contact
The self-help and support service at head quarters

Main Activities
Provides support and information on all aspects of cancer to people with cancer, their families and friends. Acts as a resource to around 450 cancer support and self-help groups, and to individuals, throughout the UK. Also helps volunteers to set up new groups.

Opportunities for Volunteers
The local groups are run by volunteers with experience of cancer. They provide support and information to others involved with cancer. There is no minimum commitment. Contact the main office as above, for details.

Opportunities for Employment
Cancer Link employs 22 staff, but opportunities for employment seldom arise.

Further Information
Leaflets, the quarterly magazine Link Up (£5 a year or free to support groups), the annual accounts and a list of local groups, are available.

Cancer Relief Macmillan Fund,
see Caring

CARE for People with a Mental Handicap (CARE), see Caring

Carers National Association,
see Lobbying & Campaigning

Catholic Marriage Advisory Council (CMAC)

1 Blythe Mews, Blythe Road
London W14 0NW
Tel: 0171-371 1341
Fax: 0171-371 4921

Contact
Elizabeth Harrison, Publicity Co-ordinator

Main Activities
Provides relationship/marriage counselling, and marriage preparation courses. Has an administrative head quarters plus over 80 local branches and fifteen regional groups.

Opportunities for Volunteers
Around 1000 volunteers work in the branches providing counselling, administrative support and fundraising. CMAC welcomes more volunteers, especially those with management skills. It trains its own counsellors. Recruitment is in-house and by application to the local centres. Minimum commitment for counsellors is three hours weekly. Travel expenses are offered.

Opportunities for Employment
CMAC employs five full-time staff. Vacancies seldom arise.

Further Information
The Annual Report, a list of local groups and various leaflets, posters and other publications are available.

Child Abuse Survivor Network

28 Mount Pleasant
London WC1X 0AP
Tel: 0171-278 8414

Contact
Willow Wallston

Main Activities
The Child Abuse Survivor network is the only national organisation dedicated to helping adult survivors of abuse in childhood. The organisation offers advice, networking, referrals and a forum for exploring the issues and problems and healing surrounding abuse. It has a local resources database, a newsletter and a pen friends scheme. All work is done by post.

Opportunities for Volunteers
Volunteers are very much welcomed to carry out administrative support, fundraising, trusteeship and public relations. Minimum commitment is between four and six hours a week. Travel expenses are offered. Word processing and book keeping skills are very useful.

Opportunities for Employment
There are no employment opportunities at present.

Further Information
Annual report available on request.

The Childlink Adoption Society, see Children

City and Hackney Alcohol Counselling Service (City and Hackney ACS)

Tower View House
134 Kingsland Road
London E2 8DY
Tel: 0171-613 1313

Contact
Valerie Hughes, Volunteer Co-ordinator

Main Activities
The City and Hackney ACS offers counselling for people with alcohol problems, their partners and relatives. The organisation also offers advice and information about alcohol to promote alcohol awareness and good health in preventative capacity.

Opportunities for Volunteers
Volunteers are extremely important to the organisation. Trained volunteer counsellors help to extend the number of counselling hours available and make the service more widely accessible. In future it is planned to develop other categories of volunteers such as those who can fundraise and give administrative support, PR and research. Main Asian languages and Turkish would be an advantage. Travel and out-of-pocket expenses are offered. For counsellors the minimum time commitment is two years. A sixty hour training programme is offered as well as on-going support. Inter-personal skills and a knowledge of alcohol and alcohol related issues an advantage.

Opportunities for Employment
There are two full-time and two part-time staff.

Further Information
A leaflet aimed at service users is available and 'A Client's Charter' is in preparation.

Contact a Family

170 Tottenham Court Road
London W1P 0HA
Tel: 0171-383 3555

Contact
Paul Soames, Assistant Director, London

Main Activities
Provides help and advice for families caring for children with disabilities or special needs. Links families together and encourages mutual support between parents. National organisation with projects in London boroughs, plus regional offices in Kent/East Sussex, Somerset, Devon, Yorkshire and Humberside, Manchester and south west London.

Opportunities for Volunteers
Volunteers are needed to run holiday playschemes at summer and Christmas time. Other useful skills include driving/escorting, committee work, finance/budgeting experience, running weekend and evening clubs. Minimum commitment is at least two hours a week for two to three months. Volunteers are particularly important to local borough based projects in London.

Opportunities for Employment
There are 24 full-time and eight part-time staff.

Further Information
Annual Report, list of local groups and further information available.

Counsel and Care

Twyman House, 16 Bonny Street
London NW1 9PG
Tel: 0171-485 1566

Contact
Ms E Richarby re volunteering; Training Officer re employment

Main Activities
Gives confidential, free, expert advice by

telephone and letter on a wide range of issues connected to people over pensionable age, and to their carers and professionals. Written advice is also available in various Asian languages. A national charity with one central office.

Opportunities for Volunteers
Up to four volunteers help to provide administrative support. They are recruited by application to head office. There is no minimum commitment. Travel and lunch expenses are offered.

Opportunities for Employment
Counsel and Care employs 21 full-time and three part-time staff. Vacancies occasionally arise. Posts are advertised in The Guardian and The Voice, based on an equal opportunities policy.

Further Information
The Annual Report and a publications list of Counsel and Care factsheets (donations appreciated, some for sale) are available.

Crossroads, *see Caring*

CRUSE *Bereavement Care, see Bereavement*

CRY-SIS Support Group, *see Family and Community Matters*

Divorce Conciliation & Advisory Service (DCAS), *see Family and Community Matters*

Drug and Alcohol Women's Network (DAWN)

c/o CLAAS, 30/31 Great Sutton Street
London EC1V 0DX
Tel: 0171-250 1627

Contact
Ros Juma, Development Worker

Main Activities
DAWN is a national network of individual women working in the fields of drugs or alcohol with women. The Network disseminates information and organises four Network Days each year. There are approximately 76 affiliated organisations.

Opportunities for Volunteers
At present there no specific opportunities, but as the organisation develops help with photocopying and maintaining the database could be very valuable.

Opportunities for Employment
There is one part-time member of staff.

Further Information
Annual Report, DAWN publications on women, drugs and alcohol, and list of network members available. Research report *When a Crèche is not enough* making recommendations on good practice in women's services is available at £4.00 including post and packing.

Drugline

9A Brockley Cross
London SE24 2AB
Tel: 0181-692 4975
Fax: 0181-692 9968

Contact
Margeret Moses, The Co-ordinator

Main Activities
Drugline offers counselling, education and advice to drug users, their families and friends. The organisation offers

information about safer sex, relapse prevention and acupuncture. There is also a legal surgery and a well user clinic and a community de-tox programme. Drugline offers its services locally in SE London but its telephone helpline is national.

Opportunities for Volunteers
Many volunteers are ex-users (of at least two years standing) who use volunteering as a stepping-stone to a paid job. Tasks include: administrative work, advice giving, project work such as escorting drug users. Travel and lunch expenses are offered.

Opportunities for Employment
There are six full-time and one part-time staff.

Further Information
Annual Report and a booklist explaining Drugline's services available on request.

Exploring Parenthood Trust,
see Family & Community Matters

Family Welfare Association
(FWA), see Family & Community Matters

Fellowship of Depressives Anonymous (FDA)

36 Chestnut Avenue, Beverley
N Humberside HU17 9QU
Tel: 01482-860619

Contact
Pat Freya, Hon Secretary

Main Activities
FDA forms and supports self-help groups for those suffering from depressive illness. Collects and exchanges information on depression. A national organisation with seventeen local groups. Annual budget is £2,500.

Opportunities for Volunteers
Two volunteers run the main office and organise fundraising. The self-help local groups are also run by volunteers, most of whom have an experience of depression – either personal or through close contact with sufferers. Recruitment is via group meetings and mail-outs. There is no minimum time commitment.

Opportunities for Employment
There are no paid staff and no employment opportunities.

Further Information
Annual Report, a list of local groups and discussion leaflets are published.

First Steps to Freedom, see
Mental Health

Gender Dysphoria Trust International (GDTI)

BM Box 7624
London WC1N 3XX
Tel: 01323-641100

Contact
Fran Springfield, Administrator

Main Activities
GDTI is a support organisation for transsexuals. Provides medical and legal information, counselling, newsletters and other publications. One national office based in Eastbourne, East Sussex.

Opportunities for Volunteers
Volunteers are essential and are needed to give administrative support. Office skills are useful and in-house training is given. One day a week is the minimum commitment. Potential volunteers should apply in writing.

Opportunities for Employment
There are no paid staff.

Further Information
Information leaflets and booklets are available.

Green Light Trust, *see*
Environment & Conservation

Guideposts Trust Ltd, *see Caring*

Guillain-Barré Syndrome Support Group (GBS Support Group)

'Foxley', Holdingham
Sleaford, Lincs NG34 8NR
Tel: 01529-304615

Contact
Mrs Glennys Sanders

Main Activities
Provides emotional support and visits, where possible, to patients and their families. Supplies literature and educates the public and the medical professions about the illness and the Group's work. Fosters research and encourages local support groups. A national organisation, with 75 local counsellors and local branches. Annual budget approximately £70,000.

Opportunities for Volunteers
The counsellors are all volunteers, as are those who visit sufferers and their relatives. Volunteers also help with administration and fundraising. Recruitment is ad hoc on application to the Group, and from among willing recovered sufferers and their relatives/friends. There is no specific time commitment. Travel expenses are offered.

Opportunities for Employment
There are no employment opportunities.

Further Information
Annual Report, a number of guides and a list of local groups are available on request. In Scotland contact Mr and Mrs S Pert, Cottage No 42, Crookfur Cottage Homes, Newton Mearns by Glasgow G77 6JQ, tel: 0141-639 8077.

The Haemophilia Society

123 Westminster Bridge Road
London SE1 7HR
Tel: 0171-928 2020
Fax: 0171-620 1416

Contact
General Secretary

Main Activities
Provides information about haemophiliacs to those who are affected and others. Cares for people with haemophilia through a wide range of activities. There are twenty eight regional groups. Annual budget is £550,000.

Opportunities for Volunteers
Volunteers are needed to fundraise. Useful qualities are enthusiasm, marketing and organisational skills. Volunteers also give advice and administrative support.

Opportunities for Employment
There are seven full-time and one part-time staff. On average one person is recruited each year.

Further Information
Annual Report available.

Headway, National Head Injuries Association Ltd, *see Social Welfare*

Herpes Association

41 North Road
London N7 9DP
Tel: 071-607 9661

Contact
Michael Wolfe or Diana Arch

Main Activities
Provides information, advice and counselling for those with herpes (HSV) or shingles (VZV), as well as information to health professionals, the media and the general public. Has a London base and local support groups.

Opportunities for Volunteers

Uses 30-40 volunteers with personal experience of herpes/shingles for the telephone help line. More volunteers needed for the help line and occasional office/clerical support. Training provided. Recruited from membership or ad hoc on application to the Association. No minimum commitment. Travel expenses paid.

Opportunities for Employment

There are three full-time staff. Opportunities are very few. An equal opportunities policy is in place.

Further Information

Membership and a quarterly journal are available plus information packs on HSV/VZV.

Ileostomy and Internal Pouch Support Group (IA)

Amblehurst House
Black Scotch Lane, Mansfield
Notts NG18 4PF
Tel: 01623-28099

Contact

David Eades, National Secretary

Main Activities

IA's primary aim is to help anyone whose colon has been, or is about to be, removed by surgical procedure or who has had an ileostomy. Promotes and co-ordinates research into bowel disease and other conditions leading to the removal of the colon, surgical procedures pertaining thereto, and related matters. Publishes a quarterly journal which is distributed free to members. There are 60 local groups throughout the UK and Ireland.

Opportunities for Volunteers

The members are all volunteers offering self-help and support to each other. Recruitment is through membership. Members must have had an ileostomy operation.

Opportunities for Employment

IA does not employ any staff.

Further Information

The Annual Report and a list of local groups are available. Pamphlets and other literature are for members only.

Jewish Bereavement Counselling Service, *see* *Bereavement*

Jewish Care, *see Caring*

Let's Face It – Support Network for Facially Disfigured

10 Wood End, Crowthorne
Berks RG11 6DQ
Tel: 01344-774405

Contact

Christine Piff, Founder, Director

Main Activities

Let's Face It offers support to people with all forms of facial disfigurement, their families and friends through a self-help support network. There are twelve regional groups and overseas links.

Opportunities for Volunteers

Volunteers are needed all the time to support fellow sufferers. The ability to care and share personal experience are useful.

Opportunities for Employment

There are no paid staff.

Further Information

Leaflets and information are available on request. For Scotland, contact: Rosemary Kelly, Canniesburn Hospital, Bearsden, Glasgow, tel: 0141-942 2255. For Northern Ireland, contact: Frances Berry, 1 Knockenden Crescent, Belfast BT6 0GP, tel: 01232-692827.

Leukaemia Care Society, *see Social Welfare*

Life for the World Trust

Wakefield Building, Gomm Road
High Wycombe, Bucks HP13 7DJ
Tel: 01494-462008

Contact
Chairman

Main Activities
Rehabilitates those affected by drug/alcohol addictions with counselling, group therapy, Bible teaching, sports, arts and practical work. National organisation with two local branches. Annual budget is £170,000.

Opportunities for Volunteers
Volunteers are required to serve on management committees. A keen interest in the nature of the project and ability to give various kinds of practical support useful.

Opportunities for Employment
There are ten full-time and three part-time staff. On average two people are recruited each year.

Further Information
Leaflets and newsletters available.

London Lesbian Line, *See Women*

London Lesbian and Gay Switchboard

PO Box 7324
London N1 9QS
Tel: 0171-837 7324 (helpline)
Tel: 0171-837 7606 (volunteering line)

Contact
via Switchboard

Main Activities
Provides advice and information (via 24 hour telephone helpline) on all aspects of lesbian and gay life including safe sex and HIV/Aids. Where appropriate, refers people to the existing network of locally based switchboards. Annual budget is £50,000.

Opportunities for Volunteers
Gay/lesbian volunteers with an ability to be empathetic and non-judgmental are needed to help staff a 24 hour telephone helpline. There is extensive induction and in-service training. Minimum commitment is 30 hours on the phone per three months period plus some non phone work. Unwaged volunteers are offered travelling expenses and subsistence.

Opportunities for Employment
There are currently no employment opportunities.

Further Information
Annual Report and further information available.

London Lighthouse, *see Aids/HIV*

Lowe Syndrome Association (LSA)

29 Gleneagles Drive
Penwortham, Preston
Lancs PR1 0JT
Tel: 01772-745070

Contact
Julie and David Oliver

Main Activities
A support group for families of children with Lowe's Syndrome. Promotes contact among families, provides information and supports research. Works to promote individual potential of sufferers. A very small organisation, it has international links with about 100 member families world-wide.

Opportunities for Volunteers
The Association is run by three volunteers.

Opportunities for Employment
There are no paid staff.

Further Information
Annual report, a newsletter three times yearly, information leaflets and conference reports are available.

Lupus UK

51 North Street
Romford, Essex RM1 1BA
Tel: 01708-731251

Contact
Mr E Hanner, Head Office

Main Activities
Lupus UK is a national registered charity operating self-help groups for people with Lupus. It provides advice and counselling, publishes regional and national newsletters, and raises funds for research and welfare support. A national organisation, with 26 local affiliates. Annual budget is approximately £100,000.

Opportunities for Volunteers
Volunteers work in head office (1) and the branches (c.150) in administration, fundraising, counselling and project work. Lupus is keen to enlist more, especially to help with support groups. Recruitment is usually in-house through application to the local groups. Contact head office for details. There is no minimum commitment. Travel expenses are offered.

Opportunities for Employment
Lupus UK employs three part-time staff and a full-time director, and has an equal opportunities policy. Opportunities for employment seldom arise.

Further Information
Annual report, range of publications and a list of local groups are available.

Manic Depression Fellowship
(MDF), see Mental Health

Manna Drop-In Centre, see
Housing & Homelessness

Mind over Matter (MOM)

14 Blighmont Crescent
Milbrook
Southampton SO15 8RH
Tel: 01703-775611

Contact
Phil Williams

Main Activities
MOM is a self-help and support group for men with testicular cancer, aiming to raise awareness of this condition. It offers telephone support nationwide. Local meeting facilities are provided by the Wessex Cancer Trust. MOM was set up in 1990 and aims to develop into a national network of support groups for men with testicular and other male related cancers.

Opportunities for Volunteers
There are five volunteers (mostly patients and their families) who support the work of the groups, fundraise and give administrative support. MOM would welcome fundraising in the Wessex area and would like to hear from anyone setting up a support group for testicular cancer.

Opportunities for Employment
There are no employment opportunities at present.

Further Information
Annual Report and leaflets are available by sending a self-addressed envelope to MOM.

Multiple Sclerosis Society, see
Social Welfare

Myalgic Encephalomyelitis Association (ME Association)

Stanhope House, High Street
Stamford-le-Hope
Essex SS17 0HA
Tel: 01375-642466

Contact
Vicki Airs, General Manager

Main Activities
Locates sufferers of ME and offers support. Disseminates information to the general public, the medical profession and other agencies. Raises funds to support existing research projects and sponsors new ones. A national organisation, it has 450 local support groups.

Opportunities for Volunteers
Head Office uses three volunteers for fundraising and counselling/advice work. Listening and secretarial skills are needed. The local support groups are run by volunteers. The Association is actively seeking more. Computer training and general support is given. Prospective volunteers should apply to head office. There is no minimum time commitment. Travel expenses are offered.

Opportunities for Employment
The Association occasionally recruits. In 1992 it was seeking people for fundraising work. Vacancies are advertised in appropriate newspapers. Consultants are sometimes used. There are eight full-time and eight part-time staff.

Further Information
Annual Report, a list of local groups and various publications - leaflets (donations appreciated) and books (for sale) - are available.

Myotonic Dystrophy Support Group, see Disability

National Agoraphobic Society

1 Church Lane
Catcliffe
Rotherham S60 5TP
Tel: 01709-820288 (24 hour helpline service)

Contact
Clive Nuttall

Main Activities
The National Agoraphobic Society aims to fill the gap left by the medical services and offer a more personal form of help and advice. A programme of help for sufferers to improve their lifestyle is offered.

Opportunities for Volunteers
Volunteer help is always welcome, especially with fundraising.

Opportunities for Employment
There are no opportunities for employment.

Further Information
Annual Report and booklets are available.

National Ankylosing Spondylitis Society (NASS), see Health & Medicine

National Association of Laryngectomee Clubs, see Social Welfare

National Association of Widows, see Women

National Autistic Society, see Caring

National Council for the Divorced and Separated (NCDS), see Family & Community Matters

National Eczema Society, *see Health & Medicine*

National Federation of Kidney Patients Associations, *see Health & Medicine*

National Marriage Guidance Council (Relate)

Herbert Gray College
Little Church Street
Rugby CV21 3AP
Tel: 01788-573241
Fax: 01788-535007

Contact
Via the Manager at the local Relate Centre

Main Activities
Centres throughout England, Wales and Northern Ireland enable Relate Marriage Guidance to offer confidential counselling, psychosexual therapy and educational services to those wanting help with adult couple relationships.

Opportunities for Volunteers
Volunteers are needed for counselling, fundraising and administrative work. Training and support are offered as appropriate.

Opportunities for Employment
Very few people are recruited each year.

Further Information
Annual Report and informational literature available.

National Rett Syndrome Association (NRSA)

15 Tanzieknowe Drive
Glasgow G72 8RG
Tel: 0141-641 7662

Contact
President, Mrs I Allan

Main Activities
Provides support to families of people with Rett Syndrome. Encourages research into the condition, provides information and promotes awareness. Undertakes fundraising. Organised nationally from the Glasgow area, membership is available. Annual budget relies on fundraising and varies.

Opportunities for Volunteers
Three voluntary workers and volunteer committee members run NRSA. They also undertake fundraising and counselling, and produce certain publications. NRSA is keen to enlist more to help with the ongoing running of the organisation, especially from among its own members. Recruitment is by application (write or phone) or in-house. Commitment is variable and no expenses are offered.

Opportunities for Employment
NRSA is a small self-help organisation. There are no employment opportunities.

Further Information
Annual Report, various brochures, the newsletter and a video on Rett Syndrome are available.

National Society for Epilepsy (NSE)

Chalfont St Peter
Gerrards Cross
Bucks SL9 0RJ
Tel: 01494-873991

Contact
Derek Westcott, Fundraising Director or Kathy McLoughlin, Volunteer Co-ordinator

Main Activities
National Society for Epilepsy carries out research, rehabilitation and long term care of people with epilepsy. There are 30 local support groups. Annual budget is £6.5 million.

Opportunities for Volunteers
Volunteers are needed for a variety of tasks eg working in a shop, sending out direct mail, Flag Day and Door-to-Door collecting, befriending, social activities and some clerical/computer work. Ability to communicate with people is important. Minimum commitment is four hours a week. Travel and Lunch expenses are offered where applicable.

Opportunities for Employment
There are 240 full-time and 40 part-time staff. Approximately 75 people are recruited each year. An essential skill is some knowledge of caring in a residential setting. Jobs are advertised in The Guardian, Community Care, Nursing Times and local papers.

Further Information
Annual Report, information and videos available on request.

The Neurofibromatosis Association

82 London Road
Kingston-upon-Thames
Surrey KT2 6PX
Tel: 0181-547-1636

Contact
John Blackwell

Main Activities
The Association supports all those affected by neurofibromatosis. Provides information for public and medical professionals and raises funds for research. There are 24 local groups in a regional self-help organisation supported by professional Family Support Workers.

Opportunities for Volunteers
Members volunteer for befriending, administrative work and fundraising. Occasional help is needed from outside the Association with mailshots etc.

Opportunities for Employment
There are four full-time and three part-time staff. The Association plans to increase the number of Family Support Workers by two (Greater London and Newcastle upon Tyne) during 1995.

Further Information
Sixteen fact sheets on neurofibromatosis are available.

New Approaches to Cancer

5 Larksfield
Egham, Surrey TW20 0RB
Tel: 01784-433610

Contact
Colin Ryder Richardson, Honorary Secretary

Main Activities
A national charity which promotes the benefits of holistic and self-help methods of healing to cancer patients. Head office

acts as the nerve centre for a network of 450 local self-help groups, holistic practitioners and clinics throughout the UK. Operates an information service directing people with cancer to local, national or international services of self-help. Annual budget is under £5,000.

Opportunities for Volunteers
New Approaches relies on volunteers and most of whom will have had personal experience of cancer. More are welcome and needed to expand the network of local groups, and to help with administration, counselling and educational work. Volunteers are recruited through application to the office and because they want to help. There is no minimum commitment and no remuneration is offered.

Opportunities for Employment
A small, part-time, paid staff runs the office. Any vacancies are usually filled by word of mouth.

Further Information
Various publications, information on local resources and a list of local groups can be provided on request. A large stamped addressed envelope is very much appreciated.

Norwood Child Care, see Social Welfare

Parentline, see Family & Community Matters

Parent Network, see Family & Community Matters

Parents Against Injustice (PAIN), see Family & Community Matters

Parents Aid, see Family & Community Matters

PSS, see Social Welfare

Portia Trust, Mental Health

Prisoners Families and Friends Service, see Family & Community Matters

Prisoners Wives and Families Society, see Family & Community Matters

Psoriasis Association

7 Milton Street
Northampton NN2 7JG
Tel: 01064-711129

Contact
Linda Henley, National Secretary

Main Activities
The Psoriasis Association offers information and self-help on all aspects of psoriasis and psoriatic arthritis. The Association supports research projects. There are 25 local branches and the annual budget is £750, 000.

Opportunities for Volunteers
Volunteers run the local branches, which typically meet regularly to provide points of social contact and information and to raise funds for research and educational projects.

Opportunities for Employment
There are three full-time and one part-time staff.

Further Information
Annual report, national journal and information leaflets available on request.

QUIT – Helping Smokers to Quit

Victory, 170 Tottenham Court Road
London W1P 0HA
Tel: 0171-388 5775

Contact
Steve Crone, Director of Services

Main Activities
QUIT specialises in helping smokers to quit. Runs a national helpline (Quitline) and training for health professionals. Annual budget is £500,000.

Opportunities for Volunteers
Volunteers are needed to work as counsellors and to do administrative tasks. Counselling training and word-processor training are offered as appropriate. Minimum commitment is eight hours a week. Travel and lunch expenses are offered.

Opportunities for Employment
There are eight full-time and two part-time staff. There are plans to recruit freelance counsellors. Jobs are advertised in The Guardian and through Charity Recruitment.

Further Information
Brochure and Quitline leaflets available on request.

The Raynard and Scleroderma Association, see Health & Medicine

Release

388 Old Street
London EC1V 9LT
Tel: 0171-729 9904

Contact
Catherine Phillips

Main Activities
Release runs a 24 hour helpline for drug users. Has a particular interest in the legal issues surrounding drug use.

Opportunities for Volunteers
Volunteers work as emergency advisors out of office hours. Induction training programmes, telephone and travel expenses are offered. Minimum commitment is six hours every two weeks for a year. Volunteers need to be able to assimilate information quickly. A sympathy with the problems which drug users face is essential.

Opportunities for Employment
There are seven full-time staff, and two part-time staff, and jobs are advertised in The Guardian.

Further Information
Annual Report is available.

St John Ambulance, see Health & Medicine

The Samaritans

10 The Grove
Slough SL1 12P
Tel: 01753-532713 (Head Office)
Fax: 01753-819004

Contact
Volunteer Unit at Head Office or local branch (look in telephone book under 'S')

Main Activities
The Samaritans offer a 24 hour confidential telephone service for those in crisis and in danger of taking their own lives. There are 200 hundred centres in the UK and Eire.

Opportunities for Volunteers
The Samaritan service is entirely provided by 23,000 volunteers who staff the telephones, raise funds and help in the day to day running of branches. Local branches organise open evenings for potential volunteers followed by selection days. Special qualities needed are the ability to listen, to be non-judgmental and accepting of people from all walks of life.

Training is provided and travel expenses are offered. Approximately three hours a week is the expected commitment.

Opportunities for Employment
There are 32 full-time staff and vacancies are advertised in The Guardian and The Independent.

Further Information
Various leaflets and packs are available.

Sickle Cell Society, see Health & Medicine

The Society for Mucopolysaccharide Diseases (The MPS Society)

55 Hill Avenue
Amersham Bucks HP6 5BX
Tel: 01494-434156
Fax: 01494-435256

Contact
Christine Lavery, Director

Main Activities
The MPS Society acts as a support group for parents with a child suffering from the illness. Raises funds for research and aims to bring about a higher level of public awareness. There are twelve local groups. Annual budget is £215,000.

Opportunities for Volunteers
Sixty trained volunteers assist families in caring for children National Weekend Conference at annual conferences, holidays and local family days. Volunteers also help in Head Office. All volunteers are carefully selected and vetted: a background in the caring professions is an advantage.

Opportunities for Employment
Employment opportunities are limited.

Further Information
Annual Report and specific disease booklets (50p per copy) available.

St Marylebone Healing & Counselling Centre

St Marylebone Church
17 Marylebone Road
London NW1 5LT
Tel: 0171-487 3797

Contact
Louisa Lennox, Co-ordinator, Crisis Listening and Befriending

Main Activities
St Marylebone Healing and Counselling Centre offers one-to-one counselling, crisis listening, befriending and group therapy. It was set up in 1986. It operates from the Crypt of St Marylebone Church.

Opportunities for Volunteers
Approximately 120 volunteers carry out counselling and befriending. Counsellors must have two years training and six months work experience. For befriending and crisis listening, volunteers need an interest in people but no formal skills or experience. Travel expenses are offered.

Opportunities for Employment
There are no employment opportunities.

Further Information
An Information Pack, Requirements to Be a Counsellor and leaflets are available from Reception.

Stepfamily, see Family & Community Matters

STEPS (National Association for Children with Lower Limb Abnormalities)

15 Statham Close, Lymm
Cheshire WA13 9NN
Tel: 01925-757525

Contact
Sue Banton

Main Activities
Support and provides information for families with children who have abnormalities of the lower limbs. Runs a family contact register and advisory service. National organisation with local branches and groups. STEPS is committed to developing teleworking using information technology to link individuals/workers in their own homes. Annual budget is £40,000.

Opportunities for Volunteers
Volunteers are needed for fundraising, advice giving, telephone helpline and administrative support. Computer and administrative skills are useful. Travel expenses are offered.

Opportunities for Employment
There are three part-time staff.

Further Information
Annual Report, list of local groups and information pamphlets for parents and professionals available.

UK Thalassaemia Society, *see* *Health & Medicine*

Urostomy Association, *see* *Disability*

Victim Support

National Office
Cranmer House
39 Brixton Road
London SW9 6DZ
Tel: 0171-735 9166
Fax: 0171-582 5712

Contact
Information Officer

Main Activities
Victim Support contacts and helps victims of crime. Aims to raise awareness of the effects of crime. There are 371 groups throughout England, Wales and Northern Ireland. Annual income is over £10 million.

Opportunities for Volunteers
Volunteers are vital to Victim Support's work. They visit and offer practical help and emotional support to victims of crime. Volunteers must be 18+ and are given a full training. References and a police check are also required. Contact co-ordinator of local victim support scheme (address in local telephone directory). Fundraising and administrative support are needed as well.

Opportunities for Employment
There are 703 staff nationally. Occasionally there are vacancies for co-ordinators in local schemes. Jobs are advertised locally.

Further Information
Annual Report available. For Scotland, contact: Victim Support Scotland, 14 Frederick Street, Edinburgh EH2 2HB, tel: 0131-225 7779.

Winged Fellowship Trust, *see* *Disability*

Youth Access, *see* *Youth*

Disability

Charities of various kinds exist to work for and with people with disabilities. They provide services and training, lobby or campaign to change attitudes towards disability, encourage empowerment, and give information and advice. The types of disabilities are very wide, including mental and physical disablement, everything from learning difficulties and head injuries to arthritis and blindness.

Some organisations are disability-led, eg the Spinal Injuries Association (SIA), others are not eg the Spastics Society, Mencap. (An indication as to whether an organisation is disability-led or not can sometimes be found in the title; those with 'of' eg British Council of Organisations of Disabled People, rather than 'for'). If you have a disability and wish to work or volunteer in a charity, disability-led organisations can be good place to start your search.

The following agencies may also be of interest:

- Employers' Forum on Disability, 5 Cleveland Place, London SW1Y 6JJ, tel: 0171-321 6591. The Forum aims to improve disabled peoples' job prospects by making it easier for employers to recruit, retain and develop people with disabilities.

- The British Council of Organisations of Disabled People, De Bradelei House, Chapel Street, Belper, Derbyshire DE5 1AR, tel: 01773-838182.

- Asian People with Disabilities Alliance, Ground Floor, Willesden Hospital, Harlesdon Road, London NW10 3 RY, tel: 0181-459 5793.

- Greater London Association of Disabled People (GLAD), 336 Brixton Road, London SW9 7AA, tel: 0171-274 0174.

Access Committee for England

12 City Forum, 250 City Road
London EC1V 8AF
Tel: 0171-250 0008
Tel: 0171-250 4119 (minicom)
Fax: 0171-250 0212

Contact
Margaret Mannion, Administrator

Main Activities
Founded in 1984 as a national focal point on issues of access for all people with disabilities, Access Committee for England works to improve access to the built environment. It advises, consults, provides information and fosters public awareness. A national committee for England, it liaises with around 400 local access support groups. Separate Access committees exist for Wales, Scotland and Northern Ireland (see below). The annual budget is £130,000.

Opportunities for Volunteers
Volunteers are needed in the London office to put material on audio-cassette for blind members, and in the local access groups for a range of tasks. Skills needed in access groups are administrative support, fundraising, lobbying, and negotiating improved access with local building owners/managers. Volunteers are required all year round, and a knowledge of access/disability issues is useful. Recruitment is ad hoc, on application. Minimum commitment varies with the individual groups, but in the London office is one afternoon a month. Travel expenses are offered in the London office; local groups usually do not offer expenses.

Opportunities for Employment
The Committee has a small staff. Posts are advertised in the national press. The administrative base for the Committee is in the Royal Association for Disability and Rehabilitation (RADAR).

Further Information
The Annual Report, free newsletter 'Access Action', free leaflets on access matters, a free summary of the National Research Project on Local Access Groups (1994), and a list of local groups in England are available. The manual for access groups 'Working Together for Access' is also available for £7.00.

Other contacts are:

Access Committee for Wales, Tel: 01222-887325

Access Committee for Scotland, Tel: 0131-229 8632

Access Committee for Northern Ireland, Tel: 01232-491011

Action for Blind People

14-16 Verney Road
London SE16 3DZ
Tel: 0171-732 8771
Fax: 0171-639 0948

Contact
Ann Lewis, Director of Personnel Services

Main Activities
Offers a range of community-based welfare support, including the provision of residential care and sheltered housing, information and advice, holidays and cash help, and employment and training schemes for blind and visually impaired people. A national organisation, concentrating on England, the annual budget is around £7 million.

Opportunities for Volunteers
A small number of volunteers is used, especially in community relations. Contact head office for details.

Opportunities for Employment
The organisation employs a total of 360 staff. Vacancies are advertised in the national (eg The Guardian), specialist and local press. Seasonal temporary work opportunities may arise in hotels used for

holidays eg in Bognor Regis and Weston Super Mare. An equal opportunities policy is being developed.

Further Information

Annual Report and a wide range of information leaflets are produced.

Action for Dysphasic Adults

1 Royal Street
London SE1 7LL
Tel: 0171-261 9572

Contact
Helen Robertson

Main Activities

Provides information, advice and occasional advocacy for people with communication problems after stroke or head injury etc. Aims to increase awareness of the condition and press for appropriate assessment, therapy and resources. There are eight local branches and four regional groups. The organisation is nationwide and the annual budget is £120,000.

Opportunities for Volunteers

Volunteers run the local groups and provide administrative assistance. Travel and out-of-pocket expenses are offered. There are not at present many resources for supervision for volunteers at Head Office but the organisation aims to take someone with dysphasia as a step towards rehabilitation in the regular work market.

Opportunities for Employment

There are four staff. An equal opportunities policy is in place and jobs are advertised in the Evening Standard (for office work) and specialist journals (for therapists).

Further Information

Annual report, series of How to Help booklets and 'Lost for Words' available on request.

Afterwards

380-384 Harrow Road
London W9 2HU
Tel: 0171-266 4311 (office)
Tel: 0171-266 2300 (support)
Fax: 0171-266 2922

Contact
Development Director

Main Activities

'Afterwards' offers an innovative service of telephone support, advice, counselling and information for people who are suddenly disabled, whatever the cause, and for those involved with them. It seeks to enable people with disabilities to play an active role in its own growth and development. Set up in late 1993, currently (1995) it covers the Greater London area only. Annual budget is approximately £44,000.

Opportunities for Volunteers

Volunteers are vital and fundamental to 'Afterwards'. Ten volunteers currently undertake much of the work, including fundraising, public relations, research, advice giving, and management. Volunteers also act as trustees. More are needed, especially for support work on phones, publicity and fundraising. Volunteers need to have listening/counselling skills, commitment, an awareness of sudden disability, and the ability to work in a team. They are recruited by various methods, including through volunteer bureaux, in-house schemes and existing services, and on application, followed by an interview. Minimum commitment is three hours a week over six months. Travel expenses are offered and a six week induction course is provided for telephone support workers.

Opportunities for Employment

One full-time and one part-time member of staff are employed. Any other opportunities depend on 'Afterwards' development plans. Any vacancies may be advertised in The Voice, the Evening Standard and the speciality press including Disability Now, and London Disability News, with a particular emphasis on recruiting people with disabilities. An Equal Opportunities Policy operates.

Further Information
A leaflet and a philosophy paper describing 'Afterwards' are available by phone or writing.

The Arthrogryposis Group (TAG)

1 The Oaks
Gillingham, Dorset SP8 4SW
Tel: 01747-822655

Contact
Jill Anderson, Chairman

Main Activities
A contact group, TAG maintains a network of contacts among arthrogrypotics and their families. It sets up regional groups, holds an annual conference, publishes a quarterly newsletter and other literature, and has an on-going research programme. A national organisation covering the whole of the UK, it has eleven regional contacts and affiliated organisations in Australia, New Zealand, Spain, Germany and Holland. Annual budget is approx. £35,000.

Opportunities for Volunteers
TAG is run by a volunteer committee and helpers, as are the regional contact groups. Member volunteers help with specific tasks, for example, the annual conference, where they care for and accompany children in the crèche or on outings. Experience of being or working with children with a disability useful but not essential. For details contact head office.

Opportunities for Employment
During 1992 TAG began employing one

part-time worker. Any further opportunities are not anticipated. TAG follows an equal opportunities policy.

Further Information
Annual Report, information leaflet, video and past conference reports are available.

Arts Disability Wales (ADW)

Chapter Arts Centre
Market Road, Canton
Cardiff EF5 1QE
Tel: 01222-377885

Contact
Jeanette Thomas, Co-ordinator

Main Activities
ADW promotes equal opportunities for disabled people in the arts in Wales. The organisation was set up in 1982 and there are thirty affiliated organisations. ADW acts as a national resource providing training, information and advice.

Opportunities for Volunteers
Volunteers give administrative support. Travel expenses are offered.

Opportunities for Employment
There are one full-time and three part-time members of staff.

Further Information
Annual report and leaflet available.

Artsline, *see Museums, the Arts and Festivals*

ASPIRE (Association for Spinal Injury Research, Rehabilitation & Reintegration)

Royal National Orthopaedic
Hospital (RNOH), NHS Trust
Brockley Hill, Stanmore
Middx HA7 4LP
Tel: 0181-954 0701
Fax: 0181-420 6352

Contact
Martina Crowley, Chief Executive

Main Activities
ASPIRE is a national charity supporting people with spinal cord injury. It works to help rehabilitate and reintegrate them. It funds a range of research projects and halfway houses, and raised £2 million to build an integrated sports and rehabilitation complex, the Mike Heaffey Centre. Apart from research projects nationally, it has a wheelchair workshop in Poland producing low-cost wheelchairs. Aspire also buys wheelchairs for individuals and funds a fertility project.

Opportunities for Volunteers
About 40 volunteers are involved in head office for administrative, fundraising and project work eg supporting the development of new facilities such as a computer workshop for vocational re-training. ASPIRE seeks more volunteers to help in all these areas, particularly during office hours, as well as for selling raffle tickets. Recruitment is ad hoc on application, via the projects, and through visitors to the sports centre. Volunteers are also needed to set up local groups throughout the UK. Commitment is variable. No expenses are offered.

Opportunities for Employment
ASPIRE actively encourages applications from registered disabled people, and has an equal opportunities policy. It employs two full-time and two part-time staff. Any posts are advertised in the disability, charity and national press, as appropriate.

Further Information
Annual Report and a brochure on ASPIRE's aims and projects are published.

Association for Spina Bifida & Hydrocephalus

42 Park Road
Peterborough PE1 2UQ
Tel: 01733-555988
Fax: 01733-555985

Contact
Roy Johnston

Main Activities
Provides support and help to children and adults with spina bifida and/or hydrocephalus. Aims to achieve quality of treatment and to break down barriers in education, housing and employment. Involved in welfare and research. A national organisation with a network of 62 autonomous, affiliated associations.

Opportunities for Volunteers
Volunteers are involved in administrative work at head quarters, and for fundraising and in the retail shops locally. In recruiting, the Association works in conjunction with Employment Action and Employment Training for the unemployed. There is no minimum commitment. Travel expenses are paid.

Opportunities for Employment
About thirty people are recruited each year, mainly for shop management positions, which are advertised in the local press.

Further Information
Besides the Annual Report, newsletters, bulletins and a bi-monthly magazine are available, together with a list of local groups.

Break, *see Caring*

British Blind Sport (BBS), *see* Sports

British Deaf Association (BDA)

38 Victoria Place
Carlisle CA1 1HU
Tel: 01228-48844 (voice/minicom)
Tel: 01228-28719 (vistel/minicom)
Fax: 01293-784647

Contact
Information Department

Main Activities
Aims to protect and advance the interests and needs of profoundly deaf people. Campaigns, monitors current research and other developments, awards minor educational grants and scholarships, and supports training courses for teachers of British Sign Language. National organisation with 178 local branches.

Opportunities for Volunteers
The Association uses volunteers to help with organising courses, workshops and conferences. More are needed, including people with hearing to help with general administration in its two offices. In general personal experience of profound deafness is preferred. There is no minimum commitment. Travel and lunch expenses are offered.

Opportunities for Employment
There are 60 staff. Opportunities are said to be limited.

Further Information
Annual Report, a list of local groups and a range of published material, including information about where to learn sign language locally, the monthly magazine and information packs, are available. In London contact: BDA, 25 Cockspur Street, London SW1Y 5BN, tel: 0171-839 5566 and minicom 0171-839 9261.

British Limbless Ex-Servicemen's Association (BLESMA), *see Social Welfare*

British Retinitis Pigmentosa Society

PO Box 350
Buckingham MK18 5EL
Tel: 01280-6363

Contact
Mrs L Cantor

Main Activities
The Society raises money for medical research into retinitis pigmentosa (RP), links members in local areas, and provides support and information of various kinds to those with RP. A national organisation, the Society has 35 local branches and twelve affiliated organisations, as well as links with similar bodies world-wide.

Opportunities for Volunteers
The branches are all run by volunteers; head office uses one. Volunteers are needed for administrative, fundraising and counselling work, year round. More are required, preferably with a knowledge of RP. Recruitment is usually in-house. Training can be given if necessary. Commitment is flexible. No remuneration is offered.

Opportunities for Employment
One full-time staff member is employed. There are no other opportunities.

Further Information
Annual report and a large selection of pamphlets are available.

British Sports Association for the Disabled (BSAD), *see Sports*

Brittle Bone Society

112 City Road
Dundee DD2 2PW
Tel: 01382-817771
Fax: 01382-816348

Contact
National Office

Main Activities
Offers practical help and advice to sufferers of osteogenesis imperfecta and their families. Also provides the very specialised equipment needed and not available from statutory sources. Raises funds to help support research. A national organisation with ten local fundraising branches in various parts of the UK, and links with sister organisations throughout the world. Membership is available at £10 a year. Income is dependent on fund-raising and donations.

Opportunities for Volunteers
The Society uses volunteers in both the national office (15-20) and the branches (10+). They are mainly involved in fund-raising. The Society also runs a charity shop which is staffed Monday to Friday by volunteers. Most of those who volunteer are relations or friends of a brittle bone sufferer. There is no minimum commitment. Out-of-pocket expenses are paid, if appropriate.

Opportunities for Volunteers
Two full-time and two part-time staff are employed in the national office. The Society seldom needs to recruit. It also funds an occupational therapist based in London who visits families of people with osteogenesis imperfecta all over the country.

Further Information
The Annual Report, a leaflet about the Society (free) and various publications about brittle bone condition (free to members, for sale to non-members) are available.

The British Disabled Water Ski Association, *see Sports*

The British Ski Club for the Disabled (BSCD), *see Sports*

Calvert Trust, *see Sports*

Camphill Village Trust (CVT)

Delrow College, Hilfield Lane
Aldenham, Watford WD2 8DJ
Tel: 01923-856006
Fax: 01923-856006

Contact
Ann Harris at above address and Andy Paton at 56 Welham Road, Norton, Yorks YO17 9DP

Main Activities
CVT provides community settings for adults with learning disabilities. It offers scope for mutual co-operation in both work areas and social life. An extended family approach ensures constant back-up support. A national organisation, covering England and Scotland, CVT has eight local projects in various areas, and sister organisations overseas. Annual budget is £7 million.

Opportunities for Volunteers
Volunteers are an integral part of CVT's work. They are used in both head office (20) and the local project centres (100) for administrative support and fundraising. Some also live and work in the individual Camphill communities with adults with learning disabilities. CVT needs more volunteers year round with skills ranging from administration to crafts. Recruitment is ad hoc on application and through in-house methods. Volunteer allowances may be paid. Extensive training and support are available.

Opportunities for Employment

These occur mainly for short-term (one year) voluntary work with paid allowances. Such positions, needing craft and administration skills in particular, typically arise in the eight project centres. Summer gardening opportunities may also be available. Contact CVT for further information.

Further Information

Annual report and pamphlets on each CVT centre are available.

Camping for the Disabled

20 Burton Close, Dawley
Telford, Shropshire TF4 2BX
Tel: 01743-761889

Contact

The office

Main Activities

Provides advice and information on camping for disabled people. Organises camping weekends, and compiles and publishes lists of suitable camp sites throughout Europe. Has a minimal annual budget of up to £1,000.

Opportunities for Volunteers

Four are used in the office and the organisation is seeking more. The main work done is administration (word processing skills required) and fundraising, with occasional involvement in camping weekends. Phone or write to the above. There is no required time commitment. Travel expenses are offered.

Opportunities for Employment

There are no employment opportunities.

Further Information

Various pamphlets are available.

CARE for People with a Mental handicap (CARE), see Caring

Cheshire, Leonard Foundation,

see Leonard Cheshire Foundation in this section

Christian Concern for the Mentally Handicapped, see Caring

Citizen Advocacy Alliance (CAA)

Douglas House, 26 Sutton Court Road
Sutton, Surrey SM1 4SL
Tel: 0181-643 7111

Contact

Sue Ashton (only for the four London boroughs below); for other areas contact National Citizen Advocacy (NCA) on 0171-359 8289

Main Activities

CAA recruits, trains and supports advocates to support people who have a learning disability. Advocates, who are volunteers, act as a friend and spokesperson on a one-to-one basis, and look after an individual's rights and interests as if they were their own. CAA covers the London boroughs of Croydon, Merton, Sutton and Richmond.

Opportunities for Volunteers

Volunteers are recruited as advocates (independent representatives), through the media, posters, and talks. More are needed. Six weeks training, one evening a week, and on-going support are provided. Long term commitment is required.

Opportunities for Employment

CAA has one full-time and five part-time staff. Opportunities for employment are limited.

Further Information

Annual Report and information leaflets are available.

Citizen Advocacy Information and Training (CAIT)

Unit 2K, Leroy House
436 Essex Road
London N1 3QP
Tel: 0171-359 8289

Contact
Sally Carr, Development Officer

Main Activities
Promotes and supports citizen advocacy through training, information and advice. Maintains a database of citizen advocacy schemes throughout the UK. Annual budget is £55,000.

Opportunities for Volunteers
Volunteers are needed to act as citizen advocates for others who need support to speak for themselves. Those contacting the office are referred to local groups throughout the UK.

Opportunities for Employment
There are two staff. Jobs are advertised in The Guardian and The Voice.

Further Information
Publications list and general information available.

CMT International UK

c/o 121 Lavernock Road
Penarth, South Glamorgan CF6 2QG
Tel: 01222-709537

Contact
Mrs M E Read, Secretary

Main Activities
Provides support, advice and information to those people who suffer from Charcot-Marie-Tooth (CMT) disease and their families. Promotes awareness of the disease, raises money for research and organises local groups where appropriate. A national organisation, it has five local support groups.

Opportunities for Volunteers
The members of CMT International UK act as the volunteers and run the main office and the local groups. A knowledge of one or all of the following would be an advantage: disability affairs, benefits, mobility, European languages. All volunteers are members of the organisation.

Opportunities for Employment
There are no paid staff and no opportunities for employment.

Further Information
The Annual Report, a quarterly newsletter and a leaflet on CMT disease are available.

The Commonwealth Society for the Deaf

Dilke House, Malet Street
London WC1E 7JA
Tel: 0171-631 5311

Contact
Ms Elizabeth Lubienska

Main Activities
The Society promotes the health, education and general welfare of the deaf in developing Commonwealth countries. It has one office in the UK and a number of local support groups/individuals.

Opportunities for Volunteers
In head office five volunteers help with the administration and fundraising. Around the country volunteers prepare and organise various special events to raise money for the Society's work. Recruitment is ad hoc on application to the Society, and through personal contacts. Commitment requested is half a day a week.

Opportunities for Employment
There are two full-time and two part-time staff. Further opportunities are unlikely.

Further Information
Annual Report and professional publications are available.

Community Transport Association Ltd, *see Education*

Crossroads (Association of Crossroads Care Attendant Schemes Ltd), *see Caring*

Crypt Foundation

Forum, Stirling Road
Chichester, West Sussex
Tel: 01243-786064
Fax: 01243-786930

Contact
Gillian Purvis

Main Activities
The Foundation provides small group homes for young adults (18-30) who wish to study any of the creative arts. One project is based in Nottingham, two in West Sussex.

Opportunities for Volunteers
Volunteers are always welcomed to serve on project management committees. Young volunteers (18-30) are needed to help care for the day to day needs of the residents. Ideal for people planning to go into one of the caring professions or with an interest in the creative arts.

Opportunities for Employment
There are approximately twenty staff.

Further Information
Annual report, Philosophy of Care brochure and job description available.

Deaf Broadcasting Council (DBC), *see Broadcasting*

DIAL UK (Disablement Information & Advice Lines)

Park Lodge, St Catherine's Hospital
Tickhill Road
Doncaster DN4 8QN
Tel: 01302-310123
Fax: 01302-310404

Contact
Ms D McGahan, Director

Main Activities
DIAL UK is a national organisation for a network of 104 disability advice centres. Each centre is run by an independent local group which affiliates to DIAL UK. Information is free, impartial, confidential and given by people with personal experience of disability.

Opportunities for Volunteers
DIAL UK relies on around 1200 volunteers in the local groups and ten in the main office to help provide its services. The work includes administration, research/writing for DIAL mailings and publications, and technical help with computing projects. Some DIAL advice centres are run entirely by volunteers. Recruitment is ad hoc by application direct to head or local DIALs and via volunteer bureaux. Volunteers are constantly needed. Minimum commitment is seven hours weekly. Travel expenses are paid.

Opportunities for Employment
Vacancies sometimes arise and are advertised in The Guardian and/or the local press. DIAL employs two full-time staff and is developing an equal opportunities policy.

Further Information
Leaflets, the Annual Report, and a list of local groups are available. Welsh and Irish groups affiliate direct to DIAL UK. Scottish groups have their own lead body: DIAL Scotland, Braid House, Labrador Avenue, Howden East, Livingston, West Lothian EH54 6BU, tel: 01506-33468.

Disability Law Service (Network for the Handicapped Ltd)

Room 241
49 51 Bedford Row
London WC1R 4LR
Tel: 0171-831 8131
Fax: 0171-831 5582

Contact
Ms Sally Mc Lean, Director

Main Activities
Disability Law Service provides free legal advice to disabled people and their families/enablers. The organisation offers telephone and written advice nationally plus representation in London area. Annual budget is £106,000.

Opportunities for Volunteers
The organisation plans to recruit volunteers as new office space has recently become available. Tasks such as administrative support, research and fundraising will be undertaken. A legal background (eg law degree) would be useful. Travel expenses will be offered.

Opportunities for Employment
There are four full-time and one part-time members of staff. There is an equal opportunities policy and jobs are advertised in The Guardian and the Law Society Gazette.

Further Information
Leaflet available on request.

Disability Scotland

Princes House
5 Shandwick Place
Edinburgh EH2 4RG
Tel: 0131-229 8632

Contact
Appeals Department

Main Activities
Disability Scotland aims to improve the active participation of people with disabilities in mainstream society and reduce their isolation. It was set up in 1982, as a national voluntary organisation with membership bodies.

Opportunities for Volunteers
There are approximately 100 volunteers, most of whom work in charity shops. Some also act as drivers and give administrative support in Head Office. Minimum time commitment is three hours a week and out-of-pocket expenses are offered.

Opportunities for Employment
There are 32 full-time staff. A formal Equal Opportunities Policy is in existence and the organisation actively recruits people with disabilities.

Further Information
Annual Report, introductory brochure etc are available from Head Office.

Disabled Housing Trust (DHT)

Norfolk Lodge
Oakenfield, Burgess Hill
West Sussex RH15 8SJ
Tel: 01444-239123
Fax: 01444-244978

Contact
Individual Unit Managers for volunteering; M J O'Connor, Operations Manager re employment

Main Activities
Provides residential care and specialist/sheltered housing to adults with physical disabilities. Also undertakes the residential rehabilitation of adults with acquired brain injuries. A national organisation, it has housing projects/units in five different parts of England. Annual budget is £3.2 million.

Opportunities for Volunteers
Around five volunteers are used in each of the residential units to support disabled

adults in using the wider community. DHT is keen to enlist more, to help with both community support and as drivers, especially in the evenings and at weekends. Recruitment is by application and through volunteer bureaux. Commitment is flexible and agreed individually. Out-of-pocket expenses are offered.

Opportunities for Employment

Around twenty people are recruited every year. During 1992 DHT was seeking recruits for its physical disability units. Driving, patience and commitment are useful skills. Vacancies are advertised in the caring press, The Guardian and local papers. DHT employs 100 full-time and 150 part-time staff and is an equal opportunities employer.

Further Information

A full range of publications, a list of local groups/units and the Annual Report are available.

Disabled Living (DL)

4 St Chad's Street, Cheetham
Manchester M8 8QA
Tel: 0161-832 3678
Fax: 0161-835 3591

Contact

Christine Trwoga, Manager Community and Leisure for volunteering; the Director re employment opportunities

Main Activities

Set up in 1897 (originally as The Cripples Help Society), Disabled Living is a Northern charity governed through a Council of Management and offering a national service. It encourages sick and disabled people to greater independence and provides advice, a continence service, holidays and outings, welfare and craftwork, and a style centre (fashion design and image advice). It also has the largest disabled living/assessment information centre in the UK with 2,000 items on permanent exhibition. Apart from linking with various UK organisations, it has links with agencies in Europe. Annual budget is £500,000.

Opportunities for Volunteers

Volunteers undertake administrative and fundraising tasks in head office and accompany groups of holiday makers and day trippers. Without them the holiday and outings service could not be provided. More are always needed. Recruitment is ad hoc, on application, via volunteer bureaux and through exhibitions and talks to various groups/organisations. Prospective volunteers must fill in an application form, provide references and have an interview. Volunteers are needed throughout the year for holidays/outings work and in autumn for other tasks. There is no minimum commitment and travel expenses and a volunteer allowance are offered. Training is given in wheelchair management, awareness and basic first aid with yearly refresher courses.

Opportunities for Employment

Up to 20 full-time and ten part-time staff are employed. Any vacancies are advertised in The Guardian, professional journals and local newspapers. Skills required depend on the job. DL has an equal opportunities policy.

Further Information

The Annual Report and various leaflets are available.

Disabled Living Foundation (DLF)

380-384 Harrow Road
London W9 2HU
Tel: 0171-289 6111
Fax: 0171-266 2922

Contact

Mary Maidment

Main Activities

Provides practical, up-to-date information

and advice on all aspects of living with disability for disabled people and their carers. Annual budget is £1.3 million.

Opportunities for Volunteers
Volunteers are very important to the DLF especially when a particular project is taken and carried through. They give administrative support and fundraise. Minimum commitment is three hours a week.

Opportunities for Employment
There are 28 full-time and five part-time staff.

Further Information
Annual Report, training course programme, Publications catalogue Legacy Leaflet and general leaflets available on request.

Disabled Motorists' Federation (DMF)

Unit 2a Atcham Estate
Upton Magna, Shrewsbury SY4 4UG
Tel: 01743-761181

Contact
Hugh Munro

Main Activities
The DMF is an umbrella organisation for independent disabled motorists' clubs. Affiliates number 21, located from Aberdeen to the Isle of Wight. DMF provides the with support, information and a free quarterly magazine, Flying Mat, to every club member. Helps new clubs to start up. RAMP project supplies free route maps marked with attended petrol stations, NKS toilets and other accessible amenities.

Opportunities for Volunteers
A volunteer Exhibitions Secretary is needed and also people willing to fundraise. Appliance and product testing, compiling camping/caravan site guides is carried out by affiliate Mobility

Information Service (at the same address). Minimum commitment is three hours a week. Computer literacy and own PC is essential. Volunteers are especially needed at major exhibition times eg 'Mobility Roadshow'.

Opportunities for Employment
There are no paid staff.

Further Information
List of local clubs and further information available on request.

The Disablement Income Group (DIG)

Unit 5, Archway Business Centre
19-23 Wedmore Street
London N19 4ZY
Tel: 0171-263 3981

Contact
Training and Development Officer

Main Activities
DIG promotes the financial welfare of disabled people through a programme of advice, advocacy, fieldwork, information, research and training. A registered national charity, it has 135 local affiliates. Annual budget is £175,000.

Opportunities for Volunteers
Volunteers act as local representatives/campaigners for DIG. They are recruited through applications to head office and in-house methods. Between two and three hours weekly are required. Travel and out-of-pocket expenses (postage, phone) are paid.

Opportunities for Employment
DIG is an equal opportunities employer, with eight, mostly long serving, staff. There are rarely any vacancies.

Further Information
Various publications, including leaflets, reports, a quarterly newspaper and DIG's journal, are available for purchase, as well as the annual accounts.

Down's Syndrome Association
(DSA), *see Health & Medicine*

DEBRA (Dystrophic Epidermolysis Bullosa Research Association)**, *see Health & Medicine*

Elfrida Rathbone

25 Leighton Road
Kentish Town
London NW5 2QD
Tel: 0171-482 5014

Contact
Jim Thompson

Main Activities
Elfrida Rathbone (Camden) supports, advises, gives information and provides training and education for young adults with learning difficulties/special needs, their families and carers.

Opportunities for Volunteers
There are two volunteers. The organisation is currently seeking volunteers, particularly in the areas of administration and fundraising. Volunteer help is essential on the management committee. Minimum commitment is five hours per week for three months. Travel, lunch and out-of-pocket expenses are offered.

Opportunities for Employment
There are eleven full-time and ten part-time staff. Posts are advertised in The Guardian, The Voice and the local press. From time to time the organisation recruits people to help with the Playscheme. A formal Equal Opportunities Policy is in operation.

Further Information
Annual Report, and publicity material on projects are available on request.

English National Association of Visually Handicapped Bowlers**, *see Recreation & Leisure*

Friends of the Young Deaf (FYD)

East Court Mansion
College Lane, East Grinstead
West Sussex RH19 3LT
Tel: 01342-323444
Fax: 01342-410232

Contact
Ann Heath, Administrator

Main Activities
The aim of FYD is to promote an active partnership between deaf and hearing people which will enable young deaf people to develop themselves and become active members of society. Provides training and recreational activities. There are five centres.

Opportunities for Volunteers
Volunteers are very important. They assist with everyday work to be project leaders and to do marketing, fundraising and give administrative support. Training is provided. Minimum commitment is at least one day a week. Most projects run from April to October.

Opportunities for Employment
There are eighteen full-time and seven part-time staff. Jobs are advertised nationally.

Further Information
Annual Report, leaflet and Signpost (Newsletter and programme) available.

Gift of Thomas Pocklington

20 Lansdowne Road
London W11 3LL
Tel: 0171-727 6426

Contact
Paul Quin

Main Activities
Provides care for blind and partially sighted people in residential care homes and sheltered flats. Also supports research into blindness. Annual budget is £2.2 million.

Opportunities for Volunteers
Volunteers are important. They help in the homes and provide social contacts for blind and partially sighted residents – reading, talking, listening, shopping for them and accompanying them on short excursions. More are needed. Recruitment is ad hoc by application to the organisation. There is no minimum time commitment and no remuneration is offered.

Opportunities for Employment
Between five and ten people are recruited each year, mainly for positions in catering, as cleaners and as care assistants. Posts for nurses occasionally arise. On-the-job training is given as necessary. Vacancies are advertised in the local press. The organisation employs 35 full-time and 80 part-time staff. An Equal Opportunities Policy is being implemented.

Further Information
The Annual Report, a list of the residential homes and information on the homes for potential residents are available.

Graeae Theatre Company

25 Baytham Street
London NW1 0EY
Tel: 0171-383 7541
Fax: 0171-267 2703

Contact
Carolyn Lucas

Main Activities
Encourages the active participation of disabled people in all types of creative performance. Annual budget £235,700.

Opportunities for Volunteers
Volunteers give administrative support when necessary. They are much appreciated.

Opportunities for Employment
There are two full-time and two part-time staff. Actors, writers and stage managers are recruited occasionally. Staff are needed for the autumn and spring tours, jobs are advertised in The Guardian, Stage, The Voice, Asian Times, Disability Now, and Disability Arts of London.

Further Information
Annual Report, information packs and workshop/performance details available. All information is available in large print, on cassette tape or in Braille.

Great Britain Wheelchair Basketball Association, see Sports

Greater London Association of Disabled People (GLAD)

336 Brixton Road
London SW9 7AA
Tel: 0171-274 0107 (voice and minicom)
Fax: 0171-274 7840

Contact
Barbara Zipser

Main Activities
GLAD works with a London-wide network of borough-based disability organisations, which are independent groups providing service and information to disabled people in their area. They also serve as local forums on disability issues.

Opportunities for Volunteers
Volunteers are integral to the work of GLAD. They provide administrative support, including large mail outs, assistance at conferences, and help with fundraising. They also tape documents, either at home or in the GLAD office, for visually impaired people. GLAD seeks more volunteers, on both an ad hoc and a regular (one day a week) basis. Support and initial training are available, together with access to learning other skills. Volunteers are recruited ad hoc through phone or written applications, via volunteer bureaux and through advertising in London Disability News, Loot newspaper, the Annual Review and local libraries. Travel and lunch expenses are paid.

Opportunities for Employment
GLAD is an equal opportunities employer and recruits perhaps two or three people yearly. Recruits must have awareness of disability; some posts are for disabled people only. Vacancies are advertised in the press, including The Guardian, London Disability News, Disability Now, The Voice, Asian Times and local papers. There are thirteen full-time and six part-time staff.

Further Information
Annual Report, a list of local groups and various publications are available.

Greater London Sports Association (GLSA), *see Sports*

The Guide Dogs for the Blind Association (GDBA)

'Hillfields', Burghfield
Reading, Berkshire RG7 3YG
Tel: 01734-835555
Fax: 01734-835433

Contact
National Fundraising Manager

Main Activities
Set up in 1931, the GDBA provides and trains dogs to act as guides for visually impaired people. A national, UK-wide organisation, it has 461 local, voluntary fundraising branches. Annual budget is £31 million.

Opportunities for Volunteers
Volunteers are always needed to fundraise and to look after puppies in their first year. They are vital to both the fundraising activities and for puppy walking (the early socialisation of future guide dogs). Leadership and/or secretarial skills are very useful. Travel and stationary costs are offered.

Opportunities for Employment
There are 720 full-time and 125 part-time staff. About 120 people are recruited each year. There are occasional needs for Rehabilitation Workers and Guide Dog Mobility Instructors. Jobs are advertised in local, national and trade press.

Further Information
Annual Report and information leaflets available.

HAPA (formerly Handicapped Adventure Playground Association), *see Children*

Hearing Dogs for the Deaf

Training Centre
London Road (A40)
Lewknor, Oxon OX9 5RY
Tel: 01844-353898
Fax: 01844-353099

Contact
Mrs D A McInnes, Administrator

Main Activities
Trains dogs to alert severely, profoundly or totally deaf people to specific sounds by a variety of means eg touch, leading them to the sound (eg door bell, a baby alarm, smoke alarm, etc). Dogs are usually selected from rescue centres, carefully chosen and thoroughly trained. A national organisation, Hearing Dogs for the Deaf has 33 local fundraising groups.

Opportunities for Volunteers
Between 200 and 300 volunteers are used in the branches, with one in head office. They undertake fundraising and puppy socialising, and speak on the work of the organisation (slides, script and instruction supplied). More are needed all year round for all these and other jobs. Recruitment is ad hoc by application to the main office. There is no minimum time commitment, except puppy socialisers must attend monthly training sessions. Travel and other out-of-pocket expenses are paid.

Opportunities for Employment
The organisation operates two centres in Oxfordshire and North Yorkshire. Posts are advertised in the specialist dog press, and/or local papers, and include office/administrative work, kennel management, dog training and placement officers. Twenty-eight full-time and five part-time staff are employed.

Further Information
Besides the Annual Report, a list of local groups, newsletters, leaflets and posters are available.

Headway (National Head Injuries Association Ltd.), *see Social Welfare*

Holiday Care Service

2 Old Bank Chambers
Station Road, Horley
Surrey RH6 9HW
Tel: 01293-774535
Fax: 01293-784647

Contact
Susan Harrington

Main Activities
Provides holiday information for disabled people, single parents and those on low incomes. Provides information about holiday insurance. Annual budget is £250,000.

Opportunities for Volunteers
Volunteers are a tremendous asset and help with day to day administration. Knowledge of word processing (Word Perfect 5.1) would be useful. Travel expenses are offered.

Opportunities for Employment
There are eight full-time and three part-time staff. Jobs are advertised in *Disability*, local and national press.

Further Information
Annual Report and accommodation leaflets for accessible hotels, guest houses and self-catering available.

House of Light Trust

The Cornerstone
115 Doncaster Road
Rotherham S65 2BN
Tel: 01709-365387

Contact
Maurice Bartley, Manager

Main Activities
The House of Light Trust maintains two community homes in Rotherham for adults with learning difficulties.

Opportunities for Volunteers
Volunteers are welcomed as residential carers working about 30 hours a week. Long term commitment, preferably a year, is desirable but this is flexible. Training and support are given. A volunteer allowance and travel expenses are offered. Volunteers must be aged eighteen or over and possess a mature attitude. Ideal for someone wishing to gain experience before entering one of the caring professions.

Opportunities for Employment
There are eight staff. Occasionally volunteers are recruited.

Further Information
Annual Report and information for prospective volunteers available on request.

Huntington's Disease Association, *see Health & Medicine*

I CAN (Invalid Children's Aid Nationwide)

Barbican Citygate
1-3 Dufferin Street
London EC1Y 8NA
Tel: 0171-374 4422
Fax: 0171-374 2762

Contact
Sharon Charteress, Information Co-ordinator

Main Activities
I CAN is a national charity for children with special education needs. The charity specialises in the education of three to sixteen year olds with speech and language difficulties. ICAN works in partnership with Local Education Authorities to provide a network of nationally recognised primary/secondary schools and an increasing number of specialist speech and language nurseries. As part of its work ICAN also manages the only school in the UK for children with asthma and eczema. I CAN also offers help, advice and information to parents.

Opportunities for Volunteers
Volunteers are used to assist in the schools and a Further Education college in care work, and must live reasonably nearby. Contact I CAN for further details.

Opportunities for Employment
Around 300 full-time staff are employed. People for various posts in care work and education, with an emphasis on special needs, are recruited each year. Jobs are usually advertised in the relevant local press. I CAN is working towards an equal opportunities policy.

Further Information
Information on various disorders, a list of the schools and the Annual Report are available.

In Touch Trust

10 Norman Road
Sale, Cheshire M33 3DF
Tel: 0161-905 2440

Contact
Ann Worthington

Main Activities
In Touch is a national information and contacts service for parents of children with special needs, covering all types of disability, physical and learning. Puts families in touch for mutual support and help. Membership includes professionals and organisations catering for childhood handicap. A national agency with one office. Annual budget £14,000.

Opportunities for Volunteers
Volunteers are not used.

Opportunities for Employment
There is one full-time organiser and one part-time assistant. There are no other employment opportunities.

Further Information
Annual Report, newsletter and information sheet are published.

The International Autistic Research Organisation/ Autism Research Ltd

49 Orchard Avenue
Shirley, Croydon CR0 7NE
Tel: 0181-777 0095 (24 hours)

Contact
The Secretary

Main Activities
Works to encourage, support and disseminate research into autism. Has one office only.

Opportunities for Volunteers
Up to three volunteers staff the office on a nearly twenty four hour basis. They also undertake fundraising. Volunteers are recruited through personal contact or application to the Secretary. Commitment is as convenient and any expenses are paid by negotiation.

Opportunities for Employment
There are no employment opportunities.

Further Information
Newsletters, general information concerning autism and the organisation's founder's initiation of a recent breakthrough in research, and the Annual Report are available.

International Disability Education and Awareness (IDEA)

William House
101 Eden Vale Road
Westbury, Wiltshire BA13 3QF
Tel: 01373-827635

Contact
Mrs M Greenhalgh, Administrator

Main Activities
Works to facilitate change in the lives of disabled people in the UK and in developing countries by promoting equal opportunities for those disabled, and by offering training in developing strategies for change. International but with only one office. Annual budget is £100,000.

Opportunities for Volunteers
IDEA uses two volunteers to help with administration and fundraising. Volunteers are recruited ad hoc by written application. The minimum commitment is four hours a week. Travel expenses are offered.

Opportunities for Employment
IDEA employs one part-time and two full-time members of staff. If any vacancies arise they are usually advertised in shop windows locally. An interest in disability and development is needed. IDEA has an Equal Opportunities Policy.

Further Information
General leaflet and annual course programme available.

Jubilee Sailing Trust, *see Recreation & Leisure*

L'Arche

10 Briggate, Silsden
Keighley, West Yorkshire BD20 9JT
Tel: 01535-656186
Fax: 01535-656426

Contact
Write to Co-ordinators in individual communities, or Rev. Tim Hollis, UK General Secretary

Main Activities
L'Arche is a national charity comprising seven communities in the UK whose aim is to establish and manage houses and work projects for people with learning difficulties. Each Community is managed by a local committee. The communities are homes and workshops where people with and without learning disabilities can live and work together in a non-competitive, caring environment based on Christian principles. Those of other faiths or none are welcomed. There are seven L'Arche communities: Bognor Regis, Brecon, Canterbury, Edinburgh, Inverness, Liverpool and London. There are over 100 worldwide.

Opportunities for Volunteers
Volunteers can join the communities as assistants or as unpaid committee members. Assistants usually live in for a year at first, and share life and work with people with learning disabilities. They are paid pocket money, and get free board and lodging. No particular skills or qualifications are needed beyond a good working knowledge of English and good general health. Induction and in-service training are given. Recruitment is through ad hoc applications, word of mouth, and various agencies and religious organisations. More assistants are needed.

Opportunities for Employment
Opportunities are primarily for assistants, as above. Between 80 and 100 are recruited each year. Positions are sometimes advertised in local papers. L'Arche is an equal opportunities employer. It also has twelve staff for administration.

Further Information
Annual Report, UK newsletter, and various publications, including one for prospective assistants, are available.

Land Use Volunteers (LUV), *see Environment & Conservation*

The Leonard Cheshire Foundation

26-29 Maunsel Street
London SW1P 2QN
Tel: 0171-828 1822
Fax: 0171-976 5704

Contact
Local Heads of individual homes; the Personnel Secretary at above address for details of young people's schemes

Main Activities
The Leonard Cheshire Foundation operates in 51 countries worldwide, providing more than 320 Homes and Services to people with physical or learning difficulties and to those with mental health problems. In the UK, services range from day care and respite care - which gives both the disabled person and their carer a much-needed break - to community based rehabilitation and Care at Home services. The latter employ professional care attendants to carry out day to day tasks in the person's own home, thereby helping them to remain as independent as possible. Each home is responsible for its own management and

finance, under a local management committee consisting of volunteers.

Opportunities for Volunteers

Many Homes and Services could not function without the help of volunteers and there is a constant need for more. There are as many as 3,000 operating in local Homes across the UK, either on the Management Committee or in connection with fundraising and administration. Many also assist clients with social and leisure activities or help the Home/Service in the areas of maintenance, gardening and driving. Volunteers are recruited through application to the individual Home and there is no minimum commitment. The Foundation operates a separate national scheme for young volunteers from 18-30 years to live-in as temporary care assistants with board, lodging and pocket money (£27 per week) paid. Few vacancies are for less than three months, and up to 38 hours a week.

Opportunities for Employment

Each Home and Service recruits its own staff through its local Management Committee. Positions include care, clerical, domestic and maintenance staff. Nurses, therapists and activity organisers may also be employed. Both full- and part-time positions are possible. Contact individual Homes. The Foundation employs around 1,600 full-time and 2,400 part-time staff in total and is an equal opportunities employer.

Further Information

A list of Homes and Services and copies of the Annual Review, international and UK magazines and various leaflets are available from Head Office.

MENCAP, Royal Society for Mentally Handicapped Children and Adults

123 Golden Lane
London EC1Y 0RT
Tel: 0171-454 0454
Fax: 0171-608 3245

Contact

Divisional advisers and managers, and local Mencap offices for volunteering (see telephone directory); Personnel Department re employment

Main Activities

Mencap is exclusively concerned with people with learning disabilities and their families. It provides support and help through its divisional offices, a network of 550 local societies, and over 700 Gateway Clubs. It runs residential, training and employment services, as well as offering leisure facilities through the National Federation of Gateway Clubs (see separate entry). Mencap also offers courses for people working in the field of learning disability, and mounts conferences and campaigns to raise public awareness.

Opportunities for Volunteers

Mencap involves volunteers in various functions, including administration, fundraising, and counselling, on management committees, and to help provide leisure opportunities for people with learning disabilities. More are wanted in all these areas, year round, as well as to help parents and other carers, and to run social activities. Volunteers are usually recruited through application to head office or any of the local autonomous groups, and via volunteer bureaux. Minimum commitment and any remuneration are decided by the individual groups.

Opportunities for Employment

With around 3,000 full-time and 1,000 part-time staff, Mencap is a large-scale employer. Considerable numbers are recruited each year due to turnover and for seasonal requirements such as summer holiday schemes. All posts are advertised externally in local and/or national newspapers, plus Care Weekly and Community Care if appropriate. An equal opportunities policy is in place.

Further Information
The Annual Report, and various publications including Mencap News (monthly), Opengate (quarterly), and a booklist on all aspects of learning disability, are available.

Mobility Information Service

Unit 2a Atcham Estate
Shrewsbury SY4 4AG
Tel: 01743-761889
Fax: 01743-761889

Contact
David Griffiths

Main Activities
Offers disabled driver assessment, mobility advice on vehicles, adaptations and travel. Helps to co-ordinate European approaches to disability. Annual budget is £20,000.

Opportunities for Volunteers
Volunteers with computer, database or language skills (French, German, Spanish) are needed.

Opportunities for Employment
There are no paid staff.

Further Information
Annual Report, new disabled driver pack and general information leaflet available.

Mobility International

Rue de Manchester 25
B-1070 Brussels, Belgium
Tel: 00-322 410 6297
Fax: 00-322410 6874

Contact
Jackie West, Acting Director

Main Activities
Mobility International has 140 member organisations worldwide, mainly in Europe, with the biggest single groups in the UK and Ireland. Promotes independence and equal opportunities internationally for people with disabilities by organising exchanges, conferences, seminars and networks. Annual budget is £750,000.

Opportunities for Volunteers
Occasionally involves volunteers. They are generally recruited in the country of the project concerned.

Opportunities for Employment
There are two full-time and two part-time staff.

Further Information
Booklets, information packs and an international membership list are available.

Mobility Trust

4 Hughes Mews
143a Chatham Road
London SW11 6HJ
Tel: 0171-924 3597
Fax: 0171-923 3938

Contact
Peter Mathon, Director

Main Activities
Assists the disabled with mobility equipment, communication devices and advice. Provides seminars and sponsors research. National organisation with five local branches.

Opportunities for Volunteers

Volunteers are needed to fundraise and give administrative support. Full in-house training is given. Volunteers should send a CV and two references.

Opportunities for Employment

There is one member of staff.

Further Information

Annual Report, list of local groups and further literature available on request.

Myalgic Encephalomyelitis Association (ME Association),
see Counselling & Self-Help

Music for the Disabled

2 Wendy Crescent
Guildford, Surrey GU2 6RP
Tel: 01483-67813

Contact

Jack and Gweneth Malby

Main Activities

Provides live music therapy and live entertainment to long-term disabled people in hospitals, nursing homes, special schools etc. There are three regional groups: Surrey, Buckinghamshire and Chichester.

Opportunities for Volunteers

Volunteers provide music therapy and entertainment. They must be trained musicians or singers. Fundraisers are also needed. The organisation is looking for people to perform in other areas of the country.

Opportunities for Employment

There are no paid staff.

Further Information

Information leaflet available on request.

Myotonic Dystrophy Support Group

c/o 175A Carlton Hill
Carlton, Notts NG4 1GZ
Tel: 01602-870080

Contact

Mrs M Bowler, Co-ordinator

Main Activities

Offers help and encouragement to sufferers and carers by providing a telephone contact line, up-to-date information on the condition, and a quarterly newsletter, and by organising regional meetings. A national organisation, there are twenty area contact people. The Group does not have an annual budget, but is funded by donations.

Opportunities for Volunteers

Volunteers are very important. All co-ordinators are either carers or people suffering with myotonic dystrophy. They offer support to other families and pass on any relevant information. They organise regional meetings. They also do administrative, fundraising and counselling work. They are recruited through in-house methods.

Opportunities for Employment

There are two part-time staff, but no further opportunities.

Further Information

Annual Report and other published information, and a list of contact people, including in Wales and Scotland, are available on request.

National Advisory Service for Parents of Children with a Stoma (NASPCS), *see Children*

National Association of Deafened People (NADP)

Longacre, Horsleys Green
High Wycombe, Bucks HP14 3UA
Tel: 01494-482355
Fax: 01494-484993

Contact
Alison Heath, Publicity Officer

Main Activities
NADP promotes the interests of deafened people (those with profound and total acquired hearing loss). Provides information and advice. There are six local support groups.

Opportunities for Volunteers
Volunteers are needed to help set up local groups and to help with exhibitions. Sympathetic and understanding attitude to deafened people and their problems essential. Currently all the volunteers are deafened people.

Opportunities for Employment
There is one part-time member of staff.

Further Information
Annual Report, list of local groups, quarterly newsletter *Network*, and publicity leaflet available on request.

National Association for Special Educational Needs (NASEN), *see Education*

National Association of Swimming Clubs for the Handicapped (NASCH), *see Sports*

National Association of Toy & Leisure Libraries / Play Matters, *see Children*

National Benevolent Fund for the Aged (NBFA), *see Elderly People*

National Deaf-Blind League

18 Rainbow Court, Paston Ridings
Peterborough PE4 7UP
Tel: 01733-573511

Contact
Jackie Scott

Main Activities
The League provides a range of services, including counselling, rehabilitation, guides and interpreters, and financial assistance where necessary. It produces a bi-weekly newspaper and a quarterly magazine. It has also built and manages accommodation for independent deaf-blind people. A national organisation, it has various local affiliates, and an annual budget of £302,000.

Opportunities for Volunteers
Volunteers are very involved in Rainbow Clubs (social clubs for deaf-blind people. They are vital for interpreting, guiding and befriending deaf-blind people. Training is provided. Administrative work and fundraising is also carried out by volunteers. The League wants to recruit more. Anyone interested should phone or write to head office. Commitment is flexible, and any out-of-pocket expenses are refunded.

Opportunities for Employment
Positions occasionally arise and are advertised in The Guardian and the local press. A genuine concern for disabled people is needed. The League employs ten full-time and eight part-time staff and has an equal opportunities policy.

Further Information
Numerous pamphlets and information sheets, plus the Annual Report are published. A list of local groups is available.

National Deaf Children's Society, *see Children*

National Disability Arts Forum

All Saints Church
Akenside Hill
Newcastle NE1 2EW
Tel: 0191-261 1628

Contact
Geof Armstrong

Main Activities
The National Disability Arts Forum aims to foster equality of opportunity for disabled people in all aspects of life. It supports the development of Disability Arts Forums and promotes innovative Disability Arts events. NDAF has a Disability Arts database.

Opportunities for Volunteers
Volunteers are being sought for administrative tasks. Induction carried out by staff. A knowledge of European languages would be an asset.

Opportunities for Employment
There are three part-time staff. The organisation only employs disabled people. Jobs are advertised in the disability press.

Further Information
The organisation has a London information office. Contact: Sian Williams, National Disability Arts Forum, 34 Osnaburgh Street, London NW1 3ND (tel: 0171-813 1431). Produces a Reference Guide called *Disability Arts... The Business*, a guide for people setting up a disability arts forum. A European Disability Arts Directory will be available in 1995.

National Federation of Gateway Clubs (Gateway)

117 Golden Lane
London EC1Y 0RT
Tel: 0171-696 5591
Fax: 0171-608 3254

Contact
National Development Officer

Main Activities
Gateway works to advance the personal development of people with learning disabilities through greater leisure opportunities, by promoting personal choice and independence, and by encouraging their full participation, integration and involvement in club and community. A national organisation, Gateway has 13 regional groupings, and 689 affiliated local branches/clubs. Annual budget is £632,000.

Opportunities for Volunteers
Volunteer are vital - over 20,000 volunteers work in the local groups. They undertake fundraising and project work, in particular as advocates/befrienders, and as youth workers in the clubs. More are welcome. They are especially needed in the evenings and at weekends, and should have a caring attitude and leisure interests (sports, arts, etc). Recruitment is ad hoc on application to local clubs or the national centre, via volunteer bureaux and through in-house schemes. Minimum commitment is two hours a week. Expenses are not usually paid.

Opportunities for Employment
Between three and five people are recruited annually, with youth and community experience preferred. There are some seasonal opportunities in summer play schemes and holiday services. Recruits need organising ability and social awareness (training provided). Posts are advertised in The Guardian and local newspapers. Gateway has an equal

opportunities policy, and employs 22 full-time and 80 part-time staff.

Further Information
Annual Report, various information packs, Gatepost magazine, the Opengate newspaper and other literature are available, plus a list of local groups. In Scotland contact: Enable, 13 Elmbank Street, Glasgow G2 4QA, tel: 0141-226 4541.

The National Star Centre, *see* *Education*

Nystagmus Action Group (NAG)

43 Gordonbrock Road
London SE4 1JA
Tel: 0181-690 6679

Contact
John Sanders, Chairman

Main Activities
Promotes self-help initiatives for nystagmus sufferers and supports the development of treatment for this eye condition. This includes funding research and providing advice and information. NAG has three affiliated organisations and a small budget.

Opportunities for Volunteers
Between six and eight volunteers work for NAG undertaking administrative support, fundraising and counselling. Their support is essential. Recruitment is in-house, through applications, and more volunteers are required, especially from January to April each year. Minimum commitment is two hours weekly. All volunteer work is unpaid.

Opportunities for Employment
NAG does not have any paid staff but is hoping to receive funding for a part-time post in 1995.

Further Information
Annual Report and leaflets are available.

One-To-One

404 Camden Road
Islington, London N7 0SJ
Tel: 0171-700 5574
Fax: 0171-700 6674

Contact
Local branch co-ordinator for volunteering; Keri Deasy, Director and Diana Battaglia for development and management

Main Activities
Provides opportunities for people with learning difficulties to participate in the life of their local communities, the support of a volunteer/friend, and aims to increase the respect in which they are held. Covers the greater London area, with four local branches, but is to go national in 1995. Annual budget is approximately £100,000.

Opportunities for Volunteers
Each branch depends on between 30 and 40 volunteers for its friendship work. The central office uses one. Volunteers also help with administrative, fundraising, counselling and leisure activities work. More volunteers are welcomed in all these areas, as well as to be advocates, and members of steering groups and management committees. Recruitment is in-house and through recruitment drives in spring and autumn. Newspaper advertisements, posters, and church, library and supermarket notice boards are all used. Application forms and personal interviews are necessary. Commitment varies, but regular contact is required between volunteer and partner (ie the person with learning difficulties). An induction and other training courses are available. Travel and certain other expenses are offered.

Opportunities for Employment
One-to-One is an equal opportunities employer with a formal recruitment policy. It has four full-time and two part-time staff, and may recruit one person a

year. Vacancies are advertised in the press, usually The Guardian.

Further Information

Annual Report, resource packs, guidelines for volunteers and an information booklet are available.

Outset

Drake House, 18 Creekside
London SE8 3DZ
Tel: 0181-692 7141
Fax: 0181-469 2532

Contact

Robbie Lloyd, Press & PR Officer

Main Activities

Outset is the national charity promoting employment opportunities and training to people with disabilities. There are ten centres, in and around London, in Luton, Middlesborough, Wolverhampton as well as a self-employment Enterprise Centre in Kent. Seven hundred disabled people a year are trained in Information Technology skills.

Opportunities for Volunteers

Outset values its volunteers for bringing a new perspective and new ideas. Experience of administration, knowledge of IT and languages are useful.

Opportunities for Employment

Outset has a hundred staff. There is a positive action recruitment policy targeted towards people with disabilities.

Further Information

The Annual Report is available as well as a list of centres.

Paddington Integration Project (PIP)

First Floor, 404-406 Edgware Road
London W2 1ED
Tel: 0171-258 1122
Fax: 0171-258 1123

Contact

The Co-ordinator

Main Activities

The Paddington Integration Project is a further education project for adults with learning difficulties. It was set up in 1984. The project aims to enable students to gain greater independence through skills learning and confidence building.

Opportunities for Volunteers

Volunteers serve on the management committee and on various projects working with the students. Support and on the job training are offered. Minimum commitment is six months or longer.

Opportunities for Employment

There are five full-time staff. An equal opportunities policy is in place.

Further Information

Further information available on request.

Paradise Community

Paradise House, Painswick
Gloucestershire GL6 6TN
Tel: 01452-813276

Contact

The Principal

Main Activities

The Paradise Community provides long-term residential care, meaningful occupation and leisure/cultural activities for adults with learning difficulties. Accommodation is provided in family homes in a rural setting. The catchment area for residents is nationwide.

Opportunities for Volunteers

There are 20 full-time volunteers who

perform caring and facility oriented activities. A seminar course is offered and board, lodging, pocket money, holiday allowance and working clothes are provided. Interest, enthusiasm and willingness to work with people are necessary attributes.

Opportunities for Employment
There are four full-time and four part-time staff.

Further Information
Annual Report, leaflets outlining the work and philosophy of the organisation are available on request.

Phab, Physically Disabled and Able Bodied

Arkwright Centre
Irchester, Northants NN9 7EY
Tel: 01933-412229
Fax: 01933-412229

Contact
Club leaders of local Phab clubs for volunteering; Paul Hope, Deputy Chief Officer re employment

Main Activities
Phab aims to promote and encourage people of all age groups with and without physical disabilities to come together on equal terms to achieve complete integration within the wider community. Set up in 1957 as a national company limited by guarantee, Phab has four regional offices and branches throughout the UK. It also has links with similar organisations in Poland and Russia. Annual income is £1.2 million.

Opportunities for Volunteers
Volunteers are integral to Phab's work since they run all the Phab clubs. Over 700 are involved in a variety of types of work and Phab is actively seeking more. Recruitment is ad hoc by application, through volunteer bureaux and via the local press. Minimum commitment is

between three and five hours a week, and out-of-pocket expenses are offered. An information pack and local training are provided. Enquiries should be made to local club leaders.

Opportunities for Employment
Phab employs paid staff and recruits between one and two people each year. There is a standard application form and a recruitment policy under development. Posts are advertised in The Guardian. There may also be local seasonal opportunities. Phab has an equal opportunities policy and actively recruits people with disabilities and those made redundant.

Further Information
The Annual Report, leaflets and copies of Phab magazine are available on request. A Phab Pack is also available for £15. Other useful addresses are:

Phab Wales, 179 Penarth Road, Grangetown, Cardiff CF1 7JW, tel: 01222-223677

Phab Scotland, Princes House, 5 Shadwick Place, Edinburgh EH2 4RG, tel: 0131-229 3559

Phab Northern Ireland, 25 Alexandra Gardens, Belfast BT15 3LJ, tel: 01232-370240

Prader-Willi Syndrome Association (UK)

2 Wheatsheaf Close
Horsell, Woking
Surrey GU21 4BP
Tel: 01483-724784

Contact
Rosemary Erskine

Main Activities
Supports families of people who have Prader-Willi syndrome. Sponsors research into the disorder. There are ten local branches.

Opportunities for Volunteers
Volunteers undertake fundraising and

counselling as well as administrative task such as filing, typing and other clerical work. Travel expenses are paid. Financial management and computing skills are required in Woking and East Molesley.

Opportunities for Employment
There are three part-time staff.

Further Information
Annual Report and information leaflets available.

Ravenswood Foundation

17 Highfield Road
Golders Green, London NW11 9D2
Tel: 0181-907 5557
Fax: 0181-209 2532

Contact
Ingrid Segal, Voluntary Co-ordinator/ Katie Taylor, PR Officer

Main Activities
The Ravenswood Foundation provides services for children and adults with learning difficulties. Runs residential, educational, training and recreational facilities. Annual budget is £11 million.

Opportunities for Volunteers
Volunteer programme offers a variety of opportunities. Befriending, visiting, driving and administrative support are needed. Full training programme. Volunteers need to be reliable, honest and friendly.

Opportunities for Employment
There are 450 full-time and 50 part-time staff. There are occasional opportunities for residential work and for school holiday schemes for children. Jobs are advertised in local and national papers, Jewish Chronicle and Community Care as appropriate.

Further Information
Annual Report, and volunteer brochure available.

Riding for the Disabled Association (RDA)

Avenue 'R'
National Agricultural Centre
Kenilworth, Warwickshire CV8 2LY
Tel: 01203-696510
Fax: 01203-696532

Contact
Contact Headquarters for a list of local groups

Main Activities
Provides riding and driving opportunities for disabled people to improve their health and well-being. There are 700 branches in the UK.

Opportunities for Volunteers
Volunteers act as instructors and helpers and also do fundraising and administrative work. An interest in disabled people is important. No previous riding experience is necessary as there is an induction course.

Opportunities for Employment
There are eight staff and very few are recruited each year.

Further Information
Annual Report and a publicity pack are available.

Royal National Institute for the Blind (RNIB)

224 Great Portland Street
London W1N 6AA
Tel: 0171-388 1266

Contact
Volunteer Co-ordinator

Main Activities
Provides a range of services for the blind and partially sighted. Advice on employment and rehabilitation is given. The organisation runs schools, colleges, hotels and hostels for the visually impaired. The annual budget is £40 million.

Opportunities for Volunteers

Volunteers help to provide the Express Reading Service, where books and other material are recorded onto tape. A clear speaking voice and a knowledge of sciences or languages would be useful. Help with fundraising and administrative support is also needed.

Opportunities for Employment

There are 200 full-time staff and jobs are advertised in The Guardian and in local media where appropriate. There are occasional seasonal requirements for staff in hostels.

Further Information

The Annual Report and list of local groups are available.

Royal National Institute for Deaf People

105 Gower Street
London WC1E 6AH
Tel: 0171-387 8033 (voice)
Tel: 0171-387 3154 (minicom)

Contact

Human Resources Division

Main Activities

The RNID represents the needs of deaf, deafened, hard of hearing and deaf-blind people. Provides a range of quality services, including interpreting service, training, information, environmental aids and residential care for deaf people with special needs. National organisation with regional offices.

Opportunities for Volunteers

Volunteers fundraise and give administrative support. Travel and lunch expenses are offered. Potential volunteers should fill out an application form and supply references.

Opportunities for Employment

Jobs are advertised in The Guardian, Evening Standard, teletext, local newspapers and professional journals as appropriate. There is an Equal Opportunities Policy.

Further Information

Annual Report, Typetalk brochure and Quality Connection Pack (RNID services) available. For Scotland, contact: 9 Clairmont Gardens, Glasgow G3 7LW, tel: 0141-332 0343. For Northern Ireland, contact: Wilton House, 5 College Square, Belfast, B11 6AR, tel: 01232-239 619.

Royal Society for Mentally Handicapped Children and Adults (MENCAP), see Mencap above

Sheffield Community Transport (SCT), see Social Welfare

St Piers Lingfield, see Children

SOS Stars Organisation Supporting Action for People with Cerebral Palsy

12 Park Crescent
London W1N 4EQ
Tel: 0171-637 9681

Contact

Head Office

Main Activities

Manages, funds and supports services for children and adults with cerebral palsy and related disabilities. Fundraising is undertaken to develop independent living and educational initiatives. There are offices in London and Redditch, and services are offered in Sussex, Essex, London and Oxford.

Opportunities for Volunteers

Fundraising and administrative support

is needed. The organisation actively seeks contacts with celebrities.

Opportunities for Employment
There are 120 full-time and 24 part-time staff, mostly with professional skills in care and education.

Further Information
Annual Report and information brochures available.

Spinal Injuries Association (SIA)

Newpoint House
76 St James's Lane
Muswell Hill, London N10 3DF
Tel: 0181-444 2121
Fax: 0181-444 3761

Contact
Mary Ann Tyrrell, Administrative Officer

Main Activities
SIA is a self-help group for people with spinal cord injuries. Provides services, holiday facilities, information, counselling and publications. National organisation with ten local groups.

Opportunities for Volunteers
Volunteers are always needed to give administrative support. Numeracy and initiative are useful qualities. Minimum commitment is six hours a week and reliability is important.

Opportunities for Employment
There are nineteen full-time staff. On average two are recruited each year. Jobs are advertised in the press.

Further Information
Annual Report, information pack and list of local groups available on request.

STEPS (National Association for Children with Lower Limb Abnormalities), *see Counselling & Self-Help*

Sue Ryder Foundation

Cavendish, Sudbury
Suffolk, CO10 8AY
Tel: 01787-280252

Contact
Mr K Wilkinson

Main Activities
The Sue Ryder Foundation is devoted to the relief of suffering on the widest scale. It is a living memorial to those who gave their lives in two world wars in defence of human values and to those who are suffering and dying today as a result of persecution. Runs 24 homes in UK for sick and disabled people. National organisation with 500 shops. Annual budget is £6.6 million.

Opportunities for Volunteers
Full-time volunteers are required to undertake a variety of duties in certain of the homes and at Head office. This work may include assisting with the care of patients, domestic duties, office work. Free simple accommodation, meals and pocket money are offered. Volunteers always needed to work in shops. Weekend secretaries (with shorthand) are especially needed.

Opportunities for Employment
There are approximately 2,000 staff, a large number being part-time. Jobs are advertised locally and nationally as appropriate.

Further Information
A leaflet outlining the Foundation's work available to all enquirers.

The Raynaud's Scleroderma Association, *see Health & Medicine*

TOC H, *see Religious Affairs*

Torch Trust for the Blind, *see Religious Affairs*

TOFS, Tracheo-Oesophagal Fistula Support, *see Health & Medicine*

Treloar Trust

Froyle, Alton
Hants, GU34 4JX
Tel: 01420-22442
Fax: 01420-23957

Contact
Trust Director

Main Activities
The Lord Mayor Treloar College provides education for 280 severely physically disabled children. 250 local groups support the work of the college. Annual budget is £600,000.

Opportunities for Volunteers
The Trust is actively seeking collectors and fundraisers who live in any part of the country. Administrative help and support are given.

Opportunities for Employment
There are eight full-time staff.

Further Information
Annual Report and College prospectus available.

UK Sports Association for People with Learning Disability, *see Sports*

United Response

162/164 Upper Richmond Road
Putney, London SW15 2SL
Tel: 0181-780 9686
Fax: 0181-780 9538

Contact
Louise Howell, Personnel Administrator

Main Activities
United Response offers community based support to people with learning disabilities or mental health difficulties. There are regional offices in Sussex, Gateshead, Wigan, Huddersfield, St. Albans, Kent, Derbyshire, Yorkshire, Suffolk and Wiltshire.

Opportunities for Volunteers
Volunteers give administrative support and do some fundraising. Some volunteers work at residential homes with clients. A medical examination and references are necessary.

Opportunities for Employment
There are over 1,000 staff with new services opening frequently. Jobs are advertised in The Guardian, Community Care, Care Weekly, the local press and The Voice.

Further Information
Annual report available.

Urostomy Association

'Buckland', Beaumont Park
Danbury, Essex CM3 4DE
Tel: 01245-224294
Fax: 01245-224294

Contact
Angela Cooke, National Secretary

Main Activities
Assists people who have to have surgery resulting in Urinary Tract Diversion/Ileal Conduit. National organisation with 22 branches.

Opportunities for Volunteers
Volunteers, who have had a urostomy, organise local branch activities and visit new urostomates.

Opportunities for Employment
There are no employment opportunities.

Further Information
Annual Report, list of local groups, information leaflets and video available on request.

Vitiligo Society, *see Health & Medicine*

Vision Homes Association, *see Housing & Homelessness*

Warwickshire Association for the Blind (WAB)

The George Marshall Centre,
Puckerings Lane, Warwick CV34 4HU
Tel: 01926-494129

Contact
Brenda Watts for general volunteering;
Ann Hadland, Guide-Help Co-ordinator
for Deafblind Services for the Volunteers
to Guide Help Scheme.

Main Activities
In collaboration with other voluntary and statutory organisations, the Warwickshire Association for the Blind (WAB) promotes good quality services for registered blind and partially sighted people in Warwickshire. This includes providing information, advice, support, practical help, and leisure and recreational services. During 1994/95 in partnership with the Services to Deaf People Social Work Team, WAB set up an innovative guide-help scheme using volunteers to help provide services for deafblind people in the county. The scheme also aims to provide a Leisure Library. Set up in 1911, WAB covers the Warwickshire area only and has affiliated local groups. Membership is open to both visually impaired and sighted people. Annual income is approximately £100,00.

Opportunities for Volunteers
Since its inception WAB has used hundreds of volunteers to support its work with visually impaired people. It acknowledges that without their help services would be poorer, or even non-existent. Volunteers help organise local groups as well as undertaking administrative work, fundraising, public relations, counselling and advice giving. They also help with projects such as those for deafblind people, the Talking Book service, the Toy Library and the Leisure Library. More are welcome and needed both in head office and the local branches, and especially for the Guide Help Scheme. Recruitment is by application, via volunteer bureaux, and through Volunteers Week, and annual public and local club meetings. Language and guiding skills are acquired through the Training Programme provided. There is no minimum commitment and travel and other expenses are offered.

Opportunities for Employment
10 full-time and seven part-time staff are employed. Any further recruitment is as needs demand. Each post is advertised in local newspapers, and the application procedure is detailed in the advertisement. WAB is working towards an equal opportunities policy.

Further Information
The Annual Report, and leaflets/pamphlets on services, equipment etc are all available by request to head office or by telephoning Ann Hadland on 01203-456045 or 01203-344 406 (Services to Deaf People).

Winged Fellowship Trust (WFT)

20/32 Pentonville Road
London N1 9XD
Tel: 0171-833 2594
Fax: 0171-278 0370

Contact
Elizabeth Clucas, Volunteer Bookings Manager

Main Activities
Provides holidays for severely physically disabled people. There are five holiday

centres in different parts of the country and 15 local support groups. Annual budget is £3.2 million.

Opportunities for Volunteers

Volunteers are essential - they give care and companionship to physically disabled people at holiday centres. They must be reasonably physically fit, aged over sixteen and be able to provide a reference. Induction course offered. Minimum commitment is one or two weeks residential.

Opportunities for Employment

There are 145 full-time staff and 35 part-time.

Further Information

Annual Report, application forms for volunteers and guests, and video available on request.

Education

Opportunities for volunteering in education, across the spectrum from pre-school to the tertiary sector, have grown considerably in recent years, particularly with the successive changes in organisation and funding introduced by the government. It is now possible to volunteer in all areas of formal education as well as in a wide variety of informal and training organisations. Whether you are interested in working with gifted children or with people who have reading difficulties; whether you want to help adults who have missed out on formal education, or to pass on your skills in retirement by teaching for the University of the Third Age (U3A), the possibilities are numerous. There are also various education/business partnership schemes which enable you to volunteer while employed, often through employee volunteering.

Your own age is not a barrier. Many young people contribute their time volunteering perhaps helping elderly people remember and reminisce about the past. Undergraduate student tutors share their knowledge with local school children. Many older and retired people, some in their seventies and eighties, volunteer in schools teaching children such skills as needlework and carpentry, befriending pupils, or helping those who need extra tuition in reading. If you are interested in volunteering in an educational organisation contact your local education authority (many have a Community Education Adviser) or local council for initial information and suggestions. You will need to decide first whether you want to volunteer with younger children or with young people in secondary education or higher.

Schools rely on volunteers. They contribute time, energy and diversity to the life of the school. Most volunteers are parents whose children are of school age, particularly in the primary sector.

Volunteering provides an ideal opportunity for parents to make a contribution to their child's school, to develop new skills and build on existing ones, and possibly make new friends too. Sometimes it can lead on to a paid post within the school.

There are a variety of opportunities from helping with reading, assisting in the classroom or playground, or helping with sports activities to fundraising for new projects and being a school governor. Both state sector and private schools use volunteers. Enquiries should usually be made through the Head Teacher. Joining the PTA/Parents Association is a good introduction and a way of gaining confidence.

Nursery schools also need volunteers and your local authority should be able to provide lists of these. Special schools, which cater for children with a wide variety of needs, such as physical disabilities and learning difficulties, use volunteers too. It may also be worth checking with your local library to see if it needs help with special reading schemes which it may be running.

Other useful contacts which can help you to identify the sorts of educational/ schools volunteering available include the Pre-School Groups Association, HAPA (formerly the Handicapped Adventure Playgrounds Association), Riding for the Disabled, and local church and community centres. Try also Volunteer Reading Help (see entry in this section), or for volunteering as a school governor contact AGIT (Action for Governors Information and Training), c/o CEDC, Lyng Hall, Blackberry Lane, Coventry CV2 3JS. Universities around the country will usually have their own voluntary service sections. Finally Community Service Volunteers (CSV) has a number of schemes that enable people of all ages to volunteer in education. These include: 'CSV Education' for young people in schools to volunteer in the community, 'Learning Together' for undergraduate students to volunteer in schools, 'Hands On' for employee volunteering, and 'RSVP' - the Retired and Senior Volunteers Programme. Contact CSV on 0171-278 6601 for details.

For some helpful books and directories see also the Useful Publications section in this directory.

ADFAM National

5th Floor, Epworth House
25 City Road, London EC1Y 1AA
Tel: 0171-638 3700

Contact
Kathy Robson, Helpline Co-ordinator

Main Activities
ADFAM works with the families and friends of drug users. Set up in 1984, it provides training, information and advice for drug-related family support services. As part of these services it runs the national telephone helpline for families of users. ADFAM is a national organisation, based in London, with an annual budget of around £125,000.

Opportunities for Volunteers
About twenty volunteers are used in head office in running the telephone helpline, which ADFAM would be unable to provide without them. Although no special skills or experience are asked for, volunteers need to be good listeners, non-judgemental and comfortable with phone work. More are wanted. They are recruited by application and training is provided. Minimum commitment is one 3-4 hour session weekly. Travel expenses are paid.

Opportunities for Employment
ADFAM has a staff of four full-time employees. Vacancies seldom occur, so opportunities are limited.

Further Information
An Annual Report, information sheets

and three-four newsletters yearly are published.

ADiTi - The National Organisation of South Asian Dance

Willowfield Street
Bradford BD7 2AH
Tel: 01274-522059
Fax: 01274-522043

Contact
Sue Hayton, Acting Director

Main Activities
Set up in 1989 ADiTi promotes and develops the practice and appreciation of South Asian dance. A national organisation, it also has a regional team for Yorkshire and Humberside. Concerned with arts development, and with an annual budget of £130,000, it is also involved in campaigning, education and giving advice.

Opportunities for Volunteers
ADiTi does not use volunteers currently.

Opportunities for Employment
There are three full-time, one part-time and a few temporary staff members. Any vacancies are advertised in newspapers such as The Guardian and the Dance Press. Skills required depend on the job. An equal opportunities policy is in place.

Further Information
The Annual Report, general information, publications and a bi-monthly newsletter are available.

African Caribbean Library Association (ACLA)

c/o Shoreditch Library
Pitfield Street
London N1 6EX
Tel: 0171-729 3545

Contact
c/o Ms Evadne Hill

Main Activities
A forum for people of African and Caribbean descent working in the field of librarianship and information, to share ideas and experiences. The aim is to advance the achievements of black people through the promotion of anti-racist materials and to support activities designed to foster racial harmony. Annual budget approximately £2,000.

Opportunities for Volunteers
A volunteer-run organisation whose members meet at various libraries nationwide, and are involved in librarianship.

Opportunities for Employment
There are no paid workers and no opportunities.

Further Information
Annual Report and list of local groups available.

Age Exchange / Age Exchange Theatre Trust, see Elderly People

Alcohol Counselling and Prevention Services (ACAPS), see Counselling & Self-help

Anthrosophical Society in Great Britain

Rudolph Steiner House
35 Park Road
London NW1 6XT
Tel: 0171-723 4400
Fax: 0171-724 4364

Contact
S. Mainzer, Secretary

Main Activities
Set up in 1923, the Society aims to foster a better understanding of the spiritual basis of many areas of life. A Library and Arts Centre, it holds information on related activities in the UK. These include: Steiner Waldorf Education, Adult Education, Schools of Art, Speech and Drama and Eurythmy, Education for Special Needs, Biodynamic Farming, Anthroposophical Medicine, a clinic, a nursing home, open days, exhibitions and so on. It provides enquirers with information, contact addresses and telephone numbers about the many autonomous institutions whose work is based on Rudolf Steiner's anthroposophy. It also has links with similar organisations in Europe and North America.

Opportunities for Volunteers
Administrative support is given by volunteers. Other needs vary according to the organisation and the area. Lunch expenses are offered.

Opportunities for Employment
There are eight staff in the head office. Most opportunities occur in communities throughout the country working with children and adults with special needs. Opportunities in catering, gardening and administration sometimes occur elsewhere.

Further Information
Annual Report and pamphlets available on request.

Baptist Youth Ministry, *see Youth*

British Association for Early Childhood Education (BAECE)

111 City View House
463 Bethnal Green Road
London E2 9QY
Tel: 0171-739 7594

Contact
Barbara Boon, Secretary

Main Activities
BAECE is concerned with all aspects of children's learning up to the age of nine. Organises conferences and carries out research. There are 52 branches which arrange meetings and seminars.

Opportunities for Volunteers
Volunteer members run local branches, provide training and social activities.

Opportunities for Employment
There are three full-time members of staff and two part-time members. Jobs are advertised in The Guardian and The Times Educational Supplement.

Further Information
Annual report and membership/information leaflet available on request.

British Association for the Advancement of Science (BA)

Fortress House
23 Savile Row
London W1X 1AB
Tel: 0171-494 3326

Contact
Dr Peter Briggs

Main Activities
Stimulates discussion about science particularly among younger people through a programme of talks, events and exhibi-

tions. National organisation with sixteen local branches.

Opportunities for Volunteers
Volunteers are needed to help with youth groups and activities. An interest in science and an ability to relate to young people useful. Travel expenses are offered.

Opportunities for Employment
There are nine full-time and six part-time staff.

Further Information
Annual Report and information leaflets available.

The British Disabled Water Ski Association, see Sports

British Dyslexia Association (BDA)

98 London Road
Reading, Berks RG1 5AU
Tel: 01734-662677 (admin)
Tel: 01734-668271 (helpline)
Fax: 01734-357927

Contact
Cleone Parker and S Flohr, Helpline Co-ordinators

Main Activities
A national organisation set up in 1972, BDA promotes awareness of dyslexia. It encourages identification of and help for the problem, and sets up training for specialist teachers. There are 30 local support groups, 100 affiliated organisations and links with similar organisations in other parts of the world.

Opportunities for Volunteers
The BDA could not work without volunteer help. Volunteers living in the Reading area are needed to work on the helpline and to give secretarial support. 35 are used in the head office. The 100 affiliated organisations are all run by volunteers. Minimum commitment is three hours a

week in term time. Telephone, typing and W/P skills are useful. Training and support are given.

Opportunities for Employment
There are six full-time staff.

Further Information
Annual Report and leaflets available on request.

British Sports Association for the Disabled (BSAD), see Sports

Business In The Community (BITC)

8 Stratton Street
London W1X 5FD
Tel: 0171-629 2209
Fax: 0171-629 1834

Contact
Ann Gordon-Owen, Human Resources Manager

Main Activities
BITC, a nation-wide organisation set up in 1981, aims to make community involvement an accepted part of successful business practice, and to increase the quality and extent of business activity in the community. It assists companies to take practical action. London-based, BITC has eleven regional offices.

Opportunities for Volunteers
BITC itself uses secondees, rather than volunteers. It runs a campaign called 'Employee Volunteering' which works with companies to help them develop programmes so that their employees get involved in the community in varied ways.

Opportunities for Employment
An equal opportunities employer, BITC recruits about fifteen people yearly. An empathy with its aims, plus understanding of the private, public and voluntary sectors is needed. Posts are advertised in

The Guardian and Daily Telegraph. BITC has around 100 full-time staff.

Further Information

A variety of pamphlets, booklets and other information, together with a corporate review are published. BITC's sister organisation in Scotland is Scottish Business in the Community, Romano House, 43 Station Road, Corstorphine, Edinburgh EH12 7AF, tel: 0131-334 9876

Campaign for State Education (CASE)

158 Durham Road
London SW20 0DG
Tel: 0181-944 8206

Contact
The Secretary

Main Activities

CASE campaigns for the right of every child to the best education. A national organisation with ten local groups and other local contacts.

Opportunities for Volunteers

Members of CASE do fundraising and administrative work, mostly in their own homes.

Opportunities for Employment

There is one full-time member of staff.

Further Information

Annual Report, list of local groups and information pamphlets available on request.

Capital Transport Campaign,
see Environment & Conservation

Community Transport Association Ltd

Highbank, Halton Street
Hyde, Cheshire SK14 2NY
Tel: 0161-366 6685/0161-351 1475
Fax: as telephone plus 0161-367 8780

Contact
Ms J Meadows, Deputy Director

Main Activities

A nation-wide, membership association with community transport members from all over the UK and set up in 1981. It offers services, advice and information to providers of community transport services and promotes good practice among such transport operators. Produces publications, organises courses and lobbies government and local authorities. National, with 600 affiliated/local organisations, the annual budget is £250,000.

Opportunities for Volunteers

The Association does not use volunteers itself, but can suggest contacts among its affiliated organisations who may need volunteer help. Volunteers are essential to the provision of voluntary sector escort transport. They need to have driving skills and the ability to assist as passenger escorts.

Opportunities for Employment

With a small staff of four full-time and three part-time employees, the Association seldom needs to recruit. Any vacancies are advertised in the press, including The Guardian, based on an Equal Opportunities Policy.

Further Information

The Annual Report and publications lists are available.

Council for Wales of Voluntary Youth Services (CWVYS), *see Youth*

Crusaders, *see Youth*

The Duke of Edinburgh's
Award, *see Youth*

The Dyslexia Institute

133 Gresham Road
Staines TW18 2AJ
Tel: 01784-463851
Fax: 01784-460747

Contact
Liz Brooks

Main Activities
Assesses and teaches dyslexics aged
between five and sixty-five years old. Set
up in 1972, it is a national organisation
concentrated in England and Scotland,
with 22 local branches.

Opportunities for Volunteers
Volunteers give administrative support,
help with fundraising and carry out
project work. A caring personality and a
good telephone manner are useful. Minimum commitment is three hours a week
in term time.

Opportunities for Employment
There are 45 full-time and 238 part-time
staff. Most are teachers. Jobs are advertised in educational papers and journals
and locally.

Further Information
Annual Report, list of local groups and
general leaflets available.

Endeavour Training

17a Glumangate
Chesterfield
Derbyshire S40 1TX
Tel: 01246-237201
Fax: 01246-203828

Contact
John Bell, Manager, Endeavour Voluntary
and Community Services

Main Activities
Endeavour is a national educational

charity, providing programmes of
practical and challenging experience to
help young people develop in mind, body
and spirit. Founded in 1955 and covering
parts of England, and Wales, it has 20
local branches supported by development
workers. The annual budget is £250,000.

Opportunities for Volunteers
Endeavour's focus is on developing local
groups of volunteers supported by full-
time, national staff. It involves around 600
volunteers and is actively seeking more.
Volunteers organise local groups and undertake projects in the local community.
They are recruited through application to
the above office and by word of mouth.
There is no minimum time commitment
and usually no expenses are offered.
Training and support are given.

Opportunities for Employment
There are 20 staff, mostly full-time.
Recruitment seldom occurs, but if any
vacancies arise they are advertised in
local and national papers such as The
Guardian. Endeavour has an equal
opportunities policy.

Further Information
The Annual Report, a list of local groups,
and information on Endeavour and its
training services are available from the
Chesterfield office.

Fairbridge, *see Youth*

Family Education Trust (FET)

322 Woodstock Road
Oxford OX2 7NS
Tel: 01865-56848
Fax: 01865-52774

Contact
Mrs Valerie Riches, Director

Main Activities
Concerned with family welfare, FET

promotes and publishes research into the social, medical, economic and psychological consequences of family breakdown, together with educational aids for schools. A UK-wide organisation set up in 1973 and run by a democratically elected committee, it has four branches and twenty affiliated organisations. Annual budget is £60,000.

Opportunities for Volunteers

Around six volunteers are used in head office for administrative, fundraising and research work. FET regularly seeks more, especially people with word processing abilities. Appropriate training and support are given. Recruitment is usually in-house and a personal interview and references are required. Minimum commitment is 30 hours weekly. Travel and lunch expenses, and a volunteer allowance are paid.

Opportunities for Employment

FET has a staff of five full-time workers, and seldom recruits. Any posts are usually filled through personal contact. A knowledge of printing and publishing is helpful.

Further Information

Annual Report, a list of local groups, and various publications (for sale) are available.

Gainsborough's House

Society, see Museums, the Arts and Festivals

GAP Activity Projects, see

Overseas & the Developing World

Godalming Museum, see

Museums, the Arts & Festivals

Green Light Trust, see

Environment & Conservation

ICOM (Industrial Common Ownership Movement)

Vassalli House
20 Central Road
Leeds LS1 6DE
Tel: 0113-246 1738/7
Fax: 0113-244 0002

Contact
Jill Gardiner

Main Activities

ICOM promotes and supports democratic employee ownership through worker co-operatives. A membership-based organisation it gives information on democratic, employee-controlled businesses and legal services for the cooperative and social economy sectors. It also provides legal and technical support services to these sectors and the voluntary sector. For example, it can offer a company formation service. It also acts as a central contact point for information and for a network of local co-operative development agencies throughout the UK, and has links with other national federations in the co-operative and social economy sectors in Europe.

Opportunities for Volunteers

There are some limited opportunities. For details and local activities, contact ICOM in Leeds.

Opportunities for Employment

ICOM has occasional vacancies. Contact the office direct.

Further Information

Annual Report, information sheets and membership details available on request.

Inter-Action

HMS President (1918)
Victoria Embankment
London EC4Y 0HJ
Tel: 0171-583 2652
Fax: 0171-583 2840

Contact

Andrew Midgeley, Administration
Manager or Derek Palmer-Brown,
Development Director

Main Activities

Inter-Action is a trust that aims to explore
new forms of creative, participatory
programmes in the inner city and to work
on new approaches to motivate learning
especially for children and adults. It is a
diverse, ever-evolving pre-pilot and pilot
project development organisation. Set up
in 1968 it is both national and international, with 30 affiliated groups and
projects in Guyana, Holland, Portugal,
Russia and Zimbabwe. Annual budget is
£1,500,000.

Opportunities for Volunteers

About ten volunteers contribute to the
work at head office. They bring skills to
the organisation and help the Trust
impart skills to the individual. They are
particularly involved in administrative
support, management and trusteeship,
fundraising, research, counselling and
advice giving. They also assist with the
approximately 12 projects underway at
any one time. The Trust wants to recruit
more, especially for project work. Recruitment is ad hoc on application to the Trust.
There is no minimum time commitment,
and travel, lunch and out-of-pocket
expenses are offered. Information
technology (IT) training is available.

Opportunities for Employment

The Trust employs 32 full-time, 6 part-
time and 4 temporary staff. Up to 12 new
staff may be recruited each year depending on the projects begun. Jobs are
advertised ad hoc. An equal opportunities
policy is in place, with particular interest
in employing young people without
formal qualifications, returners, and
people who have been made redundant.

Further Information

The Annual Report, and information on
past, present, and future projects are available by application or visiting in person.

The Jewish Lads and Girls Brigade, *see Youth*

Kent Trust for Nature Conservation, *see Environment & Conservation*

The Marine Society

202 Lambeth Road
London SE1 7JW
Tel: 0171-261 9535
Fax: 0171-401 2537

Contact

The General Secretary

Main Activities

Established in 1756, the Society is concerned with the education, training and
welfare of professional seafarers of all sea
services. It runs a library service to ships,
provides further education, operates
training ships to give basic sea education
to young people, and offers grants and
financial support of various kinds. A
national, UK-wide organisation, it has an
annual budget of £1.9 million.

Opportunities for Volunteers

Volunteers are used around the world as
individual tutors and ship librarians.
Invaluable in meeting the educational
needs of seafarers across the wide spectrum of human knowledge, tutors (with
teaching experience if possible) are
recruited only when a seafarer must study
a certain subject and requires a tutor with
the particular subject qualifications.

Various expenses are paid, subject to agreement. Recruitment is by personal introduction or application to the Society. In the UK volunteer opportunities are available in correspondence work only.

Opportunities for Employment
Between two and three people are recruited annually. With a total staff of 34 full-time and three part-time employees, the Society is an equal opportunities employer. Posts are advertised in The Times Educational Supplement.

Further Information
Annual report and literature on all aspects of the Society's work are available.

Mary Ward Centre

42 Queen Square
London WC1N 3AQ
Tel: 0171-831 7711

Contact
Olga Janssen, Vice Principal

Main Activities
The Centre provides adult and community education opportunities, offers legal and financial advice, and is involved in youth work. A single establishment in Central London, it has nine affiliated organisations. Annual budget is nearly £537,000.

Opportunities for Volunteers
The Centre occasionally uses volunteers, and may do so more in the future, following an evaluation in 1992 of its needs and staff roles.

Opportunities for Employment
Much of the Centre's work is based on the use of around 150 part-time tutors. About fifteen of these and one full-time staff member may be recruited each year. Posts are advertised in The Times Educational Supplement, other specialist press, and the local press. There is an equal opportunities policy.

Further Information
Annual prospectus available.

Midwives Information and Resource Service (MIDIRS)

9 Elmdale Road
Clifton, Bristol BS8 1SL
Tel: 0117-925 1791

Contact
Ann Thwaites

Main Activities
MIDIRS is a central source of information concerning maternity care. Produces quarterly digests, runs study days and answers queries. Based in the south west of England, MIDIRS operates nationally with regional representatives. Annual budget is £500,000.

Opportunities for Volunteers
Volunteers are used in the UK and overseas. They undertake a variety of work including talking to others about the organisation, attending conferences on MIDIRS behalf, distributing leaflets and posters, and scanning journals and abstract articles for the digest. They need to have midwifery training. MIDIRS is actively seeking midwives to act as regional representatives.

Opportunities for Employment
There are four full-time and one part-time staff. Jobs are advertised in the local press.

Further Information
Annual Report and information sheets available.

National Alliance of Women's Organisations (NAWO), see Women

National Association of Swimming Clubs for the Handicapped (NASCH), see Sports

National Association of Women's Clubs, see Women

The National Association for Special Education Needs (NASEN)

York House, Exhall Grange
Wheelwright Lane,
Coventry CV7 9HP
Tel: 01203-362414

Contact
Mike Hinson, Executive Secretary

Main Activities
Promotes the development of children and young people with special educational needs, and supports those who work with them. NASEN is a national organisation governed by a General Assembly whose members are elected by its 65 local branches. Annual budget is approximately £200,000.

Opportunities for Volunteers
At present NASEN does not use volunteers. However, the situation is under review.

Opportunities for Employment
With a settled staff of three full-time and three part-time employees, NASEN has not so far had any vacancies. Should any position arise it is most likely to be for office staff or the Executive Secretary's post (needing a professional background in special education). Any vacancy would be advertised in the local and national press. NASEN has an equal opportunities policy.

Further Information
Membership details and a list of local groups are available. NASEN publishes two quarterly journals and a magazine *Special!* Its trading company NASEN Enterprises Ltd, 2 Lichfield Road, Stafford ST17 4JX can provide a list of the publications and also of courses available.

National Confederation of Parent Teacher Associations (NCPTA)

2 Ebbsfleet Estate
Stonebridge Road
Gravesend, Kent DA11 9DZ
Tel: 01474-560618
Fax: 01474-564418

Contact
Judi Moylan, Administrator

Main Activities
Set up in 1956, the NCPTA promotes partnership between home and school. It can advise on how to set up parent-teacher associations. It is managed by an elected executive committee of volunteers, and has 11,000 affiliated organisations, covering the UK except Scotland. It also has links with the European Parents Association (EPA).

Opportunities for Volunteers
Volunteers are used to run NCPTA as elected trustees and in the local organisations. Without them the organisation would not exist. More are welcome, although the NCPTA has no way of recruiting any with special skills. For details of opportunities contact NCPTA direct.

Opportunities for Employment
NCPTA has only five full-time paid staff. Any vacancies are advertised in the local press. The Confederation is developing an equal opportunities policy.

Further Information
Annual report and basic information packs covering all aspects of membership are available. Sister organisation in Wales:

Parent Teacher Association of Wales, PTAW, 26 Hillcrest, New Inn, Pontypool, Gwent, Chairman M Osborne.

The National Star Centre, College of Further Education

Ullenwood, Cheltenham
Gloucestershire GL53 9QU
Tel: 01242-527631
Fax: 01242-222243

Contact
Mr Allan White, Vice Principal

Main Activities
A specialist college for young people with physical disabilities, the Centre's mission is to enable students to prepare for the best that adult life can offer through innovative programmes of education, training and independence. The Centre has been providing programmes for over 25 years and has a national catchment area.

Opportunities for Volunteers
Around 25 volunteers provide educational, technology and care support for students, as well as enriching their cultural experience. Regarded as very important to the College's work, volunteers are recruited through volunteer bureaux, or by applying to CSV and Gap schemes. More are required. English speakers are preferred, the minimum time commitment is three terms or 36 weeks, and volunteer allowance and lunch expenses are offered. Volunteers must be committed, and ongoing training and support are provided.

Opportunities for Employment
Paid staff are employed. The Centre regularly seeks people for technology support work. Positions are advertised locally and nationally. People with disabilities, returners and those made redundant are actively recruited, together with new graduates. The Centre has an equal opportunities policy.

Further Information
The Annual Report, Prospectus and a video of the Centre are available.

Network 81

1-7 Woodfield Terrace
Stansted, Essex CM24 8AJ
Tel: 01279-647415
Fax: 01279-816438

Contact
Val Rosier/Penny Platt

Main Activities
Network 81, set up in 1986, supports parents of children with special educational needs. It carries out assessment and review under the 1993 Education Act and Code of Practice. It also provides a helpline, local contacts, conferences. A national organisation for England and Wales, it acts as an umbrella body with local affiliates/groups.

Opportunities for Volunteers
Volunteers are essential in enabling Network 81 to have local groups. Volunteers, who need a knowledge of special educational needs, are required to run parent support groups, to work on helplines and to befriend. Befriender training courses are available.

Opportunities for Employment
There are two staff.

Further Information
Annual Accounts, list of local groups and information sheets available on request.

Notting Dale Urban Studies Centre

189-191 Freston Road
London W10 6TH
Tel: 0181-969 8942
Fax: 0181-969 7527

Contact
Martin Garman, Director

Main Activities
The Centre works with schools and colleges to investigate the urban environment and keeps information resources

about its local London area, including archive photographs, maps and publications. It also has popular darkroom photography studios. Founded in 1979 it is part of the Harrow Club W10 Trust. Annual budget is £70,000.

Opportunities for Volunteers

Volunteers undertake various kinds of work including assistance with teaching, photography, fundraising and resource production. They need to be able to use their initiative about the work. More are required, especially to organise the information resources (for which librarian or archivist skills are necessary) and to input onto the computer system. Recruitment is ad hoc, on application, and via volunteer bureaux. Minimum commitment is eight hours a week over three months. Travel and out-of-pocket expenses are offered. Training and support is given.

Opportunities for Employment

There are three full-time and one part-time members of staff. Vacancies sometimes occur and are publicly advertised, followed by an interview. The Centre has an Equal Opportunities Policy.

Further Information

The Annual Report, publications leaflet, resources list, and schools' courses offer are available on request.

Parent Partnership Project

London Borough of Lewisham
Room 311, The Town Hall
Catford, London SE6 4RU
Tel: 0181-695 6000 ext. 3236

Contact

Ms Jenny Aubrey, Parent Partnership Adviser

Main Activities

Set up in September 1994, the Project aims to give parents impartial and independent advice and guidance about the assessment of their child's special educational needs. As part of this it will recruit and train volunteers to act as named persons to give support to parents. A Borough policy on Named Persons with role definition and training package is also being developed. A local service, the Project operates in the London Borough of Lewisham only. The annual budget varies according to government grants.

Opportunities for Volunteers

Named Person volunteers are essential to the Project as every family with a special educational needs child should have a named person. Needed year round, volunteers will work direct with parents in a befriender/facilitator type role and will be involved in advice giving, counselling and support. Appropriate training in a comprehensive package will be given, but a knowledge of Special Educational Needs would be an advantage. Recruitment is via application to the Project, in-house schemes and liaison with national and local parents' groups and organisations for children who have special needs. Minimum commitment required is six months to a year, and travel expenses may be paid.

Opportunities for Employment

One full-time and one part-time member of staff are employed. Recruitment and equal opportunities policies are being developed and references will be required. Appropriate training, for example in assessment of Special Educational Needs and the Code of Practice, will be given as necessary.

Further Information

Information pamphlets are available.

The Pony Club, *see Sports*

Quay Theatre, *see Museums, the Arts and Festivals*

Raleigh International, *see*
Overseas & the Developing World

St Andrews Ambulance Association, *see Health & Medicine*

The Scout Association, *see*
Youth

Sea Ranger Association, *see*
Youth

Sing for Pleasure

c/o 25 Fryerning Lane
Ingatestone, Essex CM4 0DD
Tel: 01277-353691

Contact
Lynda Parker

Main Activities
Runs singing days, weekends and summer schools for children and adults. Provides training for teachers and choral conductors.

Opportunities for Volunteers
Volunteers serve on committees and help with clerical work.

Opportunities for Employment
Two part-time staff are employed. Monitors are required for Children's 'Superweeks' in August. Training is given and the remuneration is small.

Further Information
Annual Report and information about courses available on request.

Student Community Action Development Unit (SCADU),
see Youth

The Trident Trust, *see Youth*

United Kingdom Council for Overseas Student Affairs (UKCOSA)

9-17 St Albans Place
London N1 0NX
Tel: 0171-226 3762
Fax: 0171-226 3373

Contact
The Director

Main Activities
UKCOSA, set up in 1968, promotes the aims of international education and the interests of international students in Britain. Nationwide membership. Annual budget £500,000.

Opportunities for Volunteers
UKCOSA welcomes approaches from people interested in giving administrative and research support.

Opportunities for Employment
There are 11 full-time and one part-time staff. UKCOSA is particularly interested in recruiting new graduates if any positions become available.

Further Information
Annual Report available.

Volunteer Reading Help

Room 438, High Holborn House
49/51 Bedford Row
London WC1V 6RL
Tel: 0171-404 6204

Contact
Caroline Dale, National Organiser

Main Activities
Helps primary school age children who have a difficulty learning to read. Uses volunteers to assist individual children. A national organisation for England set up in 1973, it also has local branches in Lancashire, Nottinghamshire, Oxfordshire, Avon, Dorset, Surrey, London, Kent, Berkshire. Annual Budget is £380,000.

Opportunities for Volunteers

Volunteers are essential and the organisation recruits, trains and supports them. They work in local primary schools with individual children aged between 6 and 11 on a one-to-one basis for a year helping them to read, building their confidence and encouraging them. Minimum commitment is two to four hours a week during term time. Fundraisers are also required. People from all cultures and backgrounds between 18 and 80 are encouraged to become volunteers.

Opportunities for Employment

There are 40 part-time members of staff and one full-time member.

Further Information

Annual Report and recruitment literature available.

Wales Youth Agency (WYA),
see Youth

The Woodcraft Folk, *see Youth*

Workers' Educational Association (WEA)

Temple House
17 Victoria Park Square
London E2 9PB
Tel: 0181-983 1515
Fax: 0181-983 4840

Contact

The General Secretary

Main Activities

Set up in 1903, the WEA provides education for adults, particularly those who have been disadvantaged by the education system. A national organisation active in England and Scotland, it has thirteen districts providing courses locally and a Scottish Association. It also has links with similar organisations overseas, in-

cluding the International Federation of WEAs and the Euro-WEA.

Opportunities for Volunteers

Volunteers are essential to the WEA's work. They are needed in local branches and for outreach work in local communities. This includes organisation of and recruitment to courses, help with publicity/publications and support in classes for people with special needs. The government of the WEA at district and local level is also by voluntary members. A commitment to education and an experience of the local community are useful.

Opportunities for Employment

There are full-time and part-time staff, plus a regular need for part-time tutors.

Further Information

Enquiries to above address.

Worldaware

1 Catton Street
London WC1R 4AB
Tel: 0171-831 3844
Fax: 0171-831 1746

Contact

Derek Walker, Director

Main Activities

Aims to increase British understanding of world development issues and Britain's interdependence with developing countries. UK-wide and set up in 1977, it works with schools, colleges, the media and the business community. It also has informal links with organisations throughout the world engaged in similar educational work eg the Rossing Foundation in Namibia and the Japan Centre for International Co-operation. Annual budget is £300,000.

Opportunities for Volunteers

Well-qualified volunteers with relevant skills and experience are needed for project work eg organising an awards scheme for business. Teachers with considerable classroom experience and a thorough knowledge of the subject are especially useful. Also needed are experienced people to provide in-service education for teachers and give administrative support. Opportunities exist in head office and all over the UK. Volunteers are very important to expanding the work since funds are limited. Minimum commitment is six hours a week, preferably in term time.

Opportunities for Employment
There are seven full-time and three part-time staff.

Further Information
Annual Report and catalogue available on request.

Worldwide Education Service (WES)

35 Belgrave Square
London SW1X 8QB
Tel: 0171-235 2880

Contact
Dorrie Wheldell

Main Activities
Assists parents to educate their children (3-11 years) at home. Provides full teaching programmes, curriculum resources and tutorial support. London based with international links.

Opportunities for Volunteers
See above for parent volunteer opportunities.

Opportunities for Employment
There are six full-time and seven part-time staff. Jobs are advertised in The Guardian and the Times Educational Supplement.

Further Information
Further information and leaflets available.

Yorkshire Sculpture Park, see
Museums, the Arts and Festivals

Youth Clubs UK, see Youth

Elderly People

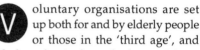 oluntary organisations are set up both for and by elderly people or those in the 'third age', and elderly and retired people also participate actively in many of them. The Abbeyfield Society for example, runs homes providing care and companionship for older people: many of the volunteers in the houses are themselves well over retiring age. The University of the Third Age (U3A) has been set up to enable older people to both learn and teach – to pass on their skills to other older people following retirement through enjoyable educational courses and classes which they run themselves.

Finding they have the time and interest many people become volunteers after retirement. They are much in demand. In fact there are many more opportunities available in a wide variety of organisations than there are available volunteers to fill them. This is partly because older people often do not know of the possibilities that exist. If retired, did you know for example that you can pass on your skills through volunteering both at home and abroad? Various organisations can advise you on the opportunities including BESO, RSVP (Retired Senior Volunteer Programme), SCORE (the Scottish Corps of Retired Executives) and VSO. See the section on Overseas and Developing Countries. If you want to work with elderly people themselves the entries in this section will help you decide. Your own age doesn't matter. Many of the voluntary organisations concerned with providing for the needs of elderly people welcome help and membership from those in both younger and older age groups.

The Abbeyfield Society

53 Victoria Street
St Albans
Hertfordshire AL1 3UW
Tel: 01727-857536
Fax: 01727-846168

Contact
Mrs Hilary Pope, Applications Secretary

Main Activities
The Abbeyfield Society , set up in 1956, is a national federation operating throughout the UK, with seventeen regions and around six hundred member/affiliated societies running nearly 1,000 houses. Abbeyfield's National Office exists to encourage and support these local societies, which set up and run family-type households that provide assisted living for older people. Each household has a live-in housekeeper and a support group of local volunteers. There are also larger houses for the very frail. The national budget is £1.1 million. Abbeyfield Societies have also been formed abroad, including Australia, Canada and the Netherlands.

Opportunities for Volunteers
As the backbone of the organisation, volunteers are crucial and central to Abbeyfield's work, and are needed all year round. Their involvement helps Abbeyfield to keep its costs down, making its houses accessible to all. Over 12,000 are used throughout the member societies, notably for administrative, fundraising and project work, particularly helping to manage the houses. Abbeyfield actively seeks volunteers for other work too, including DIY, befriending, care and accountancy. A wide range of skills is required. Volunteers are recruited through ad hoc applications, volunteer bureaux, in-house recruitment drives and word of mouth, via national office and the societies. People who have experienced career redundancies are particularly actively recruited. Depending on local need, between one and ten hours volunteering a week is required. Guidance and advice are given through the local societies with the support of the national office. Travel and other necessarily incurred expenses are paid for certain voluntary activities, such as serving on national committees.

Opportunities for Employment
Abbeyfield employs 30 staff in its national office covering a range of professional skills. Housekeepers are recruited at both national and local level. Positions are advertised in The Lady, based on an equal opportunities policy.

Further Information
The Annual Report, Annual Review, various leaflets about Abbeyfield's work, and a list of local groups are available on request. Abbeyfield can also be contacted at:

The Abbeyfield Society for Scotland, 15 West Maitland Street, Edinburgh EH12 5EA, tel: 0131-225 7801

The Abbeyfield Northern Ireland Development Society Ltd, Room 10, Carlton House, Shaftsbury Square, Belfast BT2 7LH, tel: 01232- 320386

Age Concern England

Astral House
1268 London Road
London SW16 4ER
Tel: 0181-679 8000
Fax: 0181-679 6069

Contact
Anne Hardy, Personnel Officer, Personnel Department

Main Activities
Age Concern England (the National Council on Ageing) promotes the wellbeing of older people. It is the national voice for a network of 98 national organisations and over 1,400 local Age Concern organisations nationwide. Each local Age Concern organisation is

autonomous, free to pursue its own policies and priorities, providing a wide and varying range of services for elderly people. These may include day centres, transport schemes and advice giving. Age Concern England supports this work through its team of field officers and advisors, grants, campaigning with and for older people, national policy research, analysis and development, publishing, fundraising and marketing. Annual income for 1993/94 approached £13.1 million.

Opportunities for Volunteers

There are a few opportunities at Astral House in administrative support. Recruitment is ad hoc on application, with travel and lunch expenses offered. Volunteers are also needed quite separately by local organisations which should be approached direct (contact through telephone directories, local libraries and head office).

Opportunities for Employment

An equal opportunities employer, Age Concern England has 219 full-time and 57 part-time staff, and may need to recruit a number of people each year. Most posts are advertised in The Guardian, the local press and/or professional journals as appropriate. Age Concern England is also involved in employment training. Age Concern Training offers opportunities for trainees to gain NVQs and potentially, jobs in care, business administration and related subjects at centres throughout the country. Contact Divisional Head Office, Huddersfield, tel: 01484-510740. Local organisations may also have employment opportunities and should be contacted direct.

Further Information

Annual Report and 'Working with Older People - A Careers Guide' (please send sae) are available. Sister organisations are:

Age Concern Scotland, 54A Fountainbridge, Edinburgh EH3 9PT, Tel: 0131-228 5656

Age Concern Cymru, 4th Floor, 1 Cathedral Road, Cardiff CF1 9SD, Tel: 01222-371566

Age Concern Northern Ireland, 3 Lower Crescent, Belfast BT7 1NR, Tel: 01232-245729

Age Concern England also works closely with other organisations throughout Europe and is actively involved in the International Federation on Ageing.

Age Concern, Kensington and Chelsea

19-27 Young Street
London W8 5EH
Tel: 0171-938 3944
Fax: 0171-376 2591

Contact

Mrs Jane McNeil for volunteering; Mr Desmond McGinley, Director, re employment

Main Activities

Provides a wide range of services for elderly people throughout the Royal Borough of Kensington and Chelsea in London. A local, independent part of the Age Concern movement of the UK, it was set up as a branch in 1971. Annual budget is £200,000.

Opportunities for Volunteers

As with all Age Concern activities, volunteers are the backbone of the branch's work. About 150 provide administrative support and befriending, and undertake practical tasks. More are actively sought, year round, especially for befriending and for a dementia project. An understanding of elderly people is needed. Recruitment is carried out in various ways, including through volunteer bureaux, local newspapers, newsletters and word of mouth, on application, and by phoning for an appointment. The minimum commitment asked is one hour a week. Travel and out-of-pocket expenses are offered, together with regular training and support.

Opportunities for Employment

Five full-time and 16 part-time staff are employed. One or two people may be recruited each year, the skills or experience required depending on the position. Any jobs are advertised both locally and nationally eg in The Guardian and in job centres. Age Concern has an equal opportunities policy.

Further Information

The Annual Report, a quarterly newsletter and general Age Concern literature, including leaflets, pamphlets and posters, are available by post on request or in person. A mailing list is also operated.

Age Exchange/Age Exchange Theatre Trust

The Reminiscence Centre
11 Blackheath Village
London SE3 9LA
Tel: 0181-318 9105
Fax: 0181-318 0060

Contact

Frank Thackaberry, Administrator

Main Activities

Age Exchange aims to improve the quality of life of older people by emphasising the value of their reminiscences to young and old, through pioneering artistic, educational and therapeutic activities. Set up in 1983 and based in London, Age Exchange is a national organisation with local and international contacts. In 1993/94 the annual budget was £342,000.

Opportunities for Volunteers

Volunteers are used at the Reminiscence Centre for various types of work. These include administrative support, public relations, fundraising and project work such as theatre productions, exhibitions and publications. More are needed. Recruitment is usually through in-house methods. There is no minimum commitment and

travel expenses are offered. Prospective volunteers must fill in an application form and visit Age Exchange informally.

Opportunities for Employment

There are four full-time, three part-time and around 40 sessional staff. People are recruited as and when needed, particularly for reminiscence work, acting and stage management. Drama and/or reminiscence training are required. Those experiencing career redundancies are especially actively recruited.

Further Information

The Annual Report, and reminiscence publications, resources, sessions and training courses are available, together with visits to the Reminiscence Museum.

Anchor Housing

Anchor House
269A Banbury Road
Oxford OX2 7HU
Tel: 01865-311511
Fax: 01865-310074

Contact

Naomi Simmonds, Senior Personnel Assistant

Main Activities

A charitable housing association covering England and set up in 1968, Anchor provides sheltered housing, residential and nursing care for elderly people in need. Anchor also operates a 'Staying Put' service to help older homeowners repair and improve their properties. Apart from its central office in Oxford, Anchor has divisional offices in London, Bradford and Altrincham, with a number of regional offices within each division.

Opportunities for Volunteers

There are no opportunities for volunteers currently.

Opportunities for Employment

With over 6,000 full- and part-time staff, recruitment for a variety of jobs is on-going due to natural turn-over. Posts are advertised in the local and national press, and in specific ethnic and professional publications. Recruitment is based on an evolving equal opportunities policy.

Further Information

The Annual Report and other information concentrating on specific products/ services are available on request.

Centre for Policy on Ageing (CPA)

25-31 Ironmonger Row
London EC1V 3QP
Tel: 0171-253 1787
Fax: 0171-490 4206

Contact

Gillian Crosby, Deputy Director

Main Activities

An independent policy unit, the CPA analyses and helps formulate public policy concerning elderly people, disseminates information generally as well as on good practice, and is involved in various practical projects. It has a large reference library available for use free of charge, by appointment. CPA has one national office and a budget of £500,000 annually.

Opportunities for Volunteers

There are limited opportunities for volunteers.

Opportunities for Employment

All staffing recruitment is advertised in the national or local press.

Further Information

Annual report, leaflets and a books catalogue are available.

Contact the Elderly

15 Henrietta Street
London WC2E 8QH
Tel: 071-240 0630

Contact

Paul Freeman, Volunteers Organiser

Main Activities

Set up in 1965, the organisation provides care and companionship for isolated elderly people, using groups of volunteers who arrange Sunday afternoon social meetings and provide transport. A national organisation with 190 regional groups. Annual budget £98,000.

Opportunities for Volunteers

Contact the Elderly's work is based on volunteers, over 4,000 of them. They work in both head office and the local branches. They act as volunteer hosts for afternoon tea once or twice a year, and as volunteer owner/drivers one Sunday a month. They also act as group and area leaders, and help with administrative work. They are of paramount importance as without them there would be no outings for the elderly people. More are needed. Briefing and support are given. No remuneration is offered. Volunteers must have a clean driving licence. Recruitment is through local media, leaflets and posters.

Opportunities for Employment

Contact the Elderly has three full-time staff. There are some opportunities for part-time regional recruiters.

Further Information

Contact News, leaflets, publicity material, a list of local groups and the Annual Report are available.

Daybreak (Wales) Ltd

126/128 Llanduff Road
Cardiff CF1 9PW
Tel: 01222-226429

Contact
Mrs Yvonne Apsitis

Main Activities
Daybreak provides care and support for people who are elderly and disabled and for those who care for them. The present focus of the organisation is on provision, research and quality issues of home care services. Daybreak works at the leading edge of the new Community Care activity. The annual budget is £250, 000.

Opportunities for Volunteers
There are no volunteer opportunities.

Opportunities for Employment
There are seven full-time and one part time staff. In addition, there are 180 self-employed flexicare workers. About a hundred are recruited each year. Applicants go through a careful selection and recruit procedure and should possess a caring attitude, reliability and the ability to work in a team. Training is offered. Jobs are advertised in job centres, hospitals, volunteer centres and the local press. Daybreak can be approached directly.

Further Information
Brochures and a video are available on request.

Friends of the Elderly (FOTE)

42 Ebury Street
London SW1W 0LZ
Tel: 0171-730 8263
Fax: 0171-259 0154

Contact
Mrs M H Rumney, Personnel Executive

Main Activities
FOTE cares for the elderly in such a way as to promote independent living within a residential setting. There are twelve projects nationwide and six local fundraising groups.

Opportunities for Volunteers
Volunteers fundraise and give assistance eg shopping, driving, running shops in homes, etc.

Opportunities for Employment
Jobs are advertised in national and local press and professional journals.

Further Information
Annual report and brochures on individual homes available.

Help the Aged

St James's Walk
London EC1R 0BE
Tel: 0171-253 0253
Fax: 0171-250 4474

Contact
Helen Edwards, Volunteer Co-ordinator

Main Activities
Set up in 1961, Help the Aged works to improve the quality of life of elderly people particularly those who are frail, isolated and poor. It operates in the UK, including running charity shops, and also overseas in Africa, Asia, Latin America and the Caribbean. It also has links with member organisations of Help Age International.

Opportunities for Volunteers
Volunteers are needed in head office and in regional offices such as Edinburgh, Belfast and Leeds. The jobs include home-based clerical/administrative work, helping with a variety of fundraising activities to raise money for projects working with elderly people, committee work and organising/taking part in events. Administrative support is also needed. The various fundraising departments rely heavily on volunteers. The charity's 260+ shops would not exist without volunteer helpers, while over 200,000 volunteer

house-to-house collectors contribute significantly to the overall income. Skills needed depend on the individual vacancies. General training about Help the Aged is given plus other training as required. Travel and lunch expenses are offered.

Opportunities for Employment

There are 550 full-time and 400 part-time staff. Jobs are advertised locally and in The Guardian and other publications as appropriate.

Further Information

Annual Report and information leaflets available. For Scotland, contact: Help the Aged, Heriot House, Heriothill Terrace, Edinburgh EH7 4DY, tel: 0131-556 4666.

For Northern Ireland, contact: Help the Aged, Lesley House, Shaftesbury Square, Belfast BT2 7DB, tel: 01232-230666.

Methodist Homes for the Aged / Methodist Homes Housing Association Limited

Epworth House
Stuart Street
Derby DE1 2EQ
Tel: 01332-296200
Fax: 01332-296925

Contact

Various sections for volunteering opportunities – please specify interest when contacting Head Office; Personnel Section for employment opportunities

Main Activities

Methodist Homes for the Aged is a registered charity, set up in 1943, which provides a range of accommodation and care services based on Christian principles, open to all elderly people in need, whatever their beliefs. Methodist Homes provides care for 2,500 elderly people in 39 homes, 27 sheltered housing schemes and twenty Live at Home schemes throughout the UK. A national organisation, Methodist Homes has local support groups in England, Scotland and Wales. It also has links with and welcomes visitors from caring Christian organisations in other parts of the world, and exchanges ideas and information.

Opportunities for Volunteers

At least 1,300 volunteers help in the homes, schemes and the community at large in various ways. Their work includes administrative support, counselling, fundraising, advocacy, and helping with day centre and drop-in projects. More are needed, throughout the year, especially for befriending elderly people and for a variety of voluntary tasks. Certain skills may sometimes be needed for specific tasks eg local treasurer or property steward. Regular support and training are available. Volunteers are recruited ad hoc on application, through volunteer bureaux and local media, and via local churches, especially Methodist. Commitment can be from as little as half an hour upwards. Travel expenses are paid. Local homes or schemes may be contacted direct.

Opportunities for Employment

Opportunities arise throughout the year in both head office and the various homes/schemes in various skill areas. Methodist Homes employs 430 full-time and 850 part-time staff. Senior staff are recruited through head office, while junior care, domestic and kitchen staff are recruited through the individual homes/schemes. Skills needs vary according to the post. Jobs are advertised in the national and local press, professional journals (Care Weekly, Community Care), the Methodist Recorder, and job centres. The organisation is an equal opportunities employer.

Further Information

The Annual Report, a list of local groups and various leaflets, including on the individual homes/schemes, are published.

National Benevolent Fund for the Aged (NBFA)

1 Leslie Grove Place
Croydon CR0 6TJ
Tel: 0181-688 6655
Fax: 0181-688 1616

Contact

Mrs J Wilkinson, Director

Main Activities

NBFA works to support the housebound elderly by providing free group holidays, outings and various kinds of equipment (eg emergency alarms, Transcutaneous Electrical Nerve Stimulation - TENS - machines) as necessary. It also runs an advisory service. Set up in 1958 it is a UK-wide agency with local branches. Annual budget is approximately £200,000.

Opportunities for Volunteers

Two volunteers are used in head office but, as part of a new venture, NBFA is anxious to recruit volunteers to run support groups all over the UK, as well as to help with administration and fundraising. Some training is offered. Recruitment is ad hoc on application. Commitment of half a day a week over three months is desirable but NBFA is flexible. Travel expenses are offered. Volunteers are regarded as important not only to the smooth running of the office, but also in continuing the benefits of NBFA holidays through the NBFA holiday clubs.

Opportunities for Employment

With one full-time and one part-time staff member, opportunities rarely arise (only two people recruited in the last fifteen years). Any vacancies are advertised in the national press. An equal opportunities policy is being implemented.

Further Information

The Annual Report is available.

The Royal Agricultural Benevolent Institution

Shaw House
27 West Way
Oxford OX2 0QH
Tel: 01865-724931
Fax: 01865-202025

Contact

Chief Executive

Main Activities

The Institution, set up in 1860, provides assistance for retired farmers, farm managers and their dependants. A national organisation (except for Scotland), it has a network of local branches in most counties, and residential homes at Bury St Edmunds (Suffolk) and Burnham on Sea. Annual budget is £1.4 million.

Opportunities for Volunteers

Voluntary Welfare Visitors visit beneficiaries to ensure that their needs are being met. More volunteers are required for this worthwhile and rewarding activity. It helps if they have some knowledge of farming, DSS benefits and allowances, and the needs of elderly and infirm people. Fundraising is also carried out by volunteers in the local branches, providing local publicity and thus helping to increase awareness of the Charity and its work within the local farming community. Their roles are essential.

Opportunities for Employment

There are 70 staff and opportunities arise from time to time.

Further Information

Annual Report, leaflet and list of local groups available.

The Royal Surgical Aid Society (RSAS)

47 Great Russell Street
London WC1B 3PA
Tel: 0171-637 4577

Contact
The Warden of each Home (see list below)

Main Activities
Runs four care homes for the physically frail and disabled elderly. Aims to raise care standards nationally through example, training and awards.

Opportunities for Volunteers
Volunteers can become members of the 'Friends' who are attached to each of the Homes. They help to organise fundraising events, day-trips and other activities for the residents. Homes should be contacted directly. For Worcestershire (Droitwich) tel: 01905-772710. For Sussex (Crowborough) tel: 01892-654027. For Derbyshire (near Matlock) tel: 01629-534205. For Kent (Sevenoaks) tel: 01732-741488.

Opportunities for Employment
No information available.

Further Information
Annual Report and other information available from Head Office.

Semi Care Trust (Support the Elderly Mentally Infirm)

43 Ducie Road
Barton Hill, Bristol BS5 0AX
Tel: 0117-952 5325

Contact
Oliver Holder, General Secretary

Main Activities
SEMI provides a respite service for those who care for sufferers from Alzheimer's Disease or associated illnesses. Also provides a sitting service, day care centre and counselling. Bristol based organisation. Annual budget is £220,000.

Opportunities for Volunteers
There are no volunteers currently.

Opportunities for Employment
There are twelve members of staff and 100 paid sitters. Recruits need to have a caring attitude and a knowledge of nursing if possible. Training is provided. Jobs are advertised in job centres, hospitals, shops and post offices.

Further Information
Annual Report and general information available.

Sheffield Community Transport (SCT), see Social Welfare

The Sons of Divine Providence

25 Lower Teddington Road
Hampton Wick
Kingston-upon-Thames KT1 4HB
Tel: 0181-977 5130

Contact
M Healy

Main Activities
Provides day and residential services for people who are elderly and people with learning difficulties. A national organisation with eleven local branches, especially active in Greater London, East Anglia and the North West. Also has links with similar organisations in various countries overseas, including Jordan, Kenya, Russia and Poland. Annual budget is £3 million.

Opportunities for Volunteers
Volunteers are needed to undertake care work in the residential homes, where experience is preferred, and in head office. Small numbers of committed volunteers are regarded as very helpful. Minimum commitment is flexible. Volunteer allowance and travel expenses are offered.

Opportunities for Employment
There are over 100 staff. Between ten and

twenty are recruited on average each year. Jobs are advertised in the local papers and job centres.

Further Information

Annual Report and brochures available.

Environment & Conservation

The opportunities for volunteering in environment and/or conservation work are diverse and considerable. They range from working to stop pollution to helping conserve wildlife; from campaigning to change official policy to taking local action to plant community woodland. You can become involved in global issues or local ones; you can contribute your time by volunteering actively through working on practical conservation projects or by volunteering from your own home through writing letters as part of a campaign.

Projects requiring active physical involvement include repairing footpaths, building dry stone walls, cutting marsh hay, being a warden or guide in a nature reserve, or greening derelict urban land. As long as you are fit and capable, age doesn't matter, and experience isn't necessary as training courses and other practical help are usually available. Thus you can learn new skills, perhaps a traditional craft. Courses include woodland management, coracle building, emergency first aid, successful leadership, and fundraising for conservation. Some opportunities are short-term or occasional; others need regular, consistent commitment. You can be involved every weekend or just once a year. Various organisations offer conservation working holidays of various lengths, in many different kinds of accommodation, both in the UK and overseas, and for all types of people including those with special needs and families. The entries below illustrate the wide range of opportunities.

Access Committee for England, *see Disability*

Action with Communities in Rural England (ACRE)

Somerford Court
Somerford Road
Cirencester
Gloucestershire GL7 1TW
Tel: 01285-653477
Fax: 01285-654537

Contact
Individual Rural Community Councils (RCCs)

Main Activities
A national charity and association of 38 Rural Community Councils (RCCs), ACRE works through the RCCs in each county to regenerate rural communities in England, achieve rural community development and improve the lives of rural people. Methods include promoting self-help and local initiatives. ACRE, which was established in 1987, also represents the views of the RCCs, provides advice and information of various kinds, and supports the work of Rural Voice. Each of the member RCCs acts as a local branch. ACRE and the RCCs welcome sponsorship and donations. ACRE also has partnerships with other rural organisations, and membership of the European Carrefour network.

Opportunities for Volunteers
Volunteers are actively recruited through the RCCs which, as local branches, use volunteers and should be contacted direct. ACRE itself does not generally use volunteers.

Opportunities for Employment
No information provided

Further Information
The Annual Report, a general pamphlet, a list of local groups and a full publications catalogue are available on request. RCCs also have their own publicity material and information.

British Trust for Conservation Volunteers (BTCV)

36 St Mary's Street
Wallingford, Oxfordshire OX10 0EU
Tel: 01491-839766
Fax: 01491-839646

Contact
The Information Officer at the above address

Main Activities
Set up in 1959, BTCV is the UK's leading practical conservation charity supporting the activities of over 84,000 volunteers in environmental action to improve the environment. A national network of over 90 field offices throughout England, Wales and Northern Ireland organises thousands of projects each year, from improving access to some of the country's most valued landscapes to creating a city wildlife garden or planting trees in a community woodland. In addition BTCV also runs a wide range of environmental training courses and conservation working holidays both in the UK and as far afield as Brazil and Japan. BTCV also runs a schools membership service, and provides advice and support to over 1,400 local groups and communities. It has links with similar organisations in Europe and North America. Annual income £6.8 million (March 1994).

Opportunities for Volunteers
Each year around 84,000 volunteers are equipped and trained to work on thousands of environmental projects. Opportunities exist in both head office and the local branches. Over 500 Volunteer Officers support the work of local staff and volunteers. This is an excellent way to gain experience for a career in the environmental field, supporting the activities of a field officer by leading conservation projects and organising

working holidays or training courses. Volunteers also help with administration, fundraising and publicity. BTCV could not exist without the vital support volunteers give in running the organisation. Recruitment is usually through local publicity such as posters, leaflets and the media. Among the desirable skills needed are conservation experience, fundraising and publicity. There is no minimum commitment for volunteers on weekday or weekend projects. However Volunteer Officers are expected to make a commitment of between three and 12 months.

Opportunities for Employment
BTCV employs over 190 full-time staff. Posts are advertised in the local press and The Guardian. An information pack on how to become a volunteer officer is available from the above address.

Further Information
The Annual Report, a publications catalogue, various pamphlets, and The Conserver, a quarterly magazine for members, are available. A list of local groups is available from each BTCV field office. Outside England contact the following:

Scotland - SCP (Scottish Conservation Projects), Balallan House, 24 Allan Park, Stirling FK8 2QG, tel: 01786-79697

Wales - BTCV, St David's House, New Road, Newtown, Powys SY16 1RB, tel: 01686-628600

Northern Ireland - CVNI, 137 University Street, Belfast BT7 1HP, 01232-322862

British Trust for Ornithology (BTO)

The National Centre for Ornithology
The Nunnery, Thetford
Norfolk IP24 2PU
Tel: 01842-750050
Fax: 01842-750030

Contact
Paul Green, membership unit, for volunteering; Andy Elvin, Director of Services, for employment opportunities

Main Activities
BTO promotes and encourages the wider understanding, appreciation and conservation of British wild birds, through scientific studies using the combined skills and enthusiasm of its members, other bird watchers and staff. Set up in 1933, BTO has numerous projects covering much of the UK. A national body, there are 120 volunteer regional representatives and groups, and a membership scheme. Various collaborative projects are also undertaken with European organisations. Annual budget is £1.5 million.

Opportunities for Volunteers
Head office employs a few and there are over 20,000 in the regional groups. Volunteers are needed throughout the year, UK-wide, to take part in information gathering, especially surveys. They are vital to the BTO since they gather most of the information which the staff analyses and which forms the basis for most of the organisation's work. A knowledge of and interest in birds is needed. Training is usually informal, but there are established training programmes for bird ringers. Recruitment is by application (phone or write) to the BTO, but mainly through membership and existing volunteers. BTO attracts volunteers by maximising publicity on projects and surveys, and actively encouraging staff and regional representatives, bird clubs, observatories and other interested groups. There is no minimum

commitment required. No remuneration is offered.

Opportunities for Employment
Those recruited include scientific staff who are usually graduates. Posts are advertised in specialist journals eg New Scientist, for scientific staff, and in national and/or local press for others. BTO has 59 full-time staff.

Further Information
Annual Report, list of local groups, careers and general leaflets, and numerous publications are available.

Campaign for Nuclear Disarmament (CND)

162 Holloway Road
London N7 8DQ
Tel: 0171-700 2393
Fax: 0171-700 2357

Contact
Ms Fiona Renny, Volunteers Organiser

Main Activities
CND works for international peace and complete disarmament, and for the redirection of resources now devoted to militarism to the real needs of the human community. It undertakes local and national campaigning and lobbying. A UK-wide organisation set up in 1958, it has regional offices in Scotland, Wales and Ireland, plus various local groups, and contacts with peace movements worldwide.

Opportunities for Volunteers
CND uses volunteers for administrative work, fundraising, and information and press work. They are particularly needed when a big campaign is organised. The play a very important role in the day to day business of the organisation, which wouldn't function without them. The skills needed depend on the job eg wordprocessing, proof reading, conference organising, etc. Recruitment is through application and in-house means. All prospective volunteers are sent an information pack with application form. There is no set time commitment, but most volunteers work at least one day a week. Travel and lunch expenses are offered.

Opportunities for Employment
With eight full-time and two part-time staff, annual recruitment varies greatly. Any posts are advertised in job centres, libraries, The Guardian and The Voice. Recruits need sympathy with the aims of CND. An equal opportunities policy is being implemented.

Further Information
Pamphlets and magazines, a list of local groups and the Annual Report are available.

Capital Transport Campaign

3rd Floor, Walkden House
10 Melton Street
London NW1 2EJ
Tel: 0171-388 2489/6902
Fax: 0171-388 7632

Contact
The Director

Main Activities
Campaigns to defend and improve public transport in London. The work includes campaign initiatives, lobbying politicians and transport operators, research, producing information and a bimonthly newsletter, and extensive media work. Founded in 1983, the Campaign is organised on a Greater London regional basis with individual and organisation (350) affiliates and subscribers, and the support of some local authorities (eight in early 1995). It also has some ad hoc exchanges of information with overseas organisations. Annual budget is £60,000.

Opportunities for Volunteers
The Campaign has taken on one

volunteer for two days a week (between ten and 16 hours) who carries out valuable back-up research and attends various public inquiries, press conferences, etc. Any such volunteer(s) must be able to work on their own initiative, and be able to understand and communicate policy. Travel expenses are offered. The Campaign does not expect to increase the number of volunteers currently.

Opportunities for Employment

One full-time and two part-time members of staff are employed. The organisation operates an Equal Opportunities Policy and all job vacancies must be filled in compliance with it. An application form must be completed. Any recruitment depends on vacancies. The skills needed include the ability to assess and interpret data, formulate demands, carry out research, produce written information, and plan and carry out campaigning initiatives. Job positions are advertised in newspapers – The Guardian and The Voice – and in Capital mailings.

Further Information

The Annual Report, various leaflets and briefings, and copies of the Capital Transport Bulletin (£1) are available.

Cathedral Camps

Manor House, High Birstwith
Harrogate, North Yorkshire HG3 2LG
Tel: 01423-770385

Contact

Chris Bent, Administrator/Booking Secretary at 16 Glebe Avenue, Flitwick, Bedfordshire MK45 1HS, tel/fax: 01525-716237

Main Activities

Set up in 1981, the organisation helps to preserve the great national heritage of cathedrals. Undertakes the important jobs of conservation and restoration of cathedrals and their environments,

including tasks which hitherto have been postponed due to lack of resources. Gives volunteers the opportunity to join together in a rewarding activity for the benefit of others, to make new friends, and to have an enjoyable working holiday in a cathedral environment. A national organisation, it covers cathedrals throughout the UK. Annual income is around £91,000.

Opportunities for Volunteers

The cathedral camps, which run from July to September, are organised for volunteers to engage in a wide variety of conservation and project work, often with professional conservators. The organisation, which relies on volunteers for all its camps, is keen to attract more. Disabled people are also welcome. Recruitment is through an annual brochure which is circulated to all sources of education for over 16's. Minimum commitment is the duration of a camp - four and a half working days. No remuneration is offered and a fee of £39.00 is asked for.

Opportunities for Employment

There are no opportunities for employment.

Further Information

The Annual Report and a comprehensive brochure with application form (from January each year) are available.

Centre for Alternative Technology (C.A.T.)

Machynlleth
Powys SY20 9AZ
Tel: 01654-702400

Contact

Rick Dance

Main Activities

C.A.T. promotes practical ideas and information on sustainable technologies through an education/display centre. Runs Alternative Technology Association.

Provides residential courses, mail order, information and consultancy. The Annual Budget is £1 million.

Opportunities for Volunteers

Residential and non-residential volunteers are needed to give help with conservation projects and to do maintenance and administrative work. Jobs, in the local area only, include information, gardening, building and engineering. Previous relevant experience is useful. However, short-term volunteers do not require any particular skills, but long term volunteers need knowledge/experience of the field of work eg engineering.

Minimum commitment is 40 hours a week for either one to two weeks or for at least six months. Volunteers are most needed between March and September. They contribute significantly to getting the work done, and are a means of reaching people, especially young people, in some depth. However, C.A.T. often has more applicants than it can cater for and needs more resources to enable it to improve supervision and facilities.

Opportunities for Employment

There are 21 full-time and nine part-time staff. Approximately two people are recruited each year. There is often a need for extra summer season help in the restaurant. Jobs are advertised in local media and job centres or The Guardian and specialist journals as appropriate. Speculative applications are also welcomed.

Further Information

A 'Users Guide' to C.A.T. is available on request.

Chelsea Physic Garden

66 Royal Hospital Road
London SW3 5HS
Tel: 0171-352 5646

Contact

Sue Minter, Curator

Main Activities

The Chelsea Physic Garden, which was set up in 1673, was opened to the public in 1983 (annually from April to October). It is dedicated to botanical research and education - of especial interest are rare plants and those used medicinally. There is an active friends organisation and the annual turnover is £225, 000.

Opportunities for Volunteers

There are 80 volunteers who carry out administrative work, management trustee roles, advice giving, and projects eg computer in-putting and updating. Recruitment is via REACH or local networks. Guides, who need to have good people skills and a clear voice are currently needed for work during the summer months. Horticultural volunteers must have good experience/aptitude and are interviewed by the Head Gardener. Minimum commitment is four hours per month over a period of eight months.

Opportunities for Employment

There are six full-time and three part-time staff. One student gardener is recruited annually on a yearly placement. Posts are advertised in Horticultural Week.

Further Information

The Annual Report, guidebooks and volunteer information are available.

Civic Trust
(Community Action)

35 King Street
Bristol BS1 4DZ
Tel: 0117-926 8893

Contact
Philip Bewly, Regional Officer and
Director of Community Action Unit

Main Activities
The Civic Trust was founded in 1957 and
began Community Action in 1993. The
Trust supports local projects undertaken
by local amenity societies, community
groups and others. It runs community
action programmes for the Employment
Service in Greater London, and the North
and South West, matching unemployed
participants to projects and providing
management training. It also raises
awareness and standards in the built environment, makes annual awards and
helps to develop a community voice and
concern. A national/English organisation
it is affiliated to 950 local amenity
societies.

Opportunities for Volunteers
Volunteers are needed in local projects to
which they are very important since the
community action programme is in-
tended to supplement voluntary action.
They are also often needed in the three
month run-up to National Environment
Week in May. Office skills, word processing, good telephone manner, experience
with dealing with the public and infinite
patience are useful qualities. Training
opportunities are available.

Opportunities for Employment
There are 40 staff.

Further Information
Publications list available. Associate trusts
(who may use volunteers from time to
time) include: North East Civic Trust,
Floor 4, MEA House, Ellison Place,
Newcastle-upon-Tyne; Civic Trust for

Wales, 4th floor, Empire House, Mount
Stuart Square, Cardiff CF1 6DN.

Council for the Protection
of Rural England (CPRE)

Warwick House
25 Buckingham Palace Road
London SW1W 0PP
Tel: 0171-976 6433
Fax: 0171-976 6373

Contact
Joanne Cross for volunteering in regions
and counties, Jane Lee for the London area

Main Activities
CPRE campaigns for a living and beauti-
ful countryside in England. It also acts as
a centre for advice and information, and
aims to influence public opinion and
awareness. It is active through its 44
county branches (one in each county), and
140 district committees, as well as nationally. Membership is open to all. Annual
budget £1.9 million.

Opportunities for Volunteers
Volunteers are vital to CPRE's work. There
are about 1,500 nationally and they are
needed all year round for various jobs in
head office and the local branches. These
include monitoring planning opportunities, administration (eg stuffing
envelopes!), fundraising, conservation,
and specific projects eg working on public inquiries and campaigns eg transport,
and contributing to local plans. Recruitment is ad hoc by application to CPRE.
There is no minimum commitment and
expenses may be paid.

Opportunities for Employment
CPRE employs 36 full-time staff and
recruits occasionally.

Further Information
Annual Report, list of local groups and
publications list available. Sister
organisations are the Campaign for the
Protection of Rural Wales (CPRW), the

Association for the Protection of Rural Scotland (APRS) and the Ulster Society for the Protection of the Countryside (USPC).

Earthwatch Europe

Belsyre Court
57 Woodstock Road
Oxford OX2 6HU
Tel: 01865-311600

Contact
S Moyes or V Uden

Main Activities
Earthwatch aims to improve human understanding of the planet, the diversity of its inhabitants and the processes that affect the quality of life on earth.

Opportunities for Volunteers
Approximately ten volunteers help in skilled/professional areas in the office and Earthwatch Europe is currently seeking more support. In addition over 700 are recruited to assist scientists in their field research in various overseas countries. Research Volunteers assist for two weeks and pay a part of the expedition costs and their travel expenses as well as giving their time free.

Opportunities for Employment
There are twelve full-time and five part-time staff. Computer skills and overseas languages are useful. Vacancies are advertised in Earthwatch magazine and newspapers. A formal Equal Opportunities Policy is in place.

Further Information
Annual Report, Enquiries Pack, Members Pack and follow-up literature are available on request.

Free Form Arts Trust Limited

38 Dalston Lane
Hackney, London E8 3AZ
Tel: 0171-249 3394
Fax: 0171-249 8499

Contact
Barbara Wheeler-Early, Associate Director

Main Activities
The Trust, founded in 1969, develops projects which improve the environment to benefit all members of the local community. It facilitates local involvement with inner city regeneration. Main project locations are Hackney and North Tyneside but works nationally through partnership approach. The Trust also has links with European groups, including ATD Quart Monde in France. Annual budget is £500,000.

Opportunities for Volunteers
Volunteers are needed to do research and information gathering. Previous experience useful. Lunch and travel expenses offered. Apply in writing with a CV.

Opportunities for Employment
16 full-time and five part-time staff are employed. There are also opportunities for project based employment and freelance work.

Further Information
Annual Report, information pack and videos available on request, enclosing an SAE.

Friends of the Earth (FoE)

26-28 Underwood Street
London N1 7JQ
Tel: 0171-490 1555
Fax: 0171-490 0881

Contact
Cheryl Richardson, Personnel Officer
for both volunteering and employment
opportunities

Main Activities
Established in 1971, FoE is the UK's leading environmental pressure group
campaigning on a wide range of environmental issues to bring about changes in
policy and practice, and to raise public
awareness. FoE has a network of over 250
voluntary local groups throughout
England, Wales and Northern Ireland
working with local communities on issues
of environmental importance. It is also
part of FoE International, the largest
international network of national
environmental groups in the world.

Opportunities for Volunteers
Volunteers play a vital role throughout
FoE, including the London and regional
offices and the local groups. About 50
volunteers work in the London and
regional offices mainly carrying out
administrative support work. Volunteers
need to be genuinely interested in and
committed to FoE's work, have a flexible
approach, and be able to work both as
part of a team and on their own initiative. There are also some opportunities
for volunteers with specialist skills. Volunteers receive travel and lunch
expenses. Computer training and other
support is also available. A regular
committment of at least three days a
week is preferred. For further details and
an application form please send an SAE.
FoE also needs volunteers who want to
get involved in protecting the environment in their own area for its Local
Groups. If interested in volunteering in
your local area contact the FoE switchboard on 0171-490 1555 for details of the
nearest group.

Opportunities for Employment
FoE employs approximately 100 staff in a
wide range of roles: campaigning, research, fundraising, finance,
administration, information technology
(IT), publicity, etc. FoE is an equal opportunities employer and all permanent
vacancies are advertised externally mainly
in The Guardian or local newspapers.
Posts requiring specific technical or specialist knowledge and skills eg IT, research
or fundraising posts, are generally advertised in the relevant specialist journal. If
interested in working with FoE do not
send in speculative enquiries but look for
advertisements in the national press and
apply for vacancies as they are advertised.
For further information about working at
FoE, please send an SAE.

Further Information
Annual Review, list of local groups and
publications catalogue available. Sister
organisations:

FoE Cymru, 33 The Balcony, Castle
Arcade, Cardiff CR1 2BY

FoE Scotland, 70-72 Newhaven Road,
Edinburgh EH6 5QG, tel: 0131-554 9977

The Georgian Group

37 Spital Square
London E1 6DY
Tel: 0171-377 1722
Fax: 0171-247 3441

Contact
Mrs C Lightburn, Administrator

Main Activities
Set up in 1937 and covering England and
Wales, the Group is concerned with the
appreciation and conservation of Georgian
architecture. It aims also to increase
public knowledge of the period and its
buildings. National, except for Scotland,

with three regional groups. Annual budget £200,000.

Opportunities for Volunteers

A few volunteers are used in the central office for administrative and project work. Recruitment is by application and CV direct to the Group. There is no minimum commitment and no remuneration.

Opportunities for Employment

The Group has a small team - eight full-time and two part-time staff. Vacancies seldom occur. An equal opportunities policy is being implemented.

Further Information

Annual Report, list of local groups and publications list available. In Scotland contact: Architectural Heritage Society of Scotland, The Glasite Meeting House, 33 Barony Street, Edinburgh EH3 6NX, tel: 0131-557 0019.

Green Light Trust (GLT)

Lawshall Green
Bury St Edmunds
Suffolk IP29 4QJ
Tel: 01284-828754
Fax: 01284-827078

Contact

Sue Copping, Administrator

Main Activities

Set up in 1988, Green Light Trust (GLT) specialises in environmental education through creative action. It is involved in grass roots projects planting community woodland in Suffolk, and in assisting the people of the East Sepik River area of Papua New Guinea to preserve their culture and their rain forest through sustainable and appropriate development. Its educational programme includes workshops and dramatic productions for both adults and children held throughout the UK. Based in Suffolk, it is developing a national network as well as international links, including with

organisations concerned with and in the developing world, such as the World Wide Fund for Nature (WWFN), East Sepik Council of Women (ESCOW), and Individual and Community Rights Advocacy Forum Inc. (ICRAF). Annual budget is around £35,000.

Opportunities for Volunteers

Volunteers are integral to GLT's work. Essential in such project work as local tree planting and maintenance, they also provide administrative support and undertake fundraising. Recruited ad hoc, on application and through in-house recruitment and induction schemes, volunteers are paid lunch and certain out-of-pocket expenses. Contact the administrator for details.

Opportunities for Employment

Two part-time staff are employed. The Trust is seeking recruits for fundraising work.

Further Information

The Annual Report together with brochures and flyers are available by post on request.

Greenpeace

Canonbury Villas
London N1 2PN
Tel: 0171-354 5100
Fax: 0171-696 0012

Contact

Volunteers Manager for volunteering opportunities; Personnel Assistant for employment opportunities

Main Activities

Greenpeace is involved in environmental campaigning to protect the planet against pollution and exploitation. Organised nationally with 200 local support groups. Sister organisation in Amsterdam.

Opportunities for Volunteers

Between head office and the branches, Greenpeace uses over 2,000 volunteers.

They undertake administrative support and fundraising, and have to be self-motivated and able to work in a team. Recruitment is through a variety of methods: in-house, by application (phone or write), via volunteer bureaux, and as a result of external advertising. Minimum commitment is five hours a week over three months. Induction and appropriate support are given. Travel and lunch expenses are paid.

Opportunities for Employment
Greenpeace recruits around six staff each year, through a set procedure (advertising/application/short-listing/interview). Posts are advertised in The Guardian, The Voice and appropriate trade journals. There is an equal opportunities policy in place. 78 full-time and four part-time staff are employed.

Further Information
Literature on Greenpeace generally and on specific campaigns is published. A list of local groups is available.

Groundwork

National Office
85-87 Cornwall Street
Birmingham B3 3BY
Tel: 0121-236 8565
Fax: 0121-236 7356

Contact
Stephen Grundy, Marketing Manager

Main Activities
Groundwork is a national network of local trusts empowering and enabling all sectors of the community to improve and care for the environment through partnership projects. It is the leading UK environmental partnership organisation active in 120 towns and cities throughout the country. Groundwork delivers high quality, cost effective programmes which help people improve the environment and economic prospects of their area.

Opportunities for Volunteers
Groundwork uses volunteers for a wide range of work, including in local branches. Contact direct – through national office or local telephone directories – for details.

Opportunities for Employment
Local branches occasionally recruit staff. Posts are advertised in the local and national press.

Further Information
Information packs and a list of Groundwork addresses are available.

Inland Waterways Association (IWA)

114 Regents Park Road
London NW1 8UQ
Tel: 0171-586 2510/2556

Contact
Office Manager

Main Activities
IWA promotes the conservation, restoration and development of inland waterways for the fullest commercial and recreational uses. It represents waterways users nationally to British Waterways and the government. Set up in 1946 it covers England and Wales, where there are 34 local branches, and offers individual membership and corporate membership to other waterway bodies. It is also linked with canal societies abroad.

Opportunities for Volunteers
Volunteers make the greatest contribution by volume to the IWA's work. They are needed to give administrative support at Head Office, and to be branch/regional officers and waterway 'navvies' assisting with canal camps and digs. Help is also needed with the annual Canal Clean-up as well as specific waterway restoration schemes. Training is offered as appropriate to the job. Volunteers should write to the Office Manager.

Opportunities for Employment

There are five full-time staff members and one part-time.

Further Information

Annual Report, list of local groups and fact sheets are available (send an SAE). For Scotland, contact: Scottish Inland Waterways Association, 16 Fern Avenue, Lenzie by Glasgow.

Kent Trust for Nature Conservation

Tyland Barn, Sandling
Maidstone, Kent ME14 3BD
Tel: 01622-662012
Fax: 01622-671390

Contact

Ms Claire Rintoul, Volunteer Co-ordinator for volunteering; head office re employment

Main Activities

The Trust seeks to ensure a future for the wildlife and countryside of Kent through effective conservation work. Its main areas of activity are conservation, education, marketing, publicity and fundraising. For example, it manages over 40 nature reserves. Set up in 1958, it is an independent organisation with 20 local support groups throughout the Kent area. It is also an affiliated member of the Royal Society for Nature Conservation (RSNC). Similar independent wildlife trusts, 47 in all, exist throughout the UK. The Kent Trust's annual budget is £677,000.

Opportunities for Volunteers

Volunteers are vital to the Trust's work - it could not operate without them. Opportunities exist both indoors and outdoors, close to people's homes and further afield. About 50 volunteers work in head office and between 550 and 650 in the branches. They organise local groups, undertake management and act as trustees, as well as being involved in administrative support, publicity, fundraising and active conservation work. They also help with various projects including road verge wardening and education eg running wildlife groups for children. More are welcome and needed, for a wide range of tasks, especially with local groups. Apart from on-going work, visitor centres need volunteers during summer. Recruitment is by application, through in-house schemes including advertisements in Trust publications, and by active volunteers recruiting others. Application forms are sent on request. There is no minimum commitment and expenses are offered: many volunteers donate these back. An induction course and volunteer co-ordinator support are available.

Opportunities for Employment

There are 18 full-time and eight part-time staff. Vacancies occur occasionally and the Trust may recruit one new member of staff a year. Seasonal opportunities also occur for wardens on reserves. The skills required depend on the post. Positions are advertised in The Guardian and the local press. The Trust is developing an equal opportunities policy.

Further Information

The Annual Report, a list of local groups and a publications list are available on request.

Land Use Volunteers (LUV)

Goulds Ground, Vallis Way
Frome, Somerset BA11 3DW
Tel: 01373-464782
Fax: 01373-464782

Contact

Mr J Gaskell, Co-ordinator

Main Activities

Set up in 1981, LUV selects and places qualified and experienced horticulturalists/therapists in residential projects for people with disabilities. It operates in various regional areas in England (North West, South East and the Midlands) and in Wales.

Opportunities for Volunteers
Without volunteers many of the projects could not establish horticultural therapy projects initially. Volunteers with a qualification or experience in either horticulture or therapy are needed. New graduates are especially welcome. Minimum commitment is between six and twelve months. Volunteer allowance and board and lodging provided. References are needed.

Opportunities for Employment
Many LUVs are offered full time paid employment as horticultural therapists at their project after the period of volunteering has finished.

Further Information
Annual Report and information leaflets available. For Scotland, contact: Horticultural Volunteers in Scotland, Gilmerton Community Centre, 4 Drum Street, Edinburgh, Scotland EH17 8QE.

London Wildlife Trust (LWT)

80 York Way
London N1 9AG
Tel: 0171-278 6612
Fax: 0171-837 8060

Contact
Mr Graham Turnbull, Director

Main Activities
LWT fights to save Greater London's green spaces, and promotes nature conservation and public awareness of the importance of having wildlife in urban areas. A London-wide body, the Trust works through a local group structure with a central staff team, plus staffed projects. It has 55 nature reserves and 28 local support groups. Membership is available. It also has links with European organisations such as Eurosite.

Opportunities for Volunteers
Most of the Trust's activities are carried out by volunteers. Over 4,000 person hours a year are put in by volunteers in administrative and conservation work in the Trust's central office and the local groups. The Trust actively seeks volunteers to help with managing and caring for habitats, educating the public, liaising with the media, and providing administrative support for campaigning. Recruitment is ad hoc by application. There is no minimum commitment. Travel and lunch expenses are offered, but only for whole days worked.

Opportunities for Employment
LWT may recruit a few staff each year. Special skills needed include those in business administration and ecology. Vacancies are advertised in the national press based on an equal opportunities policy. There are twenty full-time and five part-time staff.

Further Information
Annual Report and information leaflets are published. Donations for these are appreciated. A colour magazine is available three times yearly to members. List of local groups also available.

The Nansen Society

Redcastle Station
Muir of Ord
Ross-shire IV6 7RX
Tel: 01463-871255
Fax: 01463-870258

Contact
Diana Bayly, Information Officer

Main Activities
The Nansen Society offers disadvantaged young people the chance to find direction through training in a variety of environmental projects, with many of its trainees being residential.

Opportunities for Volunteers
Volunteers are very important. Disadvantaged youngsters are trained on a 1:1 basis which could not be done without volunteer help. Working with young international volunteers is very much part of the Nansen philosophy. Volunteers teach practical skills eg social skills, woodwork, outdoor education, gardening, mechanics. Experience with special needs youngsters and/or conservation gardening experience would be useful. Residential volunteers offer 40 hours a week for a minimum of three months and receive full board and lodging. Training and support are given as needed.

Opportunities for Employment
There are no employment opportunities.

Further Information
Annual report, leaflet, notes for volunteers and Development Report are available on request.

National Federation of City Farms (NFCF)

93 Whitby Road
Brislington
Bristol BS4 3QF
Tel: 0117-971 9109

Contact
Catherine Burnett, Office Manager

Main Activities
Registered as a charity in 1980, NFCF is a support and development organisation for community-run City Farming and Gardening groups. It works with people involved with the regeneration and development of our cities. A national membership organisation, it has about 70 member City Farms and Community Gardens which are independent from it. It is linked with the European Federation of City Farms. Annual budget is £102,000.

Opportunities for Volunteers
Volunteers are very important to both NFCF and its members. They are needed at Head Office to give administrative support, and undertake research and specific projects that staff cannot do. Computer experience, graphic design skills and ability to organise media events are very welcome. Initiative and self-motivation are also important. An induction and support package is offered. Volunteers are also welcome on City Farms. Contact them direct (list available from Head Office. Enclose an SAE)

Opportunities for Employment
There are two full-time and four part-time staff. Posts have been frozen for the last two years.

Further Information
Annual Report, list of local groups and leaflets available.

The National Trust for Places of Historic Interest and Natural Beauty

36 Queen Anne's Gate
London SW1H 9AS and
33 Sheep Street
Cirencester, Glos GL7 1QW

London:
Tel: 0171-222 9251
Fax: 0171-222 9251

Cirencester:
Tel: 01285-651818
Fax: 01285-657935

Contact
National Volunteers Adviser and Regional Volunteers Co-ordinators (RVCs) at Cirencester as above, tel: 01285-651818 for volunteering; Personnel Department in head and regional offices re employment – written enquiries only accepted (send sae).

Main Activities

Set up in 1895, the National Trust is concerned with the conservation of 300 historic houses, the countryside and coastlines of beauty for the benefit of the nation in England, Wales and Northern Ireland. It also provides access to these for the public. The Trust owns and protects a wide range of buildings, gardens and coastal areas. Has over two million members (1994). Organised nationally, the Trust is decentralised, with sixteen regional offices and 230 local support groups.

Opportunities for Volunteers

Volunteers are extremely important to the Trust, its 'lifeblood'. They work in partnership with Trust staff to achieve the organisation's objectives. Their efforts both help to contain costs and enable jobs to be undertaken which could not otherwise be afforded. 28,000 volunteers are involved each year at the Trust's houses and countryside properties, in offices and local communities. There are over 140 different categories of volunteering ranging from unskilled outdoor conservation work to tasks requiring professional skills and experience. Energy and enthusiasm are essential. Most volunteers work direct to National Trust staff, but some prefer to work through 70 self-administered volunteer groups. Popular tasks include being room stewards at houses, lecturers, photographers, wardens, accountants, surveyors and helping with events. The Trust has an annual programme of week-long working holidays in environmental conservation, and opportunities for long term volunteers, sometimes with accommodation. More volunteers aged over 16 years, from all backgrounds, are welcome. They are recruited by various methods: on application to the appropriate Regional Volunteers Co-ordinator, through in-house news sheets, via National Trust members, and from advertisements in papers and on Ceefax. Induction and skills training are given. Minimum commitment is a day a fortnight, seasonal, on-going or long term. Travel and other agreed expenses are paid.

Opportunities for Employment

The Trust employs around 3,000 regular staff. Vacancy lists are issued to regional offices twice monthly for personal inspection only by non-Trust staff. Seasonal work opportunities also arise in Trust properties during the open season. Skill requirements vary widely depending on the post, from gardeners to housekeepers. Jobs may be advertised in the specialist press eg Building, Chartered Surveyor Weekly, and in local and/or national papers. Equal opportunities is an integral part of the recruitment procedures.

Further Information

The Annual Report and a wide range of leaflets and pamphlets on the work of the National Trust, including on volunteering and employment, are available (send sae). In Scotland contact: National Trust for Scotland, 5 Charlotte Street, Edinburgh EH2 4DU.

National Trust for Scotland

5 Charlotte Square
Edinburgh EH2 4DU
Tel: 0131-226 5922
Fax: 0131-243 9501

Contact

Jim Ramsay, Conservation Volunteers

Main Activities

Promotes the permanent preservation of lands and buildings in Scotland of historic or national interest or natural beauty. There are 29 local support groups.

Opportunities for Volunteers

Volunteers are required for guiding, conservation work, public speaking and fundraising. Training and support are provided. Travel expenses are offered.

Opportunities for Employment
There are 350 full-time and some part-time staff. About 1000 staff are taken on during the summer to work at various properties as guides, tearoom staff, rangers, gardeners, cleaners etc. Jobs are advertised in the national press, trade magazines, The Scotsman and The Herald as appropriate.

Further Information
Annual Report, Welcome Leaflet, Conservation Volunteer Leaflet and Guide to Properties available.

Neighbourhood Energy Action (NEA)

90-92 Pilgrim Street
Newcastle-upon-Tyne NE1 6SG
Tel: 0191-261 5677

Contact
William Gillis, Deputy Director, for employment opportunities

Main Activities
NEA aims at alleviating fuel poverty and at providing warm homes in low-income households (eg those of elderly, disabled people) through practical energy efficiency improvements. Covers England and Wales, but has membership from throughout the UK, and 180 affiliated organisations. Annual budget is £1.6 million.

Opportunities for Volunteers
NEA does not use volunteers itself, but can put those interested in touch with local groups.

Opportunities for Employment
About three people are employed each year, while consultants are recruited on an ad hoc basis. NEA has a full-time staff of 40 and is an equal opportunities employer. Any vacancies are advertised in The Guardian and the local press.

Further Information
The Annual Report, a list of local groups and a publications list are available on request. NEA produces a wide range of literature on social aspects of energy, including educational materials. A sister organisation is:

Energy Action Scotland, 21 West Nile Street, Glasgow G1 2PJ, tel: 0141-226 3064.

Notting Dale Urban Studies Centre, see Education

Open Spaces Society (OSS) (formally the Commons, Open Spaces and Footpaths Preservation Society)

25A Bell Street
Henley-on-Thames
Oxfordshire RG9 2BA
Tel: 01491-573535

Contact
Kate Ashbrook, General Secretary

Main Activities
The Society campaigns to protect and preserve common land, village greens, open spaces and public paths. It advises local authorities and the public on statutory rights and the law. It also manages and preserves open spaces which it acquires by gift or purchase. It has one main office, a network of seventeen local correspondents throughout England and Wales, and an annual budget of £165,000.

Opportunities for Volunteers
The OSS relies on voluntary support financially from subscriptions, donations, and legacies. Volunteers are also extremely important to the Society's work in other ways. They are used primarily in administrative support and conservation work. As local correspondents who report

back to the Society throughout the year, they have specialist knowledge of their own areas. All volunteers need a knowledge of the footpath network and the ability to interpret maps. Support and guidance is available from OSS staff. Recruitment is ad hoc through application to OSS and an interview. Minimum commitment is variable weekly, but needed over at least a year. Travel expenses are offered.

Opportunities for Employment
OSS has a small staff of four full-time and six part-time employees, and might recruit one person a year. Experience in environmental matters is preferred. Vacancies are advertised in the national press, based on an equal opportunities policy.

Further Information
Annual Report and publications list available.

Peace People Farm Project

Kilcranny House
21 Cranaugh Road
Coleraine
Tel: 01265-58353

Contact
Anne Cummings

Main Activities
Kilcranny House is a residential centre on a small organic farm, aiming to heal divisions between people and between people and the environment through the daily discipline of non-violence. The organisation was set up in 1985 and has a capacity of 24.

Opportunities for Volunteers
Three full-time residential volunteers provide support for the paid staff. Volunteers who have skills/interest in organic farming, group work, cooking and maintenance are needed from time to time, particularly during the summer

months. Accommodation and food are offered and the minimum commitment is three months full-time.

Opportunities for Employment
Approximately two people are recruited each year. The recruitment procedure is via Action for Community Employment, NI.

Further Information
Annual Report and free pamphlet Kilkranny House – the Farm Project are available.

Pedestrians Association

126 Aldersgate Street
London EC1A 4JQ
Tel: 0171- 490 0750

Contact
Mrs Felicity Rea, Secretary

Main Activities
Campaigns for improvements in pedestrian facilities and represents the interests of walkers to central and local government and the media.

Opportunities for Volunteers
Twelve local branches (which include Wales and Scotland) are run by volunteers. Fundraising, project work and administrative support are the main activities. A voluntary committee provides speakers and delegates to meetings.

Opportunities for Employment
There are no employment opportunities.

Further Information
'Walk', the journal of the Pedestrians Association is available.

Raleigh International, *see Overseas & the Developing World*

Royal Society for the Protection of Birds (RSPB)

The Lodge, Sandy
Bedfordshire SG19 2DL
Tel: 01767-680551
Fax: 01767-692365

Contact
Volunteer Unit

Main Activities
Set up in 1889, the RSPB raises funds for the conservation of birds and their habitat. It manages 120 nature reserves, and gives advice to local authorities and landowners. A UK-wide organisation, there are various regional offices, 176 local groups for adults and over 1200 for young people.

Opportunities for Volunteers
Volunteers are very important to the RSPB, with over 7,000 already helping. They are needed for a wide variety of work, in both head office and the local branches, including a Volunteer Wardening Scheme. Opportunities also exist in fundraising and conservation.

Opportunities for Employment
There are approximately 800 established staff. Vacancies arise from time to time. There are also approximately 180 seasonal wardening contracts per year.

Further Information
The Annual Report is available for a charge.

Scottish Conservation Projects Trust (SCP)

Balallan House
24 Allan Park
Stirling FK8 2QG
Tel: 01786-479697
Fax: 01786-465359

Contact
Nancy McEwan, Administrator

Main Activities
SCP involves people in improving the environment through practical conservation work. Set up in 1984, it runs over 80 Action Breaks each year as well as national training courses. A national organisation for Scotland, it has five area offices, over 60 affiliated community groups and two trading companies, Pathcraft Ltd and Training Craft Ltd. SCP also works in partnership with other environmental organisations, including UK 2000 Scotland, Scottish Natural Heritage and Forest Enterprise. A registered charity, it receives core funding from various organisations (eg the Scottish Office), but gets much of its income from fundraising, sponsorship and donations/bequests. The annual turnover/income is £2,037,000.

Opportunities for Volunteers
Nearly seven and a half thousand volunteers are involved; they provide the key to SCP's success. They carry out most of the practical work through Action Breaks and mid-week groups. There are also long-term volunteers both in the field and in offices, and voluntary field officers. Volunteers carry out many different types of work including organising local groups, administrative support, fundraising/public relations, research, and project work including residential conservation projects. In general they need knowledge of and an interest in conservation, although volunteer field officers require practical conservation experience and a

driving licence. Recruited ad hoc and by application, Action Break brochures, group publicity leaflets, advertisements and directory entries are used to attract volunteers. The time commitment required varies and various expenses and a volunteer allowance are paid. SCP actively seeks more volunteers year round, in both Head Office and local branches. The skills required depend on the work; in-house, on-the-job training is provided, as well as one free Action Break and one training course yearly.

Opportunities for Employment
Around 65 full-time and 12 part-time staff are employed together with contracted and seasonal staff. Recruitment varies as required but SCP regularly seeks seasonal field staff for leading Action Breaks. Recruits also need administrative, computer and general office skills. Jobs are advertised in the national press, the Glasgow Herald, The Scotsman and other newspapers, and also in-house. An equal opportunities policy operates.

Further Information
A variety of information is available including the Annual Report, Action Breaks and training brochures, posters, leaflets on conservation and a list of local groups.

Tidy Britain Group

The Pier
Wigan WN3 4EX
Tel: 01942-824620
Fax: 01942-824778

Contact
Dee Bingham

Main Activities
The Tidy Britain Group campaigns for a litter free Britain. Local action groups run various litter abatement and environmental improvement projects. The budget is £6 million.

Opportunities for Volunteers
Volunteer assistance is needed at Head Office on a casual basis and in the local action groups. Thousands of people take part in the National Spring Clean Campaign. Volunteers are especially needed in the Spring, Summer and Autumn.

Opportunities for Employment
There are 103 full-time staff. On average six people are recruited each year. Jobs are advertised in The Guardian, The Daily Telegraph and/or locally.

Further Information
Annual Report and other information is available.

Tim Lilley Fundraising Consultancy

33B Medina Villas
Hove, East Sussex BN3 2RN
Tel: 01273-730042

Contact
Nick Lever

Main Activities
The Tim Lilley Fundraising Consultancy trains and supports fundraisers working on house to house campaigns for various environmental and development charities.

Opportunities for Volunteers
Volunteer fundraisers are needed to raise funds by house to house collection. They are asked to start on a voluntary basis with a view to becoming a paid fundraiser. Minimum commitment is 20 hours per week. Travel and lunch expenses are offered. Full training and support are given.

Opportunities for Employment
Successful fundraisers become paid workers as posts become vacant. Jobs are advertised in the local press when a campaign is being set up.

Further Information
The training includes a course in

communications skills and stress management.

Transport 2000

Walkden House
10 Melton Street
London NW1 2EJ
Tel: 0171-388 8386
Fax: 0171-388 2481

Contact
Head Office

Main Activities
A UK-wide organisation set up in the mid-1970s, Transport 2000 campaigns for environmentally sensitive transport. There are 30 local groups and the annual budget is £100,000.

Opportunities for Volunteers
With few staff members, volunteers are very important. However, due to limited resources in space and staff time only a small pool of volunteers can be accommodated. Administrative support is particularly needed. Computer literacy and some understanding of the transport debate are both useful. Written enquiries about opportunities are preferred to phone calls.

Opportunities for Employment
There are four full-time staff and one part-time.

Further Information
The Annual Report is available as well as a list of local groups.

Trust for Urban Ecology (TRUE)

167 Rotherhithe Street
London SE15
Tel: 0171-237 9165
Fax: 0171-237 9165

Contact
Clifford Davy

Main Activities
The Trust promotes the development of knowledge and expertise in urban ecology and conservation. It provides advice on urban green spaces and raises awareness of nature in cities.

Opportunities for Volunteers
Administrative support, project work and conservation are undertaken by volunteers at 3 main development sites and various contract sites.

Opportunities for Employment
There are five staff.

Further Information
Information leaflets are available.

Wildfowl and Wetlands Trust (WWT)

Slimbridge
Gloucestershire GL2 7BT
Tel: 01453-890333
Fax: 01453-890827

Contact
Education Officer

Main Activities
WWT saves wetlands and conserves their wildlife and their wildfowl. A national, UK-wide organisation set up in 1946, it has eight regional centres with a ninth being developed in London. Through its Wetland Link Programme WWT also has links with similar wetland education centres around the world.

Opportunities for Volunteers
Volunteers are needed at all centres and

in a variety of roles: information giving, talks, working in the grounds, research, aviculture. They are regarded as tremendously important to the Trust's activities, particularly its educational work with 600,000 visitors each year. An interest in and committment to wildlife conservation, an enthusiastic attitude and an ability to pass on information accurately are useful qualities. Various specialist skills are needed in a wide range of areas, and volunteers are matched, skill for job.

Opportunities for Employment
Approximately 200 staff are based at eight centres. Advertisements for positions are placed in national newspapers.

Further Information
Annual Report available on request.

The Wildlife Trusts (formerly the Royal Society for Nature Conservation, RSNC)

The Green, Witham Park
Waterside South
Lincoln LN5 7JR
Tel: 01522-544400
Fax: 01522-511616

Contact
Thurstan Crockett

Main Activities
Promotes nature conservation, community action and environmental education nationwide. There are 47 Wildlife Trusts and 52 Urban Wildlife Groups in the Wildlife Trusts partnership. Annual budget is £1.9 million.

Opportunities for Volunteers
Volunteers are needed for a very wide remit of work, including conservation work, fundraising and to give administrative support.

Opportunities for Employment
There are 50 full-time staff at the national office and about 500 employees in the Wildlife Trusts partnership. Approximately 30-40 people are recruited across the UK annually. Jobs are advertised in The Guardian, New Scientist and locally where appropriate. Each Wildlife Trust has its own recruitment procedure.

Further Information
List of Trusts and publications available.

The Woodland Trust

Autumn Park, Dysart Road
Grantham, Lincs NG31 6LL
Tel: 01476-74297

Contact
Mrs Jacqui Bunce, Personnel Officer

Main Activities
The Trust acquires and manages native and broad-leaved woodland for its amenity, conservation and wildlife value. It also creates new woodland and is involved in the National Forest and Community Forest initiatives. A national organisation with regionally outposted staff responsible for the management of properties in their region. Annual budget is £6 million.

Opportunities for Volunteers
Occasional opportunities arise for volunteers to act as voluntary wardens and to take part in Community Woodland Groups. An interest in Woodland Conservation is important. Wardens are required to regularly visit their site. Potential volunteers should apply to the Woodland Operations Department.

Opportunities for Employment
There are 140 full-time staff with the Trust growing significantly every year. Opportunities include out-posted Woodland Officers who facilitate the acquisition and management of the Trust's woods, and are involved in the development of new woods. There are also administrative and managerial roles within the Head Office in Grantham in a wide range of disciplines

including marketing, sponsorship and public affairs. For further information and to register an interest, please contact the Personnel Section at the above address.

Further Information
Annual Report, list of community woodland groups and information leaflets available on request.

Yorkshire Sculpture Park, *see Museums, the Arts and Festivals*

Ethnic Minorities

Academy of Indian Dance, *see Museums, the Arts & Festivals*

The Asian Women's Resource Centre, *see Women*

Centre for Armenian Information and Advice (CAIA), *see Social Welfare*

Confederation of Indian Organisations (CIO)

5 Westminster Bridge Road
London SE1 7ZW
Tel: 0171-928 9889

Contact
The Director

Main Activities
The CIO is a national umbrella body for Asian voluntary organisations. It aims to raise awareness of issues and concerns of the Asian communities. It provides advice, information, resources and consultation to groups. Annual budget is approximately £80,000.

Opportunities for Volunteers
Volunteers provide vital assistance. They work on projects and give administrative support. Travel expenses are offered. There is a full induction programme.

Opportunities for Employment
There are three full-time members of staff. An equal opportunities policy is in place and posts are advertised in newsletters and the Asian Times.

Further Information
Annual report and an information pack about the organisation are available by writing or phoning.

Migrant Resource Centre

24 Churton Street
London SW1V 2LP
Tel: 0171-834 6650
Fax: 0171-931 8187

Contact
Maria Marin

Main Activities
The Migrant Resource Centre works with and for migrants and refugees. The organisation provides advice and training. It was set up in 1984 and operates on a London-wide basis. Annual budget is £150,000.

Opportunities for Volunteers
About 30 volunteers are involved at all levels in the organisation. They help with the day-to-day work eg administrative support, advice giving, publicity, and fundraising. They also serve on the management committee. Travel and lunch expenses are offered. Potential volunteers should contact Maria Marin direct on 0171-834 2505 and ask for an application form.

Opportunities for Employment
There are two full-time, five part-time, and six temporary, staff. There is an equal opportunities policy and all posts are advertised in The Guardian and The Voice.

Further Information
Annual Report, leaflet about the Migrants Resource Centre, and research and information in various languages are available on request.

West Glamorgan Race Equality Council

10A Mount Pleasant
Swansea
West Glamorgan SA1 6EE
Tel: 01792-45035

Contact
E U Haq, Director

Main Activities
The West Glamorgan Racial Equality Council aims to promote racial equality and good relations between persons of different ethnic origins and to work towards the elimination of racial discrimination. There are seventeen local affiliated groups.

Opportunities for Volunteers
All the work of the organisation is done by volunteers. They perform a variety of tasks including management/trusteeship, public relations and organising membership drives. Currently, the organisation is looking for suitable volunteers to serve on sub-committees eg education, employment, housing and social policy.

Opportunities for Employment
There are no employment opportunities.

Further Information
Annual Report and further information available on request.

Family & Community Matters

Age Exchange / Age Exchange Theatre Trust, *see Elderly People*

Brent Family Service Unit (FSU)

60 Nicoll Road, Harlesden
London NW10 9AS
Tel: 0181-453 1226
Fax: 0181-961 9340

Contact
Ms Clare Douglas, Community Resource Worker for volunteering; Ms Suzanne Connolly, Unit Manager re employment

Main Activities
Brent FSU provides preventative social work services to families and children. Part of the national FSU network, which has 20 centres in the UK, there has been an FSU Centre in Brent for 30 years. Occasionally, people from overseas in related fieldwork areas visit the Unit. Annual budget is £170,000.

Opportunities for Volunteers
At service delivery and management level, volunteers are key contributors. The Unit Manager is accountable to a local management committee made up of volunteers. Around 16 volunteers are involved in total and, apart from management work, undertake fundraising and project work, and help with the crèche, the play scheme and family support. More are needed. Recruitment is by application and through posters distributed locally. Minimum commitment is two hours a week, and travel expenses are offered. Prospective volunteers need an interest in working with children and families, and must be supportive of the values of the organisation.

Opportunities for Employment
Three full-time and five part-time staff are employed. Further recruitment depends on vacancies, but these do occur in crèche and family work. An interest in and

ability to work with children and their parents are necessary. There is an equal opportunities application procedure. Any posts are advertised in The Guardian.

Further Information
The Annual Report, as well as leaflets on unit activities and on various specialist groups, are available by telephoning or calling in.

British Association of Settlements and Social Action Centres (BASSAC), *see Social Welfare*

Community Matters

8/9 Upper Street
Islington, London N1 0PQ
Tel: 0171-226 0189
Fax: 0171-354 9570

Contact
Katy Lofters, Administrative Officer

Main Activities
Community Matters provides information, advice, training, support and national representation for local organisations with a general concern for their community. Organisations cover the areas of education, recreation, social welfare and community building management. Covering England and Wales mainly, Community Matters is a federation of around 842 local community organisations. Local authorities who support the aims can also become members. The annual budget is approx. £350,000.

Opportunities for Volunteers
A few volunteers are used for administrative support, fundraising and public relations/marketing projects. They are recruited ad hoc and through volunteer bureaux. There is no minimum commitment. Travel and lunch expenses are paid.

Opportunities for Employment
Six full-time and three part-time staff are employed. Vacancies are few. An equal opportunities policy operates.

Further Information
Annual Report, membership brochure and publications list available.

Community Service Volunteers (CSV), *see Support for Volunteering*

CRY-SIS Support Group

B M CRY-SIS
London WC1N 3XX
Tel: 0171-404 5011

Contact
June Jordan, National Co-ordinator

Main Activities
A voluntary self-help charity providing practical self-help and emotional support for families with excessively crying, sleepless and demanding children. Members are parents who have been through similar experiences themselves. Contributions to the information available on causes of the problem, and helps to bring it to the attention of the medical profession and the public. Runs a national telephone helpline with over 250 volunteer regional advisers/contacts working from their own homes. Cry-sis is run by voluntary committees and has an annual budget of £23,000.

Opportunities for Volunteers
Volunteers run Cry-sis, as well as the telephone helpline. Contacts in each regional area are all volunteers who must have experience of a crying, sleepless or demanding child. As well as counselling, volunteers also undertake all the administrative and fundraising work. More are needed, all year round. Training and study days are provided. Minimum

commitment varies, but for contacts is twenty hours a week, two weeks at a time, on rota duty. Recruitment is through in-house schemes, ad hoc applications and parents who have had Cry-sis support. In addition each applicant is interviewed by telephone and must provide two references. Each applicant must fill in a questionnaire and sign a policy agreement. No remuneration is offered.

Opportunities for Employment
Cry-sis has only one part-time staff member. There are no other opportunities for employment.

Further Information
The Annual Report and various publications (for sale) are available. The National Co-ordinator can also provide further details.

Divorce Conciliation & Advisory Service (DCAS)

38 Ebury Street
London SW1W 0LV
Tel: 0171-730 2422

Contact
Mrs H Halpin, OBE, Director

Main Activities
Helps separating parents to make constructive plans for their children's future, as amicably as possible. Also assists individuals to clarify their thoughts about their marriages and any impending separation. Provides a counselling and conciliation service, and runs seminars and workshops. Affiliated to the National Association of Family Mediation and Conciliation Services, DCAS covers mainly inner and outer London.

Opportunities for Volunteers
Volunteers are all professionals who are available one day a week on an 'expenses only' basis. They provide counselling for DCAS and must be appropriately qualified. Qualifications may include NFCC

core training, CQSW or Marriage Guidance training. Recruitment is on application by letter. Minimum commitment is one full or two half days a week. A volunteer allowance is paid.

Opportunities for Employment
DCAS has one part-time paid employee, apart from the volunteer counsellors. There are no other employment opportunities.

Further Information
Leaflets about the service are available on request. Details on conciliation services throughout the UK from 9 Tavistock Place, London WC1H 9SN.

Exploring Parenthood Trust

Latimer Education Centre
194 Freston Road
London W10 6PP
Tel: 0181-960 1678
Fax: 0181-964 1827

Contact
Charlotte Macpherson, Administrator

Main Activities
Exploring Parenthood Trust offers advice, information and counselling on various issues of family relations, children's behaviour and development. Provides support and counselling for any parent via national advice line and regional groups in London, East Midlands, Wales and the North East. Annual budget is £250,000.

Opportunities for Volunteers
Volunteers are vital to the organisation and are needed particularly in term time to give administrative support and to train for advice work. An understanding of parents' needs, a good telephone manner and flexibility are useful qualities.

Opportunities for Employment
There are six full-time and 28 part-time

staff. On average three people are re-cruited each year. Jobs are advertised in The Guardian, The Voice and the Leicester Mercury.

Further Information
Annual Report and parent fact sheets available.

Families Need Fathers

134 Curtain Road
London EC2A 3AR
Tel: 0171-613 5060
Tel: 0181-886 0970 (national info line)

Contact
Trevor Berry, Chairman, on 0171-613 5060 or 0181-295 1956

Main Activities
Families Need Fathers is a self-help support, advice and information group for separated parents and their children, especially those seeking to maintain a parent-child relationship in the face of difficulties. Group counselling is available nation-wide. Also campaigns for changes in 'the system' and to educate people in good parenting. Covering England and Wales, it has local branches in major towns and a network of local support groups, plus contact with similar organisations in Scotland, Europe, the USA and world-wide. Mothers of children separated from them can contact the sister organisation MATCH, at BM Problems, London WC1N 3XX. The annual budget is £25,000.

Opportunities for Volunteers
Volunteers are used year round in head office and the branches for administrative support, fundraising, counselling and project work eg lobbying MPs, researching and disseminating information, publicising the issues. A national network of voluntary contacts provides advice and support. The organisation also actively seeks volunteers with good literacy skills and commitment to its aims, to staff the

London office. Recruitment is through volunteer bureaux, in-house drives and ad hoc phone and written applications. The needs of the organisation are also promoted through media features, letters to the press, etc. Commitment needs to be on-going but can be flexible. Reliability is essential. Any expenses are subject to negotiation.

Opportunities for Employment
There is only one paid member of staff in the office, but paid positions also arise in fundraising, research into family law theory and practice, and general clerical work. Jobs are advertised in the in-house journal Access and are based on a formal equal opportunities policy.

Further Information
An Annual Report and list of local groups are available. Various advice booklets and other relevant publications include Schools and Parents after Separation or Divorce, Child Maintenance - The New Law, and Surviving the Breakup.

In Scotland contact: Parents Forever Scotland, PO Box 23, Kirkcaldy, Fife KY1 1SS, tel: 01333-352034, 0131-333 1166, 0141-339 4587, 01259-217106.

Family Education Trust (FET),
see Education

Family Mediation Scotland (FMS)

127 Rose Street, South Lane
Edinburgh EH2 4BB
Tel: 0131-220 6895
Fax: 0131-220 6895

Contact
Training Officer

Main Activities
FMS is the co-ordinating body for twelve affiliated family mediation services in Scotland. Family mediation helps separating and divorced parents to come to

mutually acceptable arrangements for the care of the children.

Opportunities for Volunteers

All mediators in affiliated services are volunteers and are therefore essential to the organisation. There is a selection procedure and specialised training is required. Telephone FMS for details of local service.

Opportunities for Employment

In FMA there are four full-time and four part-time staff. There is an equal opportunities policy.

Further Information

Information leaflets on family mediation available from FMS. Contact local service for application pack.

Family Services Unit (FSU)

207 Old Marylebone Road
London NW1 5QP
Tel: 0171-402 5175/6
Fax: 0171-724 1829

Contact

National office or local units for volunteering; Personnel Department, national office re employment opportunities

Main Activities

Set up in 1948, FSU provides support for families and children living in communities in the greatest need through provision of a range of social work and practical support services. A national organisation, FSU has 19 teams in local branches in England and one in Scotland.

Opportunities for Volunteers

Part-time volunteers are used in head office, and over 200 in the branches for administrative support, fundraising and as management committee members. The local units may also have 'friends' groups of volunteer fundraisers. FSU actively seeks volunteers year round and provides induction, supervision and training if appropriate. It particularly needs fundraisers. Recruitment is via volunteer

bureaux, in-house drives and regional development initiatives. Minimum commitment is three hours a week. Travel expenses are offered.

Opportunities for Employment

FSU has 160 full- and 150 part-time staff. It recruits around 140 people a year, often for sessional work, based on an equal opportunities policy. Jobs are advertised in the national press eg The Guardian, Community Care, and local papers.

Further Information

The Annual Report, a publications list covering many aspects of social welfare issues, and a list of local groups are available on request.

Family Welfare Association (FWA)

501-505 Kingsland Road
London E8 4AU
Tel: 0171-254 6251
Fax: 0171-249 5443

Contact

Carol Ihnatowicz, Head of Personnel, for volunteering and employment

Main Activities

Set up in 1869, FWA provides practical, emotional and financial support to people in need. It runs local social work projects mainly in London, the South East, the Midlands and East Anglia. National office also offers a grant-giving and advice service. Annual budget is £4 million.

Opportunities for Volunteers

Volunteers are very important to the FWA's work. About 50 work throughout the organisation in administrative support, fundraising or assisting on local, self-help social work projects such as community mental health schemes. FWA is seeking more volunteers, particularly to work in its charity shops and to volunteer for work in various offices, especially in London. Prospective volunteers need to be able to deal with the public, work in a team and get on with people. Inter-personal skills are especially important. Training is given. Recruitment is usually on application. Individual projects may advertise for volunteers in the local press. Minimum commitment varies. Travel and sometimes other expenses are paid.

Opportunities for Employment
With 120 full-time and twenty part-time staff, FWA may recruit up to 40 staff each year for a variety of posts. Any vacancies are advertised in The Guardian and/or the social work and the local press. FWA has an equal opportunities policy.

Further Information
The Annual Report, a set of four leaflets on various FWA services and 'Family Lines' a regular publication, are available.

HALOW (Help and Advice Line for Offenders, Wives and Families)

Summerfield Fdn, 60 Dudley Road
Winson Green, Birmingham B18 4HL
Tel: 0121-454 3615

Contact
Ms Marie Curtis, Director/Co-ordinator

Main Activities
HALOW offers support, advice and infor-mation to anyone connected with a prisoner. Runs a helpline and offers coun-selling on a one-to-one basis. Has offices in the West Midlands and Bristol but deals with problems from all over the country. Annual budget is £40,000.

Opportunities for Volunteers
Counselling/advice giving and fundraising are done by volunteers.

Opportunities for Employment
There is one full-time member of staff.

Further Information
Annual Report and leaflet available on request.

Home-Start Consultancy

2 Salisbury Road
Leicester LE1 7QR
Tel: 0116-235 4988
Fax: 0116-234 9323

Contact
Albert Clark

Main Activities
Home-Start offers support, friendship and practical help to young families under stress. National body with autonomous local schemes.

Opportunities for Volunteers
Volunteers with parenting experience are needed to offer families support. A ten week induction course is offered. Volun-teers should apply to their local Home-Start scheme (list available from Head Office).

Opportunities for Employment
There are few employment opportunities although each local Home Start scheme has a secretary and an organiser.

Further Information
Annual Report and list of local schemes available.

Independent Adoption Service

121-123 Camberwell Road
London SE5 0HB
Tel: 0171-703 1088

Contact
David Bennington, Financial Administra-tor

Main Activities
Recruits and prepares families to adopt children with special needs, particularly those who have been abused, are from ethnic minorities or are older children. Families are from a 35 mile radius of Lon-don. Annual budget is £450,000.

Opportunities for Volunteers
Volunteers are needed to undertake PR, fundraising and family recruitment as well as for taking minutes and general office work. Graduates with good communication skills preferred. Expenses and a small honorarium are paid. Minimum commitment is 21 hours a week for six months.

Opportunities for Employment
There are fifteen full-time and three part-time staff. On average one person is recruited each year, either qualified social workers or experienced secretaries. Social work jobs are advertised in Community Care and Social Work Today.

Further Information
Annual Report, recruitment leaflet and annual newsletter available on request.

Junior League of London (JLL), see Women

Kith and Kids

c/o The Irish Centre
Pretoria Road
London N17 8DX

Contact
Carol Schaffer/Marjolein de Vries

Main Activities
Kith and Kids is a self-help group for parents who wish to be actively involved in the social integration of disabled children into the community. It operates in the London area only.

Opportunities for Volunteers
Volunteers are crucial to the running of the organisation. About 500 run the various projects, such as social training and respite care. Useful skills can include: drama, arts and crafts, and massage. Travel and out-of-pocket expenses are offered. Kith and Kids is actively seeking volunteers who have enthusiasm and commitment.

Opportunities for Employment
There are three members of staff. An equal opportunities policy is in place and jobs are advertised in The Guardian and The Voice. There are occasional recruitment opportunities eg on summer projects.

Further Information
Annual Report and leaflets about the organisation and the projects are available.

The Mother's Union (MU), see Religious Affairs

National Childbirth Trust (NCT), see Women

National Council for One Parent Families (NCOPF)

255 Kentish Town Road
London NW5 2LX
Tel: 0171-267 1361
Fax: 0171-482 4881

Contact
Sarah Clarke

Main Activities
Aims to improve through access to information the position of one-parent families facing problems such as poverty, unemployment, child care and housing. NCOPF provides services nationally from the London office to lone parents and advisers working with them. These include running training courses, such as 'Return to Work' for lone parents, all over the country. It also campaigns and lobbies for changes in the law.

Opportunities for Volunteers
NCOPF does not use volunteers as such. But it offers one week's work experience in the fundraising department to students involved in student rag fundraising at their colleges/universities.

Opportunities for Employment

With 26 full-time and six part-time staff, NCOPF recruits about seven people annually. Jobs are advertised internally, and in The Guardian and local papers, based on an equal opportunities policy.

Further Information

An Annual Report and publications list are available. Publications are free to single parents. Scotland has a Scottish Council for One Parent Families.

National Council for the Divorced and Separated (NCDS)

13 High Street
Little Shelford
Cambridge CB2 5ES
Tel: 01533-700595

Contact

Mrs Dorothy Squires, Chairman

Main Activities

Caters for the social and welfare needs of divorced and separated people. Runs social activities through its branches and provides counselling. Entirely self-supporting, the NCDS is run by an Executive Committee and has around 10,000 members nation-wide. There are 100 local branches, mostly in main towns, divided into seven regional groupings. Any adult who is divorced or separated may join the organisation for help, advice, support or just social contact. NCDS is funded by membership subscriptions, donations and various fundraising methods.

Opportunities for Volunteers

NCDS is run entirely by volunteers who are the members. More divorced and separated people are needed to open branches. Members are recruited through enquiries, application to the office, word of mouth and advertising.

Opportunities for Employment

There are no paid staff and no opportunities for employment.

Further Information

Various publications and a list of local groups are available.

National Family Mediation Service (NFM)

9 Tavistock Place
London WC1H 9SN
Tel: 0171-383 5993

Contact

Ms Thelma Fisher

Main Activities

NFM and its local affiliates offer help to couples during separation and divorce to make arrangements, mainly regarding their children. The organisation was set up in 1981 and there are 60 local branches.

Opportunities for Volunteers

There is one volunteer at present.

Opportunities for Employment

There are four full-time and two part-time staff. From time to time the organisation seeks recruits who have a knowledge of mediation in the area of development and training.

Further Information

Annual Report available on request as well as various leaflets and an information pack (£2.50 + post and packing).

PARENTLINE

Endway House, The Endway
Hadleigh, Benfleet
Essex SS7 2AN
Tel: 01702-559900 (Helpline)
Tel: 01702-554782 (Admin.)
Fax: 01702-554911

Contact
Carole Baisden, Director

Main Activities
PARENTLINE's 25 regional groups form a network of telephone helplines. These provide support for parents and facilitate a family's capacity to care for its children.

Opportunities for Volunteers
Volunteers are vital to the work of the organisation. Counselling, admin and fundraising are their main activities. The only experience required is that of having been a parent. Training courses are provided. Minimum commitment is between four and six hours a week.

Opportunities for Employment
There are seven staff members.

Further Information
Bi-monthly newspaper, magazines and leaflets available on request. In Northern Ireland, contact Parents Advice Centre, Room 1, Bryson House, 28 Bedford Street, Belfast.

Parent Network

44-46 Caversham Road
London NW5 2DS
Tel: 0171-485 8535
Fax: 0171-267 4426

Contact
Tim Kahn

Main Activities
Parent Network runs support and education groups for parents (known as Parent-Link). The 30 local branches situated across England, Scotland and Wales provide a 'listening ear' for parents to help them cope with the daily stresses of family life. They also offer ideas for approaching daily difficult family situations in a new way.

Opportunities for Volunteers
Most of the volunteer work is done by people already involved in Parent-Link. They help to develop local branches (fundraising, newsletters, publicity and administration).

Opportunities for Employment
There are six staff, three of whom are part time.

Further Information
An information leaflet and list of local groups available.

Parent to Parent Information on Adoption Services (PPAIS)

Lower Boddington, Daventry
Northamptonshire NN11 6YB
Tel: 01327-260295

Contact
Mrs Philly Morrall, National Co-ordinator

Main Activities
PPIAS is a self-help support and information service for adopting families. Has a particular interest in supporting new permanent families for children with special needs. National organisation with 140 local volunteer adoptive parent co-ordinators. Annual budget is £85,000. PPIAS has links with a support group for adoptive parents of children with attachment disorders – the Attachment Disorders Parents' Network (ADPN-UK). Details may be obtained from PPIAS.

Opportunities for Volunteers
Volunteers are needed to give advice and support to other adopters. Being an adoptive parent and having counselling and listening skills are essential attributes.

Travel expenses are offered and there is no minimum commitment.

Opportunities for Employment
There are three full-time and two part-time staff.

Further Information
Annual Report, list of local groups and free information packs available on request.

Parents Against Injustice (PAIN)

3 Riverside Business Park
Stansted, Essex CM24 8PL
Tel: 01279-647171
Fax: 01279-812612

Contact
Sue Amphlett, Director; Barry Barton, Family Advisor

Main Activities
PAIN is the national charity that specialises in providing advice and support to those who state they have been mistakenly involved in investigations of alleged child abuse. Provides telephone/face-to-face advice and information pack. Liaises with and advises solicitors/child care professionals and practitioners. Maintains lists of doctors prepared to give second medical or psychiatric opinions. Runs training days, seminars and workshops for professionals. Provides literature resources centre on child abuse and neglect issues.

Opportunities for Volunteers
Although no volunteers are used at present, they may be used for fundraising and administrative support.

Opportunities for Employment
There are five staff.

Further Information
Working in Partnership - coping with an investigation of alleged abuse or neglect is available at £2.50. Also available are annual report, newsletters and a comprehensive literature list.

Parents Aid

Hare Street Family Centre
Harberts Road, Harlow
Essex CM19 4EU
Tel: 01279-452166

Contact
Manager

Main Activities
Parents Aid gives advice and support by telephone and in person to families who have a child in care. Serves an area within a 10 mile radius of Harlow. Gives advice by phone to parents who are out of this area.

Opportunities for Volunteers
Volunteers fundraise, provide administrative support and do some counselling. Minimum commitment is 20 hours per week.

Opportunities for Employment
No employment opportunities at present.

Further Information
'Your Child and Social Services', a guide for families is available at £2.50 (£1 if you have a child in care). Information sheet available.

Parents Anonymous London (PAL)

61 Manor Gardens
London N7 6LA
Tel: 0171-263 8918

Contact
Mildred Lefton, Training Officer

Main Activities
PAL operates a telephone counselling service for those parents who have been or are tempted to abuse their child. A network of groups offers friendship and

support. PAL also works closely with ChildLine and the Samaritans.

Opportunities for Volunteers
Volunteers are essential and are used for counselling, fundraising and administrative work. For counselling, two rota sessions of six hours a month are expected. People with parenting experience preferred although empathetic and understanding non-parents are also accepted. A ten week induction course is offered as well as ongoing training.

Opportunities for Employment
There are no paid staff.

Further Information
The Annual Report is available.

Prisoners Families and Friends Service

106 Weston Street
London, SE1 3QG
Tel: 0171-403 4091

Contact
Sue Roberts, Administrator

Main Activities
The Service offers advice and information to any relative or friend of a prisoner. Families in inner London can be visited to offer support and friendship.

Opportunities for Volunteers
A befriending service is run by volunteers. Minimum commitment is two or three hours a week preferably over at least a year. Personal qualities of reliability, friendliness and tolerance are needed. An induction programme and support is offered. Reliability and warmth of personality are the most important qualities needed, though specialised skills may be helpful. The organisation plans to move to more spacious accommodation soon which will mean greater opportunities for volunteers to become involved in office based projects. A new Court based

initiative is planned to provide information to families.

Opportunities for Employment
There are two full-time and one part-time staff.

Further Information
Annual Report and leaflets for potential volunteers available.

Prisoners Wives and Families Society (PWFS)

254 Caledonian Road
Islington, London, N1 0NG
Tel: 0171-278 3981

Contact
Pauline Hoare, Assistant Organiser

Main Activities
The Society provides self-help, advice and support to about 2,000 prisoners' relatives each year.

Opportunities for Volunteers
PWFS has a self-help concept so user volunteers, who are generally relatives or friends of a person who has been in prison, are of great importance. They offer help and support.

Opportunities for Employment
There are two full-time staff.

Further Information
Annual Report is available.

National Society for the Prevention of Cruelty to Children (NSPCC), see Children

National Marriage Guidance Council (Relate), see Counselling & Self-Help

Stepfamily (National Stepfamily Association)

72 Willesden Lane
London NW6 7TA
Tel: 0171-372 0844 (office)
Tel: 0171-372 0846 (helpline)

Contact
Claire George, Administrator

Main Activities
Stepfamily provides support, advice and a confidential telephone counselling service for stepfamilies and those working with them. There are local support groups, training workshops and seminars. Annual budget is £160,000.

Opportunities for Volunteers
Volunteers work as Helpline counsellors. Some professional background or knowledge of counselling is essential. Help is also needed with piloting teaching materials, serving on the management committee and standing groups. Minimum commitment for Helpline counsellors is four hours a week for a year; otherwise it varies with the role. Volunteers are also required for help in the office, on short projects and specified tasks.

Opportunities for Employment
There are three full-time and two part-time staff. Approximately two project staff are recruited each year.

Further Information
Annual Report and Information Pack available on request.

Working for Childcare

77 Holloway Road
London N7 8JA
Tel: 0171-700 0281
Fax: 0171-700 1105

Contact
The Administrator

Main Activities
Working for Childcare campaigns for increased childcare provision for working parents. The organisation encourages employer subsidised care.

Opportunities for Volunteers
Volunteers are an important part of a small team and carry out administrative work.

Opportunities for Employment
There are two full-time and one part-time members of staff.

Further Information
General leaflets about the organisation, and the Annual Report, are available.

218 HEALTH & MEDICINE

Health & Medicine

Volunteering in the areas of health and medicine offers such a huge range of opportunities that the possibilities are virtually endless. Whatever illness, disease or health issue you can think of, there is almost certain to be a voluntary organisation that exists for it. The entries listed in this section cover a wide range of types but represent only a small selection of those that have been set up. If you are interested in volunteering or employment in an aspect of health or medicine not included here, to find out what, if any, organisation exists for it you could try asking

- your local authority, which should have lists of all the organisations in its area
- your GP or pharmacist
- the local hospital, which may have a Voluntary Services Department
- a voluntary organisation concerned with a similar illness, ailment or issue
- the College of Health in London
- your local reference library
- Help to Hand - listed in this directory

For organisations concerned with health and/or medical issues overseas, see also the section on Overseas & the Developing World in this directory.

Action for Sick Children, *see* *Children*

Action for Victims of Medical Accidents

Bank Chambers, 1 London Road
Forest Hill, London SE23 3TP
Tel: 0181-291 2793
Fax: 0181-699 0632

Contact
Keith Miles, Assistant Director

Main Activities
Founded in 1982 as a UK-wide body, the

organisation assists victims of medical accidents to pursue complaints and to take legal action where appropriate. It also provides details of specialist lawyers and medical experts. Annual budget is £400,000.

Opportunities for Volunteers

Volunteers are needed in head office to give administrative support. Typing ability is preferred and a legal background would be helpful. Travel and lunch expenses are offered. Applicants should write a letter giving some background details about themselves.

Opportunities for Employment

There are sixteen full-time and two part-time staff.

Further Information

Annual Report and booklet available.

Alzheimer's Disease Society (ADS)

Gordon House
10 Greencoat Place
London SW1P 1PH
Tel: 0171-306 0606
Fax: 0171-306 0808

Contact

Clive Evers, Assistant Director (Information and Education)

Main Activities

The Alzheimer's Disease Society supports families in England, Wales and Northern Ireland through a network of branches, support groups and contact people. Information and advice are given through the national office and local regional offices. Apart from publishing booklets and fact sheets on a wide range of topics, there is also a monthly newsletter free to members. The Society also campaigns and lobbies on behalf of people with Alzheimer's disease and related dementias, and their carers. It also supports research by funding several Research Fellowships,

and is in touch with European and international Alzheimer's Disease organisations. A national organisation, (except for Scotland) set up in 1979 and offering membership, it currently has thirteen regional offices including Wales and Northern Ireland, about 170 local branches and an annual budget of over £2 million.

Opportunities for Volunteers

The Society uses many volunteers, year round, for a variety of administrative, counselling, advice, practical support and fundraising work in both national office and branches. It also actively seeks volunteers to become local contact people. Recruitment is through ad hoc applications and in-house, via both national office and regional, and local branch, development officers. Specialist training on dementia and the services available to support carers is given as required. Volunteers are needed at all times but especially weekends and evenings. The precise hours vary according to location and need. Travel and lunch expenses are paid.

Opportunities for Employment

With a large complement of full-time and many part-time staff, the Society recruits between ten and twelve people nationally each year. Posts are advertised in the national and local press, particularly The Guardian, on the basis of an evolving equal opportunities policy. Contact Clive Evers as above.

Further Information

The Annual Report and a full list of publications are available on request from head office as above. For Scotland there is a separate and independent organisation called:

Alzheimer's Scotland, Scottish Action on Dementia, 8 Hill Street, Edinburgh EH2 3JZ, tel: 0131-225 1453 and helpline 0131-220 6155; fax: 0131-225 8748.

The Amarant Trust

Grant House
56-60 St John Street
London EC1M 4DT
Tel: 0171-490 1644
Fax: 0171-490 2296

Contact
Stephanie Snow

Main Activities
The Trust exists to promote a greater awareness and understanding of the menopause, to support and expand research on it, and to make information and treatment available to many more women. It organises conferences, hormone replacement therapy (HRT) clinics and voluntary self-help groups, and runs a membership scheme. A national, UK-wide organisation, currently it has three affiliated clinics and around sixty local support groups.

Opportunities for Volunteers
Volunteers are essential to the Trust's work. They run head office and also provide administrative support. The Trust is actively seeking volunteers for administrative and fundraising tasks, recruiting in ad hoc ways through application letters and informal interviews. There is no set time commitment. Travel expenses are paid.

Opportunities for Employment
None available as yet.

Further Information
Annual Report is available on request, membership costs £20 a year, and information pack (£5) and individual leaflets can be bought.

Aperts Syndrome Support Group

Fullers Barn, The Green
Loughton, Milton Keynes
Bucks MK5 8AW
Tel: 01908-608557
Fax: 01908-608557

Contact
Mrs P Walker, founder/organiser

Main Activities
The Group provides information, support and a contact list to families who have a child with Aperts. An annual picnic is arranged. Set up in 1984 it is now affiliated to the Craniofacial Support Group (CFSG) which is seeking charitable status.

Opportunities for Volunteers
The Group is very small and run by one person.

Opportunities for Employment
There are no employment opportunities.

Further Information
A 'Guide for Parents' is available to statutory bodies for a small charge.

Arthritis & Rheumatism Council for Research (ARC)

Copeman House, St Mary's Court
St Mary's Gate, Chesterfield
Derbyshire S41 7TD
Tel: 01246-558033
Fax: 01246-558007

Contact
General Secretary, head office, and appropriate regional organising secretaries

Main Activities
Founded in 1936, ARC funds medical research in various places in the UK, including medical schools, into all forms of arthritis and rheumatism. It also raises awareness of the diseases among the medical profession, sufferers and the general public through education and

HEALTH & MEDICINE **221**

publicity. A national organisation, ARC has 30 regional groups each with an organising secretary, and a network of 1,200 voluntary fundraising branches. It also has links with similar associations in Europe and North America.

Opportunities for Volunteers

Volunteers have been essential to ARC's emergence as a major medical research charity. Around 100,000 volunteers fundraise in their local areas. ARC needs more volunteers with a fundraising commitment all year round. Regional secretaries set up local branches - contact through phone books. Recruitment is through in-house methods. There is no minimum commitment and no remuneration.

Opportunities for Employment

ARC has 58 full-time staff and recruits as required, through national and appropriate regional newspapers. ARC has an equal opportunities policy. It is particularly active in recruiting school leavers and new graduates.

Further Information

Annual Report and wide range of patient literature are available. ARC also publishes an in-house magazine with a readership of 400,000.

ASH (Action on Smoking and Health)

109 Gloucester Place
London W1H 4EJ
Tel: 0171-935 3519
Fax: 0171-935 3463

Contact

Assistant Director

Main Activities

ASH is a medical charity set up in 1971, which aims to reduce and eliminate smoking by means of education and lobbying activities. There are twelve local branches. Annual budget is £400,000.

Opportunities for Volunteers

Volunteers are regarded as important and undertake valuable work. In particular they provide administrative support mostly in head office. A few of the local branches also have some scope for using volunteers. Useful skills are neat handwriting and speed. Travel and lunch expenses are offered. Minimum commitment is four hours a week.

Opportunities for Employment

There are ten staff.

Further Information

List of local groups available.

Association for Glycogen Storage Disease (UK) (AGSD (UK))

9 Lindop Road
Hale, Altrincham
Cheshire, WA15 9DZ
Tel: 0161-226 3323 (day)
Tel: 0161-980 7303 (pm)
Fax: 0161-226 3813

Contact

Ann Phillips, Chairman

Main Activities

AGSD (UK) is a support and contact group for all persons affected by GSD and their families. It acts as a focus for scientific, educational, and charitable activities concerning GSD. It works to provide information to both professionals and the general public on all aspects of diagnosis, treatment and long term outlook for GSD affected persons. Individual families in the UK and abroad are members, and AGSD (UK) has links with sister associations in Europe, North America and Israel too. Membership is £10 a year. Annual budget is £1,000.

Opportunities for Volunteers

All aspects of the Association are run by the members themselves. As volunteers they undertake fundraising and advice giving and are on the Executive Committee. They are recruited through AGSD (UK) membership. Travel expenses are paid.

Opportunities for Employment
Employment opportunities are not available.

Further Information
Annual Report, newsletters and leaflets are published.

Association for Improvements in the Maternity Services (AIMS)

40 Kingswood Avenue
London NW6 6LS
Tel: 0181-960 5585
Fax: 01753-654142

Contact
Ms S Warshal, Honorary Secretary

Main Activities
Set up in 1960, AIMS is a pressure group giving advice, information and support to parents on all aspects of pregnancy and maternity care, including parents rights. Publishes a quarterly journal. AIMS is a national organisation with five regional groups, over 800 members and an annual budget of £5,000. It also has links with the European Childbirth Education Association.

Opportunities for Volunteers
All involved are volunteers who are used and needed in all types of work - administrative, fundraising, counselling and for projects. Professional fundraising and PR skills are particularly welcomed. A knowledge of maternity services is required. Recruitment is usually in-house.

Opportunities for Employment
There are no employment opportunities.

Further Information
Annual Report and AGM minutes available. Pamphlets and quarterly journal for sale.

Association of Community Health Councils for England and Wales (ACHCEW)

30 Drayton Park
London N5 1PB
Tel: 0171-609 8405
Fax: 0171-700 1152

Contact
Local community health councils (CHCs)

Main Activities
A national organisation for England and Wales, set up in 1977, ACHCEW is a forum for its over 200 member community health councils (CHCs) and also represents users of health services at national level. It provides information and advice to CHCs, responds to policy initiatives on health and helps to promote good practice.

Opportunities for Volunteers
ACHCEW does not use volunteers itself, but its local member CHCs, of which there are over 200, may require volunteer help. Local CHCs can be contacted through the telephone directory or local library. Jobs would include assisting with the general running of a CHC office and with project work. A background knowledge of the NHS would be beneficial.

Opportunities for Employment
There are five full-time and three part-time staff.

Further Information
Available on request including Annual Report, leaflets and other publications. Individual CHCs also produce their own material. Translations are sometimes available.

Health councils also operate in Scotland and Northern Ireland.

Baby Life Support Systems, BLISS

17-21 Emerald Street
London WC1N 3QL
Tel: 0171-831 9393
Fax: 0171-404 0676

Contact

Judy Kay, Director

Main Activities

Set up in 1979, Bliss works to ensure that appropriate special care is available for new born babies by providing neonatal intensive care equipment in hospitals and funding the cost of neo-natal nurse training. It also offers support to parents through Bliss-link. It operates nationally through thirty local branches and twenty support groups and has an annual budget of £700,000.

Opportunities for Volunteers

Volunteers are actively recruited in-house, through ad hoc telephone and written applications, and via public relations. Welcomed year round, particularly for administrative support, fundraising and befriending, hundreds of volunteers are used by the branches and a few in head office. They are regarded as vital to fundraising and parent support services, while administrative help is always needed. Training and support are given, as required, through professional supervision and advice, and backup from existing volunteers. Befrienders need to have experienced their own baby receiving special or intensive care. Committment is flexible. Travel and lunch expenses are paid.

Opportunities for Employment

With 12 staff, Bliss might recruit one or two people a year. Jobs are advertised in the trade press, based on a developing equal opportunities policy. The skills needed vary, depending on the post.

Further Information

Includes annual report, brochure, leaflets and a list of local groups available on request.

British Colostomy Association

15 Station Road
Reading, Berks RG1 1LG
Tel: 01734-391537
Fax: 01734-569095

Contact

Mrs Cathy Richards, Director of Services

Main Activities

Founded originally in 1963 as the Colostomy Welfare Group the Association changed its name in 1989 and now offers support, information and reassurance to any who has, or is about to have, a colostomy. Encourages returning to an active lifestyle. Provides emotional support confidentially. National with 27 area organisers and worldwide links through the International Ostomy Association.

Opportunities for Volunteers

Volunteers are very important since the organisation's basis is voluntary. They provide practical help and emotional support. More are needed. But they must have had personal experience of a colostomy operation and be recommended by a stoma care nurse. Training is provided. Travel expenses are offered.

Opportunities for Employment

There are six full-time staff, but employment opportunities are unlikely.

Further Information

Annual Report and information pack available, plus a helpline.

British Council for Prevention of Blindness (BCPB), also known as SEE (Save Eyes Everywhere)

12 Harcourt Street
London W1H 1DS
Tel: 0171-724 3716

Contact
Jane Skerrett, Executive Officer

Main Activities
Founded in 1976, the BCPB supports research work into the prevention of blindness in the UK. It also funds projects in the developing world which treat the causes of blindness there, such as trachoma, cataract and river blindness, as well as funding eye health workers who come to the UK for six months to study at Moorfields Eye Hospital. It is affiliated to the International Agency for the Prevention of Blindness.

Opportunities for Volunteers
BCPB involves a few volunteers and is keen to increase their numbers and start a network of volunteers in England to organise fundraising activities and/or get involved in longer term ways eg organising local groups. Fundraising experience would be useful, but the Council is open to offers to organise any events eg coffee mornings, jumble sales. Volunteers would have to be self-motivated and organise in their own area as there is no space for them at head office. Recruitment is through application by phone or in writing. No expenses are offered.

Opportunities for Employment
There are two paid workers but no other opportunities.

Further Information
A brochure outlining current projects is available by writing in.

British Diabetic Association (BDA)

10 Queen Anne Street
London W1M 0BD
Tel: 0171-323 1531
Fax: 0171-636 2364

Contact
Jane Crosswell, Personnel Manager, regarding volunteering and employment

Main Activities
BDA provides vital help and support to those with diabetes and for diabetes care, and leads the funding of research into the condition. A national, UK-wide organisation founded in 1934, it celebrated its diamond anniversary in 1994. It has regional offices in Glasgow and Warrington, with West Midlands and Northern Ireland opening in 1995, and is supported by 450 local branches. It also has links with similar organisations in Europe.

Opportunities for Volunteers
Volunteers are very important to the BDA, especially as it expands its work. Both head office (3) and local branches (400+) use volunteers, mainly for fundraising, mutual support, and raising public awareness. Recruited ad hoc on application, via volunteer bureaux and through branches, more are needed in all areas. There is no minimum commitment. Travel expenses are offered.

Opportunities for Volunteers
With 72 full-time and three part-time staff, various vacancies occur each year. Posts are advertised in the national press, including The Guardian, based on a developing equal opportunities policy.

Further Information
Annual Report, a list of local groups, Balance magazine (bi-monthly) and various publications available.

British Heart Foundation (BHF)

14 Fitzhardinge Street
London W1H 4DH
Tel: 0171-935 0185
Fax: 0171-486 3815

Contact
Melanie Glanville, Recruitment and Training Officer

Main Activities
Founded in 1961 BHF aims to play a leading role in the fight against heart disease. It raises funds for research, education, training, rehabilitation and equipment. For example it is the main fundraising organisation for a number of associated though separate bodies such as ASH and the National Forum for Coronary Heart Disease. There are nine regional groups, including Edinburgh, Liverpool and Nottingham, 500 local branches and 220 charity shops. BHF is also linked with overseas organisations such as the European Heart Network and the American, Australian and Canadian Heart Associations. Annual budget is £33 million.

Opportunities for Volunteers
Volunteers are vital for both fundraising and raising awareness of what BHF does. They are needed to staff charity shops, join local branches and to help at head office. Many are heart patients themselves or have a close proximity to heart disease through family or friends. Minimum commitment is one hour a week.

Opportunities for Employment
Recruitment varies according to need.

Further Information
Annual Report and wide range of information available. For enquiries regarding shops, contact BHF Shops (telephone 0181-390 8011). For enquires about branch membership, contact Michael Collins at Head Office for a list of regional offices.

The British Kidney Patient Association (BKPA)

Bordon
Hampshire GU35 9JZ
Tel: 01420-472021/2
Fax: 01420-475831

Contact
Mrs E Ward, OBE, founder President

Main Activities
The BKPA, established in 1975, gives support, advice and practical help to kidney patients. It runs Holiday Dialysis Centres where patients can have a vacation and treatment with their families. A UK-wide organisation, membership is open to all British renal patients. BKPA also has links world-wide with other kidney patient associations.

Opportunities for Volunteers
BKPA needs volunteers in head office for fundraising.

Opportunities for Employment
Many of the staff, comprising eight full-time and eight part-time, have been with BKPA many years. Vacancies are rare. Dialysis nurses are employed from May to September for the Holiday Centres. Jobs are advertised in local newspapers and the Nursing Times.

Further Information
Annual report, various leaflets and other publications available.

British Liver Trust

Central House, Central Avenue
Ransomes Europark
Ipswich, Suffolk IP3 9QG
Tel: 01473-276326
Fax: 01473 276327

Contact
Alison Rogers, Director

Main Activities
The Trust undertakes research into the

causes, diagnosis, prevention and treatment of liver diseases. It also works to educate the public, patients and medical practitioners about liver diseases, and to support, inform and advise patients and their families suffering from liver disease. Set up in 1988, it is a national organisation with 12 local support groups. The annual budget is £300,000.

Opportunities for Volunteers

Volunteers work in head office on various ad hoc projects including administrative support and fundraising. The skills required depend on the particular job eg database input. Volunteers are recruited ad hoc and on application, no minimum time commitment is required and out-of-pocket expenses are paid.

Opportunities for Employment

Four full-time staff are employed. Opportunities for employment seldom arise, but any recruits would usually need computer (database/word processing) skills. Any vacancies might be mentioned on local radio.

Further Information

The Annual Report, a list of fact sheets, a brochure and a list of local groups are all available from head office.

British Lung Foundation

8 Peterborough Mews
London SW6 3BL
Tel: 0171-371 7704
Fax: 0171-371 7705

Contact

Office as above

Main Activities

The British Lung Foundation was established in 1985 to promote medical research into diseases of the chest and lungs, and to disseminate useful results for public benefit. It has a national office and five branches, one in each of four regional areas, plus Scotland. It also has links with the American Lung Association.

Opportunities for Volunteers

Volunteers are essential to the organisation's work and are used frequently in both national office and the branches, mainly for secretarial and administrative support. The Foundation welcomes volunteers and is actively seeking more, but prefers people who can give time on a regular basis. It recruits through ad hoc applications and advertisements placed in local public libraries and supermarkets. No specific time commitment is required and no remuneration is offered.

Opportunities for Employment

There are eleven full-time and eight part-time staff. An equal opportunities policy operates, but the Foundation seldom actively recruits.

Further Information

The Annual Report and a list of local groups are available on request. The national Breathe Easy Club for those with long term lung disorders, produces a newsletter and a range of information leaflets.

British Migraine Association

178A High Road, Byfleet
West Byfleet, Surrey KT14 7ED
Tel: 01932-352468

Contact

The Director

Main Activities

The Association, a UK-wide body set up in 1958, encourages sufferers to participate in, and financially support, research into the condition. It provides sufferers with support, understanding and information. Membership is £3 a year.

Opportunities for Volunteers

Volunteering opportunities are developing at head office.

Opportunities for Employment
Three part-time staff run the office, and vacancies rarely arise. Any recruit would need office skills and to be a migraine sufferer.

Further Information
Annual Report and information pack available.

British Organ Donor Society (BODY)

Balsham
Cambridge CB1 6DL
Tel: 01223-893636

Contact
Margaret Evans

Main Activities
BODY was set up in 1984 to provide information and emotional support for donor families, recipients and professionals. It supplies information on organ donation for the general public and promotes organ donation. A UK-wide organisation, it has a sister Society in Eire, and links with similar organisations in Australia, France and the USA.

Opportunities for Volunteers
Most of the Society's work is voluntary, so volunteer help is very important. Volunteers are needed to undertake counselling, fundraising and befriending, and to give talks and administrative support, for which the relevant skills are required. These include abilities in providing bereavement and emotional support. Opportunities exist throughout the UK, via head office.

Opportunities for Employment
There is one part-time member of staff.

Further Information
Annual Report, pamphlets and booklets 'The Gift of Life', 1 and 2, available, with the 'Gift of Life' 3 available in 1995.

British Polio Fellowship

Bell Close, West End Road
Ruislip, Middx HA4 6LP
Tel: 01895-675515
Fax: 01895-625527

Contact
Central Office for volunteering opportunities; the Chief Executive re employment

Main Activities
Set up in 1939 the British Polio Fellowship supports people in the UK and Eire who have a disability resulting from polio. A national organisation, it has a central headquarters and around 50 branches in various parts of the UK and Eire. Its income in 1993 was £1,224,000.

Opportunities for Volunteers
Volunteers are involved in administrative support, fundraising and organising local groups. They may also be welfare visitors. More are needed in different areas. Recruitment is through application to Central Office. The commitment required is flexible and those volunteers who are welfare visitors are offered travel and other expenses, and a volunteer allowance. Further details are available from Central office.

Opportunities for Employment
A small Central Office team is employed together with hotel and residential home staff. Some members of staff are recruited each year, both full- and part-time. Details are available on application. An equal opportunities policy is followed.

Further Information
General information is available from Central Office, as above.

Brook Advisory Centres

165 Grays Inn Road
London WC1X 8UD
Tel: 0171-833 8488
Fax: 0171-833 8182

Contact
Chief Executive

Main Activities
Originally founded in 1964, the Centres seek to assist young people with issues of sexual behaviour, including personal relationships, unwanted pregnancy and contraception. Centres in sixteen branch areas around the country (except East Anglia and the North East) offer young people free confidential birth control advice and supplies, and help with emotional and sexual problems. Advice and various publications are available for professionals too. Brook Advisory Centres cover Scotland, Northern Ireland and the Channel Islands also, but not Wales. National office works to a budget of £250,000, while branch budgets vary between £15,000 and £750,000.

Opportunities for Volunteers
Volunteers are regarded as vital to the work. They are used in both national office and in the branches, which are independent, mainly for fundraising and administrative support. Brook is actively seeking more, particularly people with accountancy skills and to assist with writing educational materials. Recruitment is through Volunteer Bureaux or in writing to Brook. About five to six hours commitment over one or two days a week is asked. Travel and lunch expenses are paid.

Opportunities for Employment
About twenty full- and part-time staff are employed, together with up to 500 part-time sessional health staff. Between fifty and sixty of these sessional branch workers are recruited each year, usually requiring medical, nursing and/or counselling skills. Positions are advertised in local newspapers or The Guardian. The Chief Executive can also be contacted. An equal opportunities policy operates.

Further Information
The Annual Report and a publications catalogue are available free on request.

Cancer Research Campaign

10 Cambridge Terrace
London NW1 4JL
Tel: 0171-224 1333
Fax: 0171-935 1546

Contact
Nicola Hill

Main Activities
The Cancer Research Campaign, a UK-wide organisation established in 1923, is the European leader in the development of new anti-cancer drugs and the supporter of about one third of all cancer research in the UK. CRC believes that no-one is doing more to reduce the suffering that this disease causes. It does not receive government support but raises its funds from the general public. During 1995 it will spend about £48 million on vital scientific research as a result of the time and money given by people from all walks of life. It has around 1,000 local support groups and 222 shops. Annual budget is around £48 million.

Opportunities for Volunteers
Volunteers are regarded as being very important to the Campaign's activities. They have opportunities to work in one of the Campaign's 222 shops in towns across the country. On-the-job training in a friendly environment is offered, together with the flexibility of working as few or as many hours as each volunteer wants. There are also opportunities to join one of the many local fundraising groups, or to help out at one of their fundraising

events. Again, the minimum commitment is flexible.

Opportunities for Employment

About 350 full-time and 200 part-time staff are employed by the Campaign. Jobs are advertised in The Guardian and The Daily Telegraph. The Campaign operates a formal Equal Opportunities Policy.

Further Information

The Annual Report, Welcome Pack, general information and contact numbers for local volunteer groups and Campaign shops are available.

Casualties Union

1 Grosvenor Crescent
London SW1X 7EE
Tel: 0171-235 5366

Contact

Della Svensson, Honorary General Secretary

Main Activities

The Casualties Union provides trained, acting casualties wherever first aid, nursing and rescue are taught. It is nationwide with branches and groups and was set up in 1942.

Opportunities for Volunteers

There are approximately 1,000 volunteers who assist with first aid training and provide administrative support. Training in make-up, acting and staging is given.

Opportunities for Employment

There is one part-time paid administrator.

Further Information

Annual Report, brochure and copy of journal are available from Head Office.

Child

Suite 219, Caledonian House
98 The Centre, Feltham
Middlesex TW13 4BH
Tel: 0181-893 7110 (24-hour)
Tel: 0181-844 2468 (9am-5.30pm)
Fax: 0181-893 2089

Contact

Clare Brown, Charity Co-ordinator

Main Activities

Set up in 1979 and a UK-wide organisation, Child promotes the care and treatment of infertility. It assists in the education of those suffering from infertility and provides counselling. There are 60 local support groups. Child also has links with similar organisations in America, Australia and France.

Opportunities for Volunteers

Volunteers are very important to Child because with limited funding most of the work is done on a voluntary basis. Volunteers are needed to fundraise, help run local groups and provide administrative support. Volunteers with some experience/ knowledge of infertility and with counselling and organisational skills are especially useful. A basic counselling skills course is offered.

Opportunities for Employment

There are two part-time members of staff.

Further Information

Annual Report, information leaflet and list of local groups available.

Child Accident Prevention Trust (CAPT)

4th Floor, Clerks Court
18-20 Farringdon Lane
London EC1R 3AU
Tel: 0171-608 3828
Fax: 0171-608 3674

Contact
Louise Pankhurst, Director

Main Activities
CAPT is a scientific advisory body concerned with all aspects of accidents in childhood. It aims to establish causes and patterns of accidents and find ways of reducing their number and severity. Apart from the main office in London, it has a small project in Belfast.

Opportunities for Volunteers
Volunteers are welcome and fairly important to CAPT which, as a small organisation with limited resources, can only offer limited scope in limited office space. But there is work to be done and volunteers are particularly needed to provide administrative support. Word processing skills (Word Perfect 5.1) would be an advantage. Minimum commitment is five hours a week for six months. Travel expenses offered.

Opportunities for Employment
Vacancies rare as there is a low staff turnover.

Further Information
Annual Report and list of publications available.

Cleft Lip And Palate Association (CLAPA)

1 Eastwood Gardens, Kenton
Newcastle-upon-Tyne NE3 3DQ
Tel: 0191-285 9396

Contact
Mrs Cy Thirlaway

Main Activities
CLAPA supports parents of children with the condition, and supplies information leaflets, advice and feeding equipment. It encourages research and fundraises for this. It has 56 local branches which link parents and professional workers through meetings. Also has links overseas. Budget depends on donations.

Opportunities for Volunteers
CLAPA welcomes volunteers, in head office and the branches, for administrative, advice, fundraising and project work eg applications to trusts for funds. Volunteers also help with Christmas card distribution and mail order for equipment. Recruitment is from among parents who have had support.

Opportunities for Employment
There are no opportunities as CLAPA is run by volunteers.

Further Information
Annual Report, list of local groups, leaflets and a 24-hour help line all available.

DEBRA (Dystrophic Epidermolysis Bullosa Research Association)

DEBRA House
13 Wellington Business Park
Dukes Road, Crowthorne
Berks RG11 6LS
Tel: 01344-771961

Contact
John Dart, Director

Main Activities
Offers support and welfare services to people with Epidermolysis Bullosa. Funds research into the condition. National organisation with two regional groups.

Opportunities for Volunteers
Volunteers are needed to do administrative and fundraising work. Travel expenses are offered.

Opportunities for Employment
There are four full-time and three part-time staff. Jobs are advertised in The Guardian.

Further Information
Annual Report and publications list available.

Down's Syndrome Association (DSA)

155 Mitcham Road
London SW17 9PG
Tel: 0181-682 4001

Contact
Anna Khan, Director

Main Activities
A parents' self-help organisation, DSA provides information, support and advice on all aspects of the condition. It aims to educate the public, and promote the care of people with the syndrome, as well as research into the condition. National with 75 regional groups and 19 local branches.

Opportunities for Volunteers
DSA has a few volunteers in head office and each of the branches who help with administration and fundraising. Recruitment is as required, on application. A minimum of six hours a week is required. Travel expenses are paid.

Opportunities for Employment
DSA has eight full-time and six part-time staff, and may recruit one or two people a year. Positions are advertised in The Guardian and Sunday Times. An equal opportunities policy is being implemented.

Further Information
Annual Report, list of local groups and various leaflets available. The Scottish DSA at 158 Balgreen Road, Edinburgh EH11 3QA, covers Scotland.

The Dystonia Society

Weddel House
13/14 West Smithfield
London EC1A 9JJ
Tel: 0171-329 0797

Contact
Mrs J Mason, Office Manager

Main Activities
Supports the sufferers of the neurological disorders known as the Dystonias. Aims to find cure for the disorder. There are many self-help groups.

Opportunities for Volunteers
Volunteers are needed to provide administrative support. Clerical and secretarial skills are useful as well as a good command of the English language. Fundraising volunteers are also needed for the local groups.

Opportunities for Employment
There are three full-time and one part-time members of staff.

Further Information
Annual Report and leaflets on dystonia available. For Scotland, contact Donald

Macphee, The Dystonia Society in Scotland, 121 St Vincent Street, Glasgow G2 5HW, tel: 0141-221 8422.

Elimination of Leukaemia Fund (ELF)

17 Venetian Road
London SE5 9RR
Tel: 0171-737 4141
Fax: 0171-737 7009

Contact
Martyn Hall, Director

Main Activities
ELF's primary aim is to raise funds to improve facilities for the care and treatment of people suffering from leukaemia and other blood disorders. It is involved with King's College Hospital (London), the specialist treatment centre in S E England.

Opportunities for Volunteers
Volunteers are very important. Head Office uses six for administrative work, and there are 100 volunteer fundraisers. More volunteers are needed all year round for both areas of work. They are recruited through ad hoc applications, in-house drives, and King's College Hospital notice-boards. An application form and two references are required for fund raisers. Minimum commitment is two hours a week for at least a month. Travel, lunch and other reasonable expenses are paid, plus a volunteer allowance.

Opportunities for Employment
Opportunities are few because there are only two full-time and one part-time staff. Any vacancies are advertised in The Guardian and job centres.

Further Information
Annual accounts, newsletter three times a year and general information published.

Family Planning Association (FPA)

27-35 Mortimer Street
London W1N 7RJ
Tel: 0171-636 7866
Fax: 0171-436 3288

Contact
Central Inquiries Officer

Main Activities
Promotes sexual health and family planning through information, training, education, publicity and publications.

Opportunities for Volunteers
Volunteers are occasionally needed to give administrative support. Minimum commitment is a day a week.

Opportunities for Employment
There are 38 full-time and six part-time staff.

Further Information
Annual Report, FPA publications, booklist and course brochures available.

Fight for Sight

Institute of Ophthalmology
Bath Street
London EC1V 9EL
Tel: 0171-490 8644

Contact
Anne Munby, Regional Support Manager

Main Activities
Raises funds for research into prevention, treatment and cure of eye disease and blindness. There are eight regional groups.

Opportunities for Volunteers
Volunteers are essential. Regional fundraisers are needed to organise events and flag collections. Support is provided by a full-time Regional Manager. Administrative help is needed at Head Office. Travel and any out-of-pocket expenses are offered.

Opportunities for Employment

There are four full-time and one part-time staff. Approximately one person recruited each year.

Further Information

Annual Report, leaflet and list of local groups available.

Foundation for the Study of Infant Deaths, *see Children*

The Haemophilia Society, *see Counselling & Self-help*

Headway, National Head Injuries Association Ltd, *see Social Welfare*

Health Rights Ltd

Unit 405
Brixton Small Business Centre
444 Brixton Road
London SW9 8EJ
Tel: 0171-274 4000, extension 326/417
Fax: 0171-733 0351

Contact

Jane Cowl, Information Worker

Main Activities

Promotes health as a basic right, and the rights of all people to free, quality health care. Provides information, stimulates discussion through public meetings, conferences and seminars and works with other similar groups. Membership available. London-based, with 35 affiliated organisations. Produces research and publications. Annual budget £52,000.

Opportunities for Volunteers

Three volunteers help with administrative, promotions, research and information work. Recruited through volunteer bureaux and sometimes advertising. Minimum commitment 7 hours weekly for a month. Travel and lunch expenses paid.

Opportunities for Employment

Only three part-time staff employed so opportunities are few. Any posts are advertised in The Guardian, The Voice and the Pink Paper, based on an equal opportunities policy.

Further Information

Publishes an Activities Report, membership leaflet and bulletin. Other publications available for sale.

Help to Hand

1 Fladesloe Close
Chessington, Surrey KT9 25Q
Tel: 0181-379 2454
Fax: 0181-391 5518

Contact

Pauline Hamblin, Chief Executive

Main Activities

Help to Hand produces a self-help directory on health and associated problems.

Opportunities for Volunteers

Volunteers in the Chessington, Surrey area are needed for checking entries, research and writing. Telephone and computer skills as well as good writing, spelling and a sense of humour are useful. Time commitment very flexible.

Opportunities for Employment

There are four staff.

Further Information

Help to Hand Directory available.

Herpes Association, *see Counselling & Self-Help*

Humane Research Trust (HRT), *see Animal Welfare*

Huntington's Disease Association

108 Battersea High Street
London SW11 3HP
Tel: 0171-223 7000

Contact
Director, Mark Payne

Main Activities
Provides support for those suffering from, or caring for, Huntington's Disease. Aims to enhance knowledge and understanding of the disease both among relevant professional workers and the general public. Covers England and Wales, has local branches and ten local support groups.

Opportunities for Volunteers
Both Head Office, local branches and groups use volunteers, for routine work and for particular one-off events.

Opportunities for Employment
There are eight staff. Vacancies are rare. An equal opportunities policy is under development.

Further Information
Annual Report and list of local groups available, together with a wide range of publications on the disease.

Ileostomy and Internal Pouch Support group (IA), *see Counselling & Self-Help*

Imperial Cancer Research Fund

PO Box 123
Lincoln's Inn Fields
London WC2A 3PX
Tel: 0171-242 0200

Contact
Central office or appropriate regional centre for volunteering; Personnel Department for employment opportunities

Main Activities
Entirely devoted to research into the causes, prevention and treatment of cancer in all forms. National with nine regional groups, including Scotland, and ten local branches.

Opportunities for Volunteers
The Fund uses thousands of volunteers for fundraising, in its 460 charity shops, and for administrative/secretarial work in the regional offices. Volunteers are always needed, but must be able to work in a team. Training given plus support by Area Retail or Appeals Managers. Recruitment is ad hoc on application to regional centres, via volunteer bureaux and through advertisements, posters and press releases. Minimum commitment is one four-hour shift a week in a charity shop; flexible for fundraisers. No remuneration offered.

Opportunities for Employment
The Fund is a large employer, with 1,400 full-time and 182 part-time staff. About 10 fund raisers are recruited each year; other posts arise through natural turn over. Vacancies are advertised in various print media, including national and local press, scientific journals and free magazines.

Further Information
Annual report and a wide variety of publications available from the Public Relations Department. The Fund in Scotland is at: Scottish Centre, 19 Murray Place, Stirling FK8 1DQ, tel: 01786-79137.

Institute for Complementary Medicine

PO Box 194
London SE16 1QZ
Tel: 0171-237 5165

Contact
Mrs Foulkes

Main Activities
Provides information and funds research on complementary medicine. National organisation with 300 affiliated organisations. Produces register of Complementary Practioners and Services as well as 420 public information points. Annual budget is £200,000.

Opportunities for Volunteers
Volunteers are very important and support the work throughout the country. Office skills including answering the telephone are useful. Travel expenses are offered.

Opportunities for Employment
There are four full-time staff.

Further Information
Annual Report available on request.

Institute of Cancer Research ICR

Royal Cancer Hospital
17A Onslow Gardens
London SW7 3AL
Tel: 0171-352 8133
Fax: 0171-225 2574

Contact
Amanda Wilson, Assistant Secretary

Main Activities
Post-graduate research and teaching into causes, treatment and prevention of cancer, in London and Surrey. Graduate students under take three year higher research degrees beginning each October. Budget £23 million annually.

Opportunities for Volunteers
The Institute does not use volunteers.

Opportunities for Employment
About fifty staff are recruited annually. The Institute particularly seeks high flyer, post-doctoral scientists. It has a total of 550 full-time and 40 part-time staff. Posts are advertised in specialist magazines including Science, New Scientist, Nature, British Medical Journal (BMJ) and the Lancet, and in the Evening Standard. An equal opportunities policy is being implemented.

Further Information
Annual Report available.

International Centre for Active Birth

55 Dartmouth Park Road
London NW5 1SL
Tel: 071-267 3006

Contact
Janet Balaskas, Keith Brainin, Directors

Main Activities
Provides support and advice so parents-to-be, in the UK and overseas, can empower themselves for birth and parenthood, and have the best possible experience of pregnancy, labour and birth. Offers a range of services, including workshops, courses, books and tapes, and water baths, for parents-to-be and professional health care workers also.

Opportunities for Volunteers
The Centre does not currently use volunteers.

Opportunities for Employment
There are no opportunities for employment at present.

Further Information
Various leaflets available.

Iris Fund for Prevention of Blindness

York House, Ground Floor
199 Westminster Bridge Road
London SE1 7UT
Tel: 0171-928 7743
Fax: 0171-928 7919

Contact
Mrs Vanessa Wilde, Executive Director

Main Activities
Raises money for research into the prevention and cure of blindness. Provides ophthalmic equipment for clinical, medical and surgical treatment of eye disease. Closely associated with St Thomas's Hospital, London with most events taking place in London. Funding is available UK-wide. Annual budget is approximately £900,000.

Opportunities for Volunteers
Administrative work is carried out by volunteers as needed from time to time.

Opportunities for Employment
There is one full-time and one part-time member of staff.

Further Information
Annual Report and information available.

ISD (Institute for the Study of Drug Dependence)

Waterbridge House
32-36 Loman Street
London SE1 0EE
Tel: 0171-928 1211

Contact
Jenny Sleeman, Fundraising Manager

Main Activities
Collects, supplies, researches and publishes information on all aspects of drugs. Annual budget is £1 million.

Opportunities for Volunteers
Volunteers are needed to support administration and events. Ability, a sense

of humour and good social skills, an unflappable manner and an ability to work in a group are useful. Travel expenses are offered.

Opportunities for Employment
There are 26 full-time and two part-time staff. Jobs are advertised in the national press.

Further Information
Annual Report available.

The Karuna Trust, see Overseas & the Developing World

La Leche League (Great Britain) (LLL(GB)), see Women

LEPRA (The British Leprosy Relief Association)

Third Floor, Fairfax House
Causton Road, Colchester
Essex CO1 1PU
Tel: 01206-562286
Fax: 01206-712151

Contact
Personnel Department

Main Activities
Works for the eradication of leprosy, by enabling treatment in those countries where the disease is endemic, and by educating people in the UK of the need to help and make donations. Supports leprosy control programmes, has projects in Malawi, India and Brazil, and promotes research into the disease. National with regional structure, and overseas project centres. Annual budget over £3.3 million.

Opportunities for Volunteers
Ten people help in the main office and numerous volunteers undertake administrative and fundraising work in the regions. More are needed all year round in both these areas. Good communication skills, especially on the telephone, are

required. Volunteers are recruited through ad hoc applications, volunteer bureaux, in-house methods and occasional advertising campaigns. Minimum commitment is three hours a week. Travel and lunch expenses are paid.

Opportunities for Employment
LEPRA is seeking more fund raisers, but otherwise job opportunities are few. There are 36 full-time and twenty part-time staff. Any vacancies are advertised in The Guardian, local newspapers and job centres. LEPRA is working towards an equal opportunities policy.

Further Information
House newspaper, Annual Report and various pamphlets are published. A list of local groups and posters also available.

Leukaemia Research Fund

43 Great Ormond Street
London WC1N 3JJ
Tel: 0171-405 0101

Contact
Joyce House

Main Activities
The Leukaemia Research Fund is the only national fundraising charity devoting all its resources to leukaemia and related cancers of the blood.

Opportunities for Volunteers
The Fund has 248 voluntary branches throughout the UK and members organise a variety of fundraising events. Members are vital and the Fund is actively recruiting new members for branches. Local contacts may be found in Yellow Pages or by ringing Head Office.

Opportunities for Employment
There are 26 full-time members of staff.

Further Information
Annual report and patient information booklets are available on request.

Maternity and Health Links,
see Women

Medical Aid for Palestinians (MAP)

33A Islington Park Street
London N1 1QB
Tel: 0171-226 4114

Contact
Jim Buttery, Volunteers/Appeals Officer

Main Activities
MAP aims to improve the medical conditions of the Palestinian people. It provides material, financial and personnel support in all areas of health care to Palestinian communities in the Occupied Territories, Lebanon, Egypt and Jordan. One regional office in Scotland and affiliated organisations overseas (Middle East and Canada). Annual budget is £1 million.

Opportunities for Volunteers
MAP sends specialised medical volunteers - doctors, nurses and paramedics - to Lebanon and the Occupied Territories in response to urgent requests from independent, charitable Palestinian hospitals/health institutions. Such volunteers are needed year round, and must have practical, up-to-date, hands-on medical knowledge/experience. Full support in the field is given. Recruitment is ad hoc by application and through advertising in medical journals, national press and on hospital notice boards. A CV, two referees and interview are required. Minimum contract is six months with return air fares, health insurance and reasonable living expenses paid. On return home volunteers often help MAP in other ways eg fundraising, advice.

Opportunities for Employment
A small, settled team of staff run both MAP offices and opportunities are rare. Any vacancies are advertised in the national press. Experience of development

work and a knowledge of the Palestinian situation are essential.

Further Information
Annual Report and Review, and various MAP health publications available. In Scotland: SMAP - Scottish Medical Aid for Palestinians, Suite 1, Fifth Floor, 73 Robertson Street, Glasgow, Scotland G2, tel: 0141-204 1443.

Medical Aid for Poland Fund (MAP)

16 Warwick Road
London SW5 9UD
Tel: 0171-373 5464
Fax: 0171-259 2692

Contact
Richard Sliwa, Office Manager

Main Activities
Provides medical aid to Polish hospitals

Opportunities for Volunteers
A small number of volunteers are required for administrative support in London office. Minimum commitment is one day a week. An experienced fundraiser is also needed. Volunteers are needed for sorting medical donations in the warehouse and for collecting from hospitals. The organisation is planning to have a charity shop. A knowledge of Polish is useful.

Opportunities for Employment
There are no full-time staff.

Further Information
Twice yearly review obtainable from head office.

Mental Health Foundation, see Mental Health

MIND (National Association for Mental Health), see Mental Health

Midwives Information and Resource Service, see Education

Motor Neurone Disease Association (MNDA)

David Niven House
PO Box 246
Northampton NN1 2PR
Tel: 01604-250505
Fax: 01604-24726

Contact
Gill Bausor, Branch & Volunteer Development Manager for volunteering; and Tricia Holmes, Assistant Director for employment opportunities.

Main Activities
MNDA funds research and patient care. It offers people with MND and their carers advice and information, care advisers, support groups, an equipment loan scheme and some financial assistance. A national organisation, MNDA has 100 local branches. Annual budget £2 million.

Opportunities for Volunteers
Volunteers are seen as vital to the successful running of MNDA. They are welcomed to help with fundraising, administrative support, counselling and specific projects eg marketing, data base development. They can also be on the national telephone helpline or a volunteer visitor, trained to give help and support to people with MND. National Office uses about 16 and the branches several hundred. Recruitment is through in-house schemes, volunteer bureaux, posters and radio talks. Prospective volunteers have an informal interview with a staff member first and job descriptions are drawn up. Induction, training and appropriate support are all given.

Opportunities for Employment
Recruitment, possibly four a year, includes care advisers and branch development staff. Professional posts are

advertised in The Guardian and sometimes The Independent; clerical posts in
the local press. MNDA employs eighteen
full-time and 22 part-time staff. It is implementing an equal opportunities policy.

Further Information
Annual Report, list of local groups and
pamphlets on volunteering available. In
Scotland contact:

Scottish Motor Neurone Disease Association, 50 Parnie Street, Glasgow G1 5LS, tel:
0141-552 0507

Multiple Births Foundation, see
Children

**Multiple Sclerosis Society of
Great Britain and Northern
Ireland**, see Social Welfare

Muscular Dystrophy
Group of Great Britain
and Northern Ireland

7-11 Prescott Place
London SW4 6BS
Tel: 0171-720 8055

Contact
Lyn Walker

Main Activities
Raises funds for research, provides
information about neuromuscular
conditions and offers support to families.
There are 450 local branches.

Opportunities for Volunteers
Volunteers are needed to undertake essen-
tial fundraising in local branches.
Administrative support is needed at Head
Office. Travel expenses are offered.

Opportunities for Employment
There are 37 full-time and 28 regional staff.
Ten people were recruited in 1994. Jobs
are advertised in The Guardian.

Further Information
Annual Report and a variety of publications on specific conditions.

Myalgic Encephalomyelitis
Association (ME Association),
see Counselling & Self-Help

Myasthenia Gravis
Association

Keynes House
77 Nottingham Road
Derby DE1 3QS
Tel: 01332-290219

Contact
Mrs J Wilkinson, Development Director

Main Activities
Funds research into a cure for the disease,
provides a support network for sufferers
and their families, and undertakes education to increase public and medical
awareness. A national organisation, it has
26 local groups and 60 local representatives.

Opportunities for Volunteers
Voluteers are welcomed in central
office and the branches to undertake administrative and fundraising work. Those
with personal experience of MG also act
as volunteers offering mutual support and
education. More volunteers are needed
generally. No minimum commitment is
required.

Opportunities for Employment
The Association has a small office and a
staff of four, two full and two part-time.
Posts are advertised in the national press.
An equal opportunities policy is being de-
veloped.

Further Information
Information packs for sufferers, medical
practitioners and the public available.
Annual report published.

NASPCS, The Charity for Incontinent and Stoma Children, *see Children*

National Ankylosing Spondylitis Society (NASS)

5 Grosvenor Crescent
London SW1X 7ER
Tel: 0171-235 9585
Fax: 0171-235 5827

Contact
Mr F J Rogers, Director

Main Activities
Exists to provide education and advice for sufferers and the medical profession on medical and social matters relating to the disease. Promotes better treatment facilities, and forms local branch organisations in main cities which provide weekly physiotherapy after working hours. NASS is a national organisation with 80 local branches, and has helped set up sister societies in 25 countries. Annual budget is £100,000.

Opportunities for Volunteers
About 400 volunteers run the branch committees and undertake fundraising and administrative work. There is no minimum time commitment and no remuneration offered. Physiotherapists who work for the branches are in most cases paid a small remuneration by the branches themselves.

Opportunities for Employment
NASS has only two full-time staff. There are no employment opportunities, except those for physiotherapists in the branches (see above).

Further Information
Publishes an Annual Report, a twice yearly newsletter for members and guidebook free of charge, and has various publications for sale. Also has a list of local groups and a physiotherapy video available.

National Association for Colitis and Crohns Disease (NACC)

PO Box 205
St Albans, Herts AL1 1AB
Tel: 01727-844296 (24-hour answerphone line and fax)

Contact
Mr R Driscoll, Director

Main Activities
Provides support, information and welfare for people affected by inflammatory bowel disease. Undertakes fundraising for research into the causes and treatment of colitis and Crohns disease. A national organisation, NACC has 60 area groups/branches which hold meetings and other activities. Annual budget is £450,000.

Opportunities for Volunteers
Volunteers work in head office (2) and the groups (350) in administration, fundraising and giving advice. They are also involved in producing newsletters and other publications, public relations and analysing questionnaires. NACC is actively seeking more volunteers to help in all these areas. It is also exploring the possibility of using volunteers to help with the groups which are mostly run by patients who are sometimes ill. Recruitment is through written applications to head office, volunteer bureaux and in-house drives. Commitment is negotiable and travel expenses are offered.

Opportunities for Employment
NACC employs three full-time and three part-time staff. In early 1993 it was beginning external recruitment, with an emphasis on office skills and professional experience. Seasonal work opportunities arise in the Christmas mail order scheme.

NACC operates an equal opportunities policy.

Further Information
The Annual Report, a leaflet on the disease and a list of local groups are published.

National Association of Leagues of Hospital Friends,
see Hospitals & Hospices

National Association for the Relief of Paget's Disease (NARPD)

207 Eccles Old Road
Salford M6 8HD
Tel: 0161-707 9225

Contact
Mrs P Roberts, Administrator

Main Activities
Exists to promote, encourage and assist research into the diagnosis, treatment and prevention of Paget's Disease and related disorders. Also works for the relief of sufferers and organises activities on their behalf. A national organisation, NARPD has four local support groups.

Opportunities for Volunteers
The local support groups are voluntary and run by sufferers themselves. Only sufferers can volunteer.

Opportunities for Employment
NARPD is run by two part-time staff and there are no employment opportunities.

Further Information
Annual report and various publications available including A Guide to Paget's Disease, and posters.

National Asthma Campaign

Providence House
Providence Place
London N1 0NT
Tel: 0171-226 2260
Fax: 0171-704 0740

Contact
Mrs Kim Nightingale, Branches and Membership Department, for volunteering in local branches; Miss June Nichols, Personnel and Administration Department, for volunteering in Head Office

Main Activities
Promotes and funds research into asthma and allied disorders and communicates its findings. Offers information, support and education to people with asthma, their families, health professionals and the general public. The National Asthma Campaign has approximately 180 branches around the country and an income of around £3.8 million.

Opportunities for Volunteers
The local branches are all run by volunteers. Help is needed in administration and fundraising, and also by Head Office. Volunteers interested in supporting their local branch should contact the Branch Liaison Department for further details. Recruitment for Head Office is by application at the above address. Occasional volunteer recruitment drives are held. No minimum commitment, but volunteer help is particularly needed during Asthma Week and for mail-outs during the year.

Opportunities for Employment
Permanent positions occasionally arise and are either advertised in national newspapers (eg The Guardian) or through recruitment agencies. The Campaign operates equal opportunity procedures. There are 33 full-time and eight part-time staff.

Further Information
Annual report, details of local groups, leaflets and fact sheets available.

National Benevolent Fund for the Aged (NBFA), *see Elderly People*

National Childbirth Trust (NCT), *see Women*

National Eczema Society (NES)

4 Tavistock Place
London WC1H 9RA
Tel: 0171-388 4097
Fax: 0171-388 5882

Contact
Julie Braithwaite

Main Activities
Provides information and support to people with eczema and their carers. Funds research into the disease. There are 250 local support groups. Annual budget is £500,000.

Opportunities for Volunteers
Volunteers are needed to give administrative and secretarial support. Travel and lunch expenses are offered.

Opportunities for Employment
There are eighteen full-time and two part-time staff. Jobs are advertised in The Guardian or appropriate specialist journals.

Further Information
Annual Report available. Leaflets available to members of NES.

National Federation of Kidney Patients Associations

6 Stanley Street, Worksop
Nottinghamshire S81 7HX
Tel: 01909-487795
Fax: 01909-481723

Contact
Margeret Jackson, National Co-ordinator

Main Activities
The Federation is an advice and information centre for patients and their families, students, the medical profession and the general public. It represents patients interests to the Government and media. It also campaigns for increased treatment facilities and encourages public awareness of the importance of organ donations and transplants. A national organisation, it has 48 local affiliates to which it gives support.

Opportunities for Volunteers
The Federation does not use volunteers itself, but the local Kidney Patients Associations (KPAs) do for supporting the activities and services they provide for the members. The KPAs are responsible for running their own affairs.

Opportunities for Employment
The Federation has a very small staff of one full-time and three part-time employees. There are no opportunities for employment.

Further Information
Publishes Annual report, a quarterly magazine 'Kidney Life' and various leaflets.

National Meningitis Trust

Fern House, Bath Road
Stroud, Glos GL5 3TJ
Tel: 01453-751738
Fax: 01453-753588

Contact
Bridie Taylor, National Development

Main Activities
Funds medical research and provides information on meningitis for public and professionals. Offers support to sufferers and their families. Annual budget approximately £1 million.

Opportunities for Volunteers
Volunteers are needed in Head Office to give administrative support. They are most needed in the run-up to annual Meningitis Awareness week in September/October. All the year round groups require people to fundraise, collect and distribute information. Reliability and responsible attitude are useful personal qualities.

Opportunities for Employment
There are fifteen full-time and four part-time staff. On average one or two are recruited each year. Jobs are advertised in The Guardian for senior posts and locally for junior posts.

Further Information
Annual Report, quarterly newsletter and list of local help groups available on request.

National Reye's Syndrome Foundation of the UK (Reye's Syndrome Foundation)

15 Nicholas Gardens
Pyrford, Woking
Surrey GU22 8SD
Tel: 01932-346843

Contact
Gordon Denney, Honorary Administrator and Treasurer

Main Activities
Provides funds for research into the cause, treatment, cure and prevention of Reye's Syndrome and Reye-like illnesses. Offers support to families of patients and raises awareness among professionals. The budget of approx. £24,000 is mainly for research costs.

Opportunities for Volunteers
A self-help group, all voluntary work is undertaken by interested parents within the organisation.

Opportunities for Employment
There are no paid staff and no opportunities for employment.

Further Information
Annual report, newsletter and leaflets available.

Neuroblastoma Society

41 Towncourt Crescent
Pettswood, Kent BR5 1PH
Tel: 01689-873338
Fax: 01689-873338

Contact
Mrs A Ward, Secretary

Main Activities
Raises money for medical research into neuroblastoma. Gives support to parents. There are four local branches. Annual budget is £50,000.

Opportunities for Volunteers
Volunteers are needed to help with fundraising.

Opportunities for Employment
There is one part-time member of staff.

Further Information
Annual Report, leaflets, list of local groups and parents booklets available on request.

The Neurofibromatosis Association, see Counselling & Self-Help

New Approaches to Cancer, see Counselling & Self-Help

Noonan Syndrome Society (NSS)

Unit 5 Brindley Business Park
Chaseside Drive, Cannock
Staffs WS11 1GD
Tel: 01922-415500

Contact
Sue Reynolds, National Organising Secretary

Main Activities
Provides support and information for families who have a child with Noonan's Syndrome. Promotes professional awareness and research into the condition. Parent representatives form a network of local contacts.

Opportunities for Volunteers
Volunteers are always needed to fundraise and organise events. Fundraising information and supplies are offered. Speakers for meetings are also needed.

Opportunities for Employment
There are two part-time staff.

Further Information
Annual Report, newsletter, family information pack, professional information pack

and information booklet are available on request.

Parkinson's Disease Society of the UK

22 Upper Woburn Place
London WC1H 0RA
Tel: 0171-383 3513
Fax: 0171-383 5754

Contact
Rhona Trodd, Office Manager

Main Activities
Works towards the conquest of Parkinson's Disease and alleviation of the suffering and distress it causes, through research, education and communication. Annual budget is £4 million.

Opportunities for Volunteers
Volunteers are involved either in the London Headquarters, or in helping to run one of the 220 branches throughout the UK. Particular skills such as computer literacy and typing are useful, but any voluntary help is welcomed. Following a two-day training volunteers also cover a telephone helpline weekdays from 10.00 to 4.00. Travel and basic lunch expenses are offered.

Opportunities for Employment
There are 54 staff. Jobs are advertised in the national and local press as appropriate.

Further Information
Annual Report, list of local groups and information leaflets available.

Phab, Physically Disabled and Able Bodied, see Disability

QUIT - Helping Smokers to Quit, see Counselling & Self-Help

The Raynaud's & Scleroderma Association

112 Crewe Road
Alsager, Cheshire ST7 2JA
Tel: 01270-872776
Fax: 01270-883556

Contact
Anne Mawdsley MBE, Director

Main Activities
Raises awareness of Raynaud's Disease and Scleroderma. Sponsors research and supports the welfare of patients.

Opportunities for Volunteers
Volunteers are occasionally needed for specific fundraising events. There is always one disabled volunteer on a regular basis and the premises have been specially adapted for this purpose.

Opportunities for Employment
There are four staff members and jobs are advertised through the Job Centre.

Further Information
The Annual Report and a list of publications are available.

Re-Solv

30A High Street
Stone, Staffs ST15 8AW
Tel: 01785-817885

Contact
Josie Hamer, National Training Manager

Main Activities
Reduces and prevents solvent abuse through educational programmes and sponsoring of research.

Opportunities for Volunteers
Volunteers support the work of three local branches in fundraising and administrative support. Journalistic skills, including editing and press-cutting analysis, are always welcome. Minimum commitment is three hours a week for three months. Training on the work of Re-Solv is offered.

An application form, which requires two references, is available.

Opportunities for Employment
There are fifteen staff members and approximately three people are recruited each year.

Further Information
A list of local groups is available, as well a range of publications and the Annual Report.

Research into Ageing

Baird House
15-17 St Cross Street
London EC1N 8UN
Tel: 0171-404 6878
Fax: 0171-404 6816

Contact
Elizabeth Mills

Main Activities
Supports medical research into the diseases and conditions which affect the quality of life of the elderly.

Opportunities for Volunteers
Volunteers run the numerous support groups which fundraise and provide administrative support. Basic administration skills are very welcome. In-house computer training is provided and a day a week is the commitment suggested.

Opportunities for Employment
There are seven staff in Head Office, and approximately one person is recruited each year.

Further Information
Annual Report, list of the local groups and other information are available.

Research Trust for Metabolic Diseases in Children (RTMDC)

Golden Gates Lodge
Weston Road, Crewe
Cheshire CW1 1XN
Tel: 01270-250221

Contact
Mrs Lesley Greene, Director of Support Services

Main Activities
Raises funds for research into metabolic diseases and supports families who have a child suffering from a metabolic disease. There are 21 regional branches and two specific disease groups ie for Congenital Adrenal Hyperplasis and Niemann Pick Disorder.

Opportunities for Volunteers
Volunteers undertake fundraising and administrative work.

Opportunities for Employment
There are ten staff, three based in regional offices.

Further Information
A list of local groups is available, and also newsletters, videos and pamphlets.

St Andrews Ambulance Association

St Andrews House
48 Milton Street
Glasgow G4 0HR
Tel: 0141-332 4031
Fax: 0141-332 6582

Contact
Local Groups via Head Office Recruitment Officer for volunteering; David Rickards, Office Manager re employment

Main Activities
A voluntary aid society, the Association provides first aid training to all levels and also trained first aiders at public events,

organises youth groups (Badgers and Cadets), and supplies first aid equipment, training aids and materials. Set up in 1882 it has a national network in Scotland of local branches together with Head Quarters support.

Opportunities for Volunteers
Around 3,500 volunteers in the branches play the major part in providing the Association's services in local communities. They organise the local groups, provide administrative support and are involved in management and trusteeship. They also provide first aid training, youth group leadership and first aid cover at public events, as well as undertaking fundraising and public relations. They are recruited ad hoc on application and more are always needed. Full training support is available from both the local groups and Head Office. There is no minimum commitment and out-of-pocket expenses are paid.

Opportunities for Employment
The Association employs 20 full-time, seven part-time and ten temporary staff. No further details provided.

Further Information
The Annual Report, a list of local groups and a range of other information and material are available from Head Office.

St John Ambulance (part of the Order of St John)

1 Grosvenor Crescent
London SW1X 7EF
Tel: 0171-235 5231

Contact
Local unit for volunteering; and Director of Services regarding employment opportunities

Main Activities
The organisation specialises in first aid teaching and practice. The practice covers many different areas of first aid provision,

including the St John Ambulance Brigade, care and auxiliary nursing in the community for children, elderly and handicapped people, and the Aeromedical Service 'AA St John Alert' which brings people needing urgent medical attention back to the UK. First aid training courses are taken by over 250,000 people a year. A national organisation, it has 47 regional groups and 3,500 local divisions. Annual budget c.£30 million.

Opportunities for Volunteers
St John Ambulance is staffed by volunteers who are members of it. Children from six can join; cadets are older. Volunteers are always needed, especially for weekend duties. They are needed also for administration, fundraising and ambulance duties. Training is given as required. Head office uses twenty and the divisions over 80,000 volunteers. Recruitment is ad hoc by application, through in-house schemes such as the 'Energy Scheme', and by word of mouth. Minimum commitment is two hours a week over a year. Travel expenses are paid. Local units are in the phone directory.

Opportunities for Employment
Approximately three people are recruited a year. Posts are advertised in the national press or the London Evening Standard. Sometimes Reed and Graduate Careers consultants are used. There is an equal opportunities policy. 139 full-time and 4 part-time staff are employed.

Further Information
Annual report and other literature available. For Wales contact:

St John Ambulance, Priory House, Lisvane Road, Llanishen, Cardiff CF4 5XT

For Northern Ireland contact: St John Ambulance, Erne Purdyburn Hospital, Saintfield Road, Belfast BT8 8RA.

Share Holiday Village, *see Recreation & Leisure*

Sickle Cell Society

54 Station Road
London NW10 4UA
Tel: 0181-961 7795

Contact
Jennifer Richards

Main Activities
Supports families and individuals affected by sickle cell disease. Campaigns for better services for sufferers and supports research into the disease. There are 63 regional groups.

Opportunities for Volunteers
Help is needed with events especially between June and September. Various educational projects also exist. Volunteers should send in a current CV.

Opportunities for Employment
There is one full-time member of staff. Jobs are advertised in The Guardian, The Voice and the Nursing Times.

Further Information
Information pack available on receipt of a large SAE.

TOFS Tracheo-Oesophagal Fistula Support

St George's Centre
91 Victoria Road, Netherfield
Nottingham NG4 2NN
Tel: 0115-940 0694

Contact
Dr David Dobbs

Main Activities
Promotes contact between families who have a child with TOF. Regular information is sent to family members and a national conference is held every two years. There are 30 local branches.

Opportunities for Volunteers
Volunteers run the local branches. Fundraising, counselling and communication skills are particularly useful.

Opportunities for Employment
There are three part-time staff.

Further Information
A list of local groups is available, as well as information pamphlets.

UK Band of Hope

25(F) Copperfield Street
London SE1 0EN
Tel: 0171-928 0848

Contact
Mr G Ruston, Executive Director

Main Activities
Promotes a drug-free way of life through preventive education. Activities include literature, educational talks, exhibitions and specific local projects. There are 29 affiliated organisations. Annual budget is £260,000.

Opportunities for Volunteers
Volunteers are needed to give talks to young people's groups. Training is given twice a year. Administrative support is also given by volunteers.

Opportunities for Employment
There are twelve full-time staff.

Further Information
Annual Report available.

UK Thalassaemia Society

107 Nightingale Lane
London N8 7QY
Tel: 0181-348 0437

Contact
Co-ordinator

Main Activities
Counsels and brings together people suffering from thalassaemia. Promotes education, understanding and research into the condition. National organisation with two support groups.

Opportunities for Volunteers
Volunteers are needed to give talks about thalassaemia mostly during weekdays. Help is also needed with fundraising.

Opportunities for Employment
There are two part-time staff.

Further Information
Information leaflet, videos and booklets available.

UKAN Narcolepsy Association (UK)

South Hall, High Street
Farningham, Kent DA4 0DE
Tel: 01322-863056
Fax: 01322-863056

Contact
Honorary Director

Main Activities
Promotes awareness of narcolepsy and encourages research into its causes and treatment. Supports local self-help groups. National organisation with six local support groups. Annual budget is £10,000.

Opportunities for Volunteers
Volunteers are needed to give administrative support. Book-keeping would be a useful skill. Travel expenses are offered.

Opportunities for Employment
There are no employment opportunities.

Further Information
Annual Report, brochures and reports available on request.

Vitiligo Society

97 Avenue Road
Beckenham, Kent BR3 4RX
Tel: 0181-776 7022

Contact
IA Fredriksen, Chairman

Main Activities
Supports people with vitiligo and promotes an understanding of the condition. Encourages and funds research.

Opportunities for Volunteers
Volunteers needed to do fundraising and PR, as trustees, committee members and branch organisers, and to provide specific skills. Minimum commitment is four hours a week.

Opportunities for Employment
There are two members of staff.

Further Information
General information leaflet available to enquirers. Wider range of literature for members, including quarterly newsletter.

Women's Nationwide Cancer Control Campaign (WNCCC),
see Women

Hospitals & Hospices

Hospitals use large numbers of volunteers in a wide variety of roles. Many have a Voluntary Services Department which co-ordinates the activities of volunteers. In others, the League of Hospital Friends (see entry below) and the WRVS (see entry under Social Welfare) take on some or all of the services. Usually volunteers are screened and a health check is carried out.

The first step is to contact your local hospital to see what sort of opportunities exist. Volunteering in the Health Service is not limited to hospitals alone. Many Health Centres, GP surgeries and units looking after people living in the community, such as ex-mental patients, also use volunteer help.

Each hospital will vary slightly in its volunteer requirements, but here is a selection of tasks that may be need to be done.

Ward helping includes feeding and chatting to patients and taking them shopping. Pre-medical students often do this to gain useful experience and develop their communication skills.

Drivers are used to take patients home, and to and from their appointments. Other jobs include chaplaincy visiting, reception, working in tea bars and canteens, and running trolley shops. Some hospitals have schemes for visiting elderly people. Sometimes police cadets volunteer on these as part of their community service training.

Fundraising for items of specialist equipment as well as comforts like television sets is often needed. Many hospitals have Hospital Radio stations which are staffed by volunteers.

Hospices are concerned with the care of people with a severe disease whose likely outcome is death. Some are in-patient units, others operate on a Day Care basis or Home Care services. Hospices are often very positive places to be and are committed to making the quality of life as good as they can for each patient.

Volunteers perform a variety of tasks, many of which are essential to the hospice. These include: driving, being on wards, clerical work, creative therapy, aromatherapy, fundraising, running a hospice shop, sewing, shopping for patients, gardening, and bereavement counselling. The first step is to telephone or write to the Hospice Information Service (address given below) for details of your nearest hospice and then approach it direct.

Help the Hospices

36-44 Britannia Street
London WC1X 9JG
Tel: 0171-278 1021

Contact
Chief Executive

Main Activities
Help the Hospices provides support to voluntary organisations across the United Kingdom, Northern Ireland and the Channel Islands with very modest support of the international hospice field. Annual budget is £1 million.

Opportunities for Volunteers
There are ten volunteers in Head Office who carry out: administrative support, advice giving, fundraising, management/trusteeship, PR, and research. Useful skills are: dealing with people, and expertise in fundraising, marketing, accounts and PR.

Opportunities for Employment
There are eight full-time staff and one free-lance merchandising consultant.

Further Information
Annual Report, general leaflet, Christmas and Greetings catalogues available on request.

Hospice Information Service

St Christopher's Hospice
51-59 Lawrie Park Road
Sydenham, London SW26 6DZ
Tel: 0181-778 9252, extension 262/3

Contact
Dilys Epton, Voluntary Services Co-ordinator

Main Activities
The Hospice Information Service provides information on the location and nature of hospices in the UK and overseas.

Opportunities for Volunteers
Volunteers are extremely important in all areas of the work and the information service is structured to enable them to be part of the work force.

Opportunities for Employment
There are no employment opportunities.

Further Information
Publishes an annual Directory of Hospices and a regular newsletter.

National Association of Hospice Volunteer Co-ordinators

St Leonards Hospice
185 Tadcaster Road
York YO2 2QL
Tel: 01904-708553

Contact
Mrs Pam Warn

Main Activities
The organisation aims to represent and support all voluntary service co-ordinators who are engaged in organising and co-ordinating volunteers in hospice and palliative services. A national organisation with nine regional groups.

Opportunities for Volunteers

Volunteer opportunities are via individual hospices.

Opportunities for Employment

There are no employment opportunities.

Further Information

A leaflet, 'Guidelines for Good Practice' may be obtained via the membership secretary: Glenda Leach, St Giles Hospice, Fisherwick Road, Whittington, Lichfield, Staffs WS14 9LH.

National Association of Leagues of Hospital Friends

Second Floor, Fairfax House
Causton Road, Colchester
Essex CO1 1RJ
Tel: 01206-761227

Contact

Mr R Leeson; individual Leagues of Friends

Main Activities

The National Association and its affiliated leagues aim to help patients and former patients of UK hospitals and others in the community generally who are sick, convalescent, disabled, handicapped or infirm, or who are in need of financial assistance. They support the charitable work of hospitals generally and provide volunteers. The National Association supports and advises the 1,200 affiliated local leagues. It also educates the public, promotes research, and holds conferences and other such meetings. Annual budget for head office is £100,000. The individual Leagues of Friends are autonomous. Individual and corporate membership are available.

Opportunities for Volunteers

The Leagues are dependent on volunteers to carry out their work. Around 350,000 are involved in administrative,

fundraising, visiting and other work connected to hospitals and nursing homes throughout the UK. Some are hospital visitors, some manage hospital shops, others are drivers or involved in counselling (eg bereavement). The opportunities are wide-ranging. Each League has its own recruitment methods and decides its own policy on commitment, expenses, etc.

Opportunities for Employment

The national office employs six full-time and one part-time staff. Vacancies seldom arise. An equal opportunities policy is being implemented.

Further Information

The Annual Report, affiliation packs, various pamphlets and a list of local groups are published.

St Christopher's Hospice

51-59 Lawrie Park Road
Sydenham, London SW26 6DZ
Tel: 0181-778 9252

Contact

Dilys Epton, Voluntary Services Coordinator

Main Activities

St Christopher's Hospice provides skilled medical care to improve the quality of life for patients suffering mainly from malignant diseases. The Hospice serves the local community of Bromley, Croydon and South East London with an in-patient unit of 62 beds, a Day Centre and Home Care Service for patients in their homes. St Christopher's Hospice also runs the Hospice Information Service (see above).

Opportunities for Volunteers

Volunteers are extremely important to the hospice and assist with a wide range of tasks including: reception work, running a shop, sitting with patients and/or running errands for them, clerical work, fundraising, library work, serving refreshments. There are approximately 320 volunteers at the hospice and about 300 running the Hospice's charity shops. Recruitment is on-going and potential volunteers should telephone or write to the Voluntary Services Co-ordinator for an application form.

Opportunities for Employment

The organisation employs paid staff.

Further Information

Annual Report and leaflets available.

Trinity Hospice

30 Clapham Common North Side
London SW4 0RN
Tel: 0171-622 9481
Fax: 0171-498 9726

Contact

Ms Ann Dunkley, Volunteer Co-ordinator for volunteering; the Administrator for employment opportunities

Main Activities

The Hospice cares for people suffering from advanced illness and for those caring for them. Set up in 1891, Trinity Hospice is independent, with two local support groups. Although it does not have links with similar organisations overseas, it provides help to people setting up hospices world-wide. Annual budget is £2.5 million.

Opportunities for Volunteers

About 280 volunteers assist the hospice's work, 150 in head office and 130 in its charity shops. Apart from providing administrative support, volunteers are involved in fundraising, counselling, general help in the hospice and selling in the shops. More are needed, all year round, especially as shop sales people, and drivers (current driving licence required). Volunteers are recruited ad hoc, on application and through volunteer bureaux. The time commitment varies depending on the work, and various expenses (travel,

lunch, etc) are offered. Training for shop work is provided by the shop supervisor, while the volunteer co-ordinator gives support generally. Potential volunteers fill in an application form and are interviewed.

Opportunities for Employment

Trinity Hospice employs about 100 people. The number of staff recruited each year depends on vacancies, but nurses are regularly required. The Hospice has a formal equal opportunities policy.

Further Information

The Annual Report, and general fundraising and patient information leaflets are available.

OTHER USEFUL ADDRESSES

National Association of Hospital Broadcasting Organisations

PO Box 2481
London W2 1JR
Tel: 0171-402 8815

Contact

General Secretary

This association is an umbrella group for Hospital Broadcasting organisations. There are 320 member groups. Provides computer print-out to prospective volunteers giving the nearest Hospital Radio Stations. Also provides advice on how to set up a hospital radio station.

National Association of Voluntary Help Organisations

Voluntary Services Department
Stepping Hill Hospital
Poplar Grove, Stockport SK2 7JE
Telephone 0161-419 5400

Contact
Liz Hurst

The Association promotes the image of both managers of volunteers and of volunteers in the field of health care. Sets standards of quality, promotes good practice and provides a supportive and effective information network for its members.

Housing & Homelessness

The issue of appropriate and acceptable housing for different groups of people, including the elderly, the disabled, the disadvantaged and those on low incomes, has long been the concern of various voluntary organisations and housing associations. Many of these have a Christian or religious connection. The issue of homelessness in relation to housing has become increasingly significant since the mid-1980s as the numbers of homeless people have grown. This development has spawned a considerable number of organisations, some national, many local, to cope with the accommodation and other needs of a wide range of people, many of them vulnerable.

Accommodation needs cover both providing short-term housing – eg for those sleeping rough – and developing longer term, suitable, affordable accommodation that gives people a real home and the opportunity to get back on their feet again. If you are interested in volunteering or employment in the areas of housing and homelessness, you need to decide whether you want to be involved with people in housing need in practical ways or whether you would prefer to participate in the campaigning and lobbying aspects. The kinds of voluntary opportunities available range from sitting on committees of housing associations helping to decide policy and practice to hands-on work with homeless people such as in hostels, night shelters and food kitchens. Paid work opportunities might range from running a night shelter to being an office administrator. The organisations listed below show the range of involvement possible.

Access Committee for England, *see Disability*

The Almshouse Association (The National Association of Almshouses)

Billingbear Lodge
Wokingham
Berkshire RG11 5RU
Tel: 01344-52922
Fax: 01344-862062

Contact
Mr David M Scott, Director

Main Activities
Established in 1946, the Almshouse Association is a UK-wide, non-statutory advisory body for almshouse charities. It has a membership by subscription of 2,300 groups of affiliated almshouses organisations throughout the United Kingdom, providing housing for elderly people, often in historic buildings. The Association advises and makes grants and loans to members, and reviews relevant legislation. The annual budget is £200,000.

Opportunities for Volunteers
There are none in the Association itself, but the 2,300 individual almshouse charities are administered by voluntary trustees. Various other almshouse duties can also be assisted by volunteers. The Association actively recruits people with disabilities and older people who have been made redundant.

Opportunities for Employment
The Association has a small staff of six full-time and four part-time workers. Vacancies seldom occur, the last one being early 1990. Should a position arise, candidates require knowledge of Charity Commission and Housing Corporation procedures. Posts are advertised in Housing Weekly and the Church Times, and sometimes recruitment agencies, such as Charity Recruitment, are used. A formal equal opportunities policy operates.

Further Information

The Annual Report and a list of local groups are available on request.

Carr-Gomm Society

Telegraph Hill Centre
Kitto Road
London SE14 5TY
Tel: 0171-277 5050
Fax: 0171-277 6750

Contact

Head Office for volunteering; the Personnel Director for employment opportunities

Main Activities

A special needs housing association offering good quality, supported, permanent housing. Provides shared and self-contained accommodation for single homeless and isolated people. Support is from resident staff and volunteers. The Society operates throughout England and has three regional offices. Budget is £11 million revenue and £6 million capital.

Opportunities for Volunteers

Volunteers are welcomed to provide counselling and advice, as well as support to residents, and for committee work and local lobbying/campaigning. Volunteers need an understanding of homelessness issues. Recruitment is by application and through volunteer bureaux, and involves a selection process. Minimum commitment is two hours a week on a permanent basis. Travel expenses are offered.

Opportunities for Employment

The Society has 210 full- and 140 part-time staff, and recruits a number of people each year. Applicants need skills appropriate to housing and special needs. Posts are advertised in The Guardian, Housing Association Weekly, and the local and minority press. Equality of opportunity is actively promoted.

Further Information

Annual report and promotional leaflets available.

The Central and Cecil Housing Trust (formerly Cecil Houses)

2 Priory Road
Kew/Richmond
Surrey TW9 3DG
Tel: 0181-940 9828

Contact

Ms Mags Watney, Fundraising and PR Manager

Main Activities

The Central and Cecil Housing Trust is a registered charity that runs hostels and move-on accommodation for homeless women, residential care homes for elderly people and sheltered housing for the actively retired in London. The Trust's policy is to care for those in greatest need, to provide them with secure and comfortable accommodation and to respect every individual's privacy and dignity. Set up in 1926, the Trust covers the Greater London area.

Opportunities for Volunteers

Volunteers are needed for jobs ranging from taking elderly residents of the care homes on outings and be-friending hostel residents when they are re-settled in a new home, to helping with general office work and running the charity shops. Without them the Trust could not run the shops, nor some of the fundraising and PR functions. Keen to use volunteers, both on a full- and part-time basis, throughout the organisation, the Trust would welcome enquiries from anyone interested in volunteering for it. The requirements are enthusiasm, dependability, communication skills, a pleasant personality, and the ability to make a regular commitment of service as required by the relevant department.

Opportunities for Employment
The Central and Cecil Housing Trust has about 180 full- and part-time staff. It recruits a number of staff each year. Recruitment is through local job centres and media adverts. The Trust is committed to an equal opportunities policy.

Further Information
Annual Report and information leaflet available on request.

Centre for Accessible Environments

Nutmeg House
60 Gainsford Street
London SE1 2NY
Tel: 0171-222 7980
Fax: 0171-357 8183

Contact
Sarah Langton-Lockton, Chief Executive

Main Activities
The Centre works to help ensure that the built environment is accessible to elderly and disabled people. It is an information and training resource to the construction industry, care professions and disabled people. A national, UK-wide organisation it has a membership scheme. It also has links with similar organisations in Boston and Toronto. Annual budget is £250,000.

Opportunities for Volunteers
Like most small organisations the Centre relies very much on voluntary contributions. It uses two volunteers for administrative support and others for technical (architectural) advice and training eg on building regulations. An architectural qualification, lecturing/training experience and knowledge of the construction industry are needed. The Centre recruits through volunteer bureaux, REACH and in-house. Application is by letter. There is no minimum

commitment. Travel expenses are paid.

Opportunities for Employment
The Centre has five full-time staff, and might recruit one employee a year. Vacancies are advertised in The Guardian, based on an equal opportunities policy.

Further Information
Annual report, a general leaflet and a publications list are available.

Centrepoint

Central Office
Bewlay House
2 Swallow Place
London W1R 7AA
Tel: 0171-629 2229
Fax: 0171-409 2027

Contact
Head of Personnel and Training

Main Activities
Set up in 1969, Centrepoint aims to ensure that no young person is at risk because they do not have a safe place in which to stay. It provides a range of accommodation for young people from the ages of 12 to 25. It is also active in working to prevent youth homelessness across the UK and campaigns for young people's rights. It has a central office and eleven hostels across London, with 150 bed spaces in flats and bedsits. It also works with community groups and people working with young people in schools or youth clubs across the UK, is active regionally in Oxfordshire, Warwickshire, Scotland and on Merseyside, and has links to projects in Russia. Budget is approximately £4 million annually.

Opportunities for Volunteers
Centrepoint relies on volunteers to bring an extra dimension of support, both directly and indirectly, to the young people it works with and which it would otherwise be unable to provide. Centrepoint's hostels rely on a pool of

around 130 volunteers to spend one evening a week with young people undertaking a range of activities from befriending to cooking the evening meal. Centrepoint is also looking for volunteers to work in fundraising, research, campaigning and administration from its central London office. Potential volunteers must fill in an application form, be interviewed and provide references. Full induction training is given and there is a probationary period. Minimum commitment ranges from one to six months, either one evening or a few days each week. Travel expenses are paid. More information is available from the Personnel Team on the above phone number.

Opportunities for Employment
With 180 staff, Centrepoint recruits about 60 people a year as new schemes are developed. Relevant experience is required for most posts. All positions are advertised internally and externally in The Guardian, the Pink Paper, Disability Now and The Big Issue. Centrepoint is an equal opportunities employer.

Further Information
Annual Report and other literature on young people and homelessness, including advice on leaving home, is available from central office.

CHAR, Housing Campaign for Single People

5-15 Cromer Street
London WC1H 8LS
Tel: 0171-833 2071
Fax: 0171-278 6685

Contact
Heather Carter, Administrator

Main Activities
CHAR is a campaigning organisation which works nationally with member bodies and homeless people, and aims to get provision of decent, affordable accommodation for single people.

Opportunities for Volunteers
Head Office uses a few volunteers for administrative support. They are recruited ad hoc by application to the office. Any one wishing to apply should write in with a cv and/or details of work experience and/or skills. Travel and lunch expenses are paid.

Opportunities for Employment
CHAR has 13 full-time staff, but opportunities for posts are very limited.

Further Information
Annual Report and information sheets available.

Church Army, see Religious Affairs

CRISIS

7 Whitechapel Road
London E1 1DU
Tel: 0171-377 0489
Fax: 0171-247 1525

Contact
Helen Thorp, Office/Volunteer Manager

Main Activities
Crisis is a national charity set up in 1967 and working for single homeless people throughout the country throughout the year. It operates an extensive grant programme funding 200 projects nationwide, including nightshelters, day and advice centres, and runs an Open Christmas shelter in London every December. It also undertakes research into the causes and effects of homelessness, and new ways of easing the problem. It has one regional office in Manchester. Annual budget £2.6 million.

Opportunities for Volunteers
Volunteers are very important to CRISIS, and some activities could not happen without them. They work year round in

the London (20) and Manchester (10) offices undertaking administrative support and computer duties. Others help with the weekly soup and clothing runs. 1,200 volunteers are used specifically to run the Open Christmas Shelter in London from 23-30 December. Crisis needs more volunteers for general administrative, data input, fundraising, and PR support work, especially from September to January. Training on office machines is given. Volunteers need to have an open and flexible approach. Recruitment is ad hoc and through volunteer bureaux. An application form must be filled in. Minimum commitment in office work is four hours weekly, year round. Travel expenses are paid.

Opportunities for Employment

There are 17 full-time and one part-time staff in the London office and three in the Manchester office. Positions occasionally become vacant, and about seven temporary staff are taken on from October to January. Skill needs vary. Jobs are advertised in The Guardian, The Voice and the Pink Paper, based on an equal opportunities policy.

Further Information

Annual Report, various brochures and other information available. Details for the Manchester office are:

CRISIS, 4th Floor, Fourways House, 18 Tariff Street, Manchester M1 2EP, tel: 0161-237 1607; fax: 0161-237 1609 – contact Lorraine Villa.

The Depaul Trust

The Lord Clyde Nightshelter
Tyers Street, Vauxhall
London SE11 5HU
Tel: 0171-820 0344 59 4188
Fax: 0171-735 8411

Contact

Angie Elstone, Volunteer Co-ordinator

Main Activities

The Trust was set up in 1989 and houses homeless young people aged 16 to 25 in staged accommodation varying from nightshelters to independent living. Main project locations in London: Vauxhall, Bayswater, Kilburn. Plans to expand to Manchester and Glasgow. Annual budget is £800,000.

Opportunities for Volunteers

Volunteers are relied on heavily. There are about 45 of them throughout the Trust; more are required. They are needed to provide support for regular staff and help run the 35-bed nightshelter, as well as hostels in Bayswater and Willesden. Work includes helping with meals, counselling and laundry. Empathy with and understanding of young homeless people, good physical health and some knowledge of stress and conflict management are necessary. In-service training is offered. Minimum commitment is ten hours a week (one overnight stint). However, the level of commitment for volunteers generally varies and there are many opportunities. The resettlement team also uses volunteers to help co-ordinate donations and make home visits to formerly homeless young people.

Opportunities for Employment

There are 25 full-time staff.

Further Information

Annual report and various reports about the Trust's work are available.

English Churches Housing Group (ECHG)

Sutherland House
70-78 West Hendon Broadway
London NW9 7BT
Tel: 0181-203 9233

Contact
Beverley Taylor, Assistant Director (Personnel and Administration)

Main Activities
ECHG, established in 1924, is one of the largest housing associations in England, providing emergency, supported, general needs and sheltered accommodation for over 10,000 tenants. It has six regional offices, and a subsidiary, Heritage Care Housing Association providing care services.

Opportunities for Volunteers
Volunteers are used for fundraising, and to provide care and to support staff in hostels. Recruitment is ad hoc, on application and through volunteer bureaux. There is no minimum commitment.

Opportunities for Employment
ECHG employs about 900 full-time and about 200 part-time staff. Vacancies are advertised in The Guardian, the housing press (HA Weekly, Inside Housing), the local press, trade journals and job centres. There is an equal opportunities policy.

Further Information
Annual Report and regional newsletters available.

Homes for Homeless People Project

90-92 Bronham Road
Bedford MK40 2QH
Tel: 01234-210549

Contact
Mark Howson

Main Activities
Homes for Homeless People acts as a national forum for service providers. Each of the 45 member groups is autonomous and the overall aim is to alleviate the plight of the single homeless.

Opportunities for Volunteers
Volunteers are very important and they are placed with an appropriate member organisation. They carry out: administrative support, advice giving, fundraising, counselling, project work, and organising local groups. Travel expenses are offered.

Opportunities for Employment
There are two staff members.

Further Information
Annual Report and list of member groups available.

Housing Associations Charitable Trust (HACT)

Yeoman House, 168-172 Old Street
London EC1V 9BP
Tel: 0171-336 7774
Fax: 0171-336 7721

Contact
Administration re employment

Main Activities
HACT was founded in 1960 and provides grants and loans, as well as fundraising information and advice, to voluntary housing organisations. It also gives related advice and support to grantees, as well as to grant givers/donors eg on ways of funding housing projects. Its remit is national.

Opportunities for Volunteers

There are none in HACT. But local housing organisations have contacts with various groups that use volunteers eg day centres. Contact local housing associations through the telephone directory. The National Federation of Housing Associations (NFHA) publishes *The Housing Associations Directory and Year Book* which lists housing associations in England. There are separate Federations for Wales, Scotland and Northern Ireland.

Opportunities for Employment

With 10 full-time and three part-time staff, opportunities seldom arise.

Further Information

Annual report, information leaflets, newsletter and other publications are published.

Keychange (formerly Christian Alliance)

5 St George's Mews
43 Westminster Bridge Road
London SE1 7JB
Tel: 0171-633 0533
Fax: 0171-928 1872

Contact

Personnel

Main Activities

Keychange provides residential accommodation for young single people, frail elderly people and homeless ex-offenders. It also runs day centres and clubs for all ages in inner cities. The primary aim is to follow Christ's example by giving practical help and support to people in need. Originally established in 1920, it has projects in England and Scotland.

Opportunities for Volunteers

Volunteers who are committed Christians and natural communicators can join the national Speakers' Corner team to promote Keychange's work with vulnerable people to local church and other groups.

In many of its projects Keychange needs people who can organise the occasional party or fundraising event, offer or teach practical skills (eg typing, art, cooking, cleaning, decorating, housework), teach others to read or write, serve on the local support committees, or simply befriend individuals.

Opportunities for Employment

Keychange employs both full-time and part-time staff, and has opportunities for both on its projects. Turnover varies from year to year. Jobs are advertised in the Christian, professional and local press.

Further Information

A free information pack is available on request to the London office.

Leaving Home Project (LHP)

Centrepoint, Bewlay House
2 Swallow Place
London W1R 7AA
Tel: 0171-629 2229

Contact

Youth Service Development Worker

Main Activities

Originally set up in 1984, LHP works with teachers, youth workers and others to help prepare young people for independent living. It provides training, a resource centre, information and a magazine. There is also a loan service available for the resources from the library. It covers England and Wales.

Opportunities for Volunteers

LHP is now part of Centrepoint and in its new situation is only beginning to develop using/working with volunteers, particularly for shorter projects on specific issues. LHP is looking for people with a knowledge of producing educational materials, a knowledge of schools and the youth service, and an understanding of the needs of young people.

Opportunities for Employment
There are five staff. Recruits need knowledge of education systems.

Further Information
Annual Report and a range of leaflets available.

Manna Drop-In Centre

St Stephen's Church
17 Canonbury Road
London N1 2DF
Tel: 0171-226 7526

Contact
Mark Wardle at the church

Main Activities
Set up in 1990, the Centre works with homeless people in the local area providing meals, support and befriending. It is run by a management committee from St Stephen's Church. Annual budget is £12,000.

Opportunities for Volunteers
Volunteers are central to the Centre's work. About 25 help prepare and serve food, befriend users of the Centre and play games with them, and undertake fundraising. Volunteers must be committed Christians. Recruitment is ad hoc, on application. Minimum commitment is two hours a month, by rota, and travel expenses are offered.

Opportunities for Employment
There are no paid staff.

Further Information
The Annual Report and a leaflet on the Centre are available in writing from St Stephen's.

National Association for Voluntary Hostels (NAVH)

Fulham Palace
Bishops Avenue
London SW6 6EA
Tel: 0171-731 4205
Tel: 0171-731 2888 (Placeline)
Fax: 0171-736 1292

Contact
Hazel Bonham, Administrative Secretary

Main Activities
NAVH is a membership organisation providing advice and support, and a monthly Job Centre bulletin. It also runs Placeline - a central referral agency for single homeless people.

Opportunities for Volunteers
Volunteers are needed to work on specific projects, eg residential volunteers for homeless hostels, volunteer drivers/ assistants etc. An interest in working with the homeless an advantage. Contact or register with NAVH for a monthly bulletin listing opportunities.

Opportunities for Employment
There are three full-time staff.

Further Information
Annual Report and further information including bulletin available on request.

SHAC, the London Housing Aids Council

229-231 High Holborn
London WC1V 7DA
Tel: 0171-404 7447
Fax: 0171-404 7771

Contact
Alison Burns, Volunteer Co-ordinator

Main Activities
Set up in 1970 SHAC gives housing advice, information and training to people in housing need, and the organisations that help and represent them. It also

has a register of locums. The Annual Budget is £1.2 million.

Opportunities for Volunteers
SHAC requires volunteers for all aspects of the organisation's work. It also runs SHAC DIRECT, a training scheme for volunteers to become advisors, which began in autumn 1994. Committment is necessary.

Opportunities for Employment
There are 43 full-time and seven part-time staff. About five people are recruited each year. Jobs are advertised in The Guardian and The Voice.

Further Information
A series of housing publications and a monthly bulletin are available.

The Simon Community

PO Box 1187
London NW5 4HW
Tel: 0171-485 6639

Contact
The Community Leaders

Main Activities
The Simon Community was set up in 1963 and covers the Greater London area. It works and lives with and for vulnerable homeless people, and provides houses and a nightshelter. It also campaigns on behalf of the vulnerable homeless. Annual turnover is £200,000.

Opportunities for Volunteers
Volunteers are essential to the Community's work as no paid staff are employed. More are needed and the Community is anxious to recruit people from all walks of life. Volunteer work is available in the Community's nightshelter and houses. A particular need is for people with skills eg electricians, mechanics, office administrators. Full-time workers receive a volunteer allowance and are encouraged to stay for at least six months. Part-time workers give as much time as they can. Prospective volunteers need to show initiative, be mature and enjoy a challenge. Training and support are offered. Applications in writing to the Community Leaders.

Opportunities for Employment
There are no paid staff.

Further Information
The Annual Report is available. An information pack is provided for anyone wishing to apply.

Stonham Housing Association

Octavia House
54 Ayres Street
London SE1 1EV
Tel: 0171-403 1144
Fax: 0171-378 0300

Contact
Mr A Christie

Main Activities
The Association provides housing and care for homeless people, particularly the young, mentally ill, ex-offenders and single women. A national, England-wide organisation with 200+ projects. Annual budget is £20-£30 million.

Opportunities for Volunteers
Volunteers are required to act as honorary auditors all over England for the 200+ projects. A mix of managerial and financial skills is needed and training experience is valuable. Some training is provided. Volunteers also act as committee members of the individual projects. Travel and lunch expenses are offered.

Opportunities for Employment
There are 600 full-time and 400 part-time staff. In summer temporary finance work and relief work is often available. Jobs are advertised in Job Centres, newspapers and local employment bureaux. There is an Equal Opportunities Policy.

Further Information
Annual Report, information leaflets and list of projects available. For Wales, contact: Stonham Cymru, The Maltings, East Tyndall Street, Cardiff CF1 5EA.

Thomas Coram Foundation, *see Children*

Vision Homes Association

4 Church Road, Edgbaston
Birmingham B15 3TD
Tel: 0121-455 8868
Fax: 0121-454 7247

Contact
Mrs Gayle Brown

Main Activities
The Association was set up in 1985 and covers the Midlands area. It provides and promotes provision of residential accommodation for adults who are visually impaired with multiple disabilities. It also has links with the Western Care Association, Co. Mayo, Ireland and the Lega Del Filo D'Oro, Ossimo, Italy. Annual budget is £1 million.

Opportunities for Volunteers
Volunteers with the relevant skills/ experience provide legal, financial and administrative support which is of great importance to the Association. Travel expenses are offered.

Opportunities for Employment
There are 65 full-time staff. Jobs are advertised in local and national papers.

Further Information
Annual Report and general information leaflets available.

Women's Design Service, *see Women*

Young Women's Christian Association (YWCA), *see Women*

Human Rights & Civil Liberties

Action for Victims of Medical Accidents, *see Health & Medicine*

Amnesty International, British Section (AIBS)

99-119 Rosebery Avenue
London EC1R 4RE
Tel: 0171-814 6200
Fax: 0171-833 1510

Contact
The Volunteer Organiser

Main Activities
Part of an independent, world-wide human rights movement, AIBS works for the release of 'prisoners of conscience' and for fair trials for political prisoners. It also campaigns for an end to torture, extra-judicial executions, 'disappearances' and the death penalty, and for observance of the United Nations Declaration on Human Rights. To support its active work, Amnesty fund raises, organises local groups, recruits members and publishes reports and other materials. It has offices in London, Derby and Edinburgh, over 300 local support groups and around 800 affiliated organisations.

Opportunities for Volunteers
AIBS welcomes new members to local groups throughout the UK. Volunteers constitute nearly a third of the workforce. Local prospective volunteers must apply in writing to the Volunteer Organiser. A minimum commitment of fifteen hours a week for three months is required. Travel and lunch expenses are paid.

Opportunities for Employment
No details supplied.

Further Information
A list of local groups and a leaflet on Amnesty's work are available on request. Other office addresses are:

Amnesty International Scottish Office, Edinburgh University Settlement, 5/1 Bristo Square, Edinburgh EH8 9AL, tel: 0131-650 8115.

Amnesty International East Midlands Office, St Michael's Churchyard, Queen Street, Derby DE1 3DX, tel: 01332-290852.

Anti-Slavery International (ASI)

180 Brixton Road
London SW9 6AT
Tel: 0171-582 4040
Fax: 0171-738 4110

Contact
Volunteer Co-ordinator

Main Activities
ASI aims to eliminate slavery and slave-like practices. Attempts to protect and advance indigenous peoples. Carries out research worldwide. There are five local support groups. Annual budget is £200,000.

Opportunities for Volunteers
Research/information gathering and fundraising are done by volunteers. Minimum commitment is two hours a week for three months.

Opportunities for Employment
There are five full-time and three part-time staff. Jobs are advertised in The Guardian and The Independent.

Further Information
Annual Report, membership and other leaflets available.

The Disability Law Service, *see Disability*

Fire Services National Benevolent Fund, *see Social Welfare*

INTERIGHTS – The International Centre for the Legal Protection of Human Rights

Lancaster House
31-33 Islington Street
London N1 9LH
Tel: 0171-278 3230
Fax: 0171-278 4334

Contact
Emma Playfair, Executive Director

Main Activities
Interights provides leadership in the development of legal protection of human rights and freedoms through the affective use of international and comparative human rights law. Annual budget is £400,000.

Opportunities for Volunteers
Volunteers do work on legal cases eg legal research and give administrative support. Often volunteers are law graduates with a specialism in human rights law. Word processing skills are useful but not essential. Travel and lunch expenses are offered. Minimum commitment is fifteen hours a week for three months. Applicants should write to the Executive Director with a brief letter and CV.

Opportunities for Employment
There are eight full-time and two part-time staff. Most staff have a law degree, computer literacy and a human rights law specialism. Jobs are advertised in The Guardian, The Independent and other papers as appropriate.

Further Information
Annual Report and sample copies of bulletin and information brochure available.

Liberty (National Council for Civil Liberties)

21 Tabard Street
London SE1 4LA
Tel: 0171-403 3888
Fax: 0171-407 5354

Contact
Marie Ryan, Director, Communications

Main Activities
Liberty campaigns to defend and improve civil liberties in the UK. Carries out monitoring, research and education. National organisation with sixteen local support groups and 900 affiliated organisations. Annual budget is £450,000.

Opportunities for Volunteers
Volunteers are very important to Liberty. There are sixteen paid staff and an equivalent number of volunteers. They are needed to give administrative support and to take part in campaigning. Computer and admin skills are particularly welcome. Minimum commitment is five hours a week for at least two months.

Opportunities for Employment
There are sixteen staff. On average two people are recruited each year. There is an equal opportunities policy.

Further Information
Annual Report, list of local groups and free information pack available. For Scotland, contact: Scottish Council for Civil Liberties, 146 Holland Street, Glasgow G32 4NG.

Survival International

11-15 Emerald Street
London WC1N 3QL
Tel: 0171-723 5535
Fax: 0171-242 1771

Contact
Alison Sanders

Main Activities
Survival International supports tribal people's right to survival, self determination and use of adequate land. The organisation is international with local groups in each country.

Opportunities for Volunteers
Volunteers are needed to carry out fundraising and administrative tasks. Press and Publicity Research is also needed. Minimum commitment is one day a week for at least three months. Travel expenses are offered and training is given where necessary.

Opportunities for Employment
There are eighteen staff. One or two are recruited each year on average.

Further Information
Annual Report, newsletter and brochures available.

Law & Justice

Children's Legal Centre

20 Compton Terrace
London N1 2UN
Tel: 0171-359 9392
Advice Line: 0171-359 6251
(2–5pm weekdays)
Fax: 0171-354 9963

Contact

Nicola Wyld/Maureen O'Hara

Main Activities

The Children's Legal Centre promotes the fundamental principle that children and young people should be able to participate as fully as possible in all the decisions affecting their lives according to their level of understanding. The Centre provides a free legal advice and information service by letter and telephone and publishes a range of publications promoting children's rights. Other activities include research, conferences and response to policies that affect young people.

Opportunities for Volunteers

Volunteers are important, especially for the telephone advice service. Legal qualifications required. Volunteers are recruited on an ad hoc basis or via the Volunteer Bureau. Other volunteers also give administrative support. Travel and out-of-pocket expenses are offered. The Centre is interested in recruiting volunteers with marketing or fundraising skills.

Opportunities for Employment

There are two full-time and two part-time members of staff. The Centre is working towards a formal Equal Opportunities Policy and posts are usually advertised in The Guardian or The Voice.

Further Information

The Centre publishes *Childright*, a monthly multi-disciplinary journal looking at children and young people's rights in all areas of law and policy as well as a broad range of publications including handbooks, legal information sheets, briefings and reports.

Community of the Peace People

224 Lisburn Road
Belfast BT9 6GE

Contact
Anne Mc Cann, Administrator

Main Activities
The Peace People aims to foster cross-community understanding through dialogue and action on issues of peace and justice. Since 1976 the organisation has developed several projects to address the sources of violence and conflict in Northern Ireland. Activities include: regular meetings, the Citizen newspaper, youth camps, a programme of school talks and local groups.

Opportunities for Volunteers
Volunteers are essential. They fundraise, give administrative support, carry out advice and conservation work. A volunteer allowance is offered. Minimum commitment is a year.

Opportunities for Employment
There are eleven staff. The Peace People is working towards an equal opportunities policy. Jobs are advertised in local newspapers.

Further Information
Leaflets available on request.

The Corrymeela Community

Ballycastle, Co Antrim
BT54 6QU, N Ireland
Tel: 012657-62626

Contact
Philip Freel

Main Activities
The Corrymeela Community attempts to heal the breaches in the social, political and religious fabric of society in Northern Ireland today. Groups of all sorts use Corrymeela for visits of up to a week long. The organisation also acts as a dispersed community of Members and friends who carry on the work of reconciliation in their local communities. Annual budget is £550, 000.

Opportunities for Volunteers
Volunteers are vital to Corrymeela. They run the summer programmes and visiting groups programmes and drive buses etc. English language, people skills, a commitment to working with and for people, and an acceptance of Corrymeela's ethos as a Christian community are essential. Volunteers are residential and receive a volunteer allowance and out-of-pocket expenses. Training and support are given.

Opportunities for Employment
There are twenty full-time and ten part-time staff. Jobs are advertised in the Belfast Telegraph.

Further Information
Annual report, list of local groups and further Information available on request.

English Collective of Prostitutes, *see Lobbying & Campaigning*

The Howard League for Penal Reform

708 Holloway Road
London N19 3NL
Tel: 0171-281 7722
Fax: 0171-281 5506

Contact
Frances Crook

Main Activities
Campaigns for humane and effective reform of the criminal justice and penal systems. Annual budget is approximately £250,000.

Opportunities for Volunteers
Volunteers are needed to give administrative support for one day a week. Computer, typing and filing skills are useful. Lunch and travel expenses are offered.

Opportunities for Employment
There are four full-time and two part-time staff. Jobs are advertised in The Guardian and The Voice.

Further Information
Annual Report and general information pamphlets available.

IMMUNITY Legal Centre, *see* *Aids/HIV*

International Voluntary Service (IVS)

Old Hall, East Bergholt
Colchester, Essex C07 6TQ
Tel: 01206-2982215

Contact
The Administrator

Main Activities
IVS promotes peace, justice and understanding through voluntary work. Workcamps are set up throughout the world for between two and four weeks. The organisation was set up in 1931 and there are ten local branches and three local support groups throughout England, Wales and Scotland. Annual budget is £150, 000.

Opportunities for Volunteers
Approximately five hundred volunteers each year take part in the various workcamps. Volunteers also fundraise, organise local groups, research and give administrative support. Volunteers are recruited on an ad hoc basis and via career fairs and services.

Opportunities for Employment
There are three members of staff. A

formal Equal Opportunities Policy is in operation

Further Information
Annual Report, listing for summer workcamps, and information leaflet available on request. Other addresses are:

IVS North, Castlehill House, 21 Otley Road, Leeds LS6 3AA, tel: 01532-304600.

IVS Scotland, 7 Upper Bow, Edinburgh EH1 2JN, tel: 0131-226 6722.

Latin American Women's Rights Service (LAWRS)

Wesley House
Wild Court
London WC2B 4AU
Tel: 0171-831 4145

Contact
The Co-ordinator

Main Activities
LAWRS offers advice and information to Latin American women and their families on welfare, housing, immigration, health, education, employment, domestic violence, money and debt. A counselling service for Latin American women in Spanish is also provided by three therapists on a voluntary basis.

Opportunities for Volunteers
Approximately eight volunteers give vital support. They work as interpreters/ advocates and give administrative support. A knowledge of Spanish and a familiarity with the Latin American community is necessary.

Opportunities for Employment
There are two full-time and two part-time staff.

Further Information
Annual Report, information leaflets in Spanish for clients on a variety of issues eg immigration, maternity benefits etc, are available.

Law Centres Federation (LCF)

18-19 Warren Street
London W1P 5SB
Tel: 0171-387 8570
Fax: 0171-387 8368

Contact
Lynne Evans

Main Activities
LCF promotes, co-ordinates and supports 57 Law Centres who provide free legal advice and representation. Annual budget is £190,000.

Opportunities for Volunteers
Volunteers are needed at Head Office to help with the administration of an international conference. Travel and lunch expenses are offered. Volunteers are also needed at Law Centres to act as advice workers (approaches should be made directly to a Law Centre).

Opportunities for Employment
There are four full-time and two part-time staff. On average one person is recruited each year at LCF.

Further Information
Annual Report, information and a list of law centres available.

Northern Ireland Children's Holiday Scheme (NICHS), see Youth

Portia Trust, see Mental Health

Prisoners, Families and Friends Service, see Family & Community Matters

Prisoners, Wives and Families Society, see Family & Community Matters

Lobbying & Campaigning

ADiTi - The National Organisation for Asian Dance, *see Education*

ASH, *see Health & Medicine*

British Polio Fellowship, *see Health & Medicine*

Capital Transport Campaign, *see Environment*

Carers National Association

20-25 Glasshouse Yard
London EC1A 4JS
Tel: 0171-490 8818
Fax: 0171-490 8824

Contact
Ms Julie Liggett, Administration Manager

Main Activities
Carers National Association's main aim is to make carers aware of their role and status in society and to encourage them to recognise their own needs. Set up in 1988 from a merger of two organisations dating back to 1965, Carers National is UK-wide with a number of area offices and around 120 local branches made up of carers and members. Annual turnover is approximately £2 million.

Opportunities for Volunteers
Carers National does not use volunteers at present, but is looking into the possibility of using them in the future.

Opportunities for Employment
48 full-time and 31 part-time staff are employed. Any staff vacancies are recruited through an equal opportunities recruitment procedure and application forms. Skills required vary according to the post, but Carers National has a lot of advice/information and development

workers. Posts are advertised in the national and local press, including The Guardian and The Voice.

Further Information
The Annual Report and a wide variety of leaflets are available. A publications list/order form can be obtained from the General Administrative Assistant, and information on local groups from the National Development Assistant.

English Collective of Prostitutes

King's Cross Women's Centre
71 Tonbridge Street
London WC1H 9DZ

Send mail to:
PO Box 287
London NW6 5QU
Tel: 0171-837 7509 (minicom/voice)
Fax: 0171-833 4817

Contact
Ms Nina Lopez-Jones and/or Niki Adams

Main Activities
Set up in 1975, the Collective is a network of women of different nationalities and backgrounds working at various levels of the sex industry. The Collective campaigns for the abolition of the prostitution laws, for human, legal, economic and civil rights for prostitute women, and for higher benefits, student grants, wages, housing and other resources so that no woman is forced by poverty into sex. It opposes the legalisation of prostitution. It also offers support/help and information to prostitute women on a wide range of issues including the law, child custody, benefits and health. In 1982 it initiated Legal Action for Women (LAW), a grassroots legal service for all women. Part of a national and international network, the Collective is a member organisation of the International Wages for Housework Campaign.

Opportunities for Volunteers
The Collective relies entirely on unwaged volunteers who do all the work. Travel and out-of-pocket expenses are offered.

Opportunities for Employment
There are no paid staff.

Further Information
A number of publications are available.

The Jubilee Centre

Jubilee House
3 Hooper Street
Cambridge CB1 2NZ
Tel: 01223-311596

Contact
Margeret Williams, General Manager

Main Activities
The Jubilee Centre is a research campaigning organisation aiming to bring a Christian perspective on public policy issues. It co-ordinates a number of initiatives, including the Keep Sunday Special Campaign, the Jubilee Policy Group (Christian Analysis of Public Policy) and the Relationships Foundation (building relationships in public and private life).

Opportunities for Volunteers
Volunteers are needed to give administrative support at the Centre. Secretarial skills are useful and committed Christians are preferred. One day a week is the minimum commitment. Travel expenses are offered. Potential volunteers should write to Margeret Williams enclosing a CV.

Opportunities for Employment
There are 22 full-time and eleven part-time staff.

Further Information
Annual Report, quarterly newsletter and publications list available on request.

Manna Drop-In *Centre, see Housing & Homelessness*

National Alliance of Women's Organisations (NAWO), *see* Women

National Federation of Consumer Groups (NFCG)

12 Mosley Street
Newcastle-upon-Tyne NE1 1DE
Tel: 0191-261 8259

Contact
Local consumer group or NFCG office

Main Activities
NFCG is a national federation of autonomous, voluntary, local consumer groups which investigate and campaign to improve local services, facilities and goods. In 1994 there were sixteen groups in England and Scotland, and 150 individual members. NFCG helps start new groups and is the national voice through which local consumers channel their views. Its budget is approx. £60,000.

Opportunities for Volunteers
All local groups are run by volunteers who are members. They undertake local project work eg surveys. Most groups produce newsletters etc too. Recruitment is by application and becoming a member. Some training is available. Hours are flexible. Out-of-pocket expenses are paid.

Opportunities for Employment
NFCG employs 2 full-time and 1 part-time staff. Vacancies are rare.

Further Information
Annual Report and various leaflets are available.

National Peace Council (NPC)

88 Islington High Street
London N1 8EG
Tel: 0171-354 5200
Fax: 0171-354 0033

Contact
Julia Breeze, Administration Officer

Main Activities
NPC is an umbrella organisation bringing together local, regional and national groups involved in all aspects of peacework. Co-ordinates Crisis Response Network. Working Groups at present are focusing on the Balkans crisis, the Middle East and Northern Ireland. Also for 1995: Past Hopes and New Hopes: Reconciliation: Campaigning for a Better Future. A newsletter is published monthly.

Opportunities for Volunteers
Volunteers are needed to help with a variety of tasks from design to administration. Minimum commitment is flexible. Volunteers are offered travel and lunch expenses.

Opportunities for Employment
There are two full-time and two part-time staff.

Further Information
Annual Report and information leaflets available.

OWA – One World Action, *see* Overseas & the Developing World

Peace Pledge Union (PPU)

Dick Sheppard House
6 Endsleigh Street
London WC1H ODX
Tel: 0171-387 5501

Contact
Annie Bebington

Main Activities
Peace Pledge Union is a pacifist organisation whose members work for a future without war.

Opportunities for Volunteers
Administrative support is done by volunteers. Minimum commitment is four hours a week and travel expenses are offered.

Opportunities for Employment
There are five staff, four of whom are full-time.

Further Information
An introductory leaflet about the organisation is available.

Society for the Protection of Unborn Children (SPUC)

7 Tufton Street
London SW1P 3QN
Tel: 0171-222 5845

Contact
John Smeaton, General Secretary

Main Activities
SPUC seeks to overturn the 1967 Abortion Act and restore full legal protection for unborn children. There are approximately 300 local branches.

Opportunities for Volunteers
Volunteer work at Head Office comprises office duties, telephone work, educational work and lobbying. Travel and lunch expenses are offered. In regional offices volunteer work tends to concentrate on campaigning, fundraising and leafletting.

Opportunities for Employment
There are 35 staff.

Further Information
Educational materials are available. The regional offices are: Wales: Paul Botto, 105 Bute Street, Cardiff Bay CF1 6AD; Scotland: Ian Murray, 5 St. Vincent's Place, Glasgow G1 2DH; Northern Ireland: Betty Gibson, 2 Veryan Gardens, Whitewall Road, Newtown Abbey, Belfast BT36 7HG; Cleveland: Ieleen Bridon, 4 Major Street, Stockton, Cleveland TS18 2DD.

Stonewall Lobby Group

2 Greycoat Place
London SW1P 1SB
Tel: 0171-222 9007

Contact
Suad El-Amin

Main Activities
The Stonewall Lobby Group fundraises, researches and lobbies for changes in laws, policies and practices which deny equality to lesbians and gay men and bi-sexuals. The organisation is London-based but has local affiliates nationally and a postal action network.

Opportunities for Volunteers
Help is needed to carry out parliamentary and legal strategising and research projects. Also welcome is fundraising and administrative support, design skills, a knowledge of budgeting, languages and campaigning.

Opportunities for Employment
There are six staff. The organisation only employs people who are lesbian or gay or bi-sexual.

Further Information
Annual Report is available as well as informational literature. For Scotland, please contact Scottish Homosexual Rights Group, 58A Broughton Street, Edinburgh EH1 4SA. For Northern Ireland, please contact Gay Rights Association (NIGRA), PO Box 44, Belfast BT1 1SH.

Mental Health

African-Caribbean Mental Health Association (ACMA)

35-37 Electric Avenue
London SW9 8JP
Tel: 0171-737 3603

Contact
The Administrator

Main Activities
ACMA offers various services in the field of mental health: housing, psychotherapy, befriending, legal advice. It was set up in 1982 and operates in SE London.

Opportunities for Volunteers
About 50 volunteers provide a vital link with clients and support professional workers. Tasks carried out include: counselling, management/trusteeship and administrative support. Minimum commitment is six hours a month and an induction course is offered.

Opportunities for Employment
There are fifteen paid staff. ACMA is working towards a formal Equal Opportunities Policy.

Further Information
Annual Report is available on request.

Ex-Services Mental Welfare Society

Broadway House, The Broadway
Wimbledon, London SW19 1RL
Tel: 0181-543 6333
Fax: 0181-542 7082

Contact
Brigadier A K Dixon, Director

Main Activities
Ex-Services Mental Welfare Society cares for mentally disabled ex-Servicemen and women of all ranks from the Armed Forces and the Merchant Navy. Provides welfare services, including treatment centres and a veteran's home.

Opportunities for Volunteers
Fundraising and administrative support are carried out by volunteers. Minimum commitment is flexible and lunch and travel expenses are offered.

Opportunities for Employment
There are 108 staff. Jobs are advertised in national and local newspapers.

Further Information
The Annual Report is available.

First Steps to Freedom (FSTF)

22 Randall Road, Kenilworth
Warwickshire CV8 1JY
Tel: 01926-864473
Fax: 01926-864473

Contact
Ms Lesley Hobbs, Secretary

Main Activities
FSTF provides a comprehensive service for sufferers of phobias, panic attacks and obsessive compulsive disorder (OCD). This includes a telephone helpline, one-to-one telephone counselling, and telephone help groups, as well as relaxation tapes, a pen pal list, leaflets and a newsletter. A national membership organisation, with overseas members also, FSTF became a registered charity in 1991. It has links with similar voluntary organisations in various overseas countries including America, Australia and France.

Opportunities for Volunteers
Volunteers are used both in head office (1) and in local areas (13). As helpline volunteers working from their own homes and also running the telephone groups, they are vital in providing the service. Apart from counselling work they also undertake fundraising. More are required, all year round. Volunteers need to have compassion and understanding. FSTF is also keen to recruit ex-offenders and people of various ethnic origins to help set up helpline groups for those types of people. Recruitment is ad hoc, on application and through in-house methods. Minimum commitment is four hours a week for at least 12 months, and out-of-pocket expenses are offered. Telephone training is given, together with back-up volunteer and monthly support groups. Application forms are available from the Secretary.

Opportunities for Employment
FSTF does not have any paid posts at present.

Further Information
The Annual Report and an information pack giving full details is available. Send an sae to the above address.

Hamlet Trust

9 Clifton Road
London W9 1FZ
Tel: 0171-289 1587

Contact
Robert Haywood, Assistant Programme Director

Main Activities
The Hamlet Trust supports self-help initiatives in mental health in Eastern and Central Europe.

Opportunities for Volunteers
There are few opportunities at present.

Opportunities for Employment
There are three full-time staff and the organisation is looking for suitably qualified recruits to develop an NGO agency in Eastern Europe. Knowledge/experience of mental health situation and an Eastern European language necessary.

Further Information
Annual Report, brochure 'Programme for the New Europe', are available.

Lothlorien (Rokpa Trust)

Corsock, Castle Douglas
Kirkudbrightshire DG7 3DR
Tel: 01644-440602

Contact
Brendan Hickey, Project Manager

Main Activities
Lothlorien is a supportive residential community for people with mental health problems in a rural setting. Annual budget is £100,000.

Opportunities for Volunteers
Five volunteers play a key role by living alongside people with mental health problems. An interest in gardening or another practical skill would be an asset but the main expectation is that volunteers undertake an active befriending role. Previous experience of volunteering in a caring situation would be useful. Volunteer allowance of £25 per week, free board and lodging are offered. Regular individual and group supervision are also available. Minimum commitment is six months full-time.

Opportunities for Employment
There are two full-time and one part-time staff. Employment opportunities occur very rarely.

Further Information
Volunteer information leaflet available.

Manic Depression Fellowship (MDF)

8-10 High Street
Kingston-upon-Thames
Surrey KT1 1EY
Tel: 0181-974 6550
Fax: 0181-974 6600

Contact
Myra Ford, Director/Brenda Fountain, Administrator

Main Activities
The Manic Depression Fellowship is a self-help organisation which helps sufferers of manic depression, their families and friends. It supports the establishment of self-help groups in local areas across the country. Educates the public and the caring professions. Raises funds for research into better methods of treatment. National organisation with 70 self-help groups. Annual budget is £33,460.

Opportunities for Volunteers
Volunteers organise local groups. They also fundraise and give administrative support at Head Office. Other jobs include: press and publicity, newsletters, organising one-off events, open meetings and talking to groups. Minimum commitment is two hours a week for at least three months. Word-processing, writing and basic office skills are useful.

Opportunities for Employment
There are five staff. Jobs are advertised in The Guardian and the local press as appropriate.

Further Information
Annual Report, list of local groups and information pack available.

Mental After Care Association (MACA)

25 Bedford Square
London WC1B 3HW
Tel: 0171-436 6194

Contact
Direct to individual projects (list available from Head Office)

Main Activities
Provides a wide range of community services for people with mental health needs and their carers. National organisation with annual budget of over £7 million.

Opportunities for Volunteers
Volunteers are used in local projects to befriend MACA service users.

Opportunities for Employment
Over 400 staff are employed in MACA's projects. Posts are advertised in the social work press and in local papers.

Further Information
Annual Report, list of local projects and information pack available on request.

The Mental Health Foundation

37 Mortimer Street
London W1N 7RJ
Tel: 0171-580 0145
Fax: 0171-631 3869

Contact
Jennifer Ryan, Fundraising Manager and Nicky Parsloe, Special Events Manager re volunteering; and for employment opportunities the Personnel Administrator

Main Activities
The Mental Health Foundation is a fundraising and grant giving charity in the field of mental health. It encourages and supports general medical research projects and community projects across the spectrum of mental illness and learning disabilities. It has a regional office in Glasgow, and eleven local groups. Its income is £5 million annually.

Opportunities for Volunteers
Volunteers are used for administrative support and various fundraising events and appeals. They are recruited in-house and through ad hoc applications. Travel and lunch expenses are paid.

Opportunities for Employment
With a full-time staff of 34, vacancies occur occasionally. Positions are advertised, usually in the national press.

Further Information
Booklets and Annual Report available. Scottish contact:

Lynda Somerville, 24 George Square, Glasgow G2 1EG, tel: 0141-221 2092.

Mental Health Matters

34/35 West Sunnyside
Sunderland SR1 1BU
Tel: 0191-510 3399

Contact
Jack Chetty

Main Activities
Mental Health Matters provides support and services to people with mental health problems and their carers. Services include: accommodation, day care, employment training, care crisis counselling, advice, information and self-help groups. The organisation was set up in 1983 and has local groups in the North East of England.

Opportunities for Volunteers
Approximately 100 volunteers play an important role in the organisation. Activities include: fundraising, organising local groups, management/trusteeship, advice giving and project work. A knowledge of mental health issues is essential.

Opportunities for Employment
There are 62 full-time and seventeen part-time staff. There is an Equal Opportunities Policy and the organisation actively recruits people with disabilities. Jobs are advertised in the local newspaper and professional journals.

Further Information
Annual Report and various pamphlets relating to individual services are available.

MIND (National Association for Mental Health)

Granta House, 15/19 Broadway
Stratford, London E15 4BQ
Tel: 0181-519 2122
Fax: 0181-522 1728

Contact
Personnel Department at National Mind or local associations for volunteering; and Vicky Whitfield, Personnel Officer for employment opportunities

Main Activities
MIND (NAMH - National Association for Mental Health) is a leading mental health charity in England and Wales. It has 230 local associations covering most major towns and rural areas. The organisation works for the right of people diagnosed as mentally ill to lead an active and valued life in the community. In all its activities MIND stresses the particular needs of people who face discrimination, and draws on the knowledge of people who provide and use mental health services. Services of the MIND local associations include housing, drop-ins and day centres, employment schemes, information lines, counselling and a variety of support groups.

Opportunities for Volunteers
MIND (NAMH) has limited opportunities, employing occasional volunteers for administrative and fundraising work. Recruitment is through a volunteer bureau. Local associations involve volunteers for a variety of work, and can be contacted direct through the telephone directory, MIND (NAMH) or MIND Regional Office.

Opportunities for Employment
MIND (NAMH) employment posts are usually advertised externally in The Guardian, The Voice and the Pink Paper, in line with the Code of Practice on Equal Opportunities in Employment. MIND local associations use local and national media and can be approached direct.

Further Information
MIND has six regional offices throughout England, and also a Wales office:

South East: 0171-608 0881; Northern: 0191-490 0190; North West: 01772-821734; South West: 01272-25096; Trent & Yorkshire: 01742-721742; West Midlands: 01902 24404; Wales: 01222-395123. MIND Publications: 0181-519 2122, Ext. 223 or 224.

Full listing of MIND local associations costs £2.50 from the Senior Administrator, Granta House. MIND (NAMH) has an information line (Mon-Fri 12-30 & 2-4.30) and a legal advice line (Mon, Weds, Fri, 2-4-30)

Other Contacts:
Scottish Association for Mental Health: 01450-371694/0131-229 9687

Northern Ireland Association for Mental Health: 01232-328474.

National Schizophrenia Fellowship (NSF)

28 Castle Street
Kingston Upon Thames KT1 1SS
Tel: 0181-547 3937

Contact
Head Office

Main Activities
NSF promotes a positive approach to mental illness. Provides carers groups, user projects and advice centre. We run over 200 community care projects in England, Wales and Northern Ireland. NSF campaigns and sponsors research. It is a national organisation with 160 local support groups.

Opportunities for Volunteers
Volunteers are needed for administrative support and to work on various projects.

Opportunities for Employment

There are 400 paid staff. Jobs are advertised in The Guardian, local press and Graduate magazine as appropriate.

Further Information

Annual Report and pamphlets available. For Scotland, contact: NSF (Scotland), 40 Shandwick Place, Edinburgh EH2 4RT, tel: 0131-226 2025.

Northern Ireland Association for Mental Health

80 University Street
Belfast BT7 1HP
Tel: 01232-234940

Contact

Assistant Director

Main Activities

The Northern Ireland Association for Mental Health provides a wide range of easily accessible services for those with mental health needs living in the community. The Association has a network of Beacon Centres, Beacon House clubs and residential schemes throughout the province. There are sixteen local branches and fourteen Beacon Centres. The organisation was set up in 1959 and the annual budget is £2 million.

Opportunities for Volunteers

There are approximately 420 volunteers on whom the organisation is very reliant. They organise local groups, fundraise, carry out administrative tasks and project work. Minimum commitment is two hours a month. Travel expenses are offered. Useful qualities are a caring disposition and good listening skills.

Opportunities for Employment

There are 131 staff; 73 full-time, 28 part-time, and 30 temporary. An Equal Opportunities Policy is in place and jobs are advertised in the local press.

Further Information

Annual Report, general information leaflets, list of local groups and free factsheets on mental health issues are available from the Information Department at Head Office.

Portia Trust

8 Canberra Drive
Beaconside, Staffs ST16 3PX
Tel: 01785-222272 (Jacqueline Jinks)

The Croft
Bowness-on-Solway
Cumbria CA5 5AG
Tel: 01673-51820 (Ken Norman)

Contact

Ken Norman

Main Activities

Portia Trust helps people who are in emotional/mental disturbance which may bring trouble with the law, such as baby-snatching, shoplifting, etc. The Trust has links with psychiatric nursing homes as places of retreat. There are eight branches. The annual budget is £40,000.

Opportunities for Volunteers

Volunteers are needed with counselling, legal and psychiatric skills. Also fundraisers, perhaps for occasional evening work from home.

Opportunities for Employment

There are four staff.

Further Information

Annual Report and pamphlets available.

The Richmond Fellowship

Clyde House
109 Strawberry Vale
Twickenham TW1 4SJ
Tel: 0181-744 9585
Fax: 0181-891 0500

Contact
Personnel Department

Main Activities
The Richmond Fellowship runs over fifty community-projects in the UK, working with people with mental health problems, schizophrenia, addiction and emotional problems.

Opportunities for Volunteers
Some projects take on volunteers to act as befrienders and fundraisers. Volunteers are not involved in the counselling process nor do they act as key workers.

Opportunities for Employment
There are 330 staff and vacancies are advertised in The Guardian, local press and employment centres. Speculative applications are not welcomed.

Further Information
Annual Report and other information available.

The Richmond Fellowship International

Clyde House
109 Strawberry Vale
Twickenham TW1 4SJ
Tel: 0181-744 9585
Fax: 0181-891 0500

Contact
Leela Joseet

Main Activities
The Fellowship is a psycho-therapeutic community in which clients are helped to re-enter society through a programme of group activities and individual counselling. Main project locations are in USA, Australia, India, Hong Kong.

Opportunities for Volunteers
Volunteers are used in a variety of roles. Professionals with a background in nursing, social work or psychology are needed from time to time. Also people with practical skills, such as cooking, home making, art and recreational activities. Minimum commitment is 40 hours a week for one year. Volunteer allowance, return air fare and medical insurance paid.

Opportunities for Employment
There are five full-time staff.

Further Information
Annual Report and informational leaflets available.

Schizophrenia Association of Great Britain

Bryn Hyfryd, The Crescent
Bangor, Gwynedd LL7 2AG
Tel: 01248-354048

Contact
Gyynneth Hemmings, Director

Main Activities
The Association researches into the causes of schizophrenia and provides information for sufferers and their families. Provides a telephone helpline service. Also informs the general public about the illness.

Opportunities for Volunteers
Volunteers who have schizophrenia in their family are needed to help with research. Meals and overnight expenses are offered.

Opportunities for Employment
There are two part-time staff and four researchers.

Further Information
Annual Report, newsletters and information packs available.

Museums, the Arts & Festivals

Volunteers play an important role in the arts, including drama, dance, music, and arts festivals as well as in museums and art galleries. There are a variety of roles which range from fundraising, administration and support to hands-on work.

Some museums are run totally by volunteers. Some are run with a few professional staff and a large group of volunteer supporters. Most museums do not have difficulty attracting volunteers, especially older people who may have time on their hands and have a particular interest in the museum's collection.

Volunteering is seen as an important route into professional work in museums. Students work on projects or help with the day to day running of the museum. The Tate Gallery, for example, offers student placements in various departments. Competition for these is very great so it is important to be very specific about what you want from the project.

A major way into volunteering is by joining a Friends Organisation. These groups support the museum financially, in many cases offering funds to pioneer new initiatives and purchases. Paintings in many art galleries bear plaques, saying 'Purchased by the Friends.' Contact your local Museum and see if they have a volunteer scheme or Friends Group. If not, you might consider setting one up. Contact the British Association of Friends of Museums for help and advice (address given below).

Some volunteers make a regular commitment of eg a shift or a day per week. The Victoria and Albert Museum, for instance, has over 100 volunteers who staff an information desk. Others work on various projects which will benefit the Museum and provide useful experience for the volunteer. Another way is to volunteer to work full-time for one or two weeks. Work can be very varied. The Ironbridge Gorge Museum, for example, offers volunteers the opportunity to demonstrate Victorian costumes and create street acts. Some museums, such as the Tate Gallery, offer in-depth training programmes for volunteers who work as guides and lecturers.

It is impossible to list all volunteer opportunities in the arts. A few are listed below as an indication of the sorts of opportunities which are available. The Museums Yearbook, published by the Museums Association, lists almost all museums and is available in most reference libraries. Your local public library may also be a source of information about local arts events, including festivals (see below).

Academy of Indian Dance

The Place
17 Dukes Road
London WC1H 9AT
Tel: 0171-383 4851

Contact
Helen Smart, Administrator

Main Activities
The Academy of Indian Dance strives to raise the profile of South Asian dance within the British Arts scene. The Academy works in the areas of dance training, education workshops, community outreach, and provides resources and information. It was set up in 1979 and the annual budget is approximately £140,000.

Opportunities for Volunteers
Volunteers are necessary to help staff events. They video, enrol participants and offer practical and administrative support. Travel and out-of-pocket expenses are offered.

Opportunities for Employment
There are three full-time and three part-time staff. There is a formal equal opportunities policy and jobs are

advertised in The Guardian, London based radio and Asian media.

Further Information
Information leaflets and a bi-annual newsletter are available on request.

ArtLink Live

Central Library
Albion Street
Hull HU9 3TF
Tel: 0482-883103/104
Fax: 0482-883080

Contact
Amanda Smethurst, Co-ordinator

Main Activities
Aims to take arts activity to those sections of the community which are unable, through lack of resources, to take advantage of existing arts provision. Exists as a local group affiliated to ArtLink for Humberside and North Yorkshire. Annual budget is around £4,000.

Opportunities for Volunteers
Volunteers, totalling 17 in 1995, are vital to the projects which are facilitated by them. They also form the management committee. Apart from facilitating workshops in the local community, they also fundraise and undertake public relations (PR). Arts-based and excellent communication skills are needed. Recruitment is usually ad hoc, on application and through volunteer bureaux, and more volunteers are wanted. Prospective volunteers fill in an application form and attend an interview. Travel and out of pocket expenses are paid. Disability equality and 'on-the-job' training are given together with support from the co-ordinator. Volunteers give as much time to each project as they feel able to, and each is listed on a Register for as long as they want.

Opportunities for Employment
There is one part-time paid member of

staff and no plans to increase this due to limited funds. To do the job arts administration and supervisory experience are needed, together with practical arts and communications skills. An equal opportunities policy is being developed.

Further Information
Leaflets explaining ArtLink's work and reports on projects are available. Exhibitions are held regularly.

Arts Disability Wales (ADW),
see Disability

Artsline

54 Chalton Street
London NW1 1HS
Tel: 0171-383 2653

Contact
Pauline Gutherie, Enquiries Officer

Main Activities
Artsline is London's only information and advice service on access to the arts and entertainment for London's disabled people.

Opportunities for Volunteers
Approximately six volunteers assist with advice giving, research and project work eg access visits facilitation. Some volunteers are recruited via a Community Action Employment Training Scheme. Travel and lunch expenses are offered. The organisation is actively seeking volunteers.

Opportunities for Employment
There are eight staff and vacancies are rare. Special skills needed include knowledge of the disability scene, computer skills, flexibility, administrative experience. Only disabled people are employed. There is an equal opportunities policy and jobs are advertised via newspapers, the disability press, The Voice and sometimes on the radio.

Further Information
Annual Report, leaflets and access guides to theatres, cinemas, music venues, tourist attractions and selected restaurants are available. Artsline also produces 'Play' an access guide on activities for disabled children and a guide for elderly disabled.

Berwick Studios, Printmaking Museum and Workshop

Mickley Square, Stocksfield
Northumberland NE43 7BL
Tel: 01661-844055

Contact
Christopher Bacon

Main Activities
The Berwick Studios Printmaking Museum displays the history of printmaking from the late 18th century to the present day. The museum is also a real workshop which preserves the art of hand-engraving and printing from copper plates. The Museum has a tearoom and a shop selling a wide range of hand-printed pictures of the North-East. Also runs courses in drawing and engraving.

Opportunities for Volunteers
There are currently four volunteers who are vital to the work of the museum. They carry out conservation tasks. Volunteers are always welcome. Travel expenses are offered.

Opportunities for Employment
There is one full-time member of staff.

Further Information
Information leaflet available on request.

British Association of Friends of Museums (BAFM)

31 Southwell Park Road
Camberley, Surrey GU15 3QG
Tel: 01276-66617

Contact
Sue Thorva McGowan, Honorary Secretary and local friends groups

Main Activities
BAFM supports and informs those who run membership groups and in museums whether as Friends or volunteers. The Association also works to make the views and contributions of Friends known. BAFM is totally independent and run entirely by volunteers who are active supporters of museums. Services the requirements of member groups, liaises with national museum bodies such as M&GC (Museums and Galleries Commission), AIM (Association of Independent Museums), MA (Museums Association), and encourages support for museums of all types.

Opportunities for Volunteers
Volunteers are used in head office (two) and the branches (numerous) for fundraising, conservation and various kinds of project work. Each museum friends group has its own needs and tasks. Each would welcome more volunteers. Recruitment is by application to BAFM or a local group. Minimum commitment varies. No remuneration is offered.

Opportunities for Employment
There are no paid staff and no employment opportunities.

Further Information
Various brochures (for sale), the annual 'Museum Visitor' and regular broadsheets (by subscription), and a brief annual report are published. List of local groups also available.

Drama Association of Wales

The Library, Singleton Road
Splott, Cardiff
South Glamorgan CF2 2ET
Tel: 01222-452200

Contact
Ms Nerys Jeffries

Main Activities
The organisation, supported by the Arts Council of Wales, is a Cardiff-based charity which has been actively involved in promoting amateur dramatic theatre since 1924. The members run to over 500 individual, group and corporate, who have access to the world's largest playscript and theatre information lending library, offering a postal hire and information service worldwide. It also runs training courses, organises festivals and promotes new writing with a playwriting competition and a scriptreading and publication service.

Opportunities for Volunteers
Volunteers give administrative support. A current project is the setting up of an indexing system. Volunteers can also become members of the organisation and a list of local groups can be obtained from Head Office.

Opportunities for Employment
There are four full-time and one part-time staff.

Further Information
Annual report, a magazine, and information leaflets are available.

Gainsborough's House Society

46 Gainsborough Street
Sudbury, Suffolk CO10 6EU
Tel: 01787-372958
Fax: 01787-376991

Contact

Lucy Koserski and/or Glynis Wash about volunteering; the Curator re employment

Main Activities

The Society runs a museum of works by Thomas Gainsborough, who was born in Sudbury, holds exhibitions, often of contemporary work, and runs an open access print workshop. Set up in 1958, it is a national organisation with regional (East Anglia) and local emphasis. Annual budget is £140,000.

Opportunities for Volunteers

About 100 volunteers, who are very important to the Society, are involved in management and as trustees, undertake research, and assist with stewarding the collection, gardening and other duties. More are needed, particularly for stewarding. Reliability and a welcoming personality are the only skills required as induction is given plus quarterly support meetings. Recruitment is ad hoc, via volunteer bureaux and through in-house schemes. Potential volunteers apply by phone or letter and are then interviewed. The minimum commitment is 2.5 hours a month. No expenses are offered.

Opportunities for Employment

There are four full-time and six part-time staff. Any positions that arise are advertised in The Guardian, the East Anglian Daily Times, and the Museums Journal. Recruitment is by written application with references, followed by an interview, and then a probationary period. The Society is working towards an equal opportunities policy.

Further Information

The Annual Review, publicity, membership and fundraising leaflets, and an exhibition calendar are available by sending a stamped addressed envelope.

Godalming Museum

109A High Street, Godalming
Surrey GU7 1AQ
Tel: 01483-426510

Contact

The Curator

Main Activities

The Museum aims to preserve and interpret the heritage of the Godalming area through displays and education work. Set up in 1987 as a local museum, it covers the Godalming area only.

Opportunities for Volunteers

Volunteers are vital to the Museum's work. Around 55 of them run the shop and the reception desk. They are also involved in fundraising, public relations and management. More are needed, all year round, particularly for running the shop and the reception desk. Useful skills include the ability to operate a till, answer the telephone and handle enquiries from the public. Recruitment is ad hoc, on application to the Curator. Minimum commitment is three hours a month. Expenses are not offered.

Opportunities for Employment

There is one full-time and one part-time member of staff, and no plans for further recruitment. If any vacancies arose, they would be advertised in the Museums Journal and the local paper. An equal opportunities policy is being developed.

Further Information

The Annual Report and leaflets about the Museum and the Museum Friends Group are available by writing to the Museum.

Ironbridge Gorge Museum Trust

The Wharfage, Ironbridge
Telford, Shropshire TF8 7AW
Tel: 01952-583003

Contact
Michael Ward, Manager, Blists Hill

Main Activities
The Museum conserves the social and industrial heritage of the Ironbridge Gorge.

Opportunities for Volunteers
Volunteers aged eighteen and over are needed throughout the various sites of the Museum. Jobs include: costume demonstrating, research projects, working in wardrobe department. People with drama skills are used to research and create street acts. A knowledge of English as a first language is necessary for costume demonstration. Basic dormitory style accommodation is provided. Minimum commitment is two weeks.

Opportunities for Employment
There are very few employment opportunities.

Further Information
Annual report available on request.

John King Workshop Museum

7 Billingsley Avenue
Pinxdon, Notts NG16 6QN
Tel: 01773-860137

Contact
The Steward

Main Activities
The John King Museum displays local and mining equipment from the past. It was set up in honour of John King who designed a detaching hook which was fitted to miners' cages and saved many lives throughout the world. It also has a collection of photographs and Pinxton China.

Opportunities for Volunteers
Four volunteers assist with the running of the Museum and new recruits are actively sought. Minimum commitment is three hours a week – during Sunday afternoons.

Opportunities for Employment
There are none.

Further Information
Leaflets available.

Museum of Women's Art (MWA)

Second Floor, North Suite
55/63 Goswell Road
London EC1V 7EN
Tel: 0171-251 4881

Contact
Lesley Hynes

Main Activities
MWA raises funds for the establishment of a Museum of Women's Art. The organisation also aims to raise awareness of historical and contemporary women artists and to facilitate exhibitions and study of their work.

Opportunities for Volunteers
There are six volunteers who carry out research, administration, compiling of statistics and organisation of conferences. MWA is seeking mature people with professional experience in the arts as volunteers. Book-keeping and fundraising skills would be especially welcome.

Opportunities for Employment
There is one part-time member of staff.

Further Information
Leaflet about MWA, an outline document of aims and a sponsorship pack are available on request.

Museums Association

42 Clerkenwell Close
London EC1R 0PA
Tel: 0171-608 2933

Contact
Membership Officer

Main Activities
A professional organisation that represents museums and staff in maintaining ethical standards to promote professional development. Also aims to improve the status and qualifications of its members. Based in London.

Opportunities for Volunteers
The Association does not use volunteers itself. Those interested in volunteer work in a museum should apply directly to individual museums (See Museums category in this Directory).

Opportunities for Employment
10 full-time staff are employed. Opportunities are very limited in the Association, but its magazine carries vacancies for museum staff throughout the UK.

Further Information
Besides the Annual Report a monthly journal, membership details and leaflets are available. 'Museum Visitor' is published every year and a broadsheet three times a year.

National Disability Arts Forum, *see Disability*

Quay Theatre

Quay Lane, Sudbury
Suffolk CO10 6AN
Tel: 01787-312602

Contact
Ms Nikki Murphy, Volunteer Organiser re voluntary work; Mr Simon Daykin, Director re employment

Main Activities
Set up in 1981 in a converted warehouse, the Quay is a centre for the community and dramatic arts. It puts on a wide range of plays, concerts and other performances, by local, repertory and travelling groups and performers, and has five affiliated organisations. It houses a restaurant and bar. Annual budget is £250,000.

Opportunities for Volunteers
The Quay uses about 100 volunteers, could not operate without them and is actively seeking more. Volunteers undertake administration, fundraising, public relations and research. They are also involved in committee work, run the Box Office and act as Duty Managers. They need to have in-house knowledge, but are given an induction and support programme. Most needed at evenings and weekends, a minimum of two hours a week is requested and travel expenses are paid. Recruited through a variety of methods, including volunteer bureaux, in-house recruitment drives, the Quay's newsletter and on application, volunteers are then registered by the Volunteer Organiser. A Volunteer Policy and Volunteers Charter are being implemented.

Opportunities for Employment
Five full-time and eight part-time staff are employed. Opportunities for work arise from time to time, including in running the theatre, fundraising and during the Summer Theatre School. Recruits need communication skills. Available jobs are advertised in various newspapers. An equal opportunities policy is being implemented and the Quay actively recruits school leavers, new graduates, those returning to work, and people who have been made redundant.

Further Information
The Annual Report, a 'What's On' and membership leaflet, and information for volunteers are available by post, via the phone or in person from the Box Office.

Quicksilver Theatre for Young Children

4 Enfield Road
London N1 5AZ
Tel: 0171-241 2942
Fax: 0171-254 3119

Contact
The Administrator

Main Activities
The Quicksilver Theatre for Children commissions, produces and tours plays for young children and family audiences. Performances take place in London and throughout the country in theatres, schools and arts centres. The organisation was set up in 1978 and the annual turnover is £180,000.

Opportunities for Volunteers
Volunteers give administrative support, carry out research and work on various projects. They are increasingly important as funding becomes more scarce. Lunch, travel and out-of-pocket expenses are offered.

Opportunities for Employment
There are three full-time staff and approximately ten part-time staff (often on short contracts). There is an equal opportunities policy and posts are advertised in The Stage and other professional publications as well as in The Guardian for more senior jobs.

Further Information
Annual Report and show pamphlets are available.

Riverside Studios

11 Crisp Road
Hammersmith
London W6 8RL
Tel: 0181-741 2251

Contact
Susan Dunlop, Development Officer

Main Activities
Riverside Studios is a registered charity presenting an innovative programme of drama, dance, music, poetry, cinema, exhibitions and community education. It was set up in 1983 and attracts a local, national and international audience. There is a Friends organisation. Annual budget is £1.4 million.

Opportunities for Volunteers
Volunteers supply very important administrative support in the Development and Community departments. The tasks are typically: research, PR, fundraising, project work and admin. Computer literacy, reliability and general good presentation are useful attributes. Travel allowance offered. An appeal is being run currently to renovate Riverside, which volunteers are needed to help with. Volunteers should apply in writing enclosing a CV.

Opportunities for Employment
There are 22 full-time staff and about 50 casual staff. Recruits are regularly sought for front-of-house, bar and café work. Jobs are advertised in The Guardian and internally. There is an Equal Opportunities Policy.

Further Information
Annual Report, brochures and Friends leaflet available.

Tate Gallery

London, Millbank
London SW1 4RG
Tel: 0171-828 8000

Contact
Personnel Department

Main Activities
The Tate Gallery houses the national collection of British Art and the international collection of modern Art.

Opportunities for Volunteers
There are a variety of ways to volunteer: guiding, project work and through the Friends of the Tate Gallery. Guides undergo a year long training course. They take special groups around, work on the information desk and give slide lectures. Students are occasionally taken on for specific project placements eg exhibition planning, arts marketing.

Opportunities for Employment
Employment is generally via the Civil Service.

Further Information
Other branches of the Tate Gallery offer volunteer opportunities:

Tate Gallery Liverpool, Albert Dock, Liverpool L3 4BB, tel: 0151-709 3223. Contact Administrator.

Tate Gallery St Ives, Porthmeor Beach, St Ives, Cornwall TR26 1TG, tel: 01736-796226. Contact Administrator. Opened in 1993. Volunteers are always needed to invigilate the galleries and staff an information desk.

The Upper Wharfdale Museum Society

3 Wisp Hill Croft
Grassington
Skipton BD23 5NG
Tel: 01756-752800

Contact
Mr P Fethney

Main Activities
The Upper Wharfdale Museum Society operates the Upper Wharfdale Folk Museum, assisting with the conservation of artefacts and opening to the general public. It was set up 1977.

Opportunities for Volunteers
The Museum is entirely run by twenty volunteers who carry out a variety of tasks, including conservation, PR and fundraising. Some knowledge of the museum holdings would be an asset and volunteers are especially needed in the summer and in December. Minimum commitment is four hours a month.

Opportunities for Employment
There are none.

Further Information
Leaflet available on request.

Victoria & Albert Museum

London SW7 2RL
Tel: 0171-938 8362

Contact
Angel Thurgood, Visitor Information Manager

Main Activities
The Victoria & Albert Museum houses the national collection of Art and Design.

Opportunities for Volunteers
All volunteers are Friends of the Victoria and Albert Museum. The Museum offers a four day training course for volunteers. The minimum commitment is 2.5 hours a week. There are variety of tasks,

including staffing the information desk, project work and administrative support.

Opportunities for Employment
Employment is via the Personnel Department.

Further Information
Further information and extensive publications available.

The Victorian Society

1 Priory Gardens
Bedford Park
London W4 1TT
Tel: 0181-994 1019

Contact
The Administrator

Main Activities
The Victorian Society aims to save the best examples of Victorian and Edwardian architecture and to promote an understanding of that period's history and culture. It was set up in 1958 and there are now eleven regional groups in England and Wales.

Opportunities for Volunteers
Volunteers carry out a variety of tasks including: administrative support, fundraising, casework, research, organising local groups, conservation and lobbying.

Opportunities for Employment
There are four full-time and two part-time staff. From time to time the Society recruits administrative support during mail-outs. Jobs are advertised in The Guardian and the Evening Standard.

Further Information
Annual Report, publications list, membership form and an events list can be obtained by writing or phoning the society.

Yorkshire Sculpture Park

Bretton Hall, West Bretton
Wakefield WF4 4LG
Tel: 01924-830579

Contact
Administration Manager

Main Activities
The Park is an international centre for the promotion and exhibition of sculpture, providing an important educational resource and equal opportunities for the practice, understanding and enjoyment of arts for all sectors of the community. Based in West Yorkshire, it does not have any affiliates or branches elsewhere, but is also a recreation and leisure resource concerned with the environment and conservation.

Opportunities for Volunteers
Volunteers are a developing resource within the paid/professional staffing structure. They undertake a variety of work, including administration, fundraising, organising local groups, giving advice and project work such as wardening/invigilation and education. They are recruited ad hoc, on application and through in-house recruitment drives. There is no minimum time commitment required; travel and out-of-pocket expenses are paid. The Park is seeking to increase the 20 volunteers already active, especially for summer for front-of-house and retail work. Volunteers need communication and numerical skills, and training and support are offered. Write for further details to the Administration Manager.

Opportunities for Employment
16 full-time, eight part-time and 10 temporary staff are employed. Recruitment needs vary according to the particular position, but the Park regularly seeks staff for front of house and/or seasonal work, including wardening. Posts are advertised in job centres and in newspapers such as The Guardian and the local press. An

equal opportunities policy is in place and people with disabilities are actively recruited for jobs.

Further Information

The Annual Report, and a general leaflet on exhibitions and events are available by sending a stamped, addressed envelope (sae).

Arts & Music Festivals

Volunteering at one of the many festivals that take place around the country can provide interesting fixed-term volunteer opportunities. Work often involves PR and information dissemination, administration, fundraising, stewarding and general organising of events. The British Arts Festivals Association (3rd floor, Whitchapel Library, 77 Whitechapel High Street, London E1 7QX, tel: 0171-247 4667) produces an annual brochure listing the major events but keep your eyes open for other, more local festivals. The following are a selection of some of the major festivals for 1995 (many of which are annual events but check with the festivals direct as dates will change in subsequent years).

Arundel Festival

August 25-September 3
Tel: 01903-883690

Belfast Festival at Queen's

November 6-26
Tel: 01232-667687

Canterbury Festival

October 7-31
Tel: 01227-452853

Cheltenham International Festival of Music

July 1-16
Tel: 01242-521621

Norfolk & Norwich Festival

October 5-15
Tel: 01603-764764

Swansea Festival

October 4-31
Tel: 01792-468321

York Early Music Festival

July 7-16
Tel: 01904-658338

Useful Books

Museums Among Friends

David Heaton, published by the Museums and Galleries Commission. (Can also be obtained from British Association of Friends of Museums.)

The Museums Yearbook

published by the Museums Association (see above for address) is available at a cost of £65. Also available in many public libraries.

Volunteering in Museums and Heritage Organisations, Policy, Planning and Management

Sue Miller, published by HMSO.

Overseas & the Developing World

hatever your age, whether 18 or in your eighties, opportunities exist for volunteering and working overseas in countries as close as Europe and as far away as the Asia/ Pacific area. Since conditions can be uncomfortable, sometimes even dangerous, you need to be very clear about why you want to go abroad, what you personally are able to cope with (conditions, environment, weather, etc) and what you have to offer (skills, abilities, qualifications, etc). Opportunities include both short and longer term, although the latter are usually for people with proven skills and experience that can be shared with communities overseas.

For young people without qualifications various possibilities now exist to take a 'gap year' between school and higher education or school and full-time work, for a period of up to a year. This gives the chance to develop skills, experience, confidence and understanding by living among different cultures and communities. If you decide to take a year off careful planning is essential to ensure you get the most from your time away.

Although working overseas for and with voluntary organisations is limited by the particular needs of the countries requiring assistance and workers, the organisations listed below also have a variety of opportunities for both volunteers and paid workers in the UK. Some of them are specifically Christian organisations requiring a Christian commitment from those they take on, whether to work at home or abroad.

ActionAid

Hamlyn House, Archway
London N19 5PG
Tel: 0171-281 4101

Contact
Ms Barbara Waugh, Personnel Officer
London (at above address) for volunteer-
ing in London; Ms Isobel Barndon,
Personnel Officer, ActionAid, Chataway
House, Leach Road, Chard, Somerset
TA20 1FA, tel 01460-62972 for volunteer-
ing in Chard or Bristol offices; Ms Karen
Cole, Personnel Officer, at the Chard
address re employment opportunities

Main Activities
ActionAid works with children, families
and communities in the world's poorest
countries to help them overcome poverty
and secure lasting improvements in their
lives, by assisting them develop self-
reliance. It provides emergency relief
when necessary, and raises funds in
developed countries. Established in 1972,
it has two main offices, a regional office
mainly for fundraising, about 200 local
support groups and four affiliated organisations in European Union countries.
Budget is over £20 million annually.

Opportunities for Volunteers
Volunteers are very important to the
organisation's work in the UK. Ten
volunteers are used in head office
primarily for administrative duties and 75
in Chard. Chard relies on voluntary help
particularly for appeals. More volunteers
are wanted for administration and special
projects. Languages and overseas
knowledge are useful. In-house training
is given. Recruitment is ad hoc, through
volunteer bureaux, word of mouth and
also in-house, and from all types of backgrounds. Interviews are required.
Minimum commitment is two hours a
week. Travel expenses only are paid.

Opportunities for Employment
ActionAid has 218 full-time and 45
part-time staff. It recruits varying numbers
each year. Interest in development work
is desirable. Posts are advertised internally
first and then in the press – Guardian,
Guardian Weekly and Independent. An
equal opportunities policy is being
developed.

Further Information
Annual Report and Common Cause
magazine available on request.

Action Health 2000

The Gate House, 25 Gwydir Street
Cambridge CB1 2LG
Tel: 01223-460853
Fax: 01223-301896

Contact
Director

Main Activities
An international voluntary health associa-
tion, Action Health was set up in 1984 by
a small group of health professionals from
Britain, India and East Africa. It develops
primary health care and training pro-
grammes to transfer skills in partnership
with communities around the world.
Main project locations are: India,
Tanzania, Zambia, Uganda and China.
The range of countries is likely to expand.
Annual budget is £178,000.

Opportunities for Volunteers
Volunteers have specific roles within the
organisation eg accountant, community
fundraiser. As a small agency only a
limited number can be accommodated.
But administrative help is needed, for
which administrative, keyboard and
computer skills are essential. Minimum
commitment is one day a week. Prospective volunteers should send in a CV.

Opportunities for Employment
There are four full-time and two part-time
staff. Any vacancies are advertised in The
Guardian.

Further Information
Annual Report and Newsletter available on request.

African Medical & Research Foundation (AMREF)

8 Bourdon Street
London W1X 9HX
Tel: 0171-409 3230
Fax: 0171-629 2006

Contact
Alexander Heroys, Director

Main Activities
AMREF UK exists to raise funds and give support generally to AMREF's work in Africa. AMREF's aim is to provide low cost, community based health care and health education for the peoples of eastern and southern Africa. Established in 1957, AMREF's head quarters is in Kenya and it is supported by a further nine fundraising offices in Europe and North America.

Opportunities for Volunteers
AMREF in Africa does not use volunteers. Volunteers to work in the UK office are welcome.

Opportunities for Employment
There are two full- and one part-time members of staff. Further employment opportunities in the UK are unlikely.

Further Information
The Annual Report is available on request.

Appropriate Health Resources and Technologies Action Group (AHRTAG)

29-35 Farringdon Road
London EC1M 3JB1
Tel: 0171-242-0606
Fax: 0171-242 0041

Contact
Abdul Getha, Co-Director

Main Activities
AHRTAG supports primary health care in developing countries through information services and publications. It publishes five free newsletters and runs a resources and information centre. Major overseas locations include: Africa, Middle East, South America, South-East Asia. Annual budget is £1.4 million.

Opportunities for Volunteers
Does not at present work with volunteers.

Opportunities for Employment
There are 23 full-time members of staff. On average two or three people are recruited each year. Vacancies are advertised in the press and at Job Centres as relevant to the nature of the job.

Further Information
Leaflet and publications list available on request.

Baptist Missionary Society, *see*
Religious Affairs

Book Aid International

39/41 Coldharbour Lane
Camberwell
London SE5 9NR
Tel: 071-733 3577

Contact
Maggie Gardiner, Chief Librarian

Main Activities
Selects and distributes books to developing countries for educational and other charitable purposes. The budget is £500,000 including funds for special projects.

Opportunities for Volunteers
Volunteers are always needed, preferably for at least half a day a week, to stamp books and pack them into chests. Tea and coffee are available and the work, although routine, is carried out in a friendly atmosphere.

Opportunities for Employment
There are 23 staff members, mostly librarians with overseas experience. Occasionally porters and packers are recruited for heavy work.

Further Information
An explanatory booklet 'Providing Books for Development' is available.

British Council for Prevention of Blindness (BCPB), see Health & Medicine

British Executive Service Overseas (BESO)

164 Vauxhall Bridge Road
London SW1V 2RB
Tel: 071-630 0644

Contact
Public Relations Manager, Public Relations/Marketing Department

Main Activities
BESO sends executive volunteers with professional, technical and managerial skills to help developing countries and Eastern Europe to achieve economic independence and self-sustaining growth. Founded in 1972 with support from the CBI, IOD and the British Government, BESO works in many areas, including education, social welfare, health, the environment and leisure. UK based, it has a national network of 40 regional/local groups, representation in 45 countries, links with various overseas organisations, and a budget of just over £1 million.

Opportunities for Volunteers
Volunteers are vital to BESO's work. BESO actively recruits volunteers from the UK using various methods. These include ad hoc applications, publicity, and networking with institutions and corporations. Volunteers are most needed in response to client requests, for which they must apply on specialised forms. In the UK volunteers are needed for various jobs, including administrative support. The hours required vary. About 500 volunteers are sent overseas to work each year. Positions are not advertised but BESO operates an equal opportunities policy. Those going abroad need to have sufficient professional, technical and/or managerial skills/experience (usually 20 years) in their own field to train and advise people overseas. No further training is given, nor is any remuneration offered. All volunteers are paid travel expenses and a volunteer allowance.

Opportunities for Employment
BESO employs 12 full-time and 28 part-time staff in its London office.

Further Information
Apart from general information packs, the Annual Report, fundraising and overseas packs, and a list of local groups are available on request.

Catholic Fund for Overseas Development (CAFOD)

Romero Close, Stockwell Road
London SW9 9TY
Tel: 0171-733 7900
Fax: 0171-274 9630

Contact
Richard Miller, Deputy Director

Main Activities
CAFOD was set up in 1962 and is the official relief and development agency of the Catholic Church in England and Wales. It now funds over 1000 long-term community development projects in 75 countries. It also carries out education in the UK. A national organisation covering England and Wales, it has various regional offices and 900 local support groups. It also has links throughout the world and channels funds through organisations in developing countries. Annual budget is £22 million.

Opportunities for Volunteers
Volunteers are used extensively for promotion and education work. More are needed, in England and Wales, to carry out local fundraising activities and education work. Support is given by regional fundraisers. Travel and lunch expenses are offered. Write to Head Office or local office.

Opportunities for Employment
There are 120 staff. On average ten to fifteen are recruited each year. Jobs are advertised in The Guardian and the Catholic Press.

Further Information
Annual Report, resources catalogue and leaflets available on request. For Scotland, contact: SCIAF, 5 Oswald Street, Glasgow G1 4QR, tel 0141-221 4447. For Ireland, contact: TROCAIRE, 169 Bookerstown Avenue, Co. Dublin, Ireland.

Catholic Institute for International Relations, CIIR

Unit 3, Canonbury Yard
190A New North Road
London N1 7BJ
Tel: 0171-354 0883
Fax: 0171-359 0017

Contact
Ian Linden, General Secretary

Main Activities
The ICD Department recruits skilled workers for overseas projects. The Education Programme provides information on socio-economic, church, political and human rights issues in the developing world. CIIR is also a centre for information on the developing world. Budget is £3.5 million annually.

Opportunities for Volunteers
CIIR does not use volunteers, but there is a membership scheme.

Opportunities for Employment
Head Office has 28 full- and 8 part-time staff. Posts arise for about three people in London and for project workers annually. Extensive knowledge of developing world issues is needed. Jobs are advertised in specialist journals and The Guardian, based on a developing equal opportunities policy.

Further Information
The Annual Report, CIIR News, membership details and a publications list are available, together with overseas recruitment information packs.

Christian Aid

PO Box 100
London SE1 7RT
Tel: 0171-620 4444
Fax: 0171-620 0719

Contact
Personnel Department re volunteering
and employment

Main Activities
Founded in 1945, Christian Aid provides
overseas aid and development to those in
greatest need, through fundraising in the
UK. Helps the poor, refugees and victims
of disasters through a variety of locally
based projects. There are 40 regional
offices throughout the UK. Annual
income is £40 million.

Opportunities for Volunteers
Volunteers are used in central office (20)
and the regions (over 100), for administrative support, fundraising and
educational/media work. They are recruited ad hoc on application and through
Christian Aid's supporter base. There is
no minimum commitment. Travel and
lunch expenses are paid. People also
volunteer through local churches to be
collectors during Christian Aid Week.

Opportunities for Employment
There are 200 staff. Any vacancies are advertised in The Guardian, The Voice and
the Church press, based on an equal
opportunities policy.

Further Information
Annual Report, numerous pamphlets
and other information, and a list of local
offices are available on request.

The Christian Children's Fund of Great Britain (CCF GB)

4 Bath Place
Rivington Street
London EC2N 3DR
Tel: 0171-729 8191
Fax: 0171-729 8339

Contact
Jacquelin Curtis

Main Activities
Manages and fundraises for overseas
programme which cares for children in
over 30 developing countries and Eastern
Europe.

Opportunities for Volunteers
Volunteers are needed to give help with
mail-outs, computer entries and other
clerical tasks. Minimum commitment is
two hours a week, preferably on Monday
evenings or during working hours. Travel
and lunch expenses offered.

Opportunities for Employment
There are fourteen full-time and five part-
time staff. On average one or two are
recruited each year.

Further Information
Annual Report and information leaflet
available.

Christians Abroad

1 Stockwell Green
London SW9 9 HP
Tel: 0171-737 7811
Fax: 0171- 737 3237

Contact
Claire Pedrick

Main Activities
Christians Abroad offers World Service
Enquiry - an advice and information
service for people wishing to work
overseas of any faith or none. A free information pack is offered. 'Opportunities

Abroad', a monthly vacancy list of NGO and development posts includes free entry to the register for those with professional or technical skills. Other services such as Writelines and vocational guidance interviews are offered at moderate cost.

Opportunities for Volunteers
Volunteers are important and carry out tasks at Head Office including administrative work, fundraising and PR. Travel expenses are offered.

Opportunities for Employment
There are six members of staff; five are part-time.

Further Information
Annual Report and further information about World Service Enquiry may be obtained on request.

East European Partnership

Carlton House
27A Carlton Drive
London SW15 2BS
Tel: 0181-780 2841

Contact
Recruitment Co-ordinator

Main Activities
East European Partnership offers volunteers with appropriate qualifications, skills and experience the opportunity to work on specific projects in Central and Eastern Europe. Countries include: Russia, Albania, the Czech Republic, Estonia, Hungary, Latvia, Lithuania, Macedonia, Poland, and Slovakia. The organisation was set up in 1990 as an initiative by VSO.

Opportunities for Volunteers
About 150 volunteers are recruited each year in the fields of health and social welfare, education, and business advice. A degree or professional qualification is essential plus a minimum of two years' work experience. Particularly useful skills

include: teaching qualifications and experience, business advice/support, business studies teaching experience, social work, nursing, special needs teaching. Minimum commitment is two years overseas. A volunteer allowance is offered plus a benefits package, including travel, accommodation, relocation allowance, equipment grant, NI contributions, medical insurance, language training and professional support.

Opportunities for Employment
There are ten members of staff. Jobs are advertised in The Guardian, TES and specialist press. A formal Equal Opportunities Policy is in operation.

Further Information
A handbook for volunteers, quarterly newsletter, and a list of local VSO groups are available.

GAP Activity Projects (GAP) Ltd

GAP House, 44 Queens Road
Reading, Berks RG1 4BB
Tel: 01734-594914
Fax: 01734-576634

Contact
The Registrar for young people wanting to take a 'gap' year; PA to the Director re employment

Main Activities
GAP Activity Projects is an educational charity which organises worthwhile voluntary work abroad for 17-18 year olds in their 'gap year' between school and further education/training or work. GAP has projects in over 30 countries. It offers work involving teaching English as a foreign language, assisting in English-speaking schools, caring for under-privileged and/or handicapped people, environmental conservation and outdoor education. In all its work, GAP upholds the principle of service to others through

voluntary work. A UK-wide organisation founded in 1972, GAP is unique in that it relies on the service of volunteer members of staff to set up and run its projects abroad, as well as to interview, select and brief the young people who take part in them. It has regional agents in various parts of the UK, and Overseas Agents in the countries where it has projects, all of whom work for expenses only. A number of GAP projects are run in conjunction with voluntary organisations overseas.

Opportunities for Volunteers

Young people wishing to make good use of a 'gap year' by living and working abroad, can apply to take part in a GAP project overseas. Typically a GAP placement lasts from six to nine months leaving time for the young person to travel before/afterwards. In return for full-time voluntary service, board, lodging and, in most cases, pocket money, are provided. Applications are accepted onwards from the first term of the second year of 'A' levels.

Professional people, in their spare time or retirement, may also wish to take part in this interesting, satisfying work with young people. Recruitment is through in-house methods. Travel and out-of-pocket expenses are offered. Good administrative skills and experience with young people are necessary. Special knowledge of a foreign culture and language are advantageous.

Opportunities for Employment

GAP employs only a small team of full-time staff. Recruitment depends on vacancies and expansion. The skills needed vary according to the position. In general computer, people and team-working skills are necessary. Any positions are advertised in regional newspapers and a number of recruitment consultants are used.

Further Information

The Annual Report, information leaflet and brochures are available by writing to or telephoning GAP House in Reading.

The Great Britain-China Centre

15 Belgrave Square
London SW1X 8PS
Tel: 0171-245 6885

Contact
The Director

Main Activities

The Great Britain-China Centre promotes closer cultural, academic, economic and professional relations between Britain and China. It was founded in 1974 and the annual budget is £250,000. It organises a series of lectures and events which are open to members of the Centre. It has links with several Chinese volunteer groups of semi-governmental status.

Opportunities for Volunteers

Volunteers are involved in administrative work, fundraising, research, and public relations. Languages, overseas knowledge, administrative experience, and initiative are very useful attributes.

Opportunities for Employment

There are four full-time staff. All except the Secretary speak Chinese (Mandarin). Posts are advertised in The Guardian and The Daily Telegraph.

Further Information

Annual Report, back issue of magazine, leaflet about talks/events available on request.

Health Unlimited

3 Stamford Street
London SE1 9NT
Tel: 0171-928 8105
Fax: 0171-928 7736

Contact

Lucy Medd, Office Manager

Main Activities

Health Unlimited was set up in 1984. It provides basic health care and equips local people with the primary health care knowledge, skills and resources to meet the needs of the community. It is involved in projects in Africa, Asia and Latin America, and some of its partner agencies are themselves voluntary organisations. A national organisation covering England and Scotland, it has regional offices in Bristol, Manchester and Edinburgh and Friends' groups all over the country. Annual budget is £850,000.

Opportunities for Volunteers

Volunteers are essential to Health Unlimited and particularly important in helping to raise money and the organisation's profile. More are needed to form fundraising groups locally. Briefing, fundraising advice and ideas are available. Write with a CV to head office enclosing an SAE. There are also opportunities for medically qualified volunteers to work overseas. They need six months experience of work or travel in developing countries and preferably to speak French and/or Spanish. Contact head office for details.

Opportunities for Employment

There are 30 full-time staff. Staff with medical qualifications or experience are recruited from time to time for overseas work.

Further Information

Annual Report and information leaflets available on request.

Indian Volunteers for Community Service (IVCS)

12 Eastleigh Avenue
South Harrow
Middlesex HA2 0UF
Tel: 0181-864 4740

Contact

General Secretary

Main Activities

Set up in 1981, IVCS arranges for visitors to stay in rural development projects in India. It supports a development project in North India, organises seminars and workshops in both the UK and India, and produces a joint newsletter. It also works with the International Task Force for the Rural Poor (INTAF), and has links with the Society for Agro-Industrial Education in India. It has one office in the UK and an annual budget of £3,000.

Opportunities for Volunteers

There are limited opportunities for short and long-term stays, sometimes in a voluntary capacity, in projects in India through the Project Visitors' Scheme. Voluntary work usually involves administrative office work, teaching English, and occasionally conservation work. School leavers and new graduates are particularly welcome. The emphasis is on the volunteer's learning experience. Send an SAE for information and application form.

Opportunities for Employment

At present all staff in the UK are volunteers. There is a possibility for one or two full-time paid staff, provided funds can be found.

Further Information

The Annual Report, pamphlets and newsletters are available.

International Cooperation for Development

Unit 3, Canonbury Yard
190A New North Road
London N1 7BJ
Tel: 0171-354 0883

Contact
Recruitment and Selection Officer

Main Activities
Based in London the organisation is a development agency that recruits experienced, professionally qualified people to share their skills with communities in the Third World. Main project locations: Dominican Republic, Ecuador, El Salvador, Honduras, Namibia, Nicaragua, Peru, Yemen and Zimbabwe.

Opportunities for Volunteers
Volunteers with specialist skills in health, agriculture and education are recruited at the request of Developing World partners. They must have a qualification plus two years post-qualification experience in the skill area sought, often health or agriculture related eg pharmacist, agriculturalist.

Opportunities for Employment
There are approximately eighteen full-time staff.

Further Information
Annual Report and pamphlet available on request.

International Health Exchange (IHE)

Africa Centre, 38 King Street
London WC2E 8JT
Tel: 0171-836 5833

Contact
Patrick Brook, Information Officer

Main Activities
Founded in 1980, IHE offers a unique combination of services linking health professionals and the organisations working for health improvement in developing countries. It facilitates the provision of appropriately trained health workers/personnel for programmes in such countries by helping to find positions for such people. It also promotes appropriate training for those going to work overseas, and raises awareness among health workers of developing countries' health needs. It runs a Register for health and management professionals, and provides information and advice. Has a London office only.

Opportunities for Volunteers
IHE does not use volunteers in its London office, but some of the aid agencies it works with send people overseas as volunteers. Some of the positions it finds for health professionals can also sometimes be voluntary ie at local rates of pay.

Opportunities for Employment
IHE has four full-time staff. It recruits qualified, experienced health workers to go overseas for aid agencies. These include doctors, nurses and other health professionals. Positions are advertised in IHE's bi-monthly magazine The Health Exchange.

Further Information
The Annual Report, pamphlets, and IHE's The Health Exchange, magazine are available.

The Karuna Trust

186 Cowley Road,
Oxford OX4 1UE
Tel: 01865-728794

Contact
Mr D Cowley

Main Activities
A Buddhist charity formed in 1980, the Trust's primary purpose is fundraising for social and educational projects in various parts of India. It is the northern partner of an Indian charity/NGO

(non-governmental organisation) running social welfare projects among former untouchable communities. One office only, as above.

Opportunities for Volunteers

Uses two volunteers in Oxford office for administrative work and fundraising. Does not send volunteers abroad. Recruits through ad hoc applications, volunteer bureaux and in-house. No minimum commitment but regular commitment preferred. Travel and lunch expenses are offered. Volunteers must be sympathetic to/interested in the Buddhist ethos and vision.

Opportunities for Employment

There are seven full- and two part-time staff.

Further Information

Annual Report, various pamphlets, back issues of newsletters, videos and slides are available. Speakers can be provided.

Médecins Sans Frontières (MSF) (UK)

124-132 Clerkenwell Road
London EC1R 5DL
Tel: 0171-713 5600
Fax: 0171-713 5004

Contact

Valerie Wistreich/Gabriella Breebaart for volunteering; Victoria Godsal, Office Manager for employment opportunities

Main Activities

Originally set up in 1971 by a group of former Red Cross doctors, and registered in the UK in September 1993, Médecins Sans Frontières is now the world's largest independent humanitarian organisation for emergency medical aid/relief. It provides assistance to victims of armed conflict, and of man-made and natural disasters world-wide, irrespective of race, religion, ideology or political affiliation. An international

agency, MSF has six main offices in Europe and 12 branch offices world-wide of which the UK is one. Its annual global budget is US$180 million, with 50% of funding from private donations and 90% of the total budget being used directly for medical aid.

Opportunities for Volunteers

MSF relies on volunteers for its work overseas. Each year over 2,000 volunteers are sent out, with over 100 coming from the UK during 1994. They include medical doctors, nurses, engineers and emergency aid workers from various backgrounds (eg accountants, construction workers), who work with local staff and/or collaborate with other aid organisations. Volunteers must be flexible, co-operative and diplomatic, able to work in a team with people from many different backgrounds. Two years post-qualification experience is required, while tropical medicine experience together with French and/or Spanish are useful. MSF actively seeks volunteers, especially doctors, nurses (with tropical medicine training) and logistics personnel, year round, but especially during big emergencies eg Rwanda. Recruitment is ad hoc, on application and through presentations at various medical institutions. After filling in an application form, suitable candidates are interviewed and then, if appropriate, their names are added to a register to await suitable vacancies. Two week preparation courses are run in Amsterdam. The minimum commitment required is six months. Travel, accommodation and subsistence expenses are paid, together with a volunteer allowance of £500 a month.

Opportunities for Employment

MSF (UK) employs three full-time and one part-time staff at head office, with no plans to increase these numbers. Should any vacancies arise they are advertised in The Guardian.

Further Information

The Annual Report, an Activity Report, general and specific 'recruitment for volunteers' information, and a list of MSF offices are available by phone or written request.

OWA – One World Action

5th Floor
13-14 West Smithfield
London EC1A 9HY
Tel: 0171-329 8111
Fax: 0171-329 6238

Contact

Volunteer Co-ordinator

Main Activities

A national development agency for the developing world, OWA was set up in 1989, and has an annual budget of £1 million. It has links with voluntary organisations in Europe, North America and the developing world, including WIDE (Europe), Grassroots (America), International Workers Aid, and various trade unions.

Opportunities for Volunteers

40 volunteers work in head office and undertake administrative support, fundraising, lobbying, public relations and research. They are regarded as very important to the organisation's work and need to have some overseas knowledge. Recruitment is ad hoc, on application, via volunteer bureaux and through in-house schemes. The minimum time commitment is three to six months and travel, lunch and out-of-pocket expenses are paid. OWA regularly seeks more volunteers for head office work of various kinds, including research, campaigning, marketing and general administration. Useful skills include computer, telephone answering and languages. Contact the volunteer co-ordinator for further details and an application form.

Opportunities for Employment

Seven full-time and two part-time staff are employed. Recruitment opportunities seldom arise. OWA has a formal Equal Opportunities Policy.

Further Information

The Annual Report, a newsletter and booklets are available on request.

Oxfam

274 Banbury Road
Oxford OX2 7DU
Tel: 01865-311311
Fax: 01865-312380

Contact

Volunteers Adviser or via local area Oxfam offices.

Main Activities

Tackles Developing World poverty by funding health, social development, agriculture, education and humanitarian programmes, run by project partners in 70 developing countries.

Opportunities for Volunteers

Twelve area groups and numerous local units form a network of 30,000 volunteers in the UK and Ireland who fundraise, run shops, campaign and do admin work. Minimum time commitment varies. Training is offered as well as out-of-pocket expenses such as travel and lunch. Volunteers are always needed for the 850 shops, especially during autumn. Opportunities exist locally, for fundraisers, educators and internal auditors. There is a range of opportunities at Head Office. Volunteers are not sent overseas.

Opportunities for Employment

About 1,250 staff work for Oxfam, jobs are advertised either locally or nationally as appropriate. An equal opportunities policy applies.

Further Information

A leaflet and list of locations are available from Head Office. Oxfam News, published four times a year, is distributed to shops and supporters.

The Project Trust

The Hebridean Centre
Isle of Coll, Scotland PA78 6TE
Tel: 018793-444

Contact
The Director

Main Activities
A national organisation set up in 1968, the Trust runs teaching, development and social work projects for school leavers in nineteen countries outside Europe.

Opportunities for Volunteers
Volunteers have to be in full-time education at the time of applying. They should be aged between seventeen years three months and nineteen years six months at the time of going abroad. Must be prepared to commit themselves for one year. Pocket money is offered as well as free board and lodging.

Opportunities for Employment
There are thirteen staff, generally recruited from returned volunteers.

Further Information
Recruiting pamphlet available for volunteers.

QISP – Quaker International Social Projects, *see Youth*

Raleigh International

27 Parsons Green Lane
London SW6 4HZ
Tel: 0171-371 8585
Fax: 0171-371 5116

Contact
Information Officer for volunteering; Suzy Parry, Personnel, re employment

Main Activities
Originally set up in 1984 as Operation Raleigh, Raleigh International enables youth development through involvement in challenging community and conservation projects overseas. Expeditions last for three months and go to such countries as Chile, Guyana and Zimbabwe (1995). Other project locations have included Belize and Malaysia. Raleigh has a head office in London, 40 local branches, 15 international groups and links with various countries in the developing world. Annual turnover is £3.4 million.

Opportunities for Volunteers
About 1,000 volunteers aged between 17 and 25 (or over 25 for volunteer Expedition staff) are taken on each year to work on Raleigh expeditions, undertaking conservation and other project work such as construction. More volunteers are always needed and no special skills are required. Recruitment is ad hoc, on application, through in-house schemes and via PR (public relations). The minimum commitment is three months and no remuneration is offered.

Opportunities for Employment
Raleigh International employs 45 full-time and 15 part-time staff. Any vacancies that arise are advertised in The Guardian. No special skills are required, apart from enthusiasm. An equal opportunities policy is being developed.

Further Information
The Annual Report and a list of local groups are available.

Skillshare Africa

3 Belvoir Street
Leicester LE1 6SL
Tel: 0116-254 1862
Fax: 0116-254 2614

Contact
David Harries, Recruitment Selection
Officer; Sharon Callaghan, Recruitment
Facilitator

Main Activities
A UK-wide organisation, Skillshare Africa
sends skilled and experienced people to
work in support of development in Bot-
swana, Lesotho, Mozambique and
Swaziland. Set up in 1990, it worked previously as IVS (Overseas) for over 30
years. It also has links in Europe with
other non-governmental organisations
(NGOs) and donor organisations.

Opportunities for Volunteers
Volunteer work on a wide range of
projects in the above countries is available.
Qualifications relevant to the post are required. Minimum commitment is full time
for two years. Jobs are advertised in the
national press and a volunteer allowance
is paid. Pre-departure training is offered.

Opportunities for Employment
There are 26 full-time staff and 2 part-time.

Further Information
Annual Report and Information Pack are
available.

SOS – Children's Villages UK

32 Bridge Street
Cambridge CB2 1UJ
Tel: 01223-65589
Fax: 01223-322613

Contact
Tina Barnes

Main Activities
Cares for 75,000 children worldwide in
various homes and projects. In the UK,
arranges fundraising and sponsorship of
villages, school and youth projects. There
are twelve local support groups. The
annual budget is £440,000.

Opportunities for Volunteers
Assistance is needed with fundraising and
administrative support in the office. Recruitment is usually through the local
volunteer bureau.

Opportunities for Employment
There are two full-time staff and five part-
time staff.

Further Information
Annual Report, fundraising leaflets and
information sheets on SOS projects available.

Tear Fund

100 Church Road, Teddington
Middlesex TW11 8QE
Tel: 0181-977 9144

Contact
Support Services Manager

Main Activities
Raises funds for Developing World relief
and development work with emphasis on
Christian concern.

Opportunities for Volunteers
Over 2000 voluntary representatives
organise meetings and prayer groups.
People with public speaking skills or able
to give clerical assistance are also required.
Several short term programmes overseas
exist. Applicants contribute most of the
costs of these themselves.

Opportunities for Employment
There are 118 full-time staff. Approximately 20 staff are recruited each year.
Applicants must be practising evangelical Christians.

Further Information
Annual report available. For Tear Fund
Wales: telephone 01443-402328. For Tear

Fund Scotland: telephone 0141-332 3621. For Tear Fund Ireland: telephone 01232-324940.

Third World First (3W1)

217 Cowley Road,
Oxford OX4 1XJ
Tel: 01865-245678
Fax: 01865-200179

Contact
Luis Reveoo, Director

Main Activities
3W1 raises awareness about international poverty. Fundraising is carried out for Third World projects. National organisation with 70 groups located mainly in UK colleges and universities.

Opportunities for Volunteers
Local groups of volunteers campaign and provide administrative support. Travel expenses are offered. Some knowledge of Third World issues is useful.

Opportunities for Employment
There are six full-time and two part-time staff.

Further Information
Annual Report and other information available.

Tools for Self Reliance

Netly Marsh,
Southampton SO40 7GY
Tel: 01703-869697
Fax: 01703-868544

Contact
Tim Young, Workshop Organiser

Main Activities
Collects and refurbishes unwanted hand tools for free distribution to village workshops in developing countries.

Opportunities for Volunteers
70 local support groups raise funds and collect tools for refurbishment. Volunteers

are also always required for refurbishing tools. No special skills are necessary as full training is given. Travel expenses are offered.

Opportunities for Employment
There are seven full-time staff.

Further Information
Annual Report and information sheets (including one on tool refurbishment) available.

UNICEF – The United Nations Children's Fund

55 Lincoln's Inn Fields
London WC2A 3NB
Tel: 0171-405 5592

Contact
David Bedford, Deputy Executive Director

Main Activities
Raises funds to support UNICEF'S work in 130 countries. Heightens public awareness of the special needs of children. Encourages statutory bodies and VSO to participate in this work. There are 130 local branches. Annual budget is £8 million.

Opportunities for Volunteers
Volunteers are needed for management, advocacy and fundraising tasks. Communication and organisational skills valuable. Induction and specialist training are offered as appropriate.

Opportunities for Employment
There are 54 full-time staff. On average two or three are recruited each year. Jobs are advertised in The Guardian and appropriate specialist media.

Further Information
Annual Report, list of local groups and wide variety of material covering all aspects of UNICEF's development work available.

Voluntary Service Overseas (VSO)

317 Putney Bridge Road
London SW15 2PN
Tel: 0181-780 2266
Fax: 0181-780 1326

Contact
Enquiries Unit

Main Activities
Set up in 1958, VSO enables men and women to work alongside people in about 57 developing countries in order to share skills, build capabilities and promote international understanding. VSO also has links with a wide variety of non-governmental organisations (NGOs) in the developing world and aims for a more equitable world overall.

Opportunities for Volunteers
Volunteers are fundamental to VSO's work. Around 1,700 volunteers undertake full-time professional jobs overseas for a minimum of two years. Applicants must have relevant qualifications and experience, and be between 20 and 70 years. VSO recruits in particular new graduates, people returning to work and those who have experienced career redundancy. Pre-departure training is given. Volunteers receive a modest living allowance, and accommodation and equipment grants. There is also a network of local support groups in the UK.

Opportunities for Employment
VSO has 187 full-time staff in London and 79 overseas in local field offices.

Further Information
Annual report and information leaflets available. Also a quarterly magazine 'Orbit' – annual subscription £10. Scottish representative : Kate O'Brien, telephone 0131-667 3073.

Volunteer Missionary Movement (VMM)

Comboni House, London Road
Sunningdale, Berks SL5 0JH
Tel: 01344-875380
Fax: 01344-875280

Contact
Maggie Prowse, General Co-ordinator

Main Activities
Set up in 1969, VMM recruits, prepares and places committed Christians in selected developing countries. Workers share their professional skills and their witness to Christ. Main project locations are: Kenya, Uganda, Tanzania, Zambia, South Africa and Zimbabwe. VMM has a sister organisation, VMM-USA, in America.

Opportunities for Volunteers
Volunteers as missionaries are crucial to the overseas projects. They must have professional or technical qualifications, with two years experience in their professional/vocational skill area, and must be prepared to commit themselves for two years. Many of the projects are in lonely, rural areas. There are no volunteering opportunities in the UK-based offices.

Opportunities for Employment
There are eleven full-time staff in the UK. Jobs are advertised in The Guardian, Tablet, Church of England News and Methodist Recorder.

Further Information
Annual Report and general leaflet available on request. For Scotland, contact: c/o Justice and Peace, Gillis Cottage, 113 Whitehouse Loan, Edinburgh EH9 1BB, tel: 0131-452 8559.

War on Want

Fenner Brockway House
37-9 Great Guildford Street
London SE1 OES
Tel: 0171-620 1111
Fax: 0171-261 9291

Contact
Sue Barber

Main Activities
Set up in 1952, War on Want campaigns against the causes of poverty in the developing world. Funds practical development projects in Africa, Asia and Latin America. There are over 50 local and affiliated support groups.

Opportunities for Volunteers
Volunteers are needed for general administrative work, fundraising and campaigning assistance at head office. They are very important since they work with paid members of staff and input all the staff functions. Keyboard skills are desirable, but training is given in word processing and extracting news-clips. Minimum commitment: seven hours per week over 4-6 weeks. Travel and lunch expenses paid. War on Want has a volunteer policy and draws up volunteer job descriptions.

Opportunities for Employment
Eight full-time staff work at head office. No recruitment at present.

Further Information
Annual report, information sheets and list of local groups available. The newsletter is circulated to members and supporters.

WaterAid

1 Queen Anne's Gate
London SW1H 9BT
Tel: 0171-233 4800
Fax: 0171-233 3161

Contact
Personnel Officer

Main Activities
Set up in 1981, WaterAid works with poor communities, usually through local partners (mainly non-governmental organisations – NGOs), in 15 countries in Africa and Asia to provide safe water, basic sanitation and health education. It works on a self-help basis, using technologies appropriate to local needs.

Opportunities for Volunteers
Volunteers are needed at head office for administrative support and data input. They are able to extend the work of paid staff and provide useful back-up. Good administrative and typing skills are needed for some jobs, but training will be given on a computerised database. Minimum commitment of one day a week is usually required. Lunch and travel expenses are paid.

Opportunities for Employment
There are 25 full-time staff. Numbers recruited vary. Jobs are advertised in the national press.

Further Information
Annual Review, information leaflet, fundraising newsletter and bi-annual journal available.

WOMANKIND Worldwide, *see* *Women*

World Vision (UK)

World Vision House
99 Avebury Boulevard
Central Milton Keynes MK9 3PG
Tel: 01908-841005
Fax: 01908-841014/001

Contact
Ms Marianne Dunk, Human Resources

Main Activities
World Vision is part of a worldwide partnership working towards developing world relief and development in over 90 countries.

Opportunities for Volunteers
Volunteers are regarded as a vital part of the team. They are needed for general clerical work for a minimum of four hours at a time. Travel expenses are offered.

Opportunities for Employment
About 20 people are recruited each year for overseas jobs in medicine, agricultural development and financial administration. Relevant qualifications and experience are necessary as well as a foreign language, preferably French or Portuguese.

Further Information
Annual report and information sheets available.

WWF-UK (World Wide Fund for Nature)

Panda House, Weyside Park
Godalming, Surrey GU7 1XR
Tel: 01483-426444
Fax: 01483-426409

Contact
The Regional Unit

Main Activities
WWF raises funds for international and UK conservation and environmental projects. It works on natural resource conservation, bio-diversity and pollution prevention. There are 300 local support groups.

Opportunities for Volunteers
Volunteers are needed to fundraise, to raise awareness of WWF, and to take part in local group activities eg giving talks, campaigning and publicity.

Opportunities for Employment
There are 150 staff. Jobs are advertised in The Guardian, New Scientist and local papers. There is an Equal Opportunities Policy.

Further Information
Annual Report, list of local groups and information leaflets available.

WWOOF (Working for Organic Growers)

19 Bradford Road, Lewes
Sussex BN7 1RB
Tel: 01273-476286

Contact
Don Pynches, Co-ordinator, at head office. Write, enclosing an sae.

Main Activities
Set up in 1971, WWOOF is a country-wide exchange network concerned with organic agriculture where bed, board and practical experience are given in return for work on organic farms and smallholdings. About 40 farm hosts in Southern Europe belong to WWOOF (UK), and there are also WWOOF organisations in Australia, Canada, Germany, Ghana, Ireland, New Zealand and the USA.

Opportunities for Volunteers
Volunteers are vital to WWOOF's work and opportunities are available all over the UK. Both mid-week and long term work are possible on various farms. Applicants need to be fit and willing. On long stays farmer/hosts will offer pocket money. There is a network of 17

voluntary organisers. About 30% of volunteers are unemployed.

Opportunities for Employment
There are two part-time staff.

Further Information
Annual Report and other information available on request.

Recreation & Leisure

African Caribbean Library Association, see Education

Association of Railway Preservation Societies

16 Woodbrook, Charing
Ashford, Kent TN27 0DN
Tel: 01233-712130

Contact
Raymond Williams, General Administrator

Main Activities
Preserves, co-ordinates and advises on railway preservation. Liaises with statutory bodies and individual preservation societies. Organises general meetings at national/regional venues three times a year. Also holds technical/commercial seminars. Makes representations to statutory bodies on behalf of member railways.

Opportunities for Volunteers
Individual societies need volunteers all the year round to run and maintain their sites and trains. Local training and support are given.

Opportunities for Employment
There are no employment opportunities.

Further Information
Annual Report, information leaflet and list of local societies available.

British Association of Friends of Museums (BAFM), see Museums, the Arts & Festivals

British Sports Association for the Disabled (BSAD), see Sports

Calvert Trust, see Sports

Children's Countrywide Holidays Fund, see Children

Community Transport Association Ltd, see Education

Countrywide Holidays

Birch Hays, Cromwell Range
Manchester M14 6HU
Tel: 0161-225 1000

Contact
Pauline Taylor

Main Activities
Provides walking and special interest holidays. National organisation with locations in Scotland, Lake District, Peak District, Snowdonia, Devon, Cornwall, Norfolk and the Isle of Wight. Annual budget is £2.8 million.

Opportunities for Volunteers
Volunteers are needed to act as host/hostesses on holidays. Limited travel expenses are paid. Organisational, social and walking leadership skills are essential. Minimum commitment is one week between May and September.

Opportunities for Employment
There are 100 full-time and 20 part-time staff.

Further Information
Annual Report, brochures and list of local groups available.

The Duke of Edinburgh's Award, see Youth

Duke of Edinburgh's Award / Gwobr Dug Caeredin

Oak House, 12 The Bulwark
Brecon, Powys LD3 7AD
Tel: 01874-623086

Contact
Sandra Skinner

Main Activities
The Award is a voluntary programme of leisure time activities focusing on community service, skills, physical recreation and expeditions in which young people and interested adults work together. Annual budget is £60,000 (in Wales).

Opportunities for Volunteers
There are approximately 46,000 volunteers in Wales carrying out a variety of tasks including: conservation, advice giving, counselling, organising local groups, fundraising, administrative support. The organisation is currently seeking volunteer leaders and assessors. Training is offered.

Opportunities for Employment
There are three full-time and four part-time staff. Posts are advertised in the Western Mail, Golwq and the Liverpool Daily Star.

Further Information
Annual Report, leaflets and a list of voluntary groups are available.

Earthwatch Europe, see
Environment & Conservation

Endeavour Training, see
Education

English National Association of Visually Handicapped Bowlers (ENAVHB)

11 Wordsworth Road
Clevedon, Avon BS21 6PQ
Tel: 01275-875969

Contact
Geoffrey Rawlinson, Honorary Secretary

Main Activities
The ENAVHB encourages blind people in activity and promotes awareness of the game of bowls. It has five regional groups covering England and Wales, 40 local branches, is affiliated to various organisations for blind people and has a sister organisation in Scotland. It also has links with similar voluntary organisations in other countries, including Canada, Hong Kong, Israel and Zimbabwe. A completely voluntary association, it does not have an annual budget.

Opportunities for Volunteers
Run entirely by volunteers, the ENAVHB is a self-help, self servicing group in which the participants undertake all the work that needs doing. Volunteers need to be fully committed to the organisation and no expenses are offered, except to executive levels. New volunteers are welcomed and about 20 are recruited each year. They need to have knowledge of and interest in bowls, and be keen to help others, as well as usually being individually disabled through partial sightedness.

Opportunities for Employment
There are no paid posts and no opportunities for employment.

Further Information
The Annual Report and other information are available on request to the Honorary Secretary. Other useful addresses are:

Mr J Bircham, 8 Holmes Place, Kilmarnock, Scotland.

Mr N McTavish, 27 Players Avenue, Swansea, Wales.

The Feminist Library, *see* *Women*

Festival Welfare Services (FWS)

61B Hornsey Road
London N7 6DG
Tel: 0171-700 5754
Fax: 0171-700 6964

Contact
Penny Mellor, Co-ordinator

Main Activities
FWS, a UK-wide agency which was founded in 1974, co-ordinates welfare organisations providing services at outdoor music festivals. It promotes safe and healthy festivals. The annual budget is £45,000.

Opportunities for Volunteers
Volunteers are needed to give administrative support at Head Office and are essential to the smooth running of the organisation. Minimum commitment is six hours a week for at least four weeks. In summertime, volunteers are needed to undertake general welfare duties at outdoor events/music festivals in various parts of the UK. They are crucial to the provision of these welfare services. Vegetarian food is provided and the minimum commitment is eight hours a day. Common sense and flexibility are necessary skills.

Opportunities for Employment
There are two staff.

Further Information
Annual Report and information leaflets available.

Ffestiniog Railway

Harbour Station
Porthmadog
Gwynedd LL49 9NF
Tel: 01766-512340
Fax: 01766-514576

Contact
Eamonn Seddon, Volunteer Resource Officer

Main Activities
The Ffestiniog Railway is Britain's busiest narrow gauge railway.

Opportunities for Volunteers
Both skilled and unskilled volunteers are needed. Wide variety of jobs from bramble cutting on the track to serving beer in the carriages. Overseas volunteers are welcome as are volunteers with physical disabilities. Volunteers make a contribution towards board and lodging costs. A good knowledge of the English language is necessary.

Opportunities for Employment
There are no employment opportunities.

Further Information
Annual Report and guide book available.

Godalming Museum, *see* *Museums, the Arts & Festivals*

Great Britain Wheelchair Basketball Association, *see* *Sports*

Greater London Sports Association (GLSA), *see Sports*

HAPA (Handicapped Adventure Playground Association), *see Children*

Ironbridge Gorge Museum Trust, see Museums, the Arts & Festivals

The Jewish Lads and Girls Brigade, see Youth

Jubilee Sailing Trust

Test Road, Eastern Docks
Southampton SO14 3GG
Tel: 01703-631388
Fax: 01703-638625

Contact
Miss K Harris

Main Activities
A registered charity, the Trust was founded to promote integration between able-bodied and physically disabled adults through the medium of tall ship sailing. A national organisation, the Trust has over 50 local voluntary branches.

Opportunities for Volunteers
Over 200 volunteers work in the branches carrying out vital fundraising work. The Trust Office also employs volunteers to help with periodic mail shots. Most volunteers are former voyage crew members. There is no minimum commitment. When working at the Trust office, lunch expenses are paid.

Opportunities for Employment
The Trust employs eleven people in the office and ten people on board 'Lord Nelson' for which relevant merchant navy qualifications are required. Posts are advertised in the specialised marine and the local press. The Trust has an equal opportunities policy.

Further Information
The Annual Report, a list of local groups and various publications, including voyage brochures, fundraising literature and sponsorship opportunities, are available from the Trust office.

National Association of Round Tables of Great Britain and Ireland (RTBI)

Marchesi House, 4 Embassy Drive
Edgbaston, Birmingham B15 1TP
Tel: 0121-456 4402
Fax: 0121-456 4185

Contact
Mr Richard Renold, General Secretary

Main Activities
A national association of young men's clubs for mainly business and professional men aged between 18 and 40. Aims include civic and community service, fellowship and development of members, and international understanding. Activities include regular meetings and social and community events of all kinds. Has 1,200 autonomous local clubs grouped in 53 areas, which raise c.£10 million annually for charity. Links with similar clubs world-wide.

Opportunities for Volunteers
The members are volunteers. Membership is open to men aged between eighteen and 40.

Opportunities for Employment
There are seven staff. Opportunities for employment are rare.

Further Information
Membership literature available.

National Association of Swimming Clubs for the Handicapped (NASCH), see Sports

National Association of Women's Clubs (NAWC), see Women

National Council for the Divorced and Separated (NCDS), see Family & Community Matters

National Federation of Eighteen Plus Groups (18 Plus)

Nicholson House, Old Court Road
Newent, Glos GL18 1AG
Tel: 01531-821210
Fax: 01531-821474

Contact
Headquarters for membership information

Main Activities
A self-governing social and activities organisation for adults between 18 and 30, run as a club by the members. Non-political and non-religious, 18 Plus groups offer a wide range of activities, experience in project management and opportunities to meet others. 18 Plus is a federation with about 150 branches, mainly in England, divided into thirteen areas.

Opportunities for Volunteers
There are over 1000 volunteers, drawn from the membership, who undertake administrative, fundraising and project work (eg organising events/activities, training, recruitment/development). 18 Plus actively seeks new members/volunteers, especially to open new groups. Training in practical and management skills is given. Recruitment is in-house and through head office. Commitment is variable. Travel expenses are paid.

Opportunities for Employment
Two full-time staff and one part-time. Vacancies are rare, by attrition only. Any posts are advertised locally only.

Further Information
Annual Report, a wide range of 18 Plus pamphlets, a Guide to 18 Plus and a list of local groups are available.

National Federation of Gateway Clubs (Gateway), see Disability

National Federation of Women's Institutes (NFWI), see Women

National Playing Fields Association (Scotland), NPFA (Scotland)

20 Queen Street
Edinburgh EH2 1JX
Tel: 0131-225 4307
Fax: 0131-225 5763

Contact
John E Tunnah, Director

Main Activities
A national organisation for Scotland with five regional committees, NPFA (Scotland) was set up in 1929. It is concerned with the protection and preservation of fields and recreational space, and with the provision of sports coaching opportunities in areas of greatest social need, especially for children and young people. The annual budget is £100,000.

Opportunities for Volunteers
Around 50 volunteers provide the coaching expertise for the NPFA's branch sports programmes, and help to organise the local groups. Recruitment is usually through in-house methods and volunteers should have played sport at national or international levels and hold appropriate qualifications. Travel and out-of-pocket expenses are paid.

Opportunities for Employment
The NPFA (Scotland) employs one full-time and two part-time members of staff and is unlikely to expand. It has implemented an equal opportunities policy.

Further Information
The Annual Report, technical information on playing fields and a list of local groups are available from the Edinburgh office.

The National Trust, see Environment & Conservation

National Association of Toy and Leisure Libraries / Play Matters, see Children

Quay Theatre, see Museums, the Arts & Festivals

Railworld

Oundle Road, Peterborough
Cambs PE2 9NR
Tel: 01733-344240

Contact
Rev Richard Paten, Project Director

Main Activities
Railworld aims to proclaim and promote rail transport in a global context, for the benefit of the public, the environment and the railway industry. It was set up in 1985 and there is also a Friends of Railworld group. There are various exhibitions eg Rail and the Environment, Global Rail Travel, Rail Industry Showcase, and Local Rail History, as well as outside exhibits.

Opportunities for Volunteers
There are approximately 100 volunteers who perform a variety of tasks including: administrative support, fundraising, research and PR. There is a particular need for stewards at weekends.

Opportunities for Employment
There are no employment opportunities at present but Railworld provides work for about 20 unemployed people on government training schemes.

Further Information
Data Sheet available on request.

Riding for the Disabled, see Disability

Royal British Legion, see Social Welfare

Sail Training Association, see Youth

Sea Ranger Association (SRA), see Youth

Share Holiday Village

Smith's Strand, Lisnaskea
Co Fermanagh BT92 0EQ
Tel: 013657-22122

Contact
Norma Heap

Main Activities
Share Holiday Village is a lakeside outdoor residential activity centre specially designed for the integration of disabled and able-bodied people. Activities include water sports, leisure suite, cycling, archery and orienteering. The charity was set up in 1981. Annual budget is approximately £750,000.

Opportunities for Volunteers
Three hundred and thirty volunteers are involved in the organisation. They are essential to the centre's operation and carry out a variety of tasks including: caring, respite care, maintenance, assisting with activity programmes. Volunteers are also needed to run local groups, to fundraise and to act as volunteer companions for disabled visitors. Training is provided (specialist weekends are organised at the centre). Residential volunteers are offered free meals, accommodation and travel allowance.

Opportunities for Employment
There are twenty staff. Jobs are advertised

locally and regionally. An equal opportunities policy is in place.

Further Information
Annual Report and brochure available on request.

Sing for Pleasure Trust, *see Education*

SPLASH (Single Parent Links and Special Holidays)

19 North Street
Plymouth PL4 9AH
Tel: 01752-674067
Fax: 01752-255977

Contact
Jane Guy, Chair

Main Activities
SPLASH provides low cost holidays for one parent families and adventure holidays for unaccompanied children. Holidays are all over Britain, Europe and the USA. The annual budget is £250,000.

Opportunities for Volunteers
Representatives and youth workers on children's holidays are always needed and welcomed. First Aid, life-saving and youth work experience is useful. References are required and a police check is made. Volunteers also fundraise and give administrative support.

Opportunities for Employment
There are two staff and few recruitment opportunities.

Further Information
Annual Report is available. Also available: Holiday Brochures, Child Protection Policy Statement and Guidelines for Youth Workers.

Townswomen's Guilds, *see Women*

Wandsworth Blind Bowling Club and London Blind Rambling Club

For bowls:
3 Westlands Terrace
London SW12 9PD
Tel: 0181-673 4010

For rambling:
64 Antrim Mansions
Antrim Road
London NW3 4XL
Tel: 0171-586 4548

Contact
Richard Stancombe for bowls; Ian Hamlyn for rambling

Main Activities
To encourage recreation through bowls and rambling for partially sighted and registered blind people in the Greater London area. The Bowls Club was set up in 1981, followed by the Rambling Club in 1991 which is affiliated to the Rambling Association. The annual budget of £2,000 is from the Wandsworth Recreational Fund for the Blind.

Opportunities for Volunteers
Both clubs use volunteers for fundraising and to help out at events. Sighted help is especially needed, particularly at weekends from Spring to Autumn. They are recruited ad hoc, on application, through in-house recruitment drives, and via talking newspapers for blind people and libraries. Out-of-pocket expenses are offered.

Opportunities for Employment
There are no paid staff.

Further Information
The Annual Report and a yearly newsletter for the Ramblers are available.

The Woodcraft Folk, *see Youth*

Winged Fellowship Trust, see Disability

UK Sports Association for People with Learning Disability, see Sports

WWOOF (Working for Organic Growers), see Overseas & the Developing World

Yoga for Health Organisation

Ickwell Bury
Biggleswade
Beds SG18 9EF
Tel: 01767-627271
Fax: 01767-627266

Contact
Alan Fowler, Administrative Manager

Main Activities
Yoga for Health Organisation aims to maximise the quality of life for the disabled and able bodied through the teaching of Yoga. There are 85 local branches in the UK. Annual budget is approximately £250,000.

Opportunities for Volunteers
Fundraising is occasionally done by volunteers. Minimum commitment is 20 hours a week.

Opportunities for Employment
There are ten full-time and 40 part-time staff. Jobs are advertised locally.

Further Information
Annual Report available.

Youth Hostels Association (YHA)

Trevelyan House
8 St Stephens Hill
St Albans, Herts AL1 2DY
Tel: 01727-855215
Fax: 01727-844126

Contact
Natalie Husak

Main Activities
YHA fosters care, love and knowledge of the countryside amongst young people. Provides budget accommodation throughout England and Wales. National organisation with approximately 100 local groups.

Opportunities for Volunteers
Volunteers are needed to fundraise and take part in conservation and project work, eg refurbishment of hostels. Volunteer hostel wardens are also needed and people willing to serve on committees. Enthusiasm is the most important personal quality.

Opportunities for Employment
There are 1000 staff. There are seasonal recruitment opportunities for hostel staff between April and September. Jobs are advertised in the local and national press as appropriate.

Further Information
Annual report, information leaflets, list of local groups and publication 'Who runs YHA' (for potential volunteers) available on request from Customer Services at National Office.

Religious Affairs

Africa Inland Mission (AIM)

2 Vorley Road, Archway
London N19 5HE
Tel: 0171-281 1184

Contact
Angela Godfrey, Volunteer Co-ordinator

Main Activities
Africa Inland Mission is a Protestant missionary society whose aims are evangelism and church planting. AIM operates in Africa, mainly in Kenya, but also in other countries as needs arise.

Opportunities for Volunteers
About 30 volunteers are recruited each year for teaching in rural schools and working with young people. Applicants must be between 18 and 70 and have A levels or a degree (for teaching). A knowledge of French is useful for certain countries. All volunteers must be committed Christians. Accommodation is provided but volunteers must raise their travel expenses, insurance, living costs and administration costs themselves. Advice is given on obtaining sponsorship. Orientation and de-briefing on return are provided.

Opportunities for Employment
There are no employment opportunities.

Further Information
Annual Report, and AIM International quarterly magazine are available.

Association for Jewish Youth,
see Youth

Baptist Missionary Society

PO Box 49, Baptist House
Didcot, Oxon OX11 8XA
Tel: 01235-512077
Fax: 01235-511265

Contact
Steve Woolcock

Main Activities
The Baptist Missionary Society send missionaries and professional ministers all over the world to be involved in social action and in spreading the Gospel.

Opportunities for Volunteers
The main scheme is the 28:19 Year Out Scheme for young Christians (18–25) to go overseas in teams to work with churches or on social projects. Alternatively, volunteers with special skills can be placed individually. Volunteers need to be able to help fund themselves (£1,800) but all accommodation and travel expenses are met. The minimum commitment is ten months, except for summer teams, where it is only a month.

Opportunities for Employment
There are no opportunities for employment.

Further Information
Information leaflet available on request.

Christian Action

125 Kennington Road
London SE11 6SF
Tel: 0171-735 2372

Contact
Canon Eric James, Honorary Director

Main Activities
Works to translate the teachings of Christ into practical action in local, national and international affairs. An inter-denominational fellowship of men and women, it emphasises the social and political responsibilities of Christians.

Opportunities for Volunteers
Does not use volunteers, but welcomes support, and may be able to offer suggestions for appropriate volunteering.

Opportunities for Employment
There is one full-time staff member, but no other opportunities.

Further Information
An Annual Report is available.

Church Army

Independents Road
Blackheath, London SE3 9LG
Tel: 0181-318 1226
Fax: 0181-318 5258

Contact
Head Office for volunteering opportunities generally; Andrew Smith at Danescourt House, Cardiff for Cardiff Resettlement project. Cheri Smart, Personnel Assistant at Head Office for employment opportunities.

Main Activities
Established in 1882 and part of the Anglican Church, the Church Army is involved throughout the UK in evangelism and social action. This includes homeless hostels, community, and resettlement work, as well as prison and hospital chaplaincy, homes for elderly people and counselling services. There are three regional offices and 400 officers working in different locations. Church Army organisations also work in Australia, Canada, Denmark, Jamaica, Kenya, Uganda and the USA. Annual budget is £7.5 million.

Opportunities for Volunteers
Several projects involve volunteers as a task force and the need is expanding. Work includes assisting with care, young homeless resettlement, beach mission and holiday clubs projects, especially in the summer. This gives the opportunity to explore work with an organisation like the

Church Army as well as to provide a service to clients. Other opportunities for volunteers involve fundraising and management/trusteeship and from February 1995 a new volunteer scheme for resettlement support in Cardiff. All recruitment is ad hoc, on application, through in-house recruitment drives and via advertisements in the church press. There is no minimum commitment and travel expenses are paid.

Opportunities for Employment
400 staff are employed of which 300 are full-time. Between 25 and 30 people are recruited each year, including those taken on through the training college to work as evangelists and those working seasonally in beach missions and holiday clubs. Because of the church context some tasks require a Christian commitment. Positions are advertised in The Guardian, the church press and trade papers. An equal opportunities policy operates.

Further Information
The Annual Report and pamphlets on the task force, the holiday clubs and Danescourt House are available by writing to head quarters.

Church Lads and Church Girls Brigade

2 Barnsley Road, Wath upon Dearne
Rotherham, South Yorkshire S63 6PY
Tel: 01709-876535
Fax: 01709-878089

Contact
Local units for volunteers; the General Secretary for employment opportunities

Main Activities
A uniformed Anglican voluntary youth organisation for young people between the ages of five and 21, the Brigade offers fun and friendship. Originally founded in 1891 and re-shaped in 1978, it is a national organisation with 50 regional groups and 300 local branches throughout England, Wales and Northern Ireland. It is also linked with similar Brigades in Newfoundland, the Caribbean (including Bermuda), St Helena (in the South Atlantic) and South Africa. Annual budget is £150,000.

Opportunities for Volunteers
Volunteers are vital to the Brigade which would be unable to function without them. Around 2,000 are involved in the local branches plus a few in Head Office. Apart from organising the local groups, work includes administrative support and fundraising. The Brigade is actively seeking more volunteers especially for local branch work. They are needed year-round and must be committed Christians with some youth work experience. Recruitment is ad hoc on application and through in-house drives. No remuneration is offered, but sometimes travel expenses may be paid. Training and support are available both regionally and centrally.

Opportunities for Employment
Seven full-time and one part-time staff members are employed. Other staff are occasionally recruited particularly for youth work locally. School leavers and people with disabilities are especially sought as and when opportunities arise. The Brigade has implemented an equal opportunities policy.

Further Information
The Annual Report and information about specific local branches/areas are available by writing to head office.

CONCERN Worldwide

248-250 Lavender Hill
Clapham Junction
London SW11 1LJ
Tel: 0171-738 1033

Contact
Folake Segun

Main Activities
CONCERN Worldwide is a non-denominational relief and development organisation devoted to the relief, assistance and advancement of people in need in the less developed areas of the world. The London office was set up in 1991 and there are other offices in Dublin, Glasgow, Belfast and New York.

Opportunities for Volunteers
There are approximately 150 volunteers overseas; and about four in the London office. Volunteers for the overseas programme need specific skills eg nursing, engineering etc. In London, which is a fundraising office, administrative skills are useful as well as knowledge of Apple Mac computers. Travel and lunch expenses are given, training on database entry making offered.

Opportunities for Employment
There are five members of staff. Jobs are usually advertised in The Guardian.

Further Information
Annual Report, and general information leaflets: Working with the World's Poor, The Personal Touch, Volunteering with CONCERN Worldwide available.

Crosslinks

251 Lewisham Way
London SE4 1XF
Tel: 0181-691 6111
Fax: 0181-694 8023

Contact
International Secretary

Main Activities
Crosslinks is an evangelical mission agency, committed to evangelism and Bible teaching. The society works mainly with the Church in Africa, Asia, Europe and Latin America. The society is committed to fostering partnerships between the western church and the church in the developing world. It was founded in 1922 (as the Bible Churchmen's Missionary Society). Annual budget is £1.2 million.

Opportunities for Volunteers
There are no opportunities for volunteers except occasionally on short-term summer projects.

Opportunities for Employment
There are fifteen full-time and seven part-time staff at Head Office. About 120 are employed overseas (approximately ten are recruited each year). The organisation regularly recruits teachers, theological tutors, ordained clergy and doctors. Recruits must be committed Christians, active in their local church. There is an extensive selection procedure. Languages are always an asset but previous overseas experience is not essential. Posts are advertised in in-house publications, churches and in The Times Educational Supplement.

Further Information
Leaflets about vacancies, selection procedure, and vocation weekends are available.

Crusaders, *see Youth*

Jesuit Volunteer Community in Britain (JVC), *see Social Welfare*

The Mothers' Union (MU)

Mary Sumner House
24 Tufton Street
London SW1P 3RB
Tel: 0171-222 5533
Fax: 0171-222 1591

Contact
Mr R Cozens, Deputy Chief Executive

Main Activities
The purpose of the Mothers' Union is to be specially concerned with all that strengthens and preserves marriage and Christian family life. Originally set up in 1876, the MU is organised regionally in 65 dioceses throughout the British Isles. It also exists in various countries overseas. Worldwide membership is over 750,000. Annual income is around £15 million.

Opportunities for Volunteers
The branch members are all volunteers and are integral to the MU's work. They carry out a wide variety of activities as MU members. These include caring for the local community, taking part in educational activities, fundraising for the MU's overseas work, taking part in media research projects, assisting the clergy with marriage or baptism preparation and many others. The MU's social work 'Action and Outreach' is totally carried out by the members/volunteers. The most important attributes needed are the willingness to help others and experience of being a parent, although some areas of the work may require specific skills eg debt counselling.

Opportunities for Employment
The MU employs 30 full-time staff in head office, and 66 part-time staff in the regions. On average four staff are recruited each year. They must be non-smokers. Posts may be advertised in The Guardian, The Independent, The Voice, Church Times and/or the Church of England Newspaper. Usually a recruitment agency is used. The MU has an equal opportunities policy.

Further Information
A wide variety of publications (some free), including a catalogue of these, together with the Annual Report, are available.

National Free Church Women's Council (NFCWC), *see Women*

Pax Christi

9 Henry Road
London N4 2LH
Tel: 0181-800 4612
Fax: 0181-802 3223

Contact
General Secretary

Main Activities
Pax Christi is a campaigning and educational movement for peace. Its main areas of work are Northern Ireland, disarmament and the arms trade, Eastern Europe, peace education and non-violence. It is increasingly dealing with refugee issues. Set up internationally in 1945 and in Britain in 1971, its primary focus is the Catholic Church. There are over 2000 local members in Britain and Northern Ireland. Annual budget is £65,000. It also has national sections in more than 17 countries around the world including Europe, the Asia-Pacific area and North America.

Opportunities for Volunteers
Apart from two paid staff, all in Pax Christi are volunteers. Volunteers work in head office and on various projects. For example, young people are recruited for play schemes in Northern Ireland during July and August, while volunteers also run a summer hostel in London in August. Board is provided where appropriate. A core of local volunteers provides back-up services at the above office, while summer

work camps for young people bring together teams of international volunteers and promote cultural exchange. As a membership organisation most of the campaigning/lobbying is done by the local members. Opportunities also exist at the international office in Brussels, and in some of the sister sections overseas.

Opportunities for Employment
There are two members of staff. No other details available.

Further Information
Annual Report and information leaflets available.

Scripture Union

130 City Road
London EC1V 2NJ
Tel: 0171-250 1966 / 0171-782 0013
Fax: 0171-782 0014

Contact
James Escott, Head of Human Resources

Main Activities
Set up in 1867, Scripture Union is a partnership of staff and volunteers working to make Jesus known to children, young people and families. The Union works through evangelism, schools work, bible reading and training. There are autonomous offices for Scotland and Northern Ireland. The Scripture Union also operates separately in over 90 countries world-wide.

Opportunities for Volunteers
There are opportunities in both head office and throughout the country. Volunteers are needed to help lead holidays for children and young people (all year round) and to serve on evangelism teams (summer). They must be fit, aged 18 or over and be committed Christians. Minimum commitment is at least one week. Volunteers who are able to undertake administrative support and with secretarial skills are also needed.

Opportunities for Employment
Information is available on request.

Further Information
Annual Report and extensive publications available.

SGM International

Radstock House
3 Eccleston Street
London SW1W 9LZ
Tel: 0171-730 2155

Contact
Janet Fullman

Main Activities
Originally set up in 1888, SGM International now publishes and distributes thematic selections from scripture in over 400 languages worldwide. There are nine local branches. Annual budget is £2 million.

Opportunities for Volunteers
There are no opportunities for volunteers.

Opportunities for Employment
There are 48 full-time staff. On average one or two are recruited each year. Staff must be committed Christians.

Further Information
Annual Report available.

TF8

Baptist Union, 129 Broadway
Didcot, Oxon OX11 8RT
Tel: 01235-512077
Fax: 01235-811537

Contact
Rev Lesley Edmonds, TF8 Co-ordinator

Main Activities
TF8 evolved in 1994 from Task Force which was set up in 1988. It links young people with local Baptist churches and helps to develop their ability to serve in the local Church by linking their needs/desires with the needs of the churches. It also assists

Churches to carry out projects. A national organisation with 2,000 local Baptist Churches. Annual budget is £2,000.

Opportunities for Volunteers
Without volunteers TF8 would not exist. Opportunities are available in England and Wales in particular. Enthusiasm and Christian faith are required. Volunteers are needed to help with various projects eg surveys, children's clubs, street work. Induction training is offered. Help is most needed in the summer months. Prospective volunteers should apply in writing.

Opportunities for Employment
There is one part-time member of staff.

Further Information
Annual Report, list of Baptist Churches and pamphlet available. For Scotland, contact: Baptist Union of Scotland, Baptist Church House, 14 Aytoun Road, Pollokshields, Glasgow G41 5RT, tel: 0141-423 6169. For Wales, contact: Baptist Union of Churches, 15 Lan-ger-y-caed, Ammanford, Dyfed, tel: 01792-655468. For Ireland, contact: Baptist Union of Ireland, 114 Lisburn Road, Belfast BT9 7AF, tel: 01232-663108/9.

TOC H

1 Forest Close, Wendover
Aylesbury, Bucks HP22 6BT
Tel: 01296-623911

Contact
Headquarters

Main Activities
TOC H is a Christian-based movement aimed at bringing people together to explore differences and discover a faith to live by. There are 400 local branches who take part in community projects. The annual budget is approx £1.5 million.

Opportunities for Volunteers
Projects last between two and fourteen days. They include children's play

schemes, conservation work and events with people who are disadvantaged or who have some special needs. Training is given for project leaders and volunteers are most needed in the spring and summer.

Opportunities for Employment
There are 78 staff and jobs are advertised in local and national newspapers as appropriate.

Further Information
A list of local groups is available and also the Annual Review.

Torch Trust for the Blind

Torch House, Hallaton
Market Harborough, Leics LE16 8UJ
Tel: 01858-555301
Fax: 01858-555371

Contact
Secretary

Main Activities
The Torch Trust provides Christian literature for the visually handicapped. A library service provides material in Braille, in giant print and on compact cassette.

Opportunities for Volunteers
Volunteers occasionally help with the work of the Trust.

Opportunities for Employment
There are 45 staff.

Further Information
Annual Report and pamphlets available on request.

Union of Muslim Organisations of UK and Eire

109 Campden Hill Road
London W8 7TL
Tel: 0171-229 0538 / 221 6608
Fax: 0171-792 2130

Contact
Dr Said Pasha, General Secretary

Main Activities
Set up in 1970, the Union co-ordinates the activities of UK Muslim organisations and lobbies government and MPs (members of parliament) as a representative body of the Moslem community. It organises annual conferences, seminars and public meetings. There are 199 affiliated organisations who are entitled to nominate two members on the Central Committee. The Union also has links with Islamic Centres in various countries, including in Europe. Annual budget is £45,000.

Opportunities for Volunteers
Most of the work is done by volunteers who fundraise and provide administrative support. Apart from English language, Arabic and Urdu are useful languages for volunteers.

Opportunities for Employment
There is an equal opportunities policy.

Further Information
Annual Report available.

Social Welfare

The Arts Counselling Trust, *see* *Counselling & Self-help*

Association of Jewish Refugees (AJR)

1 Hampstead Gate
1A Frognal
London NW3 6AL
Tel: 0171-431 6161

Contact
Volunteers Co-ordinator

Main Activities
AJR assists Jewish refugees from Nazi persecution. The organisation is national with much of the work being carried out in London. There is a day centre in North West London, meals on wheels and various social welfare projects.

Opportunities for Volunteers
Volunteers play an important role. They befriend, help at the Day Centre, do hospital driving, and visiting. A knowledge of German is useful. Volunteers are recruited from advertisements, talks and via members of AJR.

Opportunities for Employment
There are 22 members of staff.

Further Information
Annual report and a monthly journal are available on request.

Bangladesh Association

5 Fordham Street
London E1 1HS
Tel: 0171-247 3733

Contact
Mr M-A Khan

Main Activities
The Association undertakes social and welfare work, including in housing, among the Bangladeshi community in London, where it is a local organisation.

Opportunities for Volunteers
Volunteers are used for counselling and advice, and are recruited in-house. There are three in the Association's only office. No expenses are paid.

Opportunities for Employment
There are no paid staff and no opportunities for employment.

Further Information
There is currently no Annual Report or other literature available.

The Bourne Trust

Lincoln House
1-3 Brixton Road
London SW9 6DE
Tel: 0171-582 6699
Fax: 0171-735 6077

Contact
Welfare Officer

Main Activities
Set up in 1898, the Bourne Trust advises, counsels and assists prisoners and supports their families and dependants. National organisation with five local support groups, it is particularly active in greater London, the Leeds-Wakefield area and Devon. Annual budget is £250,000.

Opportunities for Volunteers
Volunteers are regarded as very important to the Trust's work. They are needed in to give administrative support and to work at the Advice Desk, the Creche and the Visitors' Centre. Opportunities are available in both head office and the local branches. Personal qualities of common sense, compassion and commitment are important. In-house training is offered.

Opportunities for Employment
There are six full-time and two part-time staff.

Further Information
Annual report, newsletter, leaflets and list of local groups available.

British Association of Settlements and Social Action Centres (BASSAC)

13 Stockwell Road
London SW9 9AU
Tel: 0171-733 7428 /9 /0

Contact
Mrs Vashti Ledford, Membership Officer

Main Activities
Founded in 1920, BASSAC is a national association/network of independent, multi-purpose social action organisations based in urban or inner-city areas, and committed to common principles and purposes. As an umbrella organisation it provides advice and information services to its members and represents them at national level to other voluntary sector networks, to government, the public and the private sector. BASSAC also pioneers projects which meet social needs, and provides resources and help for community initiatives. Areas of work include debt counselling, play scheme provision and work with young people at risk. There are 61 affiliated organisations as full and associate members throughout England and Scotland. BASSAC is a member of the International Federation of Settlements and has links with other networks around the world.

Opportunities for Volunteers
Around 8,000 volunteers work regularly in BASSAC centres. They are needed to assist on projects and to provide administrative support. Many exciting and varied work opportunities are available, including with children, young, disabled and elderly people, and refugees. The skills required vary greatly. Induction is given, other training may be available, and travel and lunch expenses are offered.

Opportunities for Employment
BASSAC employs five members of staff at its head office in London. Any job vacancies are advertised in The Guardian and The Voice.

Further Information
The Annual Report, various publications including information leaflets, and the newsletter are available.

British Limbless Ex-Servicemen's Association (BLESMA)

185-187 High Road
Chadwell Heath
Essex RM6 6NA
Tel: 0181-590 1124
Fax: 0181-599 2932

Contact
Head Quarters or local branch secretaries

Main Activities
Founded in 1932, BLESMA promotes the welfare of ex-Service amputees. It provides residential homes, financial assistance, and rehabilitation programmes, and carries out a regular visiting programme to members and widows. A national organisation it has an area and branch structure with 71 local branches. It also has links with similar organisations in Germany, Russia and America. Annual budget is £2,270,000.

Opportunities for Volunteers
Volunteers are vital to BLESMA's work. They assist with the running of the local branches, and in particular with administrative and welfare work. They also help with social and fundraising activities. An empathy with disabled and elderly ex-Servicemen, and counselling or welfare experience are valuable. Training is provided in local branches. Volunteers should ideally be able to give six hours a week – preferably evenings and occasional weekends.

Opportunities for Employment
There are approximately 70 staff.

Occasionally there are vacancies for residential care staff. Jobs are advertised in the local press and job centres.

Further Information
Annual Report, list of local branches and various pamphlets on amputation and mobility available.

British Red Cross

9 Grosvenor Crescent
London SW1X 7EJ
Tel: 0171-235 5454
Fax: 0171-245 6315

Contact
Ms Rosemarie Earlam, Personnel Manager re employment for national headquarters (NHQ) positions; otherwise apply to local branch

Main Activities
The British Red Cross provides skilled and impartial care to people in need and in crisis, at home and abroad. Services are provided for the sick and injured, elderly people, and people with disabilities. Training is given by the British Red Cross to the thousands of volunteers who operate these services. There are numerous branches in England and Wales. Scotland and Northern Ireland have their own Headquarters. The annual budget is over £64 million.

Opportunities for Volunteers
With over 80,000 voluntary Members, incorporating 20,000 Youth and Junior Members, operating from 92 county branches and over 1,000 local centres, there is a British Red Cross Centre near almost everybody. Volunteers have the opportunity to be trained in many of the different community care services which the British Red Cross supplies. There are also opportunities for volunteers to help with fundraising, clerical and administrative tasks. There is no minimum time commitment. Travel and lunch expenses are offered. Prospective volunteers should apply either to the Personnel Department for NHQ, or to the local branch for local work.

Opportunities for Employment
British Red Cross NHQ employs about 270 people, with a further 1,600 full-time staff throughout the UK. People are recruited every year. The range of jobs includes everything from administrative work, fundraising and marketing to nursing and community care. Recruitment is in line with best practice and equal opportunities. Vacancies are advertised in national newspapers.

Further Information
The Annual Report, Red Cross News quarterly newsletter and information leaflets are published.

Camphill – Rudolf Steiner – Schools

Murtle Estate
Aberdeen AB1 9EP
Tel: 01224-867935
Fax: 01224-868420

Contact
Staff Committee

Main Activities
The Camphill-Rudolf Steiner-Schools is a residential school for children in need of special care. It is part of an international organisation. Each Camphill community carries out its own recruitment and administration.

Opportunities for Volunteers
Volunteers are very important and a large part of the workforce is comprised of volunteers who commit themselves for one year or longer. Approximately 50 volunteers are needed each August, and then there are usually a few vacancies in October, January and April. Volunteers, who must be able to speak English, carry out education and caring roles. Board and

lodging and pocket money (currently £23 a week) are offered. Applicants should apply in writing.

Opportunities for Employment
All permanent staff have started their careers in Camphill as volunteers.

Further Information
Further information including a list of Camphill Community members available.

Centre for Armenian Information and Advice (CAIA)

105A Mill Hill Road
Acton, London W3 8JF
Tel: 0181-992 4621

Contact
General Secretary

Main Activities
CAIA supports the welfare of the most disadvantaged in the Armenian community. It provides information, a newsletter, a playgroup, clubs for senior citizens and translation services. Based in London it covers the whole of England and also has links with Armenia. Annual budget is £90,000.

Opportunities for Volunteers
Volunteers are essential to CAIA's work. They undertake administrative support and fundraising from head office. A knowledge of Armenians and the Armenian language is necessary.

Opportunities for Employment
There are three full-time and two part-time staff. Recruits must speak Armenian.

Further Information
Annual Report, leaflets on projects and Armenian Voice available.

Church Army, *see Religious Affairs*

The Clubhouse

141 Cleveland Street
London W1P 5PH
Tel: 0171-387 1360

Contact
Ian Bussell, Centre Manager

Main Activities
The Clubhouse is a local community centre in Central London offering youth clubs, a day centre for over 60's and a luncheon club, a church service and a parents and toddlers group, rooms available for booking and lunch-time sports facilities. It was set up in 1958 and the annual budget is £160,000.

Opportunities for Volunteers
There are about 30 volunteers who provide contact with the clients, research and trusteeship. They are encouraged to participate in organising and planning the work. Minimum commitment is one hour per week over a period of time and travel expenses are offered. An ability to work with people is a necessary skill and a commitment to building trusting relationships.

Opportunities for Employment
There are seven full-time and seven part-time members of staff. Staff are quite frequently recruited and jobs are advertised in the press. People are occasionally recruited on a seasonal basis eg summer youth club projects.

Further Information
Annual Report available and new publicity material in preparation.

Community Development Foundation (CDF)

60 Highbury Grove
London N5 2AG
Tel: 0171-226 5375
Fax: 0171-704 0313

Contact
Helen Wolstencroft, Head of Personnel

Main Activities
CDF's mission is to strengthen communities by ensuring the effective participation of people in determining the conditions which affect their lives. CDF does this through providing support for community initiatives, promoting best practice, and informing policy-makers at local and national level. Its activities include consultancies, training, information, research and local action projects. Established in 1968, CDF has all party support and receives substantial backing from local and central government, trusts and business. It is a leading authority on community development in the UK and the European Union. A national organisation, it has seven regional offices.

Opportunities for Volunteers
There are occasional opportunities for volunteers to undertake research, fundraising and/or typing/clerical work. A specialist knowledge of community development and/or relevant skills are necessary.

Opportunities for Employment
There are 34 full-time and 17 part-time staff. On average eight people are recruited each year.

Further Information
The Annual Review, Publications Catalogue and newsletter are available on request.

Daycare Trust / National Childcare Campaign

4 Wild Court
London WC2B 4AU
Tel: 0171-405 5617
Fax: 0171-831 6632

Contact
Carol Sherriff, Director

Main Activities
Set up in 1986, the Daycare Trust provides information and advice about affordable, accessible childcare to parents, professionals, employers and policy makers. This includes on quality services, family-friendly initiatives and equal opportunities. The Trust also offers a consultancy service. The National Childcare Campaign (established in 1980) is a pressure group campaigning for flexible, diverse, publicly-subsidised childcare and working to make adequate childcare available to all. A UK-wide organisation, the Trust also has transnational projects with such countries as Germany and the Netherlands.

Opportunities for Volunteers
Volunteers are extremely important to the work, and new graduates and those returning to work are especially welcomed. Volunteers are required for general administrative support and specific projects. Wordprocessing, library, good telephone and statistical skills are particularly useful. Sympathy for and an understanding of childcare are needed. Travel expenses are paid. The Trust also aims to support volunteers to enter paid employment where appropriate.

Opportunities for Employment
Full-time vacancies seldom arise. If posts become available, the Trust has a particular interest in recruiting new graduates and those returning to work.

Further Information
Information leaflets/packs and a list of

publications are available from Head Office.

Disabled Living, *see Disability*

Ethiopian Community in Britain (ECB)

66 Hampstead Road
London NW1 2NT
Tel: 0171-388 4944
Fax: 0171-388 3984

Contact
Dr Grima Ejere, Co-ordinator

Main Activities
The Ethiopian Community in Britain offers advice and counselling on immigration, training, housing, employment and health. A UK wide organisation, with seven local branches. ECB was set up in 1984 and its annual budget is £70,000.

Opportunities for Volunteers
Volunteers are an integral part of the team of ECB. Tasks include: administrative support, counselling, advice giving, fundraising, management and organising local groups. Travel and out-of-pocket expenses are offered. The organisation is particularly keen to recruit volunteers with secretarial and administrative skills. Induction is provided.

Opportunities for Employment
There are two full-time and two part-time staff. There is an equal opportunities policy and jobs are advertised in newspapers eg The Voice.

Further Information
Annual Report and various pamphlets available on request.

Families Need Fathers, *see Family & Community Matters*

Family Holiday Association (FHA)

Hertford Lodge
East End Road
London N3 3QE
Tel: 0181-349 4044/4047

Contact
Fiona Hills, Appeals and Allocations Officer

Main Activities
The provision of grants, via welfare agencies, to enable deprived families to have a one-week holiday break together as a family unit. The FHA has one national office and one local group in London. Its annual income is around £400,000.

Opportunities for Volunteers
Up to twenty London-based volunteers are used and are actively recruited periodically for administrative/clerical assistance and fundraising. Computer/word processing skills are an advantage. Full support is given, but no formal training. Recruitment is ad hoc through applications in writing. Travel expenses are paid.

Opportunities for Employment
There are four full-time staff, but vacancies seldom arise. Any available posts are advertised in The Guardian and The Independent. Recruitment consultants such as Charity People and Charity Recruitment have sometimes been used. FHA is working towards an equal opportunities policy. Further information on employment can be obtained only by writing.

Further Information
An Annual Report and a general leaflet outlining the FHA's work are available.

Family Services Unit (FSU), *see Family & Community Matters*

Family Welfare Association

(FWA), *see Family & Community Matters*

Fire Services National Benevolent Fund

Marine Court, Fitzalan Road
Littlehampton, West Sussex BN17 5NF
Tel: 01903-717185
Fax: 01903-731095

Contact

Benevolent Fund Secretary at local Fire Brigade

Main Activities

Set up in 1943, the Fund provides financial and material support to fire fighters, their widows and orphans, and to retired fire fighters. A UK-wide organisation, it has 65 local branches. Annual budget is £2 million.

Opportunities for Volunteers

Opportunities are available primarily in the local branches. Regarded as very important to the organisation's work, volunteers undertake fundraising and administrative work, act as local treasurers and visit beneficiaries as part of the welfare provided. They must be serving or past members of the fire service.

Opportunities for Employment

There are 22 full-time staff. On average two are recruited each year. Jobs are advertised locally or with specialist charity job agencies.

Further Information

Annual Report and leaflets available.

The Forces Help Society and Lord Roberts Workshops

122 Brompton Road
London SW3 1JE
Tel: 0171-589 3243
Fax: 0171-584 0676

Contact

Via SSAFA/FHS, 19 Queen Elizabeth Street, London SE1 2LP, tel: 0171-403 8783

Main Activities

Founded in 1899, the Society provides many kinds of help, as needed, for those who have served (members and ex-members) in HM (Her Majesty's) Forces. It builds and maintains residential care homes, purpose built cottage homes and holiday apartments for those who are disabled and their carers. Help for individuals is carried out in collaboration with SSAFA/FHS. A UK-wide organisation, the Society also has local branches, and links with Returned Services organisations in Australia, New Zealand and South Africa.

Opportunities for Volunteers

Opportunities exist in the local branches. The role of volunteers is vital. They are needed to act as caseworkers, and they form a line of communication between the individual in need and the help that can be provided. Confidentiality, ability to listen and respect for individual human dignity are important personal qualities, and the varied life experience of the volunteers is valuable. Travel expenses are offered.

Opportunities for Employment

Very few opportunities for employment exist.

Further Information

The Annual Report and a list of local groups are available.

Gingerbread

49 Wellington Street
London WC2E 7BN
Tel: 0171-240 0953
Fax: 0171-836 4500

Contact
Angela Harewood

Main Activities
Gives support, advice and information for
lone parents. There are 280 local support
groups.

Opportunities for Volunteers
Administrative support and fundraising
are done by volunteers. Minimum
commitment is one day a week for three
months.

Opportunities for Employment
There are six full-time staff and on average two people are recruited each year.

Further Information
The Annual Report and a publications list
are available.

The Guide Dogs for the Blind
Association (GDBA), see Disability

HALOW (Help and Advice Line
for Offenders, Wives and
Families), see Family & Community
Matters

Headway, National Head
Injuries Association
Limited

7 King Edward Court
King Edward Street
Nottingham, Notts NG1 1EW
Tel: 0115-924 0800
Fax: 0115-924 0432

Contact
Jan Davidson, Information Officer, at
Central Office for details of local groups

Main Activities
Founded in 1979, Headway supports
people who have suffered head injuries,
and their carers, through a network of self-
help groups and day centres. A national,
UK-wide organisation, Headway has 36
day centres and 110 local support groups.
It also has links with similar organisations
throughout the world.

Opportunities for Volunteers
Headway uses some volunteers in its
head office for administrative support,
and many in the branches for fundraising
and caring work. It recruits actively all
year through ad hoc applications. There
is no minimum time commitment. Travel
expenses are paid in certain cases.

Opportunities for Employment
There are 12 full-time staff at head office
and various staff locally. Occasional
opportunities arise, especially in local day
centres for appropriate therapists.

Further Information
The Annual Report, a newsletter, information sheets and various publications are
available.

Home-Start Consultancy, see
Family & Community Matters

ICOM (Industrial Common
Ownership Movement), see
Education

Independent Adoption
Service, see Family & Community
Matters

Institute for Social Inventions

20 Heber Road
London NW2 6AA
Tel: 0181-208 2253

Contact
Nicholas Albery

Main Activities
Promotes social inventions (projects or services which aim to improve the quality of life). National organisation with three international off-shoots.

Opportunities for Volunteers
Volunteers are needed to give administrative support, design ideas and DTP work. Minimum commitment one afternoon a week.

Opportunities for Employment
There are three staff.

Further Information
An Information Pack is available by sending four first class stamps and a self-addressed envelope.

Jesuit Volunteer Community in Britain (JVC)

St Wilfrid's Enterprise Centre
Royce Road, Hulme
Manchester M15 5PJ
Tel: 0161-226 6717

Contact
Shelagh Fawcett

Main Activities
JVC offers a one year programme to young adults (18-35 years) who do full-time voluntary work.

Opportunities for Volunteers
Volunteers are recruited each year to live in communities in inner-city areas of Birmingham, Liverpool, Manchester, Glasgow and to work in a number of voluntary agencies. Volunteers work in local community projects, homeless hostels, CABx, and women's refuges. Volunteer allowance and accommodation are offered. Minimum commitment is 37-40 hours a week for one year. JVC is sponsored and supported by the Jesuits. Young people from all sections of the community, of all faiths or no faith, are actively encouraged to apply.

Opportunities for Employment
There are four full-time staff.

Further Information
Introductory leaflets, JVC Handbook and quarterly newsletter available on request.

Junior League of London (JLL), *see Women*

Lambeth Social Services, Voluntary Sector Unit, *see Advice*

League of Jewish Women

Woburn House
Tavistock Square
London WC1H 0EZ
Tel: 0171-387 7688

Contact
Head Office

Main Activities
The League serves Jewish and non-Jewish communities on a national basis.

Opportunities for Volunteers
Volunteers are needed to help with welfare work, eg day centres, friendship clubs, hospitals, other care agencies, home visiting etc. In-house training is offered.

Opportunities for Employment
There is one full-time and one part-time member of staff,

Further Information
Annual Report and introductory leaflet available.

Leukaemia Care Society

14 Kingfisher Court
Venny Bridge
Pinhoe, Exeter,
Devon EX4 9JN
Tel: 01392-464848
Fax: 01392-460331

Contact
Sandra Brown

Main Activities
Promotes the welfare of leukaemia and allied blood disorders sufferers and their families. Provides information, support and holidays. There are 70 local support groups. Annual Budget is £2,500,000.

Opportunities for Volunteers
Volunteers are need to befriend and visit. Local training in relationship skills is offered. Minimum commitment is about seven hours a week. Telephone expenses are paid.

Opportunities for Employment
There are five full-time and two part-time staff. Jobs are advertised locally.

Further Information
Annual Report, list of local groups and selection of 'Awareness' leaflets available.

Lupus UK, see Counselling & Self-Help

The Malcolm Sargent Cancer Fund for Children

14 Abingdon Road
London W8 6AF
Tel: 0171-937 4548
Fax: 0171-376 1193

Contact
Ms Silvia Darley OBE, General Administrator

Main Activities
The Malcolm Sargent Cancer Fund for Children looks after the welfare of young people who have cancer, leukaemia or Hogdkin's Disease. Funds social workers nationwide and offers holidays in two holiday homes. Annual budget is £3 million.

Opportunities for Volunteers
Volunteers are needed to fundraise throughout England and Wales. Particular need between October and December. Travel expenses are offered.

Opportunities for Employment
There are nine staff at HQ and 46 regional social workers.

Further Information
Annual Report and information leaflets available. For Scotland, contact: Miss Venetia Fane, Drumswill, Mossdale, By Castle Douglas, Kirkcudbright DG7 2N7.

Manna Drop-In Centre, see Housing & Homelessness

Missions to Seamen (Flying Angel)

St Michael Paternoster
Royal College Hill
London EC4R 2RL
Tel: 0171-248 5202
Fax: 0171-248 4761

Contact
Local Branch (list available from Central Office)

Main Activities
Missions to Seamen is an Anglican Church Society offering practical help and spiritual support to seafarers in a 106 branches worldwide. There are 20 seafarers' centres in major ports in the UK. Annual budget is £2.25 million.

Opportunities for Volunteers
Volunteers are needed to help welcome the seafarers at the centres (the various ports) and to raise funds. Back-up from full-time staff is given. There is a Voluntary

Service Scheme for young Christians between 18 and 24 which involves working in ports in the UK and abroad in a variety of roles. (Write to Head Office for a leaflet).

Opportunities for Employment
There are 120 full-time staff. Jobs are advertised in the Church Times.

Further Information
Annual Report, Information leaflets, Missions to Seamens Newspaper available.

The Mothers' Union, *see* *Religious Affairs*

Multiple Sclerosis Society of Great Britain and Northern Ireland

25 Effie Road, Fulham
London SW6 1EE
Tel: 0171-371 8000 (info and helpline)
Fax: 0171-736 9891
24 hour counselling lines:
0171-222 3123 / 0121-476 4229 /
0131-226 6573

Contact
Marcia Dexter

Main Activities
The Society aims to fund research into the cause of and cure for multiple sclerosis – MS – and to provide welfare and support to people with MS and their families. Offers a comprehensive, national service through over 370 local autonomous branches and 20 regional groups, which between them have over 60,000 members. Membership is open to sufferers.

Opportunities for Volunteers
Volunteers are usually the members who undertake administrative, fundraising, welfare support and counselling/advice work in the branches. The Society is keen to attract more volunteer help at all times

of the year, and sometimes uses advertising campaigns to do so. Recruitment is by application to a local branch. There is no minimum time commitment. Travel expenses are paid.

Opportunities for Employment
The MS Society has 30 full-time staff. Vacancies occasionally occur and are advertised in national newspapers such as The Guardian and The Times. Consultants such as Charity People may be used. An Equal Opportunities Policy is in place.

Further Information
The Annual Report, various welfare publications and a list of local groups are available. In Scotland the Society is at 2A North Charlotte Street, Edinburgh EH2 4MR, tel: 0131-225 3600. In Northern Ireland it is at 34 Annadale Avenue, Belfast BT7 3JJ, tel: 01232-644914.

National Association for the Care and Resettlement of Offenders (NACRO)

169 Clapham Road
London SW9 0PU
Tel: 0171-582 6500
Fax: 0171-734 4666

Contact
Information Department re volunteering; Ms B O'Sullivan, Personnel Officer re employment

Main Activities
NACRO promotes the care and resettlement of offenders and the prevention of crime. It works with individuals caught up in the criminal justice process by providing practical services and also contributes to changing crime policy both locally and nationally. Has a membership scheme. A national organisation covering England and Wales, NACRO works through specialist sections providing practical or development services in over 100 projects/centres.

Opportunities for Volunteers

Volunteers can work in various ways in individual NACRO centres and projects. These include organising activities under the direction of a volunteer co-ordinator on NACRO's Youth Activity Units (YAUs). There are also opportunities for volunteering on other projects. Recruitment is through local YAUs, individual project leaders/ managers, and on application. Minimum commitment varies and expenses may be offered.

Opportunities for Employment

NACRO employs around 1,300 full-time staff and recruits approximately twenty people monthly. There is a detailed recruitment procedure in line with an equal opportunities policy. Skill requirements vary for each post and are very diverse. Any vacancies are advertised in the appropriate local press, nationally in The Guardian and in job centres.

Further Information

The Annual Report, a Directory of Services (including a list of local projects/ centres), a publications booklet, and a wide range of reports, leaflets and briefing papers giving factual information about crime, criminal justice, policies and advice, are available. Sister, but separate, organisations are:

Scottish Association for the Care and Resettlement of Offenders (SACRO), 31 Palmerston Place, Edinburgh EH12 5AP tel: 0121-226 4222

Northern Ireland Association for the Care and Resettlement of Offenders (NIACRO), 169 Ormeau Road, Belfast BT7 1SQ tel: 01232-320157

National Association for Gifted Children (NAGC), see Children

National Association of Laryngectomee Clubs (NALC)

6 Rickett Street
London SW6 1RU
Tel: 0171-381 9993

Contact

Ms Vivien Reed

Main Activities

Promotes the welfare of laryngectomees and their families, and offers help and advice. Also provides information to professionals concerned with the condition. Organised nationally, NALC has eighty local clubs/groups.

Opportunities for Volunteers

Volunteers are actually the members of the clubs, and must have personal experience of laryngectomy. They give each other mutual support and help, and undertake fundraising. Each club is self-financing.

Opportunities for Employment

There is one full-time paid staff member, and no other opportunities.

Further Information

Free literature is available for patients and professionals. There is also a helpline and a list of local groups.

National Childminding Association (NCMA), see Children

National Children's Home (NCH), see Children

National Council for One Parent Families (NCOPF), see Family & Community Matters

National Council on Gambling (NCG)

Regent's Wharf
8 All Saints Street
London N1 9RL
Tel: 0181-364 1376

Contact
National Office

Main Activities
The Council is a registered charitable trust whose objectives are to educate the public about gambling, to further research into gambling and to help those whose participation in society is impaired by gambling. It organises occasional conferences. The NCG is not against gambling in principle, but considers that society at large would benefit if an independent body kept the promotion of gambling under review.

Opportunities for Volunteers
The trustees are volunteers and the Council undertakes lobbying, publicity and raising public attention to the dangers of gambling. Any one who wishes to volunteer in this area should contact the Chairman (0181-336 9138) or the Honorary Secretary (0181-785 9460) for advice.

Opportunities for Employment
There are no opportunities.

Further Information
Information sheets are available.

National Council of Women of Great Britain (NCW), see Women

National Free Church Women's Council (NFCWC), see Women

The National Society for Mentally Handicapped People in Residential Care (RESCARE)

Rayner House
23 Higher Hill Gate
Stockport SK1 3ER
Tel: 0161-474 7323

Contact
Via Head Office

Main Activities
RESCARE exists for the relief and welfare of people with a mental handicap in all types of residential establishments including hospitals and family homes. National organisation with 93 affiliated groups.

Opportunities for Volunteers
Volunteers give advice and carry out fundraising.

Opportunities for Employment
There are three members of staff.

Further Information
Annual Report available.

National Society for the Prevention of Cruelty to Children (NSPCC), see Children

The Natural Death Centre

20 Heber Road
Cricklewood
London NW2 6AA
Tel: 0181-208 2853

Contact
Nicholas Albery

Main Activities
Aims to help the quality of dying by giving support, advice and information for those caring for the dying at home. Also gives advice on arranging funerals without undertakers.

Opportunities for Volunteers

Volunteers are needed to give administrative support. DTP or design skills would be an advantage. Minimum commitment is one day a week.

Opportunities for Employment

There are no employment opportunities.

Further Information

Information pack available. Please send four First Class stamps to cover copying costs. 'Natural Death Handbook' is published at £10.95 (includes post and packing).

Neighbourhood Energy Action

(NEA), see Environment & Conservation

The Network

PO Box 558
London SW2 2EL

Contact

Alison McFadden/Jan Guice

Main Activities

The Network aims to help people find mutual support through sharing experiences of growing up in a family where a member has emotional or mental distress. There are informal links with individuals and organisations. Annual budget is £800.

Opportunities for Volunteers

Volunteers are needed to fundraise and to act as counsellors. A knowledge of fundraising relevant to self-help groups would be useful as would counselling skills. Volunteers should write to The Network with a CV and a proposal.

Opportunities for Employment

There are no employment opportunities.

Further Information

Membership details and newsletter available on request.

Norwood Child Care

Norwood House
Harmony Way (off Victoria Road)
Hendon, London NW4 2BY
Tel: 0181-458 3282

Contact

Volunteer Co-ordinators re volunteering; Linda Davis, Director of Administration re employment opportunities

Main Activities

Providing social services to all Jewish children and their families, who are disadvantaged or handicapped in any way. These include fostering, adoption, respite care, counselling, child protection and special education services. Although a national organisation, the services are offered mainly in London and the South East through area based teams, in seven local branches and two affiliated organisations. Norwood Child Care works closely with other voluntary agencies, including those in the Jewish community and with local authorities. The annual budget is £3 million.

Opportunities for Volunteers

Volunteers are used in head office (6) and the branches (190) for administrative support, fundraising and counselling. They are also required for befriending children and families, helping in day centres, schools and nurseries, as drivers and to take children on outings. The organisation needs them all year, but especially as drivers in school holidays. Volunteer co-ordinators give training and support. Recruitment is ad hoc on application and through volunteer bureaux, in-house drives and word of mouth. An application form, assessment interview and references are required. Minimum commitment is two hours a week for at least two months. Travel expenses are offered.

Opportunities for Employment

There are 47 full-time and 51 part-time

staff. About five or six staff are recruited annually. A knowledge of the Jewish community is necessary. There is an equal opportunities policy and posts are advertised in social work publications, the Jewish Chronicle and local papers.

Further Information
The Annual Report, a list of local groups and publicity material (pamphlets, leaflets, etc) are available.

Parentline, *see Family & Community Matters*

Parents Anonymous London, *see Family & Community Matters*

Parents at Work (formerly the Working Mothers Association)

77 Holloway Road
London N7 8JZ
Tel: 0171-700 5771/2
Fax: 0171-700 1105

Contact
Ms Angela Seesurrun, Administrator

Main Activities
Set up in 1985 as the Working Mothers Association, Parents at Work is a self-help organisation for working parents and their children. It provides an informal support system, offering information and advice. A UK-wide organisation, there are 174 local support groups.

Opportunities for Volunteers
Parents at Work relies on volunteers to help in all areas of its work. They are needed to give administrative assistance, help with mail-outs, answer the telephone and undertake research and marketing. Typing and word-processing skills are useful.

Opportunities for Employment
There are seven full-time staff. Jobs are advertised in the local press. New graduates, returners and those made redundant are particularly actively recruited.

Further Information
Information leaflets available.

Prisoners Families and Friends Service, *see Family & Community Matters*

Prisoners Wives and Families Society, *see Family & Community Matters*

PSS

18 Seel Street
Liverpool L1 4BE
Tel: 0151-707 0131
Fax: 0151-707 0039

Contact
Jill McKenzie for volunteering; Eileen Johnson, Manager, Central Resource Unit re employment opportunities

Main Activities
PSS pioneers new ways to support people in the community, covering a wide range of issues including family matters, elderly people, children, bereavement and disability. Services include small group homes, adult placements, neighbourhood care, domiciliary support, counselling, day facilities, and neighbourhood and family centres. Set up in 1919, PSS has a national and European role in pioneering and disseminating new ways of working, with direct services focusing on the North West of England and North Wales. It also networked various innovative projects for the 1993 European Year of Older People and Solidarity between Generations in Belgium, France, Holland and Italy. Annual income/turnover includes £4

million in direct expenditure, with services and activities valued at £6 million.

Opportunities for Volunteers

Volunteers are vital and always needed: PSS could not provide some of its services without their help. Around 700 assist with organising local groups, fundraising, advice giving, and counselling. The skills needed vary according to the project. PSS is actively seeking more volunteers for a variety of projects and work in both Head Office and the local branches. Volunteer organisers support and train volunteers in individual projects. Recruitment is usually ad hoc on application with occasional advertising. The procedure is to write, phone or visit Head Office in person. The minimum commitment varies with the particular project. Travel, lunch and out-of-pocket expenses are offered.

Opportunities for Employment

295 staff are employed: 142 full-time, 143 part-time and ten temporary. Around 55 people are recruited each year, with the skills and experience required varying according to the work/position. PSS's recruitment policy aims to ensure the appointment of staff with appropriate knowledge, skills, behaviour, attitudes, and the ability to provide a quality service. Staff must also be cost effective and satisfy the equal opportunities policy requirements. Jobs are advertised in the Merseyside and local press, and occasionally in The Guardian, as well as in job centres and sometimes other voluntary organisations.

Further Information

The Annual Report, leaflets about individual projects, and a list of local groups are available on request to Head Office.

QISP Quaker International Social Projects, see Youth

Ravenswood Foundation, see Disability

Royal British Legion

48 Pall Mall
London SW1Y 5JY
Tel: 0171-973 0633
Fax: 0171-973 0633

Contact
General Secretary

Main Activities
Promotes the welfare of ex-Service men and ex-Service women and dependants of those who have served. There are over 3000 branches, seven residential homes, three convalescent homes, a housing association, a poppy factory and other industries.

Opportunities for Volunteers
Volunteers are needed to act as welfare caseworkers, for which training is provided. Fundraisers and collectors are needed between September and November for the Poppy Day Appeal.

Opportunities for Employment
There are 186 staff, jobs are advertised in the press and applicants should ideally have a service background.

Further Information
The Annual Report is available.

Royal British Legion Women's Section

Haig House, 48 Pall Mall
London SW1Y 4JY
Tel: 0171-973 0633

Contact
National Secretary

Main Activities
Aims to improve the welfare of the ex-Service community. Of particular concern are ex-Servicewomen, widows and

dependants of past and present members of HM Forces.

Opportunities for Volunteers
There are 1800 local branches and volunteers are needed for fundraising and welfare visiting. Applications should be made via Head Office and membership has be submitted to local branch for acceptance.

Opportunities for Employment
There are thirteen members of staff, and recruitment takes place through agencies.

Further Information
The Annual Report is available as well as recruitment leaflets.

Royal National Lifeboat Institution (RNLI)

West Quay Road, Poole
Dorset BH15 1HZ
Tel: 01202-671133
Fax: 01202-670128

Contact
Richard Mann, Regions Manager

Main Activities
RNLI provides a lifeboat service in order to preserve life from disaster at sea. National organisation with approximately 2,000 branches.

Opportunities for Volunteers
Volunteers are need to help with fundraising. Minimum commitment is one hour a week.

Opportunities for Employment
Vacancies are advertised through the general press.

Further Information
Annual Report and information leaflets available on request.

Royal National Mission to Deep Sea Fishermen

43 Nottingham Place
London W1M 4BX
Tel: 0171-487 5101
Fax: 0171-224 5240

Contact
Ian Ogilvie, Director of Fundraising

Main Activities
Carries out Christian-based pastoral and social welfare work among fishermen and their families. It was set up in 1881 and is nationally based with centres in fishing ports: Truro, Southport, Lowestoft, Glasgow and Cwmran.

Opportunities for Volunteers
Volunteers with either computer skills or pastoral experience are of great value. Knowledge of or interest in the fishing industry is not essential but would be an advantage. Fundraisers are also needed especially between April and November.

Opportunities for Employment
There are 70 full-time and 70 part-time staff and approximately ten people are recruited each year.

Further Information
The Annual Report is available as well as a list of local groups.

The Royal Society for the Prevention of Accidents (ROSPA)

Cannon House, The Priory
Queensway, Birmingham B4 6BS
Tel: 0121-200 2461

Contact
Personnel Department

Main Activities
Works to prevent accidents at home, on the road, at work or in leisure activities. There are three regional groups. Annual budget is £6 million.

Opportunities for Volunteers
Volunteers give time on advisory committees.

Opportunities for Employment
No information available.

Further Information
Annual Report available.

Salvation Army

101 Queen Victoria Street
London EC4P 4EP
Tel: 0171-236 5222
Fax: 0171-236 6272

Contact
Direct to local corps (number in local telephone directory)

Main Activities
The Salvation Army is a Christian organisation which believes in putting faith into action via a diverse range of social and welfare projects. International organisation with 900 worship centres in the UK.

Opportunities for Volunteers
Volunteers are needed in local corps. For example, providing support services at local community level, driving, catering etc.

Opportunities for Employment
There are 1,807 Salvation Army ordained officers and 2,627 employees. Jobs are advertised in the national press and Salvation Army publications.

Further Information
Annual Report and list of local corps available.

Shaftesbury Society

16 Kingston Road
London SW19 1JZ
Tel: 0181-542 5550
Fax: 0181-545 0605

Contact
Gill Faragher

Main Activities
The Shaftesbury Society helps the disabled to fulfil as independent a life as possible. Provides hostel accommodation for homeless and helps them find jobs and long-term accommodation. National organisation.

Opportunities for Volunteers
Volunteer fundraisers are vital. People are needed to give administrative support at Head Office. Carers are also needed in residential homes for those with physical or learning difficulties.

Opportunities for Employment
There are 1300 staff. Employment vacancies list is available. Jobs are advertised in The Guardian, Care Weekly and the local papers.

Further Information
Annual Report, and information sheets for carers, training schemes and work of society available.

Sheffield Community Transport (SCT)

31 Montgomery Terrace Road
Sheffield S6 3BU
Tel: 0114-276 6148
Fax: 0114-278 7173

Contact
Elspeth Mallowan, Volunteer Co-ordinator (Development); Linda Moran, Personnel Officer

Main Activities
A local organisation with national affiliations set up in 1988, SCT provides a range

of transport services to over 4,000 individual passengers and 600 community groups, most of whom have some mobility difficulty or who find using public transport inappropriate. Services include: dial-a-ride minibuses (City-Ride), Community Group Travel, Social Car Scheme (Community Car Scheme), Excursion Club for Individuals (Miles of Mobility Club), and a Vehicle Brokerage Scheme. SCT is a member of the Community Transport Association which networks, provides training for and campaigns on issues around accessible transport. SCT's annual budget is around £400,000.

Opportunities for Volunteers
About 120 volunteers working directly for SCT are involved and provide around 70% of SCT's service delivery to passengers and groups. They work as drivers of either SCT's mini-buses and cars or their own cars and also work as passenger escorts. Drivers need to be over 21, have held a clean current full UK licence and driven for more than two years. They are offered training in safe driving, minibus emergency procedures, wheelchair safety restraint systems, moving and handling and an introduction to first aid. There is also an active social life within the volunteer team. They are recruited through volunteer bureaux, in-house recruitment drives and on application. Bus fares and car mileage expenses, and refreshment/meal expenses are reimbursed. Volunteers are needed all year round, day and evening, weekday and weekend. New volunteers are very welcome. Potential volunteers complete an application form and are interviewed. There is an induction period and probationary review.

Opportunities for Employment
There are 20 staff, 16 full-time and 4 part-time. Vacancies up to Sc6 are advertised locally in the Sheffield Star. SO1 and above are advertised in The Guardian. A formal Equal Opportunities Policy operates.

Further Information
The Annual Report and various pamphlets and leaflets are available.

Sick Children's Trust

1A Doughty Street,
London WC1N 2PH
Tel: 0171-404 3329
Fax: 0171-831 3182

Contact
Jan Vernon-Smith, Director of Fundraising

Main Activities
The Sick Children's Trust provides free accommodation for families whose children need treatment for a life-threatening illness in a hospital far from home. There are four homes-from-home in London and one at St James's Hospital, Leeds. The next Home will open at the Royal Victoria Infirmary, Newcastle in 1995. There are two day-facilities in Kent.

Opportunities for Volunteers
Volunteers are needed in Head Office to help with newsletter, press and PR, database entries and events. Nationwide fundraisers and PR workers are needed. Travel expenses are offered. Training and support as required.

Opportunities for Employment
There are six staff in Head Office and four House Managers. Two new full-time staff were recruited in 1994.

Further Information
Annual Report, information leaflets and details for potential volunteers are available.

Sickle Cell Society, see Health & Medicine

Society of Voluntary Associates (SOVA)

350 Kennington Road
London SE11 4LH
Tel: 0171-793 0404
Fax: 0171-793 4410

Contact
Gill Henson

Main Activities
SOVA trains local volunteers and involves them in work with offenders and their families. National organisation with branches in: London, Rotherham, Barnsley, Sheffield, Wales, Derby, Kent, Hartlepool, Middlesex.

Opportunities for Volunteers
Volunteers are needed for the various projects eg helping prisoners partners, literacy, letter writing. Two/three hours a week is the minimum commitment. Travel and lunch expenses are offered. Patience, tact and understanding are useful personal qualities. Training is provided and supervision and support are on-going.

Opportunities for Employment
There are 24 full-time staff and seventeen part-time. About 20 people are recruited each year. Recruits need to have an understanding of the criminal justice system. Jobs are advertised in The Guardian, local newspapers and Job Centres.

Further Information
Annual Report and further information available on request.

Soldiers', Sailors', and Airmen's Families Association (SSAFA/FHS)

Queen Elizabeth the Queen Mother House
19 Queen Elizabeth Street
London SE1 2LP
Tel: 0171-403 8783
Fax: 0171-403 8815

Contact
Ann Needle, Organisation and Recruitment Officer

Main Activities
Offers advice, friendship and practical help to Service and ex-Service men, women and their families. There are 900 branches in the UK and ex-patriate communities abroad.

Opportunities for Volunteers
Help is needed to undertake case work and give administrative support. Also needed are treasurers, visitors and drivers. All out-of-pocket expenses are paid (travel, telephone calls, stamps) and training is given.

Opportunities for Employment
There are 66 full-time staff.

Further Information
A list of local groups is available as well as informational literature.

Sue Ryder Foundation, see Disability

Thomas Coram Foundation for Children, see Children

Women's Royal Voluntary Service (WRVS)

Head Office
234/244 Stockwell Road
London SW9 9SP
Tel: 0171-416 0146
Fax: 0171-416 0148

Contact
Mr Les Barclay

Main Activities
Assists government in supporting the vulnerable. Provides meals on wheels and canteens and shops in hospitals, prisons and courts. Is involved with family welfare, clubs for elderly people crisis support schemes and much more. National organisation with more than 120 local branches. Annual budget £6 million.

Opportunities for Volunteers
Volunteers are always vitally needed to take part in the activities of the WRVS (see list above). Minimum commitment is one hour a week. Also needed are volunteers with finance, computer and management skills. Contact local WRVS (in local telephone directory).

Opportunities for Employment
There are approximately 100 full-time and 1,000 part-time staff. Jobs are advertised in many local papers and on the radio.

Further Information
Annual Report, list of main locations of WRVS activities and further information available from Head Office. For Scotland, contact: Mrs E Ross, WRVS, 19 Grosvenor Crescent, Edinburgh EH12 5EL. For Wales, contact: Mrs M Gibbons, WRVS, 26 Cathedral Road, Cardiff CF1 9LT.

Young Women's Christian Association (YWCA), *see Women*

Sports

Sport – as a form of physical activity and fun - is the most popular field of voluntary effort. Volunteers organise thousands of clubs, societies and associations all over the country covering all types of games and recreation, for male and female, young and old, able-bodied and disabled. Many of these organisations employ paid staff too. The listings below represent only a very small selection of the many groups that exist. A significant number of them are particularly concerned with providing sports and games of various kinds for disabled people and/or with developing opportunities to participate for those who are disabled.

If you are interested in a sport or an area of the UK not covered here you could also check

- with your local library – including such publications as The Education Yearbook, which has a section on Sport
- with your local sports centre
- the notice boards in local community and arts centres, and village halls.

British Blind Sport (BBS)

67 Albert Street, Rugby
Warwickshire CV21 2SN
Tel: 01788-535960
Fax: 01788-536142

Contact
Head Office for volunteering;
Tim Hamper, Director re employment

Main Activities
BBS is the governing body in the UK for sport for blind people. Set up in 1976 as a UK-wide national agency, it has 800 members covering individual people and clubs. It is also affiliated to the International Blind Sport Association (IBSA). Annual budget is £250,000.

Opportunities for Volunteers

Volunteers are very important to the BBS since without them it could not run its events. They guide the blind participants and help with coaching. The skills they require are a knowledge of sport and of blind people. Volunteers are mostly drawn from among the membership, but can also be recruited ad hoc through application. Travel, lunch, out-of-pocket and accommodation expenses are offered. Sports training can be provided.

Opportunities for Employment

Two full-time and two part-time staff are employed. Others are recruited on a seasonal basis during the summer, especially for 'Have-a-Go' days. Posts are advertised in local newspapers, and people with disabilities are actively recruited.

Further Information

An Information Pack costing £3 can be obtained by contacting head office.

The British Disabled Water Ski Association

The Tony Edge National Centre
Heron Lake, Hythe End
Wraysbury, Middlesex TW19 6HW
Tel: 01784-483664
Fax: 01784-482747

Contact

Sylvia Nicholl, National Administrative Officer

Main Activities

Founded in 1979, the Association teaches people with a disability, including amputees as well as those who are blind, deaf or partially paralysed, to ski using fully qualified instructors. Apart from the national centre in Middlesex, it also operates a North West Centre in Rochdale, and has four other regional facilities covering the South West, Yorkshire and Humberside, the Midlands and Scotland. Residential groups can be catered for over three day

periods. Membership of the Association is available at a nominal cost. It is affiliated to the British Water Ski Federation and has links with similar organisations in Australia, Europe (France, Italy, Switzerland), Singapore and the USA. A registered charity, it relies on donations for its income.

Opportunities for Volunteers

The Association could not operate without volunteers and is actively seeking more, especially to teach water skiing, particularly during the summer season, but also for fundraising and advice giving. Volunteers must be able to water ski and/or fundraise. No remuneration/expenses are offered.

Opportunities for Employment

There are three full-time staff. No further details provided.

Further Information

A leaflet, information sheet and list of local groups are available on request.

The British Ski Club for the Disabled (BSCD)

Springmount, Berwick St John
Shaftesbury, Dorset SP7 0HQ
Tel: 01747-828515

Contact

The Membership Secretary or Chairman

Main Activities

Set up in 1974 the Club aims to help people, both young and old, with a variety of disabilities, to gain confidence by participating in as many sporting activities as possible, especially ski-ing and skating. Ski-ing sessions are available on artificial slopes at centres in England, Scotland and Wales, and ski-ing holidays are also organised. The BSCD is a national organisation with regional affiliates and local groups. A registered charity, it operates a membership scheme and also accepts donations to help cover costs. It is linked with similar organisations in

Europe and North America, including the Canadian Association for Disabled Skiers.

Opportunities for Volunteers

Volunteers are essential to the Club's work. Apart from organising local groups, they are involved with administrative support, fundraising, public relations, and committee management and trusteeship. If competent skiers or with sports ability, they are also involved in project work as guides for disabled people and in running courses to train guides. The Club actively seeks more volunteers, preferably already able to ski, to act as guides, especially for winter holidays. Training is provided. Recruitment is ad hoc on application to the address above, and by word of mouth. There is no minimum time commitment, some out-of-pocket expenses are paid, and subsidies are available for those assisting with holiday parties.

Opportunities for Employment

The Club does not have any paid staff.

Further Information

A list of local groups and holidays is available from the Chairman.

British Sports Association for the Disabled (BSAD)

The Mary Glen Haig Training Suite
Solecast House, 13-27 Brunswick Place
London N1 6DX
Tel: 0171-490 4919
Fax: 0171-490 4914

Contact

Gordon Neale, Senior Manager Operations and/or Allison Wood, Senior Manager Administration and Finance

Main Activities

The BSAD, a registered charity, aims to provide, develop and co-ordinate a wide variety of sports and recreation opportunities for people with disabilities of all ages, ranging from the beginner to the elite disabled sportsman and sportswoman.

The Association's work includes providing various innovative training opportunities, events, challenges and awards initiatives, as well campaigning for increased disability awareness. BSAD also provides an information and advice support service. To achieve its objectives it also works in partnership with other relevant agencies, including the British Paralympic Association (BPA) and the Sports Council. Founded in 1961, BSAD is a national organisation with ten regional branches incorporating around 550 clubs, schools and affiliated associations, as well as about 50,000 individual members. It also has contacts with sports for disabled organisations around the world, including developing nations. Its funding includes grants from governing bodies, charitable trusts, commercial sponsorship and private donations. BSAD's annual budget is £1.03 million.

Opportunities for Volunteers

Volunteers are the life blood of the BSAD, and the Association recognises their valuable and fundamental role. They facilitate the Regional Executives in all regions, and the local club structure and events. They also organise the local groups, provide the management and trustees, give administrative support and undertake fundraising and research. The skills BSAD volunteers need depend on the jobs they do. More are required in both Head Office and the regional/local areas. Selection and recruitment are undertaken in a professional way, including through volunteer bureaux, on application and via in-house schemes. No minimum time commitment is asked for and expenses may be offered. Enquiries should be directed to Head Office or the regional bodies (Peterborough, Sutton Coldfield, Darlington, Maidenhead, Winchester and Eastbourne).

Opportunities for Employment

26 full-time and two part-time staff are employed. Annual recruitment varies, but

occurs in the areas of administrative assistance, clerical work, fundraising and events. Vacancies are advertised in The Guardian, the Evening Standard, and/or the regional and local press. BSAD is particularly interested in recruiting people with disabilities and has an equal opportunities policy.

Further Information
The Annual Report, Policy Charter booklet, leaflets, posters and other literature are available on request from Head Office.

Calvert Trust

Little Crosthwaite, Keswick
Cumbria CA12 4QD
Tel: 017687-72254
Fax: 017687-73941

Contact
Centre Director

Main Activities
The Trust provides outdoor adventurous activity courses for people with disabilities. The focus of a course can be recreation, education, rehabilitation or personal development. Founded in 1974, the Trust operates throughout the UK with the local administration of course centres and three local branches. The annual budget is £300,000 approximately at each centre.

Opportunities for Volunteers
About 25 volunteers support the Trust's work, especially as riding assistants and by providing care support. New volunteers are welcomed, but they need experience in working outdoors and with people with disabilities. The minimum time commitment is two hours a week or a week at a time. The work is occasional and seasonal eg summer. Recruitment is ad hoc on application to the Trust and through in-house schemes. No expenses are offered.

Opportunities for Employment
30 staff are employed, 20 full-time, eight part-time and two temporary. There are

some seasonal recruitment opportunities for trainee instructors, who need outdoor work experience and enthusiasm for working with people with disabilities. Posts are advertised in the Times Educational Supplement. The Trust has an equal opportunities policy and actively recruits people with disabilities.

Further Information
The Annual Report is available from the Charities Commission and brochures about the work from the Trust.

English National Association of Visually Handicapped Bowlers, *see Recreation & Leisure*

Great Britain Wheelchair Basketball Association (GBWBA)

c/o 104 London Road
Chatteris, Cambs PE16 6SF
Tel: 01354-695560
Fax: 01354-695752

Contact
Club Secretary via club handbook or Steve Spilka, General Secretary, as above

Main Activities
The GBWBA administers the sport of wheelchair basketball in Britain, and encourages people with physical lower limb disability to participate in a team sport. Set up informally in the 1950s, the Association was formally constituted in 1982. A UK-wide organisation it has 35 associated clubs, links with other clubs world-wide, and is affiliated to the International Wheelchair Basketball Federation. Annual budget is £70,000.

Opportunities for Volunteers
The Executive Officers are all volunteers and individual clubs also use volunteers to act as escorts assisting wheelchair users. Volunteers also organise the local clubs,

are managers and trustees, give administrative support and undertake fundraising. More are welcome. There is no minimum time commitment and expenses may be offered. An interest in sport would be an advantage.

Opportunities for Employment

There is one full-time staff member, the National Development Officer, but no other opportunities. The GBWBA has implemented an equal opportunities policy.

Further Information

The Annual Report, handbook, information pack and 'Rebound' the quarterly newsletter can all be obtained from the General Secretary.

Greater London Sports Association (GLSA)

Ground Floor
436 Essex Road
London N1 3XP
Tel: 0171-354 8666
Fax: 0171-354 8787

Contact

Angus Robertson, Director

Main Activities

The GLSA is concerned with developing, co-ordinating and promoting sport and recreation for people with learning disabilities in Greater London. Set up in 1981, it is a regional body with ten affiliated organisations and also members (groups and individuals). Its annual budget is £200,000.

Opportunities for Volunteers

About 50 volunteers are involved and are very important to the Association's work, particularly during events and activity days when they help to organise, marshal and support competitors and participants. They also provide administrative support and undertake management/trusteeship duties. More are actively sought, especially

to help with the ten main events each year and with general administration. It is also possible that volunteers with particular skills such as PR and fundraising could be of great assistance. A knowledge of sports/coaching is useful, but briefing support is given by staff. Recruitment is ad hoc, on application in writing or by phone, and through approaches to schools and colleges. No minimum commitment is required, and travel and out-of-pocket expenses are offered.

Opportunities for Employment

Three full-time and two part-time staff are employed. Perhaps one person is recruited each year. All posts are advertised in local and regional papers, and in The Voice; application is by specific form only. Skills required vary depending on the post. A formal equal opportunities policy operates.

Further Information

The Annual Report, a membership leaflet, information sheets on the work of GLSA and a list of local groups are available on request.

National Association of Swimming Clubs for the Handicapped (NASCH)

The Willows, Mayles Lane
Wickham, Hampshire PO17 5ND
Tel: 01329-833689

Contact

Mike O'Leary, Co-ordinator

Main Activities

NASCH aims to encourage and develop swimming for disabled people. Set up in 1966, it is a national organisation with 125 affiliated clubs throughout the UK.

Opportunities for Volunteers

NASCH depends on volunteers and would be unable to operate without them. About 1,200 are involved in organising and running the local clubs and in training other helpers. Recruitment is ad hoc on application, no minimum commitment is required and no expenses are paid.

Opportunities for Employment
There are no paid staff.

Further Information
The Annual Report, other information and a list of local groups are available on request.

National Playing Fields Association (Scotland), *see Recreation & Leisure*

The Pony Club

B.E.C., Stoneleigh, Kenilworth
Warwickshire CV8 2LR
Tel: 01203-696697
Fax: 01203-696836

Contact
Local branches for volunteering; Miss C Moir, Executive Secretary re employment

Main Activities
Aims to encourage young people to ride and enjoy all sport connected with horses. Provides instruction in riding and the proper care of horses, and promotes high ideals of sportsmanship, citizenship and loyalty to cultivate strength of character and self-discipline. Set up in 1929 the Club is UK-wide, has an elected and appointed Council, and 369 affiliated local branches/clubs. It also has links with similar clubs in Europe and North America. Annual budget is £900,000.

Opportunities for Volunteers
Essential to the work of the Club over 3,000 volunteers organise and administer the branches, provide advice and teach members. More volunteers are needed, year round, especially for instructing. A knowledge of the horse world is required. Recruitment is usually by word of mouth.

Travel and out-of-pocket expenses (for administrators) are offered, and training courses are available.

Opportunities for Employment
There are five full-time members of staff. People are regularly recruited for work in administration and seasonally for summer camps, especially those returning to work. Posts are not advertised. A knowledge of horses is necessary.

Further Information
The Annual Report and a leaflet listing Pony Club books are available. Send a stamped addressed envelope (sae) to head office.

Wandsworth Blind Bowling Club and London Blind Rambling Club, *see Recreation & Leisure*

UK Sports Association for People with Learning Disability

Solecast House
13-27 Brunswick Place
London N1 6DX
Tel: 0171-250 1100
Fax: 0171-250 1100

Contact
Roger Biggs, Director

Main Activities
The UK Sports Association for People with Learning Disability is an umbrella organisation for all interested regional and national organisations involved in the provision of sport for people with learning disability. The Association develops and co-ordinates sporting opportunities for people with learning disability. There are ten regional groups.

Opportunities for Volunteers
The Association aims to progress its objectives through working with volunteers

Support for Volunteering

and is committed to assisting volunteers to develop their experience, knowledge and ability. Volunteers are always needed for fundraising and administrative work. Special skills eg accounting, typing, press and PR are also useful. Minimum commitment negotiable.

Opportunities for Employment

There are five full-time staff and two are recruited approximately each year.

Further Information

Annual Report and list of local groups available.

Youth Clubs UK, *see Youth*

Another place to look for volunteer work is in your local volunteer bureau. The role of the nationwide network of volunteer bureaux is to promote voluntary service in the community.

The opportunities for volunteering vary with each bureau and each local community. They may include not only charities and voluntary organisations but hospitals, schools, social services and community projects of every kind. You can contact your nearest Bureau by phone (the number will be in your local telephone book) about the volunteering opportunities in your area. Or you can just drop in for a chat. The personnel in the bureau will be probably ask you a bit about yourself and may ask you to fill in a simple form. They can then match your interests, needs and lifestyle with the volunteer jobs available.

The national network of Volunteer Bureaux (VBx) promotes volunteering and good practice in the involvement of volunteers in organisations. Volunteer Bureaux act as central recruiting and interviewing agencies for volunteers, introducing them to organisations who need volunteer help. They actively publicise the need for volunteers and give support and training to organisations developing new projects with volunteers. The range of opportunities available to volunteers is enormous. There are practical things such as gardening or decorating for a housebound elderly person to very intensive support such as helping people get over a bereavement. There is work with all types of people - homeless people, children, people with disabilities and so on. Or you might prefer to help in an office, making the most of existing skills or developing new ones. Volunteer work is also a useful way of refreshing skills and regaining confidence for those who are planning to return to the workforce after a break.

Often there are volunteer opportunities within the individual bureau. Volunteers work on the reception, assist with administrative duties, answer the telephone and help with organising special events and projects.

As well as dealing with individual volunteers, Volunteer Bureaux also play an important role in supporting organisations who use volunteers. They provide networking opportunities, workshops and training to improve an organisation's effectiveness in recruiting and retaining volunteers. Often they initiate special projects such as how to recruit the 'over fifties' or how to involve more business employees in voluntary work.

Each Bureau is managed by a Management Committee consisting of representatives from voluntary organisations, social services and other local authority staff, and elected members. Funding usually comes from the local council, with further financial help from trusts, special grants and local businesses.

Central to the philosophy of Volunteer Bureaux are the beliefs that everyone has the right to volunteer without experiencing unfair discrimination, and that volunteering is a matter of free choice. VBx actively promote the concept that volunteering is an invaluable, integral part of society which assists in effecting social change and improving the quality of life of people in the community.

As well as volunteer bureaux, there are a number of voluntary organisations that specifically support volunteering. They, too, need volunteers, or can sometimes suggest suitable organisations to approach.

Community Service Volunteers (CSV)

237 Pentonville Road
London N1 9NJ
Tel: 0171-278 6601
Fax: 0171-837 9621

Contact
Press and Information Officer

Main Activities
CSV creates opportunities for people to play an active part in the life of their community through volunteering, training, education and the media. Centred in London, CSV has regional offices and project locations throughout the UK.

Opportunities for Volunteers
CSV actively promotes four types of opportunities of volunteering:

CSV's Volunteer Programme attracts over 3,000 young volunteers each year to work with people who need their help. Community Services Volunteers (aged between sixteen and 35) are placed in over 800 projects nationwide, from helping people live independently in their own homes, to working with adults and children with disabilities and befriending the homeless. CSV actively seeks and welcomes volunteers all year round, and liaises closely with the Careers Service.

CSV's Retired and Senior Volunteer Programme (RSVP) involves over 2,500 volunteers aged 50+ on projects in education, the environment and community care in the local community. On average volunteers give four hours a week. Out-of-pocket expenses are paid.

CSV's Employee Volunteering Programme encourages employees to volunteer in their community with the support of their employers.

CSV's Learning Together initiative involves over 5,000 student tutors each year volunteering in local schools for a morning or afternoon each week.

Opportunities for Employment
Approximately five hundred employees work throughout the UK in CSV's five divisions, including the Volunteer Programme. Staff are recruited as necessary. There is an equal opportunities policy and posts are advertised in The Guardian and local newspapers.

Further Information
Annual Report, a general information leaflet and other printed information are available from the above address. Wales, Scotland and Northern Ireland are covered by CSV in London.

Federation of Independent Advice Centres (FIAC)

13 Stockwell Road
London SW9 9AU
Tel: 0171-274 1839
Fax: 0171-737 4065

Contact
Dorothy Newton

Main Activities
FIAC is an umbrella organisation for independent advice centres. It provides them with various services, including professional indemnity insurance, recruitment, and training courses. A national federation, it has 727 affiliated organisations.

Opportunities for Volunteers
FIAC does not use volunteers itself. It acts as a referral agency to put prospective volunteers in touch with member organisations who do use them.

Opportunities for Employment
There are thirteen full-time staff, and two part-time staff, but employment opportunities seldom occur.

Further Information
The Annual Report is available on request. There is a mailing service and information pack for member organisations.

National Association of Councils for Voluntary Service (NACVS)

3rd floor, Arundel Court
177 Arundel Street
Sheffield S1 2NU
Tel: 0114-2786636

Contact
Assistant Director, Finance and Administration

Main Activities
NACVS is a membership body for Councils for Voluntary Services in England. It supports CVSs and local voluntary action. Provides advice, information, training and consultancy and promotes local voluntary action at a national level. 230 affiliated organisations. Annual budget is £200,000.

Opportunities for Volunteers
Volunteers give administrative support. Travel expenses are offered. Apply in writing.

Opportunities for Employment
There are eight core staff.

Further Information
Annual Report available.

National Association of Volunteer Bureaux (NAVB)

St Peter's College, College Road
Saltley, Birmingham B8 3TE
Tel: 0121-327 0265

Contact
Ms H Reeve and NAVB for names etc of local Volunteer Bureaux (VBx).

Main Activities
NAVB is a national network of autonomous local volunteering development agencies or Volunteer Bureaux - VBx. The national office serves, supports and represents the interests of the VBx. There are 323 VB members (including branch offices) in England, ten in Wales and three in Northern Ireland. NAVB's annual budget is £200,000 (1994).

Opportunities for Volunteers
The national office uses volunteers direct from the VBx network. Individual VBx involve volunteers directly in their own work and by placing volunteers with other agencies. Every VB has a data bank and information about a vast range of volunteering opportunities locally, covering all types of work/service/activity to enable all people to get involved in voluntary activity of their choice. VBx are the local experts on all aspects of volunteering, including recruitment. They play a vital role in local communities. VBx also advise other agencies on good practice in volunteering and are advocates for the rights of volunteers, including the reimbursement of expenses incurred in being a volunteer. Potential volunteers are usually interviewed. Some VBx operate a 'drop-in volunteer job shop'.

Opportunities for Employment
NAVB employs five full-time staff. Member VBx employ an average of 1.4 full-time equivalents. Vacancies occur occasionally as a result of staff turn-over. NAVB has an equal opportunities policy and employment recruitment procedures which specify how jobs will be advertised.

Further Information
Annual Report, various leaflets and an annual VBx Directory (at £6.50) are published. NAVB works also with Wales Association of Volunteer Bureaux (WAVB), with the Volunteer Development Agency NI in Northern Ireland and with Volunteer Development Scotland (VDS). Relevant addresses are:

Volunteer Development Agency NI (VDA NI), Annsgate House, 70-74 Ann Street, Belfast BT1 4EH, tel: 01232-236100

Volunteer Development Scotland (VDS), 80 Murray Place, Stirling FK8 2BX, tel: 01786-79593.

National Council for Voluntary Youth Services

Coburn House
3 Coborn Road
London E3 2DA
Tel: 0181-980 5712
Fax: 0181-983 4822

Contact
Susanne Rauprich, Chief Executive

Main Activities
The National Council for Voluntary Youth Services comprises the network of National Voluntary Youth Organisations and Local Councils for Voluntary Youth Services. The organisation aims to meet the needs of youth organisations. Provides information service to, and about, Voluntary Youth Service.

Opportunities for Volunteers
Volunteers are needed to provide administrative support, do fundraising and project work. Travel expenses are offered.

Opportunities for Employment
There are two staff.

Further Information
Annual Report and further information leaflet available.

Returned Volunteer Action

1 Amwell Street
London EC1R 1UL
Tel: 0171-278 0804

Contact
Rod Leith

Main Activities
This is a membership organisation of returned overseas voluntary workers who wish maintain their interest in the developing world. Offers advice and information to prospective volunteers going overseas.

Opportunities for Volunteers
Volunteers are needed for various projects at Head Office.

Opportunities for Employment
No information available.

Further Information
Annual Report and bulletin of overseas voluntary work opportunities available.

Swanley District Volunteer Bureau, see Charity Support

The Volunteer Centre UK

Carriage Row
183 Eversholt Street
London NW1 1BU
Tel: 0171-388 9888
Fax: 0171-383 0448

Contact
Information Officer

Main Activities
The Volunteer Centre UK is an umbrella organisation with over 600 members who are all volunteer-involving. Promotes volunteering for the benefit of individual volunteers and the community. Encourages good practice in the organisation of volunteering.

Opportunities for Volunteers
Volunteers are very important and give support at all levels of the organisation. Volunteers are also needed during UK Volunteers Week (1-7 June). Support is offered. Project based to meet work and volunteer needs. Travel and lunch expenses offered. Write, in the first instance, with personal details and interests to Sheila Edwin at the above address.

Opportunities for Employment
There are 25 full-time and fifteen part-time staff. About three people are recruited each year. Jobs are advertised in The Guardian and local papers.

Further Information

Annual Report, catalogue of services and membership leaflets available. For information about volunteering in Wales, Scotland and Northern Ireland, contact: Wales Council for Voluntary Action, Llys Ifor, Crescent Road, Caerphilly, Mid Glamorgan CF8 1XL, tel: 01222-869224; Volunteer Development Scotland, 80 Murray Place, Stirling FK8 2BX, tel: 01786-79593; The Northern Ireland Volunteer Development Agency, Anne's Gate House, 70-74 Ann Street, Belfast, tel: 01232-236100.

Women

Asian Women's Resource Centre (AWRC)

134 Minet Avenue
Harlesden
London NW10 8AP
Tel: 0181-961 6549/5701
Fax: 0181-838 1823

Contact

Ms S Ganger

Main Activities

A women's collective, the AWRC offers a practical service and free advice on a wide range of issues, including welfare benefits, housing, immigration, employment and domestic violence. It also undertakes developmental work in the areas of youth, health, children, employment and sexual health, and provides advocacy and counselling services. Founded in 1980 by Asian women, it is an autonomous Asian women's group, managed by its members. It covers the Greater London area, but receives enquiries from all over the UK, and is funded by the London Borough Grants Unit (LBGU). It also has links with international women's groups, including in Bombay, India and Zimbabwe. Annual budget is £77,000.

Opportunities for Volunteers

Currently the volunteers involved are students on placement and women users of the Centre. AWRC plans to develop a pool of volunteers for the future, especially to give administrative support. Minimum commitment is three hours a week, and travel expenses are offered.

Opportunities for Employment

Four full-time staff are employed. Workers in the area of sexual health are required, for which experience is necessary, together with knowledge of one Asian language. Vacancies are advertised in The Guardian, the Asian Times, and Eastern Eye. AWRC has an equal opportunities policy.

Further Information
The Annual Report and a publicity leaflet in six Asian languages are available.

Drug and Alcohol Women's Network (DAWN), *see Counselling & Self-help*

The Feminist Library

5 Westminster Bridge Road
London SE1 7XW
Tel: 0171-928 7789

Contact
The office

Main Activities
A lending and reference library, and information centre for women. Set up in 1975, it has an extensive collection of books, journals, articles and pamphlets on women's issues and contemporary feminism. Located in London and run by volunteers, it serves mainly London members, but has visitors from around Britain and overseas.

Opportunities for Volunteers
Run entirely by a team of sixty women volunteers, the Library is always actively seeking more, to help run it, produce the newsletter, and for fundraising and administration. Volunteers are especially needed at weekends. Recruitment is through volunteer bureaux and advertising in women's and minority publications. Volunteers should have an interest in feminism. Full training is given, as required. Minimum commitment is three hours monthly. Travel expenses are paid.

Opportunities for Employment
There are no employment opportunities.

Further Information
A general information leaflet and a copy of the constitution are available on request, plus access details for women with disabilities.

GFS Platform for Young Women

Townsend House
126 Queen's Gate
London SW7 5LQ
Tel: 0171-589 9628
Fax: 0171-225 1458

Contact
Director, Parish and Community Work

Main Activities
The organisation supports housing, community projects, parish based clubs, and adventure opportunities for young women. The aim is to enable to girls and women to develop their potential spiritually, socially and personally. The organisation is nationally based with local groups and projects. There are 200 local branches and fifteen local support groups.

Opportunities for Volunteers
There are approximately 600 volunteers involved in branch work and about 40 at Central Office. Volunteers carry out a variety of tasks including administration, fundraising, management and trusteeship, as well as support of staff and clients. Minimum commitment is generally flexible but about three hours a week would be expected of parish based volunteers. Travel and out-of-pocket expenses are offered. The organisation is currently seeking volunteers for youth work and for fundraising. An ability to work with people is necessary and GFS leadership course and local training are offered.

Opportunities for Employment
There are 40 full-time and 20 part-time members of staff. There is an equal opportunities policy. Posts are advertised in The Guardian, The Voice and the NFHA Weekly.

Further Information
Annual report, information leaflet and newsletter are available from Central Office. In Ireland, including Northern

Ireland, contact GFS Ireland, 36 Upper Leeson Street, Dublin 4, Eire.

The Guide Association, *see Youth*

Junior League of London (JLL)

9 Fitzmaurice Place
London W1X 6JD
Tel: 0171-499 8159

Contact
Leesa Wilson-Goldmuntz

Main Activities
JLL is a self-governing, self-funded organisation of women volunteers committed to promoting voluntary service and improving the community through the effective action of trained volunteers. It was set up in England in 1979 as a Service League, and became a Junior League in 1985 with a Head Office in London and projects within a 30-mile radius. JLL is part of an international organisation, the Association of Junior Leagues International. As well as JLL, there are more than 280 Junior Leagues throughout Canada, Mexico and the USA. Funding comes from membership subscriptions and fundraising of various kinds. The annual budget is approximately £80,000.

Opportunities for Volunteers
Since the Junior League exists to promote volunteering and co-operative endeavour, volunteers are central to it. Women volunteers carry out all tasks including hands-on work in community projects to help families in need. A six month training programme is offered, during which volunteers learn a variety of skills, together with an on-going support structure. A commitment to voluntary and community service is essential, and enquiries are welcomed from women who

wish to make that commitment. Minimum time commitment is two to four hours a week. Information meetings are held in spring and summer.

Opportunities for Employment
There are two part-time members of staff.

Further Information
Brochure, list of local community projects and Media Kit are available on request.

La Leche League (Great Britain), (LLL(GB))

BM 3424
London WC1N 3XX
Tel: 0171-242 1278 (24 hours)

Contact
The Chairwoman

Main Activities
Founded in 1971, LLLGB provides information and help on breast feeding through various methods, especially personal help. It trains and accredits mothers as leaders to advise. It also organises local groups offering mother to mother support and information. Numerous leaflets and other publications are produced or can be supplied. A national, UK-wide organisation with international links through La Leche League International, LLLGB has a network of about 75 local groups, and an annual budget of nearly £24,000.

Opportunities for Volunteers
LLLGB carries out its work through volunteer leaders accredited as counsellors. Leaders run monthly mother-to-mother support meetings, administer local groups, offer telephone help and undertake health professional liaison work. Leaders need to have had a positive breast feeding experience and be happy to support other mothers. Volunteers are also used throughout the branches for administration and fundraising work. LLLGB needs volunteers constantly and

actively seeks women, primarily through in-house recruitment via local group leaders. Women are trained to become leaders through its leader accreditation process, based on their own successful breast feeding relationship. There is no minimum commitment and no remuneration is offered.

Opportunities for Employment
There is one part-time administrator and are no employment opportunities.

Further Information
Annual Report, numerous pamphlets and publications, and a list of local groups are available on request. A newsletter is sent to members. Membership of various kinds is available.

Latin American Women's Rights Service (LAWRS), *see Law & Justice*

London Lesbian Line – also known as Women's Referral and Information Services (WRIS)

BM Box 1514
London WC1N 3XX
Tel: 0171-251 6692

Contact
Angie Brew or Bev Hockley

Main Activities
Provides a phone service/helpline run by lesbian volunteers, offering help, advice and information. Primarily for lesbians, and women of any age and girls who think they might be lesbians. Advice given on all issues. London Lesbian Line is a lesbian collective with an annual budget of £30,000.

Opportunities for Volunteers
About 30 volunteers run London Lesbian Line undertaking administrative, fundraising, counselling and project

work. This includes giving information and listening on the telephone helpline, as well as expanding the collective of volunteers and publicising the service. More volunteers, who must be lesbians, are welcome. Recruitment is by application to the office above, word of mouth, lesbian organisations and publicity at women's events. Minimum commitment is three hours a fortnight, especially in the evenings and/or Monday and Friday afternoons. Training for the Helpline and other on-going support given. Travel expenses are paid for any woman unwaged/low waged.

Opportunities for Volunteers
There are two part-time workers who job-share. Vacancies rarely arise. An Equal Opportunities Policy operates.

Further Information
The Annual Report, a list of local branches, an information pack about the Line, and detailed information on other services/organisations for lesbians are available. Lesbian Lines also exist in such cities as Edinburgh, Cardiff and Belfast. Contact London office for details.

London Rape Crisis Centre

PO Box 69
London WC1X 9NJ
Tel: 0171-916 5466 (admin)
Tel: 0171-837 1600 (counselling)

Contact
Write to the project/Centre

Main Activities
The Centre provides counselling for women and girls who have been raped/sexually assaulted. Runs training courses for groups within the voluntary sector. Gives advice on legal and medical issues.

Opportunities for Volunteers
Volunteers are needed as counsellors on a helpline. A three month training course is offered plus back-up. A commitment

to working in a women-only organisation is necessary. Minimum commitment is four duties a month with one overnight. Travel, lunch and creche expenses are offered.

Opportunities for Employment

There are two full-time and five part-time staff.

Further Information

Annual Report and leaflet available on request.

Maternity and Health Links

Old Co-op, 38-42 Chelsea Road
Easton, Bristol BS5 6AF
Tel: 0117-955 8495

Contact

Asma Ahmad/Shaheen Chaudhry

Main Activities

Maternity and Health Links provides interpreting and advocacy for non-English speaking clients using the health services. It gives English tuition during pregnancy for non-English speaking, pregnant women. It also promotes cultural awareness amongst professionals. Based in Bristol at present, it focuses on the local area.

Opportunities for Volunteers

Volunteers provide much needed health-related English tuition to pregnant minority ethnic women. This empowers the women so they are better able to access the health services. More volunteers are needed. Some adult teaching experience and personal experience of motherhood are useful, together with knowledge of maternity services. Fluency in an Asian or other language in addition to English is an advantage. Minimum commitment is two hours a week.

Opportunities for Employment

There is one full-time member of staff and eight part-time members.

Further Information

Annual Report, leaflet and video (in English and Asian languages) available on request. A teaching video on home tuition is also available for training.

Meet-a-Mum Association (MAMA)

14 Willis Road
Croydon CR0 2XX
Tel: 0181-665 1972

Contact

Briony Hallam

Main Activities

MAMA puts mothers in touch with other mothers in their area for friendship and support. It also provides support and information for mothers suffering from post-natal depression. National organisation with over 60 local support groups.

Opportunities for Volunteers

Volunteer supporters are very important to MAMA. They help at Head Office with administration, they act as trustees, they support mothers with post-natal depression and they run local groups. Experience of post-natal depression is useful. Training, support and travel expenses are offered. Minimum commitment is two hours per week.

Opportunities for Employment

There are none.

Further Information

Annual Report, leaflets, booklets are available. Please send an SAE.

Museum of Women's Art (MWA), *see Museums, the Arts & Festivals*

National Alliance of Women's Organisations (NAWO)

279-281 Whitechapel Road
London E1 18Y
Tel: 0171-247 7052

Contact
Administration Manager

Main Activities
Founded in May 1989, NAWO is a comprehensive, umbrella alliance offering advocacy, information, advice and support to all women's organisations. It brings together a wide diversity of women's groups committed to and working towards the elimination of all forms of discrimination against women. It also seeks to empower them in order to achieve true equality and justice for all women. It undertakes policy work in Britain and Europe. England based, with over 200 full and associate member organisations from around the UK representing over six million women, it has a nascent federal structure through a working party consisting of NAWO and sister alliances in Scotland, Wales and Northern Ireland. It is also linked to the European Women's Lobby in Brussels. Its budget is around £150,000 (1994) annually.

Opportunities for Volunteers
Volunteers are essential to NAWO's work. They are used for administrative support, fundraising, project work (eg women in rural areas, black and ethnic minority women), research and in the library/ resource centre. Up to eight volunteers work in the office. All volunteers must be committed to the women's agenda. Volunteers are actively recruited year round, through ad hoc methods, advertisements in Everywoman and the NAWO newsletter, and placements from programmes like Working for a Charity. They are interviewed and must supply a reference. Computer literacy is preferred. Training and support are given as needed. Preferred commitment is one day a week or more over at least 4-6 weeks. Travel and lunch expenses are offered.

Opportunities for Employment
There are four paid staff. Vacancies sometimes occur and occasionally short term contracts are available. Applicants must be committed to the women's agenda. Posts are advertised in The Guardian, The Voice and Everywoman, based on an equal opportunities statement of intent.

Further Information
The Annual Report is available copies permitting, together with a publications list and general leaflet.

National Association of Ladies Circles of Great Britain and Ireland (NALC)

NALC HQ Office
Provincial House, Cooke Street
Keighley, West Yorkshire BD21 3NN
Tel: 01535-607617
Fax: 01535-662312

Contact
General Secretary, Head Office; local branch secretaries

Main Activities
NALC provides opportunities for social contact, friendship and service for women through meetings, social functions, community service projects and fundraising. A national, UK-wide organisation set up in 1936, it is divided into 53 regional areas with 860 individual branches, is affiliated to Ladies Circle International (LCI) and has links in many countries worldwide.

Opportunities for Volunteers
All members are volunteers and NALC welcomes new ones. It recruits through

personal introduction and branch secretaries. Work includes fundraising and community service at branch level. No expenses are paid.

Opportunities for Employment
There are no opportunities as all members are volunteers.

Further Information
Details of NALC can be obtained through head office.

National Association of Widows (NAW)

54-57 Allison Street
Digbeth, Birmingham B5 5TH
Tel: 0121-643 8348

Contact
Lynne Davies, Research and Information Officer

Main Activities
NAW offers specialist advice, information and friendly social support to all widows whether or not they are members, and irrespective of age. It has also set up a younger widows contact list. A national organisation covering England and Scotland, and set up in 1971, it has 70 local branches. It also has links with Russia where a Widows Association has been set up in St Petersburg with NAW's support.

Opportunities for Volunteers
As a self-help organisation, NAW is run by its members who are all volunteers. Prospective volunteers, who must be widows themselves, are needed to give advice and support in the local branches. An ability to listen is very valuable. Seminars and workshops are provided.

Opportunities for Employment
There are two members of staff.

Further Information
Annual Report, Newsletter, list of local groups and information leaflets available.

National Association of Women's Clubs (NAWC)

5 Vernon Rise
King's Cross Road
London WC1X 9EP
Tel: 0171-837 1434

Contact
Mrs S Nicholas, General Secretary

Main Activities
NAWC (established in 1935) and its member clubs aim to improve the conditions of life for women by advancing their education and providing facilities for leisure and recreation. The clubs are self-governing and run programmes which include classes, home craft demonstrations and speakers. The Association covers England and Wales, has 23 regional groupings, 338 local clubs and 19 affiliated organisations. Its annual budget is nearly £115,500.

Opportunities for Volunteers
Around 500 volunteers are used in the clubs, and one in head office, for fundraising and promotional work. They also recruit new members, open new clubs and service existing clubs. Recruited through in-house leaflets, the minimum commitment is 3 hours weekly. Travel expenses are paid.

Opportunities for Employment
There is one full-time and five part-time staff. Staff are needed mainly for clerical work. Vacancies seldom occur, are advertised in the in-house magazine and NAWC's own members are preferred.

Further Information
An Annual Report and a leaflet are available.

National Childbirth Trust (NCT)

Alexandra House, Oldham Terrace
Acton, London W3 6NH
Tel: 0181-992 8637
Fax: 0181-992 5929

Contact
Shirleyanne Seel

Main Activities
Founded in 1956, the NCT offers information and support in pregnancy, childbirth
and early parenthood. It provides ante-
natal classes, counselling and support
groups, and aims to enable every parent
to make informed choices. In particular
it runs a support group for parents
with disabilities. A national, UK-wide
organisation, it is divided into seven
regional groups with 400 local branches,
and an annual budget of £750,000. It also
has links with voluntary organisations in
Europe, especially in training ante-natal
teachers and counsellors.

Opportunities for Volunteers
Volunteers carry out the main thrust of the
NCT's work. They are used in head office
and the local branches for administrative
support, fundraising and counselling
(breast feeding, mother-to-mother). NCT
actively seeks volunteers (preferably
parents) eg to train as counsellors, ante-
and post-natal teachers, and to run
groups, especially during the day.
Training is given. It recruits through in-
house methods as all volunteers must be
members. Commitment is variable and
travel expenses are paid.

Opportunities for Employment
18 full-time and nine part-time staff are
employed. Turnover is low. If vacancies
occur they are advertised in The Guardian
or local press, based on an evolving equal
opportunities policy.

Further Information
An Annual Report, various leaflets, a
quarterly magazine and a list of local
group areas are available. Branches
receive a monthly mailing.

The National Council of Women of Great Britain (NCW)

36 Danbury Street
London N1 8JU
Tel: 0171-354 2395
Fax: 0171-354 9214

Contact
Miranda Park, Office Manager

Main Activities
NCW aims to improve the quality of life
for all, and for women in particular. This
includes making representations to government and other bodies on legislation
and policy. It acts as a co-ordinating body
to which societies with similar aims can
affiliate. Membership also comprises
individual women. NCW works for
international understanding and peace
too, and is affiliated to the International
Council of Women which comprises 76
member countries. A national organisation set up in 1895, and covering England,
Wales and Scotland, it has 67 branches
around the country and over 100 affiliates.
The annual budget is £50,000.

Opportunities for Volunteers
NCW is a voluntary organisation. All
members are volunteers and give as much
or as little time as they wish. The NCW
relies completely on their work. They
assist in the administration of head office
and organise numerous conferences,
study days, etc. Recruitment is through
in-house schemes. Expenses are not paid.
Local branches are run by members and
can be contacted direct.

Opportunities for Employment
NCW has one full-time and one part-time
member of staff. Opportunities for employment are unlikely.

Further Information
Annual Report, a brochure and a list of local groups are available.

National Federation of Women's Institutes (NFWI)

104 New Kings Road
London SW6 4LY
Tel: 0171-371 9300

Contact
Local branches for volunteering; and Rhiannon Bevan, General Secretary, for employment opportunities

Main Activities
An educational and social voluntary organisation, the NFWI offers women the opportunity for friendship and learning together to improve the quality of life in the community, especially in rural areas. Training courses are offered in a wide variety of subjects, including home economics and social welfare. Local branches hold monthly meetings with speakers. NFWI organises co-operative markets in rural towns, has a publishing company, and its own Denman College which provides further education through short residential courses. It also contributes to international understanding among country women. A national organisation, it has 70 county offices, nearly 9,000 local WI branches, and a budget of £2.5 million annually.

Opportunities for Volunteers
All local WIs are run by volunteers who are needed constantly for management, leadership and organisation at local, county and national levels. Recruitment is usually in-house and volunteers need communication, organisational and interpersonal skills, as well as commitment to WI aims. Time commitment varies widely. Travel expenses are paid. Individual WI county federations can be contacted through local telephone directories.

Opportunities for Employment
With 69 full-time and 24 part-time staff, the NFWI recruits about five people each year. All posts are advertised internally and externally, and, depending on the post, through either the national (Guardian, Times) and/or local press, and professional journals. Recruits must have a commitment to women, the voluntary sector and the aims of the WI. NFWI is working on developing an equal opportunities policy.

Further Information
The Annual Report and relevant pamphlets are available. The Home and Country magazine costs £1.40 a month to non-members and is available through newsagents. Other useful addresses are:

Scottish Women's Rural Institutes, 42 Heriot Row, Edinburgh, Scotland EH3 6EU

The Federation of Women's Institutes of Northern Ireland, 209-211 Upper Lisburn Road, Belfast, Northern Ireland BT10 0LL.

National Free Church Women's Council (NFCWC)

27 Tavistock Square
London WC1H 9HH
Tel: 0171-387 8413

Contact
Pauline Butcher, Secretary

Main Activities
NFCWC is concerned with women's ministry within free Churches. Set up in 1907, it promotes the welfare of elderly people, women and girls, provides residential homes and runs a variety of other projects. Run by a national Executive Committee and covering England and Wales, it has 40 local groups.

Opportunities for Volunteers
Volunteers are needed to serve on local management committees, and to manage the projects. Fundraising and project work eg hostels for young mothers, residential

homes for elderly people are also under-taken by volunteers. Travel expenses are offered. Volunteers should apply directly to local groups (list available from Head Office). A sympathy with Christian ethics is required.

Opportunities for Employment
There is one member of staff.

Further Information
Annual Report is available on request.

National Women's Register (NWR)

National Office, 9 Bank Plain
Norwich, Norfolk NR2 4SL
Tel: 01603-765392

Contact
Judy Ross

Main Activities
The National Women's Register (NWR) is a nationwide organisation providing in-formal meetings for women, from all walks of life and of any age. Discussions on non-domestic topics take place dur-ing the meetings. The aims of NWR are friendship, self-development and mental stimulation. There are 700 local branches.

Opportunities for Volunteers
Volunteers are essential. All are members of NWR. A small elected group under-takes the day-to-day management of NWR on behalf of its Trustees. Volunteers are needed to establish new groups, seek sponsorship, organise NWR conferences and produce magazines. Enthusiasm is a useful attribute and computer literacy and/or publicity experience would be welcome for some volunteer jobs.

Opportunities for Employment
There are two part-time staff.

Further Information
Annual Report, Member Magazine and list of local groups available.

The Pankhurst Trust

The Pankhurst Centre
60-62 Nelson Street
Chorlton-on-Medlock
Manchester M13 9WP
Tel: 0161-273 5673

Contact
Racholle Warburton, Administrator

Main Activities
The Trust maintains a centre in Emmeline Pankhurst's house, restored as a memo-rial to the suffrage movement. The Trust (set up in 1980) and the Centre (opened in 1987) provide a variety of resources for women and women's groups, both locally and nationally.

Opportunities for Volunteers
As a self financing organisation the Trust relies heavily on volunteers to undertake much of the day to day tasks and activi-ties. A range of opportunities exists, including administration, working in the arts and craft shop, decorating, garden-ing, cleaning, and exhibition design. Minimum time commitment is four hours, during the week, between 12 and 3pm. Volunteers must be committed to women's issues and equal opportunities.

Opportunities for Employment
There are three staff.

Further Information
Annual report available.

Parents at Work (formerly the Working Mothers Association), *see Social Welfare*

Positively Women, *see Aids/HIV*

Townswomen's Guilds (TG)

Chamber of Commerce House
75 Harbourne Road, Edgbaston
Birmingham B15 3DA
Tel: 0121-456 3435
Fax: 0121-452 1890

Contact
Head Office

Main Activities
The TG advances the education of women irrespective of race, creed or party. The 2000 local branches meet for social and recreational projects. The annual budget is £400,000.

Opportunities for Volunteers
Help is needed for project work, administrative support or fundraising. Training is provided where relevant.

Opportunities for Employment
There are twelve staff.

Further Information
'Townswoman', a monthly magazine is available on request as is a recruitment leaflet.

WOMANKIND Worldwide

122 Whitechapel High Street
London E1 7PT
Tel: 0171-247 9431
Fax: 0171-247 3436

At the time of going to press, WOMANKIND Worldwide's new address was not known. From the beginning of April their new telephone number will be 0181-563 8607/8/9

Contact
Emanuela Brahamsha, Project, Research and Information Officer

Main Activities
WOMANKIND raises funds for women's self-help projects in developing countries. It also promotes awareness of the role women play in the development of their country. There are three local support groups. Annual budget is £500,000.

Opportunities for Volunteers
Volunteers are vital to the running of WOMANKIND. Their help with administrative support, outreach and fundraising is always needed. They can also assist with running campaigns. Minimum commitment is four hours a week. Enthusiasm is the most important quality, but computer, language and fundraising skills are all very useful. Volunteers are especially needed around International Women's Day (8 March).

Opportunities for Employment
There are six staff. Jobs are advertised in The Guardian and in local colleges where appropriate.

Further Information
Annual Report and other literature available on request.

Women's Design Service (WDS)

Johnson's Yard, Second Floor
4 Pinchin Street
London E1 1SA
Tel: 0171-709 7910

Contact
Carolyn Clarke, Information Officer

Main Activities
The Women's Design Service offers advice and information on issues concerning women and the built environment. It works in partnership with community groups, the voluntary and private sectors, and local authorities. Set up in 1986, it is funded by the London Borough Grants Unit (LBGU). London-based, 80% of its work is in the London area, and 20% nationally. It also has links with similar organisations in Europe and North America. The annual budget is £80,000.

Opportunities for Volunteers
WDS uses a small number of volunteers. They undertake administrative support, research, and specific project work eg as

researchers/assistants for community advice/tenants. Knowledge of built environment issues, architecture and local government is necessary. Although recruitment is ad hoc, on application (by writing with a cv) and through in-house schemes, volunteers are only accepted when they have particular skills related to one of the WDS's research projects. The minimum commitment required varies, but must be over at least two to three months. Travel and out-of-pocket expenses are offered.

Opportunities for Employment

Four part-time staff are employed. Recruitment occurs occasionally. The application procedure includes an equal opportunities application form, short-listing and interviewing. Usually a knowledge of architecture, tenants rights and related issues is required. Any vacancies are advertised in the national press including The Guardian and The Voice.

Further Information

The Annual Report, an information pack and a publications list are available on request. WDS has a series of books, pamphlets and in-depth studies of topical issues available for sale.

Women's Health

52-54 Featherstone Street
London EC1Y 8RT
Tel: 0171-251 6580

Contact

Pat Thompson, Volunteer Co-ordinator

Main Activities

Women's Health is an information and resource centre, committed to providing information in a supportive manner and helping women to make informed decisions about their health. It is a national organisation. The Helpline and Resource Centre are open Monday, Wednesday, Thursday and Friday 1-4 pm.

Opportunities for Volunteers

Volunteers are vital and carry out a variety of tasks including: administrative work, research, public relations and project work eg researching leaflets. Travel and lunch expenses are offered. People are needed to help also with despatching orders, entering statistics on a database and library work. Potential volunteers should apply in writing.

Opportunities for Employment

There are two full-time and six part-time staff. There is an equal opportunities policy and all jobs are advertised in the national press – The Guardian and The Voice.

Further Information

Annual Report, publicity leaflet and a newsletter (quarterly by subscription) are available on request.

Women's Nationwide Cancer Control Campaign (WNCCC)

Suna House
128/130 Curtain Road
London EC2A 3AR
Tel: 0171-729 4688/1735

Contact

Judy Harding

Main Activities

WNCCC supports and encourages the provision of facilities for the early diagnosis of cancer, with particular reference to the disease in women, furthering the education of the public. There are three local branches and 30 affiliated organisations as well as 250 individual members. Annual budget is £200,000.

Opportunities for Volunteers

Volunteers are very necessary and are much valued. There are 50 in Head Office and 20 in the local branches. They carry out a variety of tasks including:

administrative work, fundraising and organising local groups. Minimum commitment is one day a week. Volunteers are especially needed for the preparation of press kits and information packs and also for computer in-putting.

Opportunities for Employment
There are four staff.

Further Information
Annual report and a full information pack containing selection of literature available.

Women's Voice

PO Box 5
Boreham Wood
Herts WD6 3PP
Tel: 0181-236 0050

Contact
Hilary Tipping

Main Activities
Women's Voice was set in 1991 to provide rehabilitation for victims of domestic violence and their children. The organisation trains 'front-liners' to deal with the victims as well as carrying out community education. Local affiliate groups are planned for the near future.

Opportunities for Volunteers
There are 30 volunteers plus accredited counsellors whose work is crucial to the organisation. They carry out: telephone helpline duties, administrative work, counselling, fundraising, and management trusteeship roles. Minimum commitment is six hours per week.

Opportunities for Employment
There are no paid staff.

Further Information
Posters, information sheets and a self-help tape and pack are available by post.

Young Women's Christian Association of Great Britain (YWCA of GB)

Clarendon House
52 Cornmarket Street
Oxford OX1 3EJ
Tel: 01865-726110
Fax: 01865-204805

Contact
Ms G Tishler

Main Activities
The YWCA of GB is an informed and active membership movement that promotes women and young people in decision making and leadership, and encourages them to gain greater control over their own lives. It provides secure, affordable housing for women and young people, and encourages their development through a national programme of youth, community and education work. A national organisation set up in 1855 and covering England, Scotland and Wales, it has 200 local branches. It is also affiliated to the World YWCA which has members from 91 countries. Annual budget is £10 million.

Opportunities for Volunteers
Vital to the YWCA's work, volunteers are needed in both head office and the branches in a variety of roles: administrative support, fundraising, advice giving and for specific projects. Volunteer skills are used and developed. Training is also offered eg on trustee responsibilities. Volunteers should join the YWCA (£6 pa).

Opportunities for Employment
There are 250 full-time and 250 part-time staff. About 100 are recruited each year. Jobs are advertised nationally, locally and in the Christian press.

Further Information
Annual Report, list of local groups and information leaflets available.

Youth

The organisations concerned with youth are numerous. They include clubs, religious associations (Jewish, Christian, Moslem, etc), adventure holiday agencies, and those bringing together young people and commercial businesses. Whether you are a young person or someone keen to help develop young people's skills and experience, the opportunities and possibilities for volunteering are similarly numerous.

In recent years a number of new schemes aimed at and for young people have been set up or developed. 'Volunteers', an initiative devised with joint funding by the Prince's Trust Community Venture offers anyone between 16 and 24 the chance to undertake voluntary work for the benefit of the local community and the environment, in a training programme running for between 12 and 18 weeks. Supported by a large range of employers, it aims to develop skills and teach independence, and provides a certificate of recognition from the National Council for Vocational Qualifications (NCVQ) at the end. Conversely, 'Young Enterprise', a nation-wide business/education partnership offers young people between 15 and 19 the opportunity to form and run their own companies while still at school or college. Volunteer advisers from business (industry and commerce) guide and advise each company, while boards of volunteers from business and education provide overall co-ordination. The Scheme has been extended as 'Young Enterprise Europe', consisting of member countries from all over Europe, with the same common purpose for young people of 'learning by doing' in an international perspective. Contact Young Enterprise on 01865-311180.

If neither of these schemes is quite what you are looking for, there are many alternative options. For example, you could either join or volunteer with one of the many clubs and groups specifically for young people, such as the Guide Association or the YMCA (Young Men's Christian Association). The entries below will provide you with some ideas and guidance. See also the section on 'Youth Service' in the annual Education Year Book.

Association for Jewish Youth (AJY)

AJY House, 128 East Lane
Wembley, Middx HA0 3NL
Tel: 0181-908 4747
Fax: 0181-904 4323

Contact
Mr M Shaw, Executive Director

Main Activities
Set up in 1899, AJY is a national Jewish youth organisation, providing fieldwork service and advice to Jewish youth clubs, centres, projects and movements. It has 150 affiliates all over the country, but 70% of its work is located in Greater London, the Home Counties and in all Jewish communities. It also has links with sister organisations in Europe and North America. Annual budget is £280,000.

Opportunities for Volunteers
AJY has 25 volunteers working in its head office in administrative support and fundraising. Volunteers also help with voluntary youth work in the clubs and centres of the Jewish Youth Service. Volunteers are regarded as essential and desirable. More are welcome, particularly to organise new activities and events for young Jewish people. A youth work training scheme is available. Recruitment is in-house and by application direct to AJY. Minimum commitment is three to four hours weekly. No remuneration is offered.

Opportunities for Employment
AJY employs eight full-time and four part-time staff. It recruits between two and three people each year, mainly qualified youth workers. Posts are advertised in The Guardian and selected periodicals. An equal opportunities policy is being implemented.

Further Information
The Annual Report, a list of local groups, information leaflets and the quarterly journal/magazine are available.

Baptist Missionary Society, see
Religious Affairs

Baptist Youth Ministry

Baptist House, 129 Broadway
Didcot, Oxon OX11 8RT
Tel: 01235-811537
Fax: 01235-811537

Contact
TF8 Co-ordinator

Main Activities
The Baptist Youth Ministry works throughout England and Wales in 31 regional areas and 2,111 local churches, as well as internationally around the world. Its work with children and young people includes education and advice.

Opportunities for Volunteers
Baptist churches depend on volunteers for most of their work. This includes organising local groups, involvement in management and trusteeship, providing administrative support and counselling, and undertaking fundraising. Volunteers are required seasonally for summer holiday camps/programmes, and evangelism programmes through TF8.

Opportunities for Employment
Two full-time staff are employed. Positions are advertised within Baptist churches. An equal opportunities programme has been implemented.

Further Information
The Annual Report is available .

British Youth Council

57 Chalton Street
London NW1 1HU
Tel: 0171-387 7559
Fax: 0171-383 3545

Contact
General Secretary; member organisations

Main Activities
The Council is a national, umbrella body, set up in 1948, with a membership structure and about eighty member organisations. Through these organisations it represents the views and interests of young people aged 16 to 25 to Government and decision makers. The Council also has links with other National Youth Councils throughout the world. Its budget is £150,000 annually.

Opportunities for Volunteers
Member organisations use volunteers for the delivery of most services. These include administrative support, fundraising and counselling. Volunteers are also responsible for project work, and all committees and decision-making fora. Head Office uses about twenty volunteers from member organisations. Volunteers are recruited ad hoc on application and through in-house schemes. The minimum commitment varies. Travel and lunch expenses are paid.

Opportunities for Employment
The Council employs four paid staff. It seldom needs to recruit. Any positions are advertised in The Guardian, The Voice and the Pink Paper, following written guidelines and an equal opportunities policy.

Further Information
Annual Report and information leaflets are available, plus a detailed publications list.

For Northern Ireland Youth Forum, Tel: 01232-232432.

Catholic Youth Services (CYS)

39 Fitzjohns Avenue
London NW3 5JT
Tel: 0171-435 3596
Fax: 0171-435 3596

Contact
Reg Harrow

Main Activities
CYS, set up by the Catholic Bishops' Conference of England and Wales to promote the church's work among young people, provides a training consultancy and information service for (Catholic) youth workers in England and Wales. Its national head quarters delivers services to local (diocesan) groups. There are twenty two dioceses. The Training and Development Unit is in Birmingham. CYS has an annual budget of around £108,000.

Opportunities for Volunteers
CYS does not use volunteers itself, but can provide contacts with organisations which do.

Opportunities for Employment
CYS employs four people at headquarters. Posts occasionally become available. Jobs are advertised in newspapers, through diocesan correspondents, and in The Universe and The Catholic Herald, based on a developing equal opportunities policy.

Further Information
An Annual Report and a mission statement are available. For Scotland and Northern Ireland contact Carmel Heaney, Inter-Church House, Lower Marsh, Waterloo, London; Tel: 0171-620 4444.

Church Lads and Church Girls Brigade, *see Religious Affairs*

Council for Wales of Voluntary Youth Services, CWVYS

Llys Leslie
Lon-y-LLyn, Caerphilly
Mid Glamorgan CF8 1BQ
Tel: 01222-880088
Fax: 01222 880824

Contact
Executive Officer

Main Activities
CWVYS is the representative body of voluntary youth organisations working in Wales. Its main roles include support, information, advocacy, development and networking with and on behalf of its member bodies. These are both Welsh national and local voluntary youth organisations, with 28 affiliated in all. CWVYS's operational activities are supported by the Wales Youth Agency. Similar organisations to CWVYS have been set up in England, Scotland and Northern Ireland (see below).

Opportunities for Volunteers
CWVYS does not itself involve any volunteers.

Opportunities for Employment
No details supplied.

Further Information
The Annual Report, a list of local groups, a pamphlet and a directory are available through the Executive Officer. Addresses for similar agencies are:

NCVYS, Coborn House, Coborn Road, Bow, London E3 2DA, England

Youthnet N. I., Lamont House, Purdy's Lane, Belfast BT8 4TA, Northern Ireland

Scottish Standing Conference of Voluntary Youth Organisations, Central Hall, West Tollcross, Edinburgh EH3 9BP, Scotland.

Crusaders

2 Romeland Hill
St Albans
Hertfordshire AL3 4ET
Tel: 01727-855422
Fax: 01727-848518

Contact
Elizabeth Dore, PA to National Director

Main Activities
Founded in 1906, Crusaders is an inter-denominational youth organisation reaching today's young people with Christian values and the gospel message through youth groups, events and holidays. It also provides active teaching materials, leadership training and youth centres. Among the opportunities offered are leadership training for young people from 15-19 years, and Crusaders Overseas Expeditions - Crusoe - for 2-4 weeks for those aged 16+. Apart from the national Head Office, there are, UK-wide, three regional offices, 26 local support groups, 450 local branches and an International Department with links with voluntary organisations in Guatemala, Latvia, Romania and Zambia. The annual budget is £1,600,000.

Opportunities for Volunteers
Around 2,500 volunteers support Crusaders' work, 10 in Head Office, the rest in the branches. Volunteer youth leaders are the mainstay of Crusaders youth groups and activities. Volunteers also organise the local groups, are involved in management/trusteeship, provide administrative support and undertake fundraising and public relations. More are actively sought for year round work and the holiday programme. They need to identify with the aims of a Christian youth organisation and have some skills in Christian youth work. Training is offered in leadership, first aid and catering. Recruitment is by application, through in-house drives and from advertising. The

minimum time commitment varies from short to long term, but at least three hours a week are required. Remuneration may be offered.

Opportunities for Employment
Crusaders employs 35 full-time and 15 part-time staff. Around 200 people are recruited annually as holiday leadership staff via applications and interviews. Skills in youth work are needed, including enthusiasm and energy. Positions are advertised in the media, particularly Christian magazines. An equal opportunities policy operates.

Further Information
Apart from the Annual Report, a resources catalogue, information pack, promotional literature, holidays catalogue, short term opportunities brochure 'Go Global', and a video are available. Regional contacts are:

Dell Jones, Crusaders in Wales, Regal House, Gelligaer Lane, Cathays, Cardiff CF4 2JS, tel: 01222-882726

Kevin Simpson, Scottish Crusaders, 23 Royal Exchange Square, Glasgow G1 3AJ, tel: 0141-248 6380

Trevor Taylor, Northern Ireland Secretary, 27 Hawthornden Road, Belfast BT4 3JU, tel: 01232-656302

The Duke of Edinburgh's Award

Gulliver House, Madeira Walk
Windsor SL4 1EU
Tel: 01753-810753
Fax: 01753-810666

Contact
Through local youth service or via head office for volunteering; Justine Rego, Administration Officer re employment

Main Activities
An award linked with a programme of leisure activities to challenge and develop all young people between the ages of 14 and 25. A national organisation set up in 1956, the Award has 10 regional offices which license local authorities/groups to run the scheme. Of these there are 358 operating authorities together with 11,347 operating units throughout the UK. The organisation also has links with similar schemes in Canada, Eire, India, Kenya, Lesotho and St Kitts, and with over 58 other countries world-wide. Annual budget is £4.1 million.

Opportunities for Volunteers
Volunteers are essential to the Award which is largely operated by them. Head office involves ten, the branches 20, while another 46,000 run the scheme throughout the country. More are actively sought. The type of work includes organising the local groups, being local committee managers and trustees, and undertaking public relations. The volunteers also run the project work, instructing and assessing the particular activities of those taking part. Some experience and qualifications may be needed where the activity brings in a safety issue. Recruitment is ad hoc on application, via volunteer bureaux, and sometimes through promotional literature. A minimum commitment of once a week for three months is required. Whether remuneration/expenses are offered varies according to the operating authority, as does training and support.

Opportunities for Employment
The Award employs 81 full-time and 15 part-time staff. It recruits around five people each year who are appointed on the basis of application form and interview. Jobs are advertised in the local and national press, and there is a formal equal opportunities policy.

Further Information
The Annual Report and general information leaflets are available from head office. Other useful addresses are:
Gwobr Dug Caeredin, 12 The Bulwark,

Brecon, Powys LD3 7AD, tel: 01874-623086

The Duke of Edinburgh's Award, 69 Dublin Street, Edinburgh EH3 6NS, tel: 0131-556 9097

The Duke of Edinburgh's Award, 109 Royal Avenue, Belfast BT1 1EW, tel: 01232-232253

Duke of Edinburgh's Award / Gwobr Dug Caeredin, see Recreation & Leisure

Endeavour Training, see Education

FAIRBRIDGE

1 Westminster Bridge Road
London SE1 7PL
Tel: 0171-928 1704
Fax: 0171-928 6016

Contact
Local Team Managers for volunteer opportunities; Jo Eades, PR Manager and Di Scott, Administrator re employment opportunities.

Main Activities
Fairbridge provides a progressive programme of personal development training and long term support to young people (14-25 years) deemed to be 'at risk'. Set up in 1981 it is a national organisation with 13 regional centres in inner cities throughout the UK, including Cardiff, Edinburgh, Glasgow and Belfast. The annual budget is £3 million.

Opportunities for Volunteers
Volunteers have a limited role to play because training team staff must be suitably qualified and experienced in outdoor activities. However one or two volunteers work with each local team plus one in head office. The work includes fundraising, advice giving, conservation

and organising local groups for which outdoor activity qualifications are needed. Recruitment is typically in-house, usually of trainees who have come up through the system. The time commitment varies – full-time is preferred – and travel expenses may be paid. Fairbridge is developing its long term support programme for young people who have completed the first two stages of training. There will be opportunities for volunteers in team centres to assist in developing young people action plans.

Opportunities for Employment
There are 125 full-time staff. About 20 people are recruited each year as opportunities arise, through a standard application form and interview process. The skills required depend on the position, but experience of the client group is necessary. Posts are usually advertised in The Guardian. Fairbridge has implemented a formal equal opportunities policy.

Further Information
The Annual Report, a corporate folder with inserts (fact sheets, strategy, etc), leaflets, posters and Challenger magazine are available from Central Office.

Festival Welfare Services (FWS), see Recreation & Leisure

GAP Activity Projects (GAP) Ltd, see Overseas & the Developing World

The Guide Association

17-19 Buckingham Palace Road
London SW1W 0PT
Tel: 0171-834 6242
Fax: 0171-828 8317 or 0171-834 5171

Contact
Commonwealth Headquarters (CHQ) as above for volunteering; Personnel Department at CHQ re employment

Main Activities
Aims to enable girls to mature into confident, capable, caring women determined to realise their potential in their career, home and personal life, and willing to contribute to their community and the wider world. Membership is available to any girl over 5 years. Activities are divided by age groups into Rainbows, Brownies, Guides, Rangers and Young Leaders. In the UK the Guide Association is divided into nine country/regions, further subdivided into counties, divisions and districts. Local branches number 35,021 with 1028 local support groups. Full membership is 750,000. Income for 1993 was £4.36 million. CHQ is also headquarters for Guides throughout the Commonwealth.

Opportunities for Volunteers
The Guide Association is dependent on around 85,000 volunteers – young and adult leaders (Guiders, Commissioners, etc.). The work undertaken includes being Unit Guiders working with groups of girls and young women in accordance with the Guiding method, and outreach work to develop Guiding in inner cities. Young people undertake service projects. Volunteers also work in administration and counselling. The Guide Association actively seeks more women year round to run local units. They must be able to work with young people and apply the Guiding method. Extensive training courses are available, together with a District/Division Commissioner support network.

Recruitment is by application and in-house. Current members recruit new ones, and young members progress to adult leadership roles. Minimum commitment is about four hours a week. Essential expenses can be reimbursed.

Opportunities for Employment
The Guide Association employs 157 full-time staff and nine part-time. During 1993 it recruited 22 people. Seasonal work opportunities are available at Training and Activity Centres as Outdoor Activity Instructors. All vacancies are advertised internally, prior to being advertised and/or placed with agencies. Various newspapers and trade journals are used, including The Guardian, The Daily Telegraph, The Times, Design Week, Book Seller, The Lady and the local press.

Further Information
The Annual Report and numerous publications are available.

Jewish Lads and Girls Brigade (JLGB)

Camperdown, 3 Beechcroft Road
South Woodford, London E18 1LA
Tel: 0181-989 5743/8990
Fax: 0181-518 8832

Contact
Richard Weber/Lester Harris

Main Activities
Set up in 1895, the JLGB is a national voluntary youth organisation with over 60 local branches throughout the UK, and loose contacts with similar organisations in Israel. Annual budget is £350,000.

Opportunities for Volunteers
Volunteers are needed centrally and throughout the UK to give administrative support and to offer their knowledge and skills to help organise activities indirectly for or face-to-face with young people. They are vital to the organisation's work as the JLGB is totally dependent on the

time given by its volunteer youth workers who run all groups and activities. No special skills are required, but there is a selection process. Travel expenses are offered.

Opportunities for Employment

There are no employment opportunities, but a small professional staff supports the volunteers.

Further Information

Annual Report, information leaflets and list of local groups available.

London Union of Youth Clubs

64 Camberwell Road
London SE3 0EN
Tel: 0171-701 6366
Fax: 0171-701 6320

Contact
Simon Abbott

Main Activities

The Union brings skills and resources to mixed clubs and groups in London, and provides a resource for work with young women.

Opportunities for Volunteers

Volunteers are needed to help stage special events.

Opportunities for Employment

There are six full-time staff.

Further Information

Annual Report and affiliation pack sent to groups on request.

The Methodist Association of Youth Clubs (MAYC)

2 Chester House, Pages Lane
Muswell Hill, London N10 1PR
Tel: 0181-444 9845
Fax: 0181-365 2471

Contact
The Administrator

Main Activities

MAYC enables young people to achieve their full potential as members of their church and citizens of the world. MAYC was set up in 1945 and is made up of about 2,500 local youth groups. It organises the largest annual non-uniformed youth event in Europe – the London Weekend in May. Other initiatives include MAYC World Action which aims to provide young people with opportunities to effect change on the major issues of our day eg homelessness.

Opportunities for Volunteers

Most of MAYC's youth workers are volunteers working locally, usually from their Methodist church.

Opportunities for Employment

There are sixteen full-time staff. Posts are advertised nationally in The Guardian, Methodist Recorder and other press.

Further Information

The Annual Report and a variety of publicity material, including a handbook, are available.

NABC Clubs for Young People (NABC-CYP)

369 Kennington Lane
London SE11 5QY
Tel: 0171-793 0787
Fax: 0171-820 9815

Contact
Bill Almond

Main Activities
To promote the spiritual, moral, cultural and physical development of young people through leisure-time activities. A national body, the NABC-CYP is divided into five regional groupings, with 55 local branches and 2,000 affiliated organisations. It's annual budget is about £1,000,000.

Opportunities for Volunteers
There are many opportunities for volunteers in clubs throughout the UK.

Opportunities for Employment
NABC-CYP employs 16 full-time staff, and recruits perhaps two or three people each year. Posts are advertised in The Guardian and local press. NABC-CYP has a full equal opportunities policy.

Further Information
An Annual Report and relevant literature are available.

The Nansen Society, see
Environment & Conservation

National Federation of Young Farmers Clubs (NFYFC)

YFC Centre, National Agricultural Centre
Stoneleigh Park, Kenilworth
Warwicks CV8 2LG
Tel: 01203-696544
Fax: 01203-696559

Contact
Bryan Lovegrove, Marketing Field Officer

Main Activities
Set up in 1921, the NFYFC covers England and Wales. Through participative youth work Young Farmers Clubs – YFCs – seek to meet the needs of rural young people. They organise education, training and social programmes which encourage community involvement and concern for the environment. Home stay and study tours to all parts of the world are also arranged. YFC members are young people aged from ten to 26 with similar interests. There are 924 clubs forming 50 county federations, each of which is affiliated to the National Federation. NFYFC also has links with similar organisations world-wide.

Opportunities for Volunteers
NFYFC is made up from a volunteer base. The members of the branches, numbering around 32,000, are all volunteers. Apart from running the branches, they work in conservation, community and countryside projects and charity fundraising. Recruitment is usually in-house. Many new members join each year. There is no minimum time commitment.

Opportunities for Employment
NFYFC employs fifteen full-time staff. It seldom recruits, and employment opportunities are few.

Further Information
The Federation publishes an Annual Report, a leaflet on the YFC, the YFC Charter and a tabloid style newspaper.

National Playing Fields Association (Scotland), *see Recreation & Leisure*

The National Star Centre, *see Education*

National Youth Agency (NYA)

17-23 Albion Street
Leicester LE1 6GD
Tel: 0116-247 1200
Fax: 0116-247 1043

Contact
Carolyn Oldfield, Information Officer

Main Activities
NYA provides information and support for all those concerned with the social education of young people. It also has some contacts with similar organisations overseas. Annual budget is £2 million.

Opportunities for Volunteers
There are no specific volunteer opportunities but a leaflet 'Voluntary Work and Young People', is available free to young people, £1 to others. This lists full-time volunteer placements and sources of further information in other organisations.

Opportunities for Employment
There are 60 full-time staff. NYA has an Equal Opportunities policy. Jobs are advertised in The Guardian, Times Educational Supplement, own publication and specialist press as appropriate.

Further Information
For Wales, contact: Wales Youth Agency, Leslie Court, Lon-y-Llyn, Caerphilly CF8 1BG, tel: 01222-880088. For Scotland, contact: Scottish Community Development Council, West Coates House, 90 Haymarket Terrace, Edinburgh EH12 5LQ, tel: 0131-313 2488.

Northern Ireland Children's Holiday Scheme (NICHS)

547 Antrim Road
Belfast BT15 3BU
Tel: 01232-370373

Contact
Paddy Doherty / Jackie Chalk

Main Activities
NICHS is a cross-community youth organisation working with under-privileged young people from both sides of the religious divide through programmes designed to counter prejudice, fear and mistrust. NICHS's ultimate aim to promote tolerance and understanding between the communities in Northern Ireland. There are thirteen regional fundraising committees.

Opportunities for Volunteers
NICHS involves about 150 volunteers a year. They fundraise carry out management tasks and work on various projects eg youth projects and staffing residential events. Useful skills include: a knowledge of First Aid, life saving, driving, catering, games, arts and crafts. Locally based volunteers offer a minimum of three hours per month. UK volunteers offer a ten day period during the summer months and also help to raise funds for NICHS. Training is provided for the residential projects.

Opportunities for Employment
There are five permanent members of staff and five who are recruited through a one year Government funded programme – Action for Community Employment.

Further Information
Annual Report and information leaflets available on request.

The Prince's Trust and the Royal Jubilee Trusts

8 Bedford Row
London WC1R 4BA
Tel: 0171-430 0524

Contact
Via local committee (list available from Head Office)

Main Activities
The Trusts enable disadvantaged young people to develop themselves and be of service to others through grants made by the Trusts' 59 local committees.

Opportunities for Volunteers
Volunteers are used to assess grant applications. They require a knowledge of and sympathy with issues affecting young people. There are also opportunities to give fundraising and administrative help.

Opportunities for Employment
There are 35 staff. Any job vacancies are advertised in either local or national newspapers as appropriate.

Further Information
Annual Report and guides to grant-making policies available.

QISP – Quaker International Social Projects

Friends House, Euston Road
London, NW1 2BJ
Tel: 0171-387 3601
Fax: 0171-388 1977

Contact
UK Volunteer Administrator

Main Activities
Runs international community projects, bringing together up to twenty volunteers of different nationalities to work together. Projects include mental health, working with children, community arts and the environment. Locations are in the UK.

There are also opportunities abroad for experienced volunteers.

Opportunities for Volunteers
The projects on which the volunteers work are residential and last between two and three weeks. Volunteers must be aged eighteen (sixteen for youth projects).

Opportunities for Employment
Three full-time staff are employed.

Further Information
A newsletter, published twice a year, gives details of projects.

Raleigh International, see Overseas & the Developing World

Sail Training Association

2A The Hard, Portsmouth
Hampshire PO1 3PT
Tel: 01705-832055/6
Fax: 01705-815769

Contact
Esther Tibbs, Marketing Services Manager

Main Activities
Founded in 1956, the Association provides adventure holidays on board the tall ships 'Sir Winston Churchill' and 'Malcolm Miller'. Young people go to sea for two weeks enjoying challenges and enriching experiences. There are 65 local support groups UK-wide. Annual budget is £1,100,000.

Opportunities for Volunteers
Volunteers are essential to the Association, which is dependent on them. They are frequently needed to paint and maintain sailing ships. Meals and accommodation offered while on board. Fundraisers and supporters to spread the word about the Association's work are also required. Volunteers need an enthusiasm for what the sea has to offer.

Opportunities for Employment
There are 26 full-time staff.

Further Information
Lists of local groups, voyage programme and Annual Report available.

St Andrews Ambulance Association, see Health & Medicine

The Scout Association

Baden-Powell House
Queen's Gate, London SW7 5JS
Tel: 0171-584 7030
Fax: 0171-581 9953

Contact
Local Scout Groups for volunteering; Mrs E Shingleton-Smith, Personnel Officer re employment

Main Activities
The Scout Association is part of an educational youth movement. It promotes the development of boys and girls, and young people, aged 6-20 years through an enjoyable and attractive scheme of progressive training. Part of an international movement, Scouting has over 17 million members world-wide in 150 countries and territories. The World Association of the Scout Movement includes information sharing and training, and support for community development with Scout organisations in the developing world. It also collaborates on projects with such organisations as UNICEF and Save the Children Fund. The UK Scout Association has 540,000 members from all major faiths. It offers equal opportunities to all young people no matter what their social, religious or ethnic background, and encourages them to grow spiritually and develop within their own faith. It also has a positive policy of integration, and welcomes children and young people who have physical and mental disabilities. Set up in 1907 it is decentralised in around 10,000 Scout Groups, supported locally by 110 District and County organisations, and affiliated with the World Association and the Guide Association. Annual budget is £10 million.

Opportunities for Volunteers
Over 100,000 volunteers are involved in all types of work including administrative support, fundraising, management, counselling, community project work and public relations. They organise local Scout Groups and as volunteer leaders provide all face-to-face youth work and much of the training, as well as working as administrators and managers at all levels. More are always needed. The skills required depend on the appointment, but for local Scout Groups volunteers must be able to work with young people undertaking also managerial and administrative tasks. Recruitment is ad hoc on application, through in-house schemes and by encouraging parents of young people already involved. Time commitments depend on the appointment and out-of-pocket expenses are offered. Structured training programmes are run for leaders.

Opportunities for Employment
370 full-time, 35 part-time and seven fixed term staff are employed. Between 25 and 30 staff are recruited each year and posts regularly occur for office, hotel/catering and camp site staff. Positions are advertised in The Guardian, The Voice, the 'Scouting Magazine' and free London magazines. Packs are sent out to enquirers including the equal opportunities policy, followed by interviews with suitable applicants. The Association actively recruits school leavers in particular.

Further Information
The Annual Report, fact sheets, bulletins, resource materials, 'Scouting Magazine' and names of local contacts are available through the Resource Centre, Gilwell Park, Chingford, London E4 7QW, tel: 0181-524 5246.

Sea Ranger Association (SRA)

Registered address:
HQTS 'Lord Amory'
631 Manchester Road
London E14 9NU

Secretary: Mrs M White
29 South View Park, Plympton,
Plymouth, Devon PL7 4JE
Tel: 01752-330413

Contact
The Registered Office as above

Main Activities
The SRA involves young people from 10 to 21 years in community service as well as outdoor activities (canoeing, camping, rowing, sailing), and also gives them the opportunity to develop other skills. Established in 1973 and covering England only, it has an elected national Council of Management with autonomous regional (7) and local groups (45) operating within the framework of SRA rules and regulations. The annual budget is under £10,000.

Opportunities for Volunteers
Volunteers are involved in various types of work including organising the local groups, committee management and trusteeship, administrative support, fundraising, and public relations. More are needed, especially people with youth leadership skills. Recruitment is via in-house drives and ad hoc through application to the registered office. Travel and out-of-pocket expenses are offered.

Opportunities for Employment
There are no paid staff.

Further Information
The Annual Report, a general leaflet, and a list of regional officers are available by request from Mrs V Corner Halligan, 4 Grand Drive, Raynes Park, London SW20 0JT.

Student Community Action Development Unit (SCADU)

Oxford House
Derbyshire Street
London E2 6HG
Tel: 0171-739 9001/4565/0918
Fax: 0171-729 0435

Contact
Kelly Drake/Julie Christie, Development Workers

Main Activities
SCADU is a UK-wide organisation set up in 1981. It promotes and liaises with Student Community Action (SCA) groups in institutions of higher education. This includes acting as a resource, information and training agency for SCA local groups and student volunteers. SCADU also sends out termly information mailings and organises national conferences within the SCA network. There are 125 local groups in all. Annual budget is £78,000.

Opportunities for Volunteers
Although SCADU does not use volunteers itself, it can refer people to the appropriate SCA group. Volunteers are crucial to these local groups.

Opportunities for Employment
There are three members of staff. An equal opportunities policy exists.

Further Information
Annual Report and information leaflets available on request.

The Trident Trust

Saffron Court
14b St Cross Street
London EC1N 8XA
Tel: 0171-242 1616
Fax: 0171-430 2975

Contact
Personnel Director

Main Activities
The Trust aims to raise the motivation, self-confidence and achievement of all young people within the framework of the National Curriculum and the National Education and Training Targets through personal challenge, community involvement and work experience. Set up in 1972 the Trust has three regional offices and 70 project offices throughout England and on Jersey (Channel Islands). A sister charity Trident Transnational offers young Europeans the possibility of UK work experience with UK employers.

Opportunities for Volunteers
The Trust involves volunteers in various ways and as a charity is always pleased to welcome volunteers in any capacity. For the Trust's project work in local branches in England it is helpful for volunteers to have a commercial/ industrial background at a middle/senior level. Communication and interpersonal skills, mobility and a car are also required. The minimum time commitment varies from project to project and can be individually negotiated.

Opportunities for Employment
There are 350 staff covering full- and part-time posts. Between five and ten people are recruited each year. Skills required are the same as those for volunteers and posts are advertised in the local press. The Trust has an equal opportunities policy.

Further Information
The Annual Report, a list of local groups and leaflets for students, parents, schools, colleges and employers are available from Trident's head office and from local Project offices.

Turkish Youth Association

628–630 Green Lanes
London N8 0DS
Tel: 0181-888 3080

Contact
Mr R Ozturk, Director

Main Activities
The Turkish Youth Association provides services which are specific to the needs of Turkish/Turkish Cypriot young people. They include youth services, counselling, education and health projects which are culturally appropriate and specific.

Opportunities for Volunteers
There are ten volunteers. They are very important and contribute extensively to the development of the work. Spoken Turkish as well as English is essential. Volunteers carry out a variety of tasks including administrative support, fundraising and management/trusteeship. Travel and lunch expenses are offered.

Opportunities for Employment
There are four full-time and four part-time staff.

Further Information
Information leaflets are available through the Administrator.

Wales Youth Agency (WYA)

Leslie Court
Lon-y-llyn, Caerphilly
Mid Glamorgan CF8 1BQ
Tel: 01222-880088
Fax: 01222-880824

Contact
The Senior Administrative Officer

Main Activities
WYA aims to promote, support and assist both the voluntary and maintained sectors

of the youth service to develop and improve the quality of youth work practice in Wales. This includes assisting the development of the youth work curriculum, identifying training needs, encouraging partnership between statutory and voluntary organisations, and providing information for youth workers and young people. WYA also supports the work of the Council for Wales of Voluntary Youth Services (CWVYS) and the Wales Youth Forum (WYF). Established in 1992 as a non Departmental Public Body, the WYA is governed by a Management Board and supported by national sub-committees, planning and working groups. It also has contacts with similar youth organisations in England, Scotland and Ireland, as well as with the European Youth Centre, the European under 26 Discount Card and various youth exchange schemes. The annual budget is £380,000.

Opportunities for Volunteers
The Agency does not itself involve any volunteers.

Opportunities for Employment
Nine full-time and three part-time staff are employed. WYA only recruits if any positions become available, for which youth work experience and/or an educational qualification are necessary. Posts are advertised in the Times Educational Supplement. An equal opportunities policy is in practice.

Further Information
The Annual Report, WYA leaflet and occasional publications (eg briefing papers, youth information) are available from the Information Officer. A bi-monthly Information Pack and the quarterly magazine 'Ymlaen' are also available for youth workers.

The Woodcraft Folk

13 Ritherdon Road
London SW17 8QE
Tel: 0181-672 6031
Fax: 0181-767 2457

Contact
Tony Billinghurst, National Secretary

Main Activities
Set up in 1925 and UK-wide, Woodcraft Folk provides weekly meetings and residential camps for children and young people. It aims to promote awareness of issues such as environment, democracy and co-operation. There are regional offices in Bristol and Birmingham, 721 local branches and exchanges of information and young people with Europe and the developing world. Annual budget is £160,000.

Opportunities for Volunteers
Fundraising and administrative support always needed in the head office. Opportunities also exist for specific work with groups of young people in branches, where volunteer involvement is essential.

Opportunities for Employment
There are thirteen full-time staff. Approximately three are recruited each year. Jobs are advertised in The Guardian.

Further Information
Annual Report and information available.

Young Men's Christian Association (YMCA)

National Council of YMCAs
640 Forest Row
London E17 3DZ
Tel: 0181-520 5599
Fax: 0181-509 3190

Contact
Human Resources Department

Main Activities
YMCA is a Christian charity committed

to helping people particularly in times of need. It provides 20,000 training places and 7,000 beds. A national organisation with 200 Local Associations.

Opportunities for Volunteers
Volunteers are needed for fundraising, administrative work, shop work, publicity, committee and executive work. Depending on type of work a volunteer allowance may be offered.

Opportunities for Employment
Contact Local Association.

Further Information
Annual Report, information leaflets and list of local groups available.

Young Women's Christian Association (YWCA), *see Women*

Youth Access

Magazine Business Centre
11 Newark Street
Leicester LE1 5SS
Tel: 0116-255 8763
Fax: 0116-254 7800

Contact
Lindy Nichols, National Administrator

Main Activities
Youth Access is a UK-wide support and membership organisation for youth information, advice and counselling services. Specifically it provides training on a national basis to raise the quality of information, advice and counselling offered to young people, and acts as a national referral service for them to local counselling and advisory agencies in their own area. There are 230 affiliated organisations. Annual budget is £150,000.

Opportunities for Volunteers
Volunteers are needed to fundraise for the national organisation.

Opportunities for Employment
There are three full-time staff.

Further Information
Annual report available.

Youth Clubs UK

11 St Bride Street
London EC4A 4AS
Tel: 0171-353 2366
Fax: 0171-353 2369

Contact
Mr John Bateman, Chief Executive

Main Activities
Established in 1911, Youth Clubs UK exists to support and develop high quality voluntary work and educational opportunities for all young people. A national organisation, it has three divisions (Scotland, Northern Ireland and Wales), eight regional groups, 41 local support groups, and 7,000 local branches. It also has links with similar organisations in Europe, and is a member of the European Confederation of Youth Clubs. Annual budget is £2 million.

Opportunities for Volunteers
Around 200 volunteers are used in the branches, together with a varying number in Head Office. They are of key importance in delivering youth work at the local level. Apart from organising local groups, volunteers are involved in administrative support, fundraising, management and as trustees. More are required with an interest in and empathy with young people. They are recruited ad hoc, on application and through in-house schemes. Travel expenses are offered, an induction programme is provided and follow-up is available if required.

Opportunities for Employment
Both full-time (36) and part-time (20) staff are employed together with a varying number of temporary and other paid employees. About four people are recruited annually following advertising, shortlisting and interviewing. A job description

and person specification is key to the process. Seasonal opportunities exist for residential centre helpers. Employees must have experience of work with young people. Positions are advertised in various media, including The Guardian, and an equal opportunities policy operates.

Further Information

The Annual Report, handbook, list of local groups and magazine are available from Head Office. A stamped addressed envelope (sae) is required.

Useful Publications

Below is a selection of publications that you may find helpful. Many of them are available from your local library, or can be ordered through inter-library loan.

Directories

Directory of London Disability Organisations

International Directory of Voluntary Work (published by Vacation Work Publications)

The Third World Directory by Lucy Stubbs (published by the Directory of Social Change, 1993) – lists over 200 development organisations, volunteering opportunities and sources of funding

Volunteer Work (published by the Central Bureau for Exchanges and Visits, London) – lists longer term volunteer work (3-36 months), often residential, in a range of countries, including the developing world

Fundraising

Organising Local Events by Sarah Passingham (published by the Directory of Social Change) – a guide for anyone organising a local fundraising event, covering: permission, publicity, finding volunteers, budgeting, insurance, and safety and practical tips

Tried and Tested Ideas for Raising Money Locally by Sarah Passingham (published by the Directory of Social Change) – a practical fundraising guide for community groups, local charity projects and schools. Includes a selection of money-spinning ideas which work, as well as a clear breakdown of how to go about them

Managing/Campaigning

The Campaigning Handbook by Mark Lattimer (published by the Directory of Social Change) – describes ways in which ordinary citizens can change society. Written for pressure groups, charities and social activists, it covers the main skills of modern campaigning

Essential Volunteer Management by Steve McCurley and Rick Lynch (published by the Directory of Social Change) – covers the art of volunteer management, creating motivating jobs, screening and interviewing, supervision, orientation and training, volunteer and staff relations

Other Publications

A considerable range of published material is available covering many aspects of the voluntary sector, including:

Finding Your Personal Route into the Voluntary Sector, a series of 20 leaflets produced for Charityfair, series editors Jan Brownfoot and Frances Wilks (published by the Directory of Social Change)

Active Citizens: New Voices and Values by Nick Fielding, Gillian Reeve and Margaret Simey (published by Bedford Square Press)

Charity Choice (published by Abercorn Hill Associates)

Charity Magazine (published by the Charities Aid Foundation)

Charity Status: a Practical Handbook (published by the Directory of Social Change)

The Education Yearbook edited by Michaela Evans et al (published by Longmans)

The Effective Trustee: Roles and Responsibilities (published by the Directory of Social Change)

The Gap Year Guidebook (published by Peridot Press)

Go for It! Martyn Lewis's Essential Guide to Opportunities for Young People by Martyn Lewis (published by Lennard Publishing)

Good Deeds in Old Age: Volunteering by the New Leisured Class by Susan Maizell (published by Lexington Books, USA)

How to Work for a Charity on a Paid or Voluntary Basis by Jan Brownfoot and Frances Wilks (published by the Directory of Social Change)

Lending A Hand – a pack of information material on volunteering (published by the Community Education Unit, Yorkshire Television)

The Museums Yearbook 1993/94 edited by Sheena Barbour (published by The Museums Association)

Prospects – Scotland's Action and Opportunites package for older people (published by Scottish Community Education Guidance)

Self Help Groups – Getting Started, Keeping Going by Judy Wilson (published by Longman)

Starting and Running a Voluntary Organisation (published by the Directory of Social Change)

Starting and Running a Voluntary Group by Sally Capper, Judith Unell and Anne Weman (published by Bedford Square Press)

Third Sector (magazine)

Volunteers in Museums and Heritage Organisations: Policy, Planning and Management (published by HMSO)

Voluntary but not Amateur (published by the London Voluntary Service Council)

The Voluntary Agencies Directory (published by Bedford Square Press)

Useful Addresses

Training Courses

Working for a Charity
44-46 Caversham Road,
London NW5 2DS
Tel: 0171-911 0353

Directory of Social Change
24 Stephenson Way
London NW1 2DP
Tel: 0171-209 4949

**Institute of Charity
Fundraising Managers**
Market Towers,
1 Nine Elms Lane
London SW8 5NQ
Tel: 0171-627 3436

The Industrial Society
3 Carlton House Terrace
London SW1Y 5AF
Tel: 0171-839 4300
*provides communications and
self-marketing training*

C.I.T.E. (Associates) Ltd
23 Newman Street
London W1P 3HA
Tel: 0171-636 5544
*provides free training on self-
marketing for those who have
been unemployed for more than
six months*

Local Job Clubs provide free
advice and help for those
who have been unemployed
for more than six months

Specialist Recruitment Agencies

CR Charity Recruitment
40 Rosebery Avenue
London EC1R 4RN
Tel: 0171-833 0770

Charity Appointments
3 Spitals Yard
London E1 6AQ
Tel: 0171-247 4502

Charity People
First Floor, Station House
150 Waterloo Road
London SE1 8SB
Tel: 0171-620 0062

Index